The more we split and pulverize matter artificially, the more insistently it proclaims its fundamental unity.

Teilhard de Chardin
The Phenomenon of Man

Developmental Therapy

Theory into Practice

Allen E. Ivey

Developmental Therapy

 Jossey-Bass Publishers

San Francisco • London • 1986

DEVELOPMENTAL THERAPY
Theory into Practice
by Allen E. Ivey

Copyright © 1986 by: Jossey-Bass Inc., Publishers
433 California Street
San Francisco, California 94104
&
Jossey-Bass Limited
28 Banner Street
London EC1Y 8QE

Library of Congress Cataloging-in-Publication Data

Ivey, Allen E.
  Developmental therapy.

  (The Jossey-Bass social and behavioral science series)
  Bibliography: 359
  Includes indexes.
  1. Developmental therapy. I. Title. II. Series.
[DNLM: 1. Counseling—methods. 2. Human Development.
3. Psychotherapy—methods. WM 420 I95d]
RC489.D46I94   1986   616.89   86-45618
ISBN 1-55542-022-2

Manufactured in the United States of America

The paper in this book meets the guidelines for
permanence and durability of the Committee on
Production Guidelines for Book Longevity of the
Council on Library Resources.

Copyright acknowledgments appear on page 385.

JACKET DESIGN BY WILLI BAUM

FIRST EDITION

Code 8639

The Jossey-Bass
Social and Behavioral Science Series

Consulting Editor
Counseling Psychology

Ursula Delworth
University of Iowa

Contents

Preface

As most therapists, I have been a firm believer in developmental theory since I first encountered its fundamental concepts thirty years ago in the works of Freud, Erikson, and Piaget. Developmental theory made sense to me; I could see examples of oral dependency, adolescent identity, and childlike concrete thinking in my own clients. But at the same time, I found it difficult to apply such conceptual approaches to daily therapeutic practice, and so I did not pursue the question of how to relate developmental theory to practice.

The relationship of therapeutic practice and developmental theory has remained disturbingly remote. Whether we are social workers or psychologists, mental health counselors or psychiatrists, therapeutic teachers or nurses, we all work with issues of human development. Therapy and counseling are, after all, ultimately concerned with client development. How can developmental theory be integrated into therapeutic practice? To answer that difficult and complex question is the aim of this book. I seek to join, in this work, basic developmental theory, particularly that of Piaget, with the rigor of daily practice in therapy and counseling.

In concrete terms, how does developmental theory relate to practice in the interview session? To answer this question, I decided to study intensively the two major developmental theorists, Freud and Piaget. This study led forward and backward. First, I found it helpful to return to the Greeks; Plato's conceptions of consciousness indicated to me that most developmental theorists have a common ground. (Later, my study of Freud led me to Lacan's controversial reinterpretation of Freud.) As I explored the foundations of developmental theory in the work of Loevinger, Kegan, Kohlberg, and Gilligan, I found that the concepts of Piaget formed an integrating theme.

This discovery led to my writing this book; I believe that this integrating Piagetian theme has general utility for and relevance to the helping professions. Piaget's orientation to development shows that children move from sensori-motor and preoperational thinking through concrete operations and, finally, to formal thinking. I noted parallels between Piagetian thinking and Plato's four levels of consciousness as described in *The Republic*. (Although much of the book is derived from the thinking of Plato and Piaget, the concepts are not necessarily those of either, and the definitions and usage herein are unique to this book.)

I hypothesized that adults might metaphorically move through the same systematic stages of cognitive development as do children. If this was so, we should be immediately able to *observe* cognitive-developmental changes in our clients in the therapy process. A review of my microcounseling videotapes confirmed this assumption—clients present preoperational problems at the beginning of an interview. The term *preoperational* is highly descriptive of virtually all clients who come for help— they would not be in therapy if they could "operate" on the environment and feel or think well about themselves in the process. Whether we as therapists are dealing with our clients' irrational ideas, behavioral deficits, or unconscious thought processes, each description of the client represents a form of preoperational behavior, thought, or feeling.

Further examination of the videotapes revealed additional Piagetian/Platonic observations. Once a preoperational idea is clearly defined, it seems helpful to move the client "back" one step to "ground" the problem or concern in sensori-motor reality. Specifically, what does the client "see, hear, and feel" as he or she experiences the problem? As Plato notes, we base our thinking on the images we first receive in the deceptive world of appearances.

Once sensory or perceptual data are grounded in "reality" (or the first stage of the world of appearances), it becomes possible to facilitate client development to the concrete operational stage. At the risk of oversimplification, therapists have accomplished both sensori-motor and concrete operational tasks when they ask clients for specific, concrete examples of their problems. The classic question "Could you give me a specific example?" often facilitates the confused, preoperational client in moving to more solid, sensori-motor functioning and then to linear explanations of concrete problems. It is then possible to work through the question of how one can "concretely operate" on the problem. Therapists can do this by using a variety of therapeutic techniques and theories, most notably those associated with assertiveness training, reality therapy, and rational-emotive therapy.

Beyond concrete operations are formal operations—the examination of patterns. We examine life patterns using theories such as those presented by Rogers and Frankl and many psychodynamic theorists. At this point the work of the first developmental psychologist, Freud, becomes especially helpful, particularly as reconstructed by Lacan in his "return to Freud."

In Piagetian thinking, formal operations represent the "highest stage." Is there a "highest stage" of development? This book seriously questions this idea. Is it better to sense a flower directly (sensori-motor), place it in an arrangement (concrete operations), write a poem about one's feelings toward the flower (formal operations), or engage in a critical, egalitarian discourse on the nature of flowers (dialectics)? The search for "truth" and the highest good is indeed elusive.

Lacan implicitly suggests that there is a fourth stage of development—that of the dialectic in which the therapist and client become more coequal in the search for truth. However,

as Plato suggests in his comments on advanced stages of thinking (the "intelligible" world as compared to that of mere "appearances"), truth may slip away as quickly as it is discovered.
The dialectical fourth stage of therapy requires more attention
than therapists and theorists have accorded it to date.

The theory put forth in this book has highly specific implications for therapeutic practice. First, it is possible to identify the cognitive-developmental level of the client. Second, we
can match our verbal and nonverbal interventions to the specific
cognitive level of the client, thus facilitating exploration and
later cognitive-developmental processes. In effect, it is feasible
to match counseling skills and theory to the observable developmental level of the client.

One important extension of this approach is that different therapeutic modalities are especially effective for particular
cognitive levels. Thus relaxation training, Gestalt exercises, and
structured behavioral modification methods are attuned to the
sensori-motor level of development, while assertiveness training
and many of the cognitive-behavioral methods of Meichenbaum
are especially suitable for clients at the concrete operations
level. Thinking and feeling therapies may be appropriate for
those at the formal operational level of cognition.

This book is organized into eight chapters, which attempt
to present some highly complex and holistic ideas in linear
form. The last section of each chapter outlines a standard format that has proven useful in microtraining methodology. A
core construct from the chapter is presented in brief form, and
this is then followed by one or more practice exercises that
illustrate the construct. This instructional model has its origins
in Bandura's social learning theory but also represents Brentano's intentionality in action—thought (the construct of the
chapter) and action (the practice exercise) in relationship become one in *praxis.*

The first chapter provides an overview of the developmental therapy approach and relates the ideas of Plato and Piaget. Chapters Two and Three explore person-environment issues
and basic Piagetian constructs as they might appear analogically

in adult clients. Chapter Three contains highly specific suggestions for facilitating client cognitive development through the
several stages.

Chapter Four may be described as the heart of this book.
Figure 8 represents the basics of the developmental therapy approach as presented in a visual summary coupled with written
explanation of the process. Chapter Five supplements these concepts by exploring the nature of the change, developmental, or
transformational process. (These key words are used interchangeably.) Chapter Six examines how to assess client cognitive level and presents a detailed examination using a typescript
of a developmental therapy session. This chapter includes a
scale for the measurement of client progress.

The final two chapters extend the concepts of developmental therapy. Chapter Seven explores the implications of
Gilligan's relational theories of female development, the ideas of
Lacan, and the integrated work of Gregorc. Therapy is a whole;
it is not as linear and directed as traditional developmental theorists would have us believe. Thus, the intent in exploring the
ideas of these three highly diverse theorists is to integrate their
differences. Chapter Eight examines development over the total
life span and gives special attention to an adaptation of Bowlby's concepts of separation and attachment and also to the concept of development of the unconscious.

The concepts of developmental therapy reflected in
Plato's "Allegory of the Cave" initiated my exploration of this
topic many years ago. The Epilogue presents this perhaps most
famous writing of Plato and includes a developmental therapy
analysis that relates this philosophic work to practical issues of
therapy and practice.

Thus, this is a book for therapists and theorists, researchers and pragmatists. Developmental therapy suggests that it is
indeed possible to apply developmental theory directly to therapeutic and counseling practice and to measure that process.
Developmental therapy, particularly as presented in Chapter
Four and as reflected in the concepts of style-shift counseling,
is an integrating force for many diverse approaches to therapy.

In all, the central purpose is to facilitate client developmental processes.

For, is not all therapy and counseling ultimately about client development?

Amherst, Massachusetts   Allen E. Ivey
September 1986

Acknowledgments

As a first-year student at Stanford University in 1951, the high-light of my week was Jerry A. O'Callaghan's class in Western civilization. He introduced us not only to history, but also to art, music, and philosophy. The most fascinating and puzzling portion of the course came early in our discussion of Plato's "Allegory of the Cave" from *The Republic*. The prisoners' search for truth and the light within and outside the cave has been my own goal ever since. At one time the words of the Allegory were repeated as the first statements of Chapter One. As the book progressed, the importance of the Allegory remained, but has been moved to serve as an Epilogue. Jerry O'Callaghan is now retired from governmental work and serves as volunteer historian with the Bureau of Land Management. Dr. O'Callaghan, thank you for starting me toward the light.

In an *American Psychologist* review of my 1971 book, *Microcounseling*, Norman Sprinthall provided kindly support, and the title of his review, "Sooner or Later . . .", was perhaps the first indication that this book on developmental therapy was necessary. In his supportive review, he commented that the microskills model had utility but that "sooner or later, a theoretical justification for the model was required."

This book has its origins in a dream I had in 1968 just as

our group at Colorado State University was completing its first monograph on microcounseling and microskills. The dream resulted in an article, "Communication as Adaptation," which was co-authored with James Hurst. This article provided the conceptual foundations of the relationship of counseling process and outcome that form the foundation of Chapter Two and were prescient of the Platonic concepts of knowledge (*episteme*) and intelligence (*noesis*) that are so important to the book.

In June of 1983, I was invited to speak on microcounseling to students and faculty at the University of Oporto, Portugal. Norman Sprinthall had spoken on developmental psychoeducation to this same group some four months previously. Again, my presentation was well received, but I was bombarded by student and faculty questions about the relationship of microskills and therapy to the developmental process. Bartolo Campos, professor and head of the psychology and education department, and assistant professor Oscar Goncalves were particularly helpful in stimulating questions.

During the fall of 1983, I decided to take a course in Piagetian theory from George Forman, a past president of the Jean Piaget Society and a fellow faculty member at the School of Education at the University of Massachusetts. Later that fall, I was invited to serve as Lansdowne Scholar at the University of Victoria, British Columbia. There at a faculty presentation, I outlined the specific concepts that form the core of this book. My discussion with Donald Knowles, a faculty member there, was especially helpful, and his wonderful little book (co-authored with Nancy Reeves) *But, Won't Granny Need Her Socks?* holds a special place on my bookshelf.

The following January was a very hard time in Amherst, Massachusetts. It was cold and bleak. My favorite person, Mary Bradford Ivey, was visiting her mother in Florida. So in seven exhausting days, I input the entire first draft of this manuscript on my word processor and forwarded what was then entitled *Genetic Epistemology* to Jossey-Bass Publishers.

Their acceptance was not an end point, but a beginning. William Henry, Ursula Delworth, and Gracia Alkema have challenged me to be precise, to meet deadlines, and to expand concepts to a more pragmatic level. They also did not like the old title. There is no doubt that without their constant support, encouragement, and urging, this manuscript would never have been finished. The most sincere thanks to them—and they were right about the title! The manuscript was given its final polish by Evelyn Mercer Ward, who copyedited it. My appreciation goes to her for her thoughtful and careful work.

The spring of 1984 brought new challenges. I attended a course taught by John Muller of Austen Riggs Center, Stockbridge, and William Richardson of Boston College at the University of Massachusetts on Jacques Lacan's seminar on Edgar Allan Poe's "The Purloined Letter." Some Piaget was mixed in with the Lacan, and developmental therapy expanded still further. Then followed a second course with John Muller and Donald Levine, of the Department of Comparative Literature, in which we reviewed Hegel, dialectics, and Lacan. Two additional courses with Jennifer Stone of the university's comparative literature department resulted in the addition of even more complexities to the manuscript. Out of these experiences came the material in Chapter Four on "The Purloined Consciousness" and certainly some Lacanian "midspeak," which will require some decoding on the part of the reader.

At the same time that I was exposed to Lacan, I visited Chuck Easton's used bookstore in Mt. Vernon, Washington, and found Cornford's translation of Plato's *Republic*. Easton was my former high school band leader (he may recall me as a less-than-adequate tuba player). The route toward publication is indeed devious. On this trip I reread Plato's "Allegory of the Cave" and noted important parallels between Plato's conceptions of development and those of Piaget. In the class I taught that presented these ideas, a graduate student, Tod Rossi, severely criticized my linear presentation and told me of his study with Joyce Elbrecht of Ithaca College. Elbrecht's conception, as communicated by Rossi, was an important breakthrough and enabled me to move away from a linear presentation of the developmental model and to emphasize the recycling nature of experience—the beginning again.

During the fall of 1985, Oscar Goncalves from the University of Oporto came to the University of Massachusetts on a Fulbright grant. Weekly breakfast discussions with Oscar at "Rooster's" were critical to the evolution of ideas about the developmental therapy orientation and its dialectical relationship with the work of Piaget, Plato, Freud, Lacan, and others. There is a lot of Oscar in this book.

During 1985 and 1986, I made constant revisions, seeking commentaries from my colleagues; the manuscript just would not stand still and be finished. It still is not finished; the developmental therapy conceptions are rich in ideas that have an effect and change other ideas written earlier. Clearly, developmental therapy is only in its beginning stages.

Many people were helpful in the process of writing this book. Fred Sweitzer (University of Hartford, human services) and Mitchell Kosh (DeSisto Schools) were especially helpful and lavish with extensive written and verbal feedback. Eric Hewton and Peter Kutnick of the University of Sussex provided incisive commentaries. Marie Litterer brought T. S. Eliot to my attention and showed me how his poetry captured in a few short lines much of the essence of this book. Alfred Alschuler, Gerald Weinstein, and George Forman of the University of Massachusetts kindly commented on portions of the manuscript. A number of students of the University of Massachusetts provided useful ideas, especially Miguel Rivera, Edward McCreanor, Patrick Fleming, Margaret Flaherty, and William Mailler. Electra Petropulos helped by translating Greek used by Lacan and thus led me to a deeper understanding of Plotinus and of Lacan's relationship to Heidegger. John Ivey of the London School of Economics provided extensive and helpful editing and textual criticism. William Matthews, my colleague in counseling psychology, offered his support, criticism, and fresh ideas. Terry D. Anderson of Fraser Valley College, British Columbia, has been a consistent friend and colleague in this process. His conceptions of style-shift counseling were important in the construction of Chapter Four. Frank Reilly's warmth and wisdom have brought me to new levels of understanding of John Bowlby's separation and attachment conceptions. Carol B. Germain of the University of Connecticut School of Social Work provided extremely useful criticisms of my use of object relations theory and helped me forge a closer intellectual bond with John Bowlby.

Malcolm Pines of Tavistock Clinic, London, offered commentary and suggestions early in my work on the manuscript. And, as the book was nearing its final stages, he provided some last-minute clarifications and ideas that have been most important. His standards of excellence and personal support are warmly appreciated. Lois Grady was especially helpful, and the representation of the developmental sphere, which is central to this book, was her visual conception of early chapters I shared with her. My original developmental model was linear, then changed to a cyclical quadrant, then to a spiral, and then to a cycle on a spiral; finally Lois integrated the several dimensions into one unified visual concept.

Maurice and Fran Howe of Melbourne, Australia, have actively been involved in the dialectics of developmental therapy throughout the entire process of writing this book. Their emotional and intellectual support is especially treasured. Kenneth and Marjorie Blanchard of Blanchard Training and Development, San Diego, have been with me in important ways throughout this process. Discussion with them concerning their Situational Leadership model has been most helpful in formulating some of the early ideas of therapeutic style matching.

Machiko Fukuhara of Jissen Women's University, Tokyo, Japan, granted me permission to use her interesting paper on and diagrams of the development of a single client during seven interviews. Her work helped me realize that development may well be a cross-cultural, multicultural phenomenon.

Special thanks also go to my DEC-Rainbow 100 and to the Wordstar (R) package. A computer certainly makes things easier, but when one loses half a chapter with the push of a button, one certainly wonders whether the whole package is a developmental step forward or three steps backward!

It also is appropriate to acknowledge the most important contributor to this support network—Mary Bradford Ivey. Mary is not only my wife, she is also my co-author, a spirited coach and consultant, an endlessly talented listener, and a therapist.

She exemplifies all that developmental therapy stands for in every way. Her therapeutic style is analyzed in detail in Chapter Six, and the reader may understand the joy her presence brings me.

Developmental Therapy: Theory into Practice is the result of the thoughts and efforts of many people. Lacanian theory discusses how our discourse may be considered "the discourse of the Other." According to my interpretation of the discourse of the Other, the generation of an independently authored book is somewhat of a misnomer. The dialectics of relationship and interdependence suggest that no one is alone, even in the painful, lonely process of authorship.

Given the dictates of our particular culture, however, this book is ultimately my responsibility. The particular interpretations and integration of concepts herein are my own, and as the reader may note, I have been liberal in my constructions and interpretations of existing theories; the search for unifying constructs requires flexibility and adaptation. However, the development of these ideas would not have been possible without this large and supportive group of people and the relationships we share with each other. This book is about our interdependence and need to be aware of the complexity of interactions with others. This book is not an end; rather, I hope it serves as some small beginning step toward a more unified view of the developmental process that is therapy.

The Author

Allen E. Ivey is professor and codirector of the Counseling Psychology Program at the University of Massachusetts, Amherst. He received his A.B. degree, Phi Beta Kappa, in psychology from Stanford University in 1955. After a year as a Fulbright scholar at the University of Copenhagen, he completed his Ed.D. degree (1959) in counseling at Harvard University.

Ivey is perhaps best known for his twenty years of writing and research in microcounseling, the delineation of specific skills of helping via video analysis. Developmental therapy and its special applications in psychoanalytic and multicultural dimensions occupy much of his current activity.

Ivey, a diplomate in counseling psychology of the American Board of Professional Psychology, is past president of the Division of Counseling Psychology of the American Psychological Association (APA) and is currently a member of the APA Council and a fellow of the APA. He has served as a Fulbright Senior Lecturer and Distinguished Visitor in Psychology at Flinders University, South Australia (1982), and has lectured throughout Europe, the Pacific, and Japan. Ivey's clinical experience includes the founding of counseling centers at Bucknell University (1959) and Colorado State University (1963) and consulting appointments at the Veterans Administration in Northampton, Massachusetts (1969–1972, 1985–present). He has authored more than 10 books (translated into 7 languages) and more than 120 articles. Among these are *Microcounseling* ([1971] 1978), with J. Authier, *Counseling and Psychotherapy* ([1980] 1987), with M. Ivey and L. Simek-Downing, and *Face to Face: Management Communication Skills* (1979), with J. Litterer.

Developmental Therapy

Theory into Practice

To Mary Bradford Ivey—scholar, co-author,
and friend—a multiplicity in One

1

Developmental Therapy

An Introduction

The following is taken from an initial interview with a ten-year-old client:

Client: (*In tears.*) My life is a mess. I just can't do anything. It's awful.

Therapist: Sounds like you feel pretty bad. What's bothering you?

Client: It's total—impossible.

Therapist: Could you tell me one specific thing that is impossible?

Client: My room! (*More tears.*) It's like my life. It's a total mess. I can't find anything.

Therapist: Tell me about your room . . .

And so it begins—the process of therapy. Many, perhaps most, clients come to therapy and counseling with lives that are messy and disorganized. Their development has been stymied and they are "stuck" and immobilized. The task of therapy is to free the client for intentional movement and development.

In this case, the client is confused and lost in a world of multiple and mixed sensory impressions. The therapist refuses to accommodate the confusion and instead starts immediately to organize and assimilate data, thereby initiating the process of development. The young client starts with total confusion; the therapist listens and reflects the emotions underlying the confusion and then raises the client's cognitive level with the simple but critical question "Could you tell me one specific thing that is impossible?" By asking for a concrete example of the impossible, the therapist has already lessened the client's confusion and the session begins to have a focus. At a later point in therapy, underlying issues and the full complexity of "life's mess" can be more fully understood.

A room is a metaphor that may be used by more than one client. We live in arbitrary spaces given to us by our culture and family script. We can only develop within the confines of the room provided for us. The confused, mixed messages that culture and family provide often stultify growth rather than facilitate it. Therapy and counseling aim to make sense of the room life gives us and to develop our potential as full human beings.

Developmental Therapy as Integrated Practice

Developmental theory has been too long separated from clinical practice. This book presents a systematic model of developmental practice that is an adaptation of Platonic philosophy and the developmental psychology of Jean Piaget. Developmental therapy focuses on both the process and outcome of development and suggests specific therapeutic techniques that may be employed to facilitate growth and change.

Clients bring various developmental issues into the counseling and therapy environment. The therapist can first assess the client's developmental level and then use developmentally appropriate interventions to facilitate personal growth. Different theories offer varying levels of utility at different stages of client growth. A framework for integrating theoretical constructs in a client's therapy so that it fits the particular pattern of developmental progression will be presented in this chapter.

First, however, developmental therapy must be briefly defined. Developmental therapy, as constructed here, is a new, integrative position, which I present as having four key perspectives:

1. *A philosophical position* that is based on an alternative reading of Plato, which considers the paradox of develop-

ment best summarized, perhaps, by T. S. Eliot at the end of "Little Gidding."

> We shall not cease from exploration
> And the end of all our exploring
> Will be to arrive where we started
> And know the place for the first time.
>   [1943, p. 39]

Life is simultaneously a journey, a destination, and a state of being. The journey is development; the destination is an inevitable repetition of our return to where we began (but with a new state of awareness); and the state of being is our ontology, our total experience of the past, present, and future.

2. *A theory of human development in the counseling and therapy process* that is a unique synthesis of the work of Plato, Piaget, and other developmental theorists. The theoretical model presented here is *not* that of Plato or Piaget; rather, it is a new model that has evolved from and adds new dimensions to their work.

Central to the developmental therapy model is the belief that developmental progressions recycle back to the beginning, back to where we started; but our awareness of this progression and our return to the starting point is paradoxically a continuing new awareness.

3. *A practice of therapy and counseling* that is based on my previous work in the skills and structure of counseling and psychotherapy (Ivey, 1971; Ivey and Authier, 1978; Ivey, 1983a, 1983b; Ivey, Ivey, and Simek-Downing, 1987). In this continually evolving and changing model of therapeutic action, theory is brought into practice with the anticipation of predictable results in the client as a result of the therapist's specific interventions. In the developmental therapy model, specific developmental and cognitive changes in the client can be anticipated through specific action on the part of therapist and counselor.

4. *A coconstructed model of the therapy session* in which the therapist is as impacted by the client as the client is

by the therapist. Underlying this model is a belief in the co-construction of reality, a dialectical model in which truth comes not from one source but through coevolution with the client in the therapeutic environment.

These are the four major concepts of developmental therapy. The following sections will define development, consider how Piagetian theory relates to adult development, and illustrate parallels between Piaget's developmental theory and that of Plato. The combination of Piagetian and Platonic concepts ultimately results in the general model of development that undergirds the conceptions of this book.

Development: A Definition

Development is the goal of counseling and psychotherapy. Whether we as therapists seek to facilitate a client's ego development, identity development, or to encourage the development of human relations skills, we are concerned with developing change and growth in the client. Therapists often talk about cognitive and affective development as being the central goal of therapy. College student personnel staff are concerned with student development, management consultants with organizational development and human resources development.

Development involves changing and developing new behaviors and systems that are more effective in the real world. Development also requires the individual to change less easily identifiable ideas, beliefs, attitudes, and even unconscious processes. Development is a generic process critical to and underlying human growth, change, and transformation.

The *Oxford English Dictionary* (compact edition, 1971) offers eleven distinct meanings for the word "development." Development is first defined as a process and an outcome: "The process or fact of developing; the concrete result of this process." Development as a process *and* as an outcome is critical to the thesis of this book: counseling and psychotherapy are developmental processes that lead to a wide array of developmental outcomes among clients. This seemingly simple statement can become more complex when one considers that the processes of counseling and psychotherapy are simultaneously outcomes of theoretical and empirical practice. For example, psychoanalytic therapeutic practices and processes are the outcomes of previous work by Freud and his descendants. The unity of process and outcome is a basic, underlying theme of this book.

Clients come to therapy with processes that have ceased to be effective. A phobia is a process that is an outcome of other factors and processes in the client's life. Client development is clearly a unity of process and outcome. As therapists, our task is to free the client of ineffective processes in order to encourage further development. The outcome of development is more development—more of the same process of the continuous clarification of ideas and reality.

Finally, development is closely associated with a variety of words, each of which provides useful distinctions but addresses similar phenomena. Words such as "change," "growth," "creativity and creation," "transformation," and "evolution" all relate to central aspects of development and at times will be used interchangeably with the word "development."

The working definition of development presented here depends on the interplay of process and outcome. As both a process and outcome, the construct "development" has many possible meanings and applications. The frameworks and paradigms for examining such a complex construct are also many.

Some Alternative Constructions of Development

There are many ways to portray development, and a number of developmental theorists have addressed this task. They portray the developmental process in varying visual models, all of which are interesting and valid.

Development is often presented as a hierarchy, where the individual moves from "lower" to "higher" levels of complexity and organization. Figure 1 presents three well-known developmental models that follow this structure—a structure that has value because it is familiar and clear. It is possible to anticipate developmental movement and look forward to specific goals in the change process. Models such as those portrayed in Figure 1

Figure 1. Three Models of Development

Moral Development (Kohlberg, 1981)	Ego Development (Loevinger, Wessler, and Redmore, 1970)	Intellectual and Ethical Development (Perry, 1970)
	Presocial	
Obedience and punishment	Symbolic impulsive	Basic duality
	Self-protective	Multiplicity pre-legitimate
	Conformist	Multiplicity subordinate
Naive egoistic		Multiplicity coordinate or relative subordinate
	Conscientious	Relativism correlate, competing, or diffuse
Good persons	Autonomous	Commitment foreseen
Authority and social order maintaining		Initial commitment
Contractual, legalistic		Orientation in implications of commitment
Conscience or principle	Integrated	Developing commitments

are often used as goals for training others in moral, ego, or intellectual development.

The disadvantage of the linear model is that it sometimes assumes that "higher" is better, an assumption that the cyclical and relational developmental theorist Gilligan (1982) seriously questions in her ground-breaking book on the moral development of women entitled *In a Different Voice*. Gilligan suggests that linear, hierarchical models may be appropriate for men but do not adequately account for the complex, relational world of women. In the Gilligan model, development is construed as a matter of recycling an issue or developmental task and more fully coming to terms with the complexity of relationships. Gilligan questions the hierarchical male model.

Kegan (1982) challenges the hierarchical model still further by offering a spiraling model of development. He proposes that development recycles back on itself, and with every recycling, a new developmental level is reached. He adapts and extends Piagetian theory in his discussion of the incorporative, impulsive, imperial, interpersonal, institutional, and inter-individual self. Kegan also points out that development occurs in a sociopolitical and cultural context. Specifically, what is stage-appropriate development in one culture may be inappropriate in another.

Although the Gilligan model has had a profound impact and describes much of women's development in new and important ways, it does not sufficiently allow for relational developmental processes that may occur for men as well as for women. Some women do move through the Kohlbergian hierarchies of moral development. The Kegan spiraling model combines the advantages of the linear and the cyclical models. Kegan writes of periods of truce, where the developmental spiral in effect stays relatively still for a time and gains a sense of itself before moving on again.

My goal in this book is to incorporate as much as possible of these highly useful models of development—the linear and hierarchical, cyclical, and spiraling models of the development process—into one conceptual model of development that also takes into account critical sexual, cultural, ethical, and political differences. A distinction made by the present model of development is an emphasis on simultaneity—all things happening at once. We do develop in orderly progressions, we do seem to turn back on ourselves in repeating patterns, and yet the whole seems always more than the sum of its parts.

Development Theory, Piaget, and Therapeutic Movement

Developmental theory has been conceptualized from different perspectives. Erikson's ([1950] 1963) psychoanalytic developmental conceptions, Kohlberg's (1981) moral development theory, and Loevinger, Wessler, and Redmore's (1970) ego development concepts are but three examples of important, influential perspectives on this area. However, most of the work in development has remained theoretical and has had relatively little influence on daily clinical practice.

Development inevitably seems to be conceptualized as a

series of levels or steps that individuals move through in a relatively systematic fashion. It is expected that the individual must learn to stand solidly on one developmental step before moving on to the next. Piaget's developmental theory stresses this point. For example, in *The Moral Judgment of the Child* (1965), he comments that a child cannot develop more complex ideas of morality unless basic stages have been solidly established.

Two central types of development should be stressed. We most often think of development as moving ahead to the next stage, to the next problem or opportunity. This may be termed *vertical development*—the ascent of varying developmental steps. But *horizontal development,* the building of an adequate foundation, is usually required before moving to another stage. For example, in therapy we often observe clients' sudden insights; in the process it appears that important developmental gains have been made. However, the next week we may find that no change has been implemented and that the important insight has been forgotten or repressed. In such cases, horizontal development and understanding need further explication before an advance can be made to the next stage of development.

The importance of horizontal development and its later influence is perhaps most clearly exemplified in Erikson's eight stages of development (1950). A person must work through issues of "basic trust versus basic mistrust" as an infant if he or she is later to be effective in negotiating the developmental task of "autonomy versus shame and doubt." Also, if an adolescent is to develop a clear self-concept or identity, earlier stages must have been successfully worked through.

Figure 2 outlines Erikson's eight stages of individual development. Erikson notes that all stages are operative throughout one's life, although one development issue is usually primary at each stage. Thus, a teenager who is working through identity versus role confusion issues still has continuing concerns about trust, autonomy, and initiative, and these are constantly reworked. In addition, matters of intimacy, generativity, and ego integrity cannot be fully separated, and the manner in which the youth works through identity will have an impact in later developmental stages. Thus, the Erikson model represents an early attempt to portray development both as linear and hierarchical (Kohlberg) as well as relational (Gilligan).

Figure 2. Erikson's Stages of Development

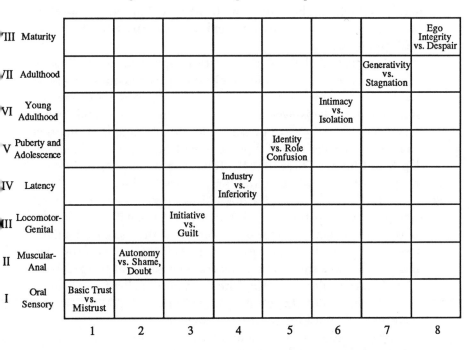

	1	2	3	4	5	6	7	8
VIII Maturity								Ego Integrity vs. Despair
VII Adulthood							Generativity vs. Stagnation	
VI Young Adulthood						Intimacy vs. Isolation		
V Puberty and Adolescence					Identity vs. Role Confusion			
IV Latency				Industry vs. Inferiority				
III Locomotor-Genital			Initiative vs. Guilt					
II Muscular-Anal		Autonomy vs. Shame, Doubt						
I Oral Sensory	Basic Trust vs. Mistrust							

Source: Reprinted from *Childhood and Society* by Erik H. Erikson, by permission of W. W. Norton & Company, Inc. Copyright renewed 1968 by Erik H. Erikson. Permission also kindly granted by Hogarth Press, London, England.

Piaget's well-known framework of development includes (1) the sensori-motor stage, where the infant learns to integrate perceptual and motor schema into an ever-increasing whole; (2) the preoperational stage, the time of early language learning and representations; (3) the concrete operations stage, where the young child learns to act on the world and think about that world; and (4) the final stage, usually reached in early adolescence, in which the young person becomes more fully in touch with affect and feelings and is able to reflect on the self and to "think about thinking." Piaget's work is usually regarded as concerning primarily children and youth. Kegan's (1982) recent adaptation of Piagetian thinking extends this model and specifically discusses dialectics as a possible "post-formal" mode of thinking. Despite the conceptual power of Piagetian thought, relatively little has been done with the model in terms of practical applications in counseling and therapy, particularly with adult populations.

Analogues of the Piagetian stages appear again and again in adult development and in psychotherapy and counseling processes. Movement through the stages of development may be more rapid, perhaps even instantaneous, in the adult, but there is evidence that they are present, identifiable, and useful in the therapeutic process. This argument will be presented in more depth in Chapter Three, but the following summary provides an overview of the developmental therapy orientation.

1. *Preoperational Factors.* Most, perhaps all, clients in therapy seek help for *preoperational* problems. They are unable to operate or act on their environment with desired effectiveness. They may lack the appropriate behavior or be prone to magical or fuzzy thinking that leaves them stuck at the preoperational stage of development. The ten-year-old client mentioned at the beginning of this chapter was clearly not able to operate in a predictable fashion on the environment.

The preoperational mode of thought can, and does, continue beyond Piaget's age seven.

2. *Sensori-Motor Factors.* Effective therapists are interested in knowing how the client constructs the preoperational problem. They want to know how the client *sees, hears, and feels* the problem through sensory-based data. This grounding in sensory-based data provides the therapist with the specific schema on which he or she can later help the client move toward more effective ways of being. In the search for concrete perceptions (whether behavioral or cognitive), the therapist moves back from preoperational thinking to more basic elements of perception. Since the therapist in the case of the ten-year-old asked for concrete specifics, she was simultaneously obtaining sensory impressions of the child and starting to concretely organize the facts and feelings of the situation.

3. *Concrete Operations.* Counselors begin the transformation process and assist their clients to think concretely about their situations by asking the question "Could you give me a specific (concrete) example?" Using a variety of techniques (for

example, assertiveness training, identification of irrational ideas and thought processes), therapists help clients learn to identify the linear causes and effects of their problems and to act on them more efficiently. With a ten-year-old client, a therapist is likely to stop therapy, since formal operations are not really possible. With an older client, more cognitive awareness may be needed.

4. *Formal Operations.* Some therapists emphasize reflecting on problems (to think about thinking), and the client is encouraged to find a self-concept (Rogerian person-centered theory) or to analyze thoughts and emotions (psychodynamic methods). Furthermore, those therapists who emphasize a cognitive-behavioral approach seek to unite thought with behavior. Not only must we think about behavioral change but we must also take concrete action.

As can be seen from the above, each client presents basic cognitive or behavioral styles that can be identified and modified using the highly specific developmental techniques of existing systems of counseling and therapy.

Much of the understanding of Piagetian theory is based on the assumption that formal operations is the final stage of development. Kegan's dialectic, or post-formal, stage is considered by many Piagetians simply as an extension of the formal operations stage, because once a person is able to engage in formal operations, it is possible to conduct an almost infinite series of increasingly sophisticated cognitive operations. For example, formal operations requires one to think about thinking. The next step is to think about thinking about thinking, and this can continue to many levels of abstraction.

The concept of dialectics makes an important contribution to Piagetian developmental theory; dialectics is also rooted in Platonic thought.

Plato as a Developmental Theorist

The transition to enlightenment, according to Plato, involves four levels of cognitive development. Each level of consciousness builds on previous perceptions of reality and prepares the way for the next higher level. Cornford has outlined Plato's levels of consciousness, and Figure 3 reveals interesting and useful parallels between Piagetian constructs of development and Platonic thought.

**Figure 3. Structural Similarities of Piagetian and Platonic
Developmental Frameworks**

Level	*Piaget*	*Plato's States of Mind*
World of appearances	Sensori-motor Preoperational Concrete operations	Imagining (*eikasia*) Belief (*pistis*)

Line between outer
  visible world and
  the world of ideas
	⎯⎯⎯⎯⎯⎯⎯⎯⎯⎯⎯⎯⎯⎯⎯⎯⟶	

Intelligible world	Formal operations (Post-formal)	Thinking (*dianoia*) Knowledge (*episteme*) Intelligence (*noesis*)

The Platonic model is first divided into the "world of appearances" (the outer visible world) and the "intelligible world" (the world of ideas). There are useful correspondences between Plato's concepts and the distinctions made in psychology between behavior and cognition. The world of appearances can be seen, felt, touched, and concretely believed in or acted on. In the most general sense, the world of appearances is roughly equivalent to the word "behavior," but this level is also concerned with elementary cognitions. The intelligible world corresponds to more sophisticated cognitions. The intelligible world is in truth more complex than visible appearance would suggest. Thus, the reality of life and of behavior goes far beyond mere visible appearance. Awareness of reality requires understanding and experience in both the visible and intelligible worlds. Understanding of *both* the visible (concrete and behavioral) world and the intelligible (cognitions) world is necessary for reality coping, although in much of Plato there is the implication that the "highest good" is represented by the intelligible world of the more complex cognitions.

Irigary (1985) sharply criticizes Plato and the concept of

"highest good." She sees this as an example of a male-ordered universe. Several alternative readings of Plato are possible. The position taken here is that *both* linear and holistic interpretations of Platonic thought are useful. (Also see further comments on Irigary in the Epilogue of this book.)

There are four levels that Plato termed "states of mind" that are derived from the idea of visible and intelligible worlds and are important for theory and practice. In turn, each state of mind has an "object" toward which it is directed. Plato calls the first state of mind (or cognition) *eikasia* (or imagining), and this level may be considered analogous to that of Piaget's sensori-motor functions. In this state the individual is bombarded by a sensory world of images, and the unenlightened mind believes that these appearances are true reality. At the sensori-motor stage, the young child experiences the "bumbling confusion" of the world's images, and the first task for the child is to sort out and make sense of these images. Adults and children who fail to make sense of the images remain preoperational and magical in their functioning. An example would be a child of five who notes the shadow following him or her while walking. The child may reason in this way: "That shadow knows where I am going and keeps following me." Most children at some point try to run away from their shadows. Children have explanations that work, but they do not have accurate representations of reality.

Many clients come to therapy with such magical images, and their cognitive level is again parallel to that of imagining (*eikasia*). For example, the neurotic patient who believes he or she is being followed or who has to wash his or her hands frequently to avoid germs is reacting to magical images. The ten-year-old presented at the beginning of this chapter is initially embedded in a sensori-motor world of confused and blurred images. Through intelligent questioning, the therapist readily moved the child to a more concrete, less diffuse level of cognition.

The next level of cognition is *pistis,* or belief in visible things. Plato talks about "correct beliefs without knowledge." Here the child or adult becomes aware of visible concrete objects, their names, and the cultural ordering of reality. The individual is able to act, but has limited knowledge or cognition of reasons for action. This second level of consciousness may be illustrated by the child who holds concrete beliefs and acts appropriately but does not know the reason why. A client in therapy may either act appropriately or inappropriately, but he or she will be responding to visible appearances. He or she may be thinking about a problem but will fail to think about thinking. Therapies that operate at the level of belief or action include much of traditional behavioral therapy, the skills training movement, and Glasser's (1965) early work in reality therapy.

The state of mind at the third level is termed *dianoia,* or thinking. Plato believed that mathematics represents best the way to describe the object of the abstract thinking process. Through mathematics, we build abstract models that serve as bridges to help explain the world of appearances. In a similar fashion, we build models of humankind (for example, psychoanalytic, Rogerian, religious, or economic) to explain what happens in our world. Clients, just like therapists, can build models to explain reality. And just as models of mathematics are incomplete, so are our models of human abstraction. Again, Plato points out the limitations of model building by reminding us that mathematical models are built on unprovable assumptions. "The premises may be true and the conclusions may follow, but the whole structure hangs in the air until the assumptions themselves have been shown to depend on an unconditional principle. . . . *Dianoia* suggests discursive thinking or reasoning from premise to conclusion" (quoted in Cornford, [1941] 1982, p. 223). A similar point can be made about theories of counseling and therapy that themselves are models of reality. Much of therapeutic theory fails to examine the premises on which it is built. This third level of cognition is perhaps best illustrated by formal-operational adolescents who are learning to see others' perspectives and to discover that there may be more than one way to interpret a situation. This development of alternative perceptions is, in truth, a sort of model building that goes on in the mind. A major developmental task of the adolescent is to learn to understand the perspective of the other. Empathy similarly requires counselors and therapists to think about their clients' thought processes and models.

Rogerian and psychodynamic therapy are prime examples of abstract models of helping in this category. The object of these therapies is to think about abstractions. To what degree these therapists pay attention to their premises is an interesting question. Many theorists all too frequently hold an egocentric commitment to their position that resembles the single-mindedness of the early adolescent. In their model building, these therapists and theoreticians often forget that the models are built on premises and assumptions just as are mathematical models. However, since the vast majority of the client population operates in the *dianoia,* or thinking level of consciousness, "thinking therapies" are likely to be highly favored.

George Kelly (1955), a personality theorist, describes humankind as scientists who are constantly hypothesizing (model building) about their environment, testing their hypotheses, and revising them on the data received in an ever-expanding set of personal constructs. His work is closely attuned to the final set of Platonic constructs.

The fourth state of consciousness is concerned with the search for "Forms." The object of the states of mind is the ultimate search for truth and for "the Good." The debate about the most correct and comprehensive psychological theory can be considered an example of the search for the Form of the Good. Rather than define goodness, Plato prefers to outline the process of finding the Form through the dialectic. Dialectic has become a word with confusing associations. Cornford ([1941] 1982) states: "In the *Republic,* it simply means the technique of philosophical conversation (dialogue) carried on by a question and answer and seeking to render, or to receive from a respondent, an 'account' (*logos*) of some Form."

Thus, dialogue (dialectic) centrally involves a discussion or search for truth or goodness (which are themselves undefined). This simple concept of dialectic as dialogue is important. By this definition, ordinary conversations, counseling and therapy, and academic debate join together as varying forms of dialectic. Dialectic or dialogue is not above or beyond most people; it is part of everyday life. True dialogue, however, is more complex than simple conversation; dialectic requires a special type of interaction. True dialectics requires the participant (ideally, both participants) to have "dialectical awareness." Specifically, this is the awareness of the existence of the dialectic itself and of the elusive nature of truth.

Important in dialogue and the search for Forms (models, theories, meanings) is the examination of premises and assumptions. Whereas the search in the consciousness level of *dianoia* is for models but not for the premises on which the models are built, the emphasis at this fourth level (*episteme*) is on examination of foundation ideas. Here there is a level of abstraction in which the individuals involved in dialogue or dialectic are "thinking about thinking about thinking," similar to continuing reflections in a set of mirrors. Two people may debate about the notion of the goodness or value of the analytic construct of repression. At the *dianoia* level of consciousness, they may argue or dispute the question of whether or not such a construct is useful and in fact whether repression exists at all. This is a typical and long-debated question in the field (for example, see Lieberson, 1985, for a review of the issue of the goodness of the Forms invented by Freud). At the fourth level of *episteme*, the discussant becomes concerned with the definition of premises: "What is goodness?" "What is value?" "Can we agree on a common definition of repression even though our definition may be incomplete?" Too many psychological battles are argued at lower levels of cognition; more dialogue and examination of premises are needed.

Therapies that operate at the level of the dialectic are only now beginning to be conceptualized. Feminist therapy (Ballou and Gabalac, 1984) is perhaps the clearest example of a systematic format for helping that relies on an egalitarian model. In this model, the therapist attempts to be the client's equal and to seriously examine the premises and assumptions on which individual problems may be conceptualized. Specifically, feminist therapy seeks out contradictions in typical male-oriented, defined therapy and considers truth from a markedly different perspective to the many orientations of counseling.

Yet, is the final definition of truth, goodness, or Form possible? Plato wisely never used hard-and-fast technical terms (see Cornford, [1941] 1982). He changed meanings of terms to fit special needs and situations. The closer one gets to truth and final answers, paradoxically, the more one is aware of complexity and of the ultimate looseness or permeability of words and constructs. Again, there exists a close parallel between some of Kelly's (1955) thinking and ancient Greek philosophy. In this area a special awareness of the nature of dialectics and their implications for therapeutic practice is of central importance.

Dialectics and Therapeutic Method

Most development theorists tend to believe that reality is constructed within the person. However, the dialectical view is that reality is coconstructed: It takes two to construct an idea, a concept, or a thing. The "two" in this case can be two concepts in one person's mind. Thus, coconstruction of reality can exist either inside or outside the individual. Dialectical reasoning can exist within one individual or between two individuals.

Piaget perhaps best illustrates the coconstruction of reality in his first major work, *The Language and Thought of the Child* ([1930] 1955).* His study of children's conversations is a classic of coconstruction, but is not typically considered a prime example of dialectics. Piaget ([1930] 1955) notes the process of dialectic discovery of two children and how the *structure* of their thoughts might resemble that of an adult thinking about him- or herself in therapy or a therapist thinking about how to handle a forthcoming interview.

When . . . can conversation properly be said to take place between children? Whenever—to fix an arbi-

---

The Thought and Language of the Child was first published in French in 1923 and appeared in English in 1926. Piaget was criticized for some of the ideas in this book, which is perhaps the most dialectical of his works. When it was published in second edition in 1930 (the reference used in this book), he speaks of these criticisms and aims for greater clarity of expression. It is believed by some that the criticisms led Piaget away from a dialectical, person-environment approach to development to an examination of the inner cognitive world of the child.

trary minimum—three consecutive remarks about the same subject are made by at least two interlocutors.

1. Remark by A.
2. Remark by B adapted to 1.
3. Remark by A adapted to 2 [p. 71].

Pie [6;5 (6 years, 5 months)] :   Now, you shan't have it (*the pencil*) because you asked for it.

Hei [6;0] :   Yes I will, because it is mine.

Pie: 'Course it isn't yours. It belongs to everybody, to all the children.

Lev [6;0] :   Yes, it belongs to Mlle. L. and all the children, to Ai and to My too.

Pie: It belongs to Mlle. L. because she brought it, and it belongs to all the children as well [p. 88].

This simple three-step framework represents the dialectic or dialogue. It also represents "communication as adaptation" (see Chapter Two), which is parallel to the organism-environment transaction of biological evolution. By setting up an opposition or separation of two ideas, one person can construct reality in her or his head or two children can learn from one another or client and therapist can produce developmental change.

In psychotherapy, a client may make a statement. It is the task of the therapist to make a statement in reaction to the client. If the statement is helpful, the client may modify his or her construction of reality. If not, it becomes incumbent on the therapist to acknowledge this failure and to change his or her behavior. In therapy, failure to change is the responsibility of the therapist, not the client. Similarly, resistance is a problem of the therapist or counselor, not of the client. The dialectic of the therapist with the ten-year-old child illustrates this point. The therapist asked the ten-year-old child, "What's bothering you?" when the child described life as a mess. The child continued to repeat that life was a mess until the therapist realized the failure of the child to respond and then reformulated the question in more concrete terms that the child could respond to.

This constructivist view helps explain problems that clients bring to the therapeutic session. Often, for these clients, the process of constructive development has stopped. The individual may take an action (in the world or within his or her head) and experience a reaction but will *fail* to note the reaction. Thus the third requirement for construction noted by Piaget is absent. One of the goals of therapy is to open the individual's mind to constructive development and dialectics.

Dialectics involves a search for more workable answers and a search for truth. The young children in Piaget's example are hunting for the abstract concept of ownership—who owns the pencil. In the process, they discover that truth is somewhat elusive, although they seem to move toward a workable joint resolution. In a similar and parallel situation, we can imagine a client stuck originally with one version of truth (for instance that it is unfair for his wife to ask him for assistance in the kitchen) and then moving through the dialectic to an awareness of alternative constructions and beliefs about household work.

The word "dialectics" offers many possibilities for definition and usage. Alternative uses of the concept will be made in this book at different times. The first and most important meaning of dialectics is the idea of coconstruction of reality. Dialectics, in its most basic form, involves two (or more) people constructing truth or knowledge in an interaction. Piaget seems to move away from this important idea in the edition published in 1926, when he describes coconstruction clearly and returns to a "constructivist" position. In a constructivist dialectic, one person constructs the world within the self through interaction with the environment. Thus, the two most basic forms of dialectic involve coconstruction with others and an internal construction within the self.

Dialectics in practical formulations also appears in what the profession calls person-environment interaction. The relationship of person to environment and the change each causes in the other is a critical dialectical formulation. The therapist-client relationship can also be considered a dialectical, coconstructed approach to knowledge and truth. Other important dialectics discussed in this book are those of assimilation and accommodation, separation and attachment, and conscious and unconscious. In each of these dialectics, two concepts are defined in opposition to one another. It is the relationship of these oppositions that provides dialectical movement or evolving synthesis.

As this book progresses, the word "dialectic" is used in several different contexts in different ways. Two major formulations underlie these distinctions. First, the dialectic is a constant process that is always present and active (as the example of the young children described by Piaget shows). In such cases the dialectic occurs without conscious awareness on the part of the participants. This same lack of awareness of process may occur between client and therapist as well as in virtually any interaction we may have. Second, one may become aware or conscious of the dialectical process. This awareness shows up particularly in therapies, such as family therapy and feminist therapy, which attempt to examine the interview process as a person-environment interaction. Needless to say, the examination of transference and counter-transference issues or of relationship issues may involve this same awareness of the dialectic. In summary, the dialectic is always present even though we may be unaware of it. The words "person-environment" interaction, more familiar to the counseling and therapy professions, may often be used as substitute wording for "dialectic."

The "truth value" of a thought or action is critical to an examination of the outcome of psychotherapy. Plato examines this matter in some depth, which provides some guidance about the ultimate purpose of therapy.

The Nature of Dialectic Truth

Dialectics implies joint construction of reality. Two differing constructs are used by Plato to discuss the highest levels of dialectic truth. The distinction between *episteme* and *noesis* is important for an understanding of the complexity of Plato's highest level of consciousness.

Episteme may be equated to the word "knowledge." Knowledge may be the result of a search for truth. Examples of knowledge include the Newtonian theory of physics, Kelly's view of personality development (but not his process of thinking), and even the manner in which recipes for Italian pasta may be organized. In each of these models of knowledge, it is possible to examine underlying premises on which the theory is built. Knowledge is often distorted into a final "truth" that becomes fixed. Some religions and some theories of therapy represent this form of knowledge. The issue is clouded by the question "Does absolute, ever-changing truth exist?" Those who argue that it does have taken the leap of faith into knowledge.

Noesis may be translated as *intelligence* and represents a very different view of the dialectic from that of knowledge. The intelligent thinker recognizes truth as more elusive, believing that knowledge will pass away and change into new forms. Einstein brought a new view to physics by challenging and changing the assumptions of Newton. Paradoxically, Einstein's view, even though it may retain the idea of the relativity of truth, itself turns into knowledge. Knowledge and intelligence appear to be in their own unique dialectical relationship.

This may be illustrated by Kelly's work, which is indeed knowledge. Yet, as we use his theory of personal constructs, we find that his theory constantly changes and develops. Kelly's work is both everlasting and changing.

The concepts of knowledge and intelligence are directly applicable to psychotherapy theory and practice. Clients and therapists who seek certain knowledge can remain focused on a single world view or interpretation of events. A larger goal for therapy is intelligence—the awareness that truth will change with new data and understanding. In other words, every time a client solves a problem, a new problem will present itself.

"It is not things, but our view of things." This paraphrase of the first century Stoic philosopher Epictetus perhaps best summarizes the abstract issues within the world of knowledge and intelligence. Clients often come to therapy confused about reality, and their alternative conceptions of reality have gotten them into difficulty. Frankl's logotherapy, cognitive approaches, and many other orientations are concerned not so much with the visible world of behavioral change as with changing the way individuals think about themselves and their situations. For clients in therapy, the task is to facilitate dialectical movement toward development of increasingly adequate modes of dealing with truth. It is typical for clients to seek ultimate "perfect" truths. This search for *episteme,* or knowledge, may indeed be useful, but it may block and make difficult the awareness of *noesis,* the more elusive, changing truth of intelligence.

Therapeutic theory is by definition "above the line"—it is concerned with the intelligible world. However, much of theorizing fails to deal with the reality faced by the client. This is particularly apparent in the all-too-constant search for the single "best" method or theory, which fails to take into account that different individuals may have widely varying needs. However, the field seems to be currently moving toward a more eclectic or metatheoretical position as it redirects its search for commonalities among theories and increasingly recognizes that the "final truths" of therapy are less final than was once believed.

What is not always clear in Plato is that the distinction between appearance and intelligibility, although useful, is only a distinction. Plato apparently needed the distinction between concepts and objects to give substance to the dialectic. In his later works, *Sophist* and *Parmenides,* he argues against this separateness. For example, he argues that knowledge of nature is more attainable than is stated in the *Republic.* The ultimate integration of appearances and reality sought by Plato underlies a special purpose of this book—that, although many distinctions are made, ultimately a unified view of the person and of psychology is emphasized. Differences, distinctions, and dialectics are useful but may obscure underlying unity. (The concept of unity in spite of distinctions and differences will be explored in the final chapter.)

This discussion of the nature of dialectic truth is aimed at a specific criticism of the traditional interpretation of Plato and also of Figure 3, where Plato and Piaget are compared. The particular interpretation of Plato presented here is that there is no necessarily "higher" form of knowledge or intelligence; rather knowledge and intelligence exist themselves in a dialectical relationship. "Higher" and "better" depend on one's frame of reference and belief system. Thus, the linear model of Figure 3, although useful descriptively, is incomplete. Therefore, an integrated, visual model is proposed here as a metamodel of development.

The Development of Consciousness
as a Metagoal of Psychotherapy

An integrated model for the development of consciousness is presented in Figure 4. This model shows the developmental therapy orientation in a simultaneously linear, cyclical, and spiraling model within a spherical framework. Note that this visual model is an attempt to bring together linear and hierarchical, relational, and spiraling models. Furthermore, the model does not consider one mode as being "higher" than another. The Platonic concept of intelligence (*noesis*) is placed at the core of the model. Once one has arrived at knowledge (*episteme*), further knowledge and experience tend to "deconstruct" through *noesis* (intelligence). New developmental tasks await. It can be argued that the core of our being is the search rather than the finding.

The developmental therapy model should be viewed as dialectic in orientation—dialectic because of the constancy of the person-environment transaction. Specifically, the client is represented by the spiral of development. The client is presented within a spherical visual presentation within which are four main dimensions, or worlds, of images and perceptions, visible things and concrete action and thought, abstraction and thinking, and dialectical awareness of complexity and interaction. It is the client's dialogue or dialectic with this environment that leads to development, change, and growth—or that may result in stabilization and homeostasis, stuckness, or immobility and pathology.

As the visual model illustrates, we first receive data through our sensory modalities of seeing, hearing, and touch. These data are then organized into schemata or systems that permit predictable concrete operations on the environment. It then becomes possible to reflect on one's actions and thinking through formal operations or abstract thought. At the fourth and final level, dialectics makes possible the awareness of the total process and outcome of interactions.

The fourth level of development is not necessarily final, since the individual may return to the beginning and, as T. S. Eliot suggests, "arrive where we started and know the place for

Figure 4. A Spherical Model of Development

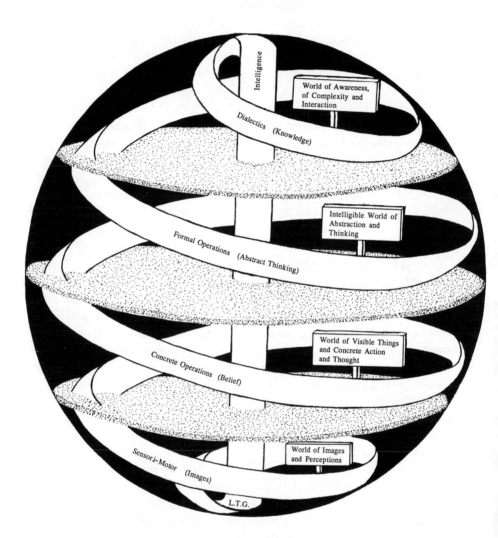

Note: All dimensions of development are active simultaneously, but one aspect may be the central point of focus at one point in time. An adequate foundation of skills and knowledge is required at each level before a solid transformation to the next stage is possible.

Source: This spherical model was originally drawn by Lois T. Grady and is used here by her permission.

the first time." The arrival back to the first level and the facing of a new developmental task represents developmental spiraling and involves an awareness of the process and a return to the beginning, with a new awareness (*noesis* or intelligence) that the beginning is not the same. Another type of dialectical awareness (*episteme* or knowledge) leads one to return to the initial point without awareness that one is back to the beginning and merely circling.

If one imposes the Gilligan relational or holistic model on this spherical model, the return to the beginning is not mere recycling but rather brings with it a keen awareness of relationships and how all dimensions of development can be simultaneously present. The sphere may expand and change shape because of dialectical relationships with others and with the environment. The ecology movement, for example, may represent this type of awareness of the return to the beginning but without the need to continue upward.

Let us assume that our ten-year-old client has become twenty and still lives in a messy room. The way one keeps his or her room often is a metaphor for life-style. The client may begin the session much as presented at the beginning of the chapter—"My life is a mess"—and then continue with vague hand wringing. The therapist can ask for concrete images and specifics of the client's life and can focus the session by specifying the concrete aspects of *one* situation.

After focusing the session on one item (such as the messy room), the therapist can work toward helping the client clean up the room by having the client think about what to pick up first and by suggesting that the client assertively go out and clean up the room.

Once having cleaned up the room, the client may be encouraged to reflect on how it felt to clean the room and to search for other life situations in which the client needs to "clean up his or her act." By removing oneself from the world of appearances, this reflective process involves the client in the world of abstraction and thinking. Out of these reflections, patterns of life-style can be discovered.

If therapy progresses, the client may start to think about

patterns of patterns and to obtain knowledge about how he or she functions. This new knowledge of how one interacts with the world may provide an important lever for many changes. However, the knowledge itself may present a contradiction, and the client gains intelligence and awareness that the new knowledge was only knowledge and that its truth value has slipped away. In this case, the client is ready to face a new developmental task in therapy. If the client remains fixed at the knowledge level, a repeating pattern of circling and more variations on the "life is a mess" theme may be expected. This recycling could be a problem or it could be a new relational understanding. Again, upward is not necessarily better.

With intelligence (*noesis*), the client is ready to recycle back for yet another developmental task. Perhaps having cleaned up the room, the client is now ready for the more complex and confusing task of cleaning up a difficult relationship with a lover or child. There appears to be no specific end to development. Although development is a process, it is also an outcome of constantly changing meaning and activity. The outcome of knowledge about cleaning one's room now leads to a new intelligence about the need to clean up one's life in general.

One definition of "cure" in therapy is that there is no cure and that one must always intelligently face change and the need for adaptation to new environmental realities and contingencies. With this dialectical awareness, clients may also discover that they are embedded in their own texts, their own life situations, and they may enter into the world of reflecting about reflections about reflections and so on. This constant reflection ultimately leads one back to the world of images and the need to organize these images systematically in order to cope with the being. Neither the world of concrete appearances nor that of abstract ideas can exist independently. Appearance and reality—abstractions and concrete things—represent unities in which both dimensions are needed to define the other.

Theory into Practice

The broad conceptual framework of this book has been presented in this chapter. However, developmental therapy is not just a theory: it is a *praxis,* an integration of theory with practice.

The story of a Samurai swordsman provides a metaphor for such *praxis*:

> Japanese master swordsmen learn their skills through a complex set of highly detailed training exercises. Through theoretical analysis and examination, the process of masterful swordsmanship is broken down into specific components and studied carefully, one at a time. In this process of technical mastery, the naturally skilled person often finds handling the sword awkward. The skilled individual may even find his performance dropping during the practice of single skills. *Being aware of what one is doing can interfere with coordination and smoothness.*
>
> Once the individual skills are practiced and learned to perfection, the Samurai retire to a mountaintop to meditate. They deliberately forget about what they have learned. When they return, they find that the distinct skills have been naturally integrated into their style of way of being. The Samurai then seldom have to think about skills at all. They have become Samurai swordsmen [Ivey, 1983a, p. 37, based on a personal communication from Lanette Shizuru, University of Hawaii, December 1980].

This same model is valid for learning tennis, ballet, cooking, and many other life activities. Practice leads to integration and a natural way of being. *Praxis* may be described as the integration of skills and theory and the elimination of artificial epistemological separations.

With the goal of integrating theory and practice, each chapter in this book will include a "Theory into Practice" section that follows a standard format proven useful in microtraining methodology (Ivey, 1971; Ivey and Authier, 1978). A core construct will be presented in brief form, followed by one or more practice exercises that illustrate the construct. The instructional method has its origins in social learning theory (Bandura and Walters, 1963) but is also Brentano's (1874) intentionality in action. Thought (the construct presentation) and action (the practice exercise) in relationship become one in *praxis*. The purpose of the outline that follows is to move cognitive material toward action and behavior.

Several important dialectics are presented in these exercises: (1) the coconstructions of therapist and client, (2) the change in internal constructions of the client (and perhaps the therapist as well), (3) the interaction of the observer observing both therapist and client, and (4) the group reflections (or observations) of the observer observing therapist and client.

Construct 1: Development is the aim of counseling and psychotherapy. Change, growth, creativity, transformation, and evolution are all about development. Staying put, refusing or being unable to change are what development is not.

   1. *Learning Objective:* To be able to define and provide examples of varying models of development as contrasted with immobility and stuckness.
   2. *Cognitive Presentation:* The basic framework of developmental therapy was presented as consisting of four main dimensions: (1) a philosophical position, (2) a theory of human development, (3) a practice of therapy and counseling, and (4) a coconstructed model of the therapy session. Development was defined and several alternatives and important conceptions of the developmental process were summarized.
   3. *Experiential Exercises or Homework:* One or more of these following exercises can be used to make the abstract conceptions of the first pages more personally relevant:
       a. Identify in yourself instances of developmental arrest and nonmovement. Write these down and share them with a colleague.
       b. Identify in yourself instances of developmental change and growth. Where were you and where are you now? What happened? What helped you move?

    c.   Consider the example of the ten-year-old in the opening pages of this chapter. Imagine yourself at some stage with the "life is a mess" problem. Engage in a role-played therapy session with a colleague in which you imagine yourself in some sort of impossible "life is a mess" situation. What happens to facilitate your becoming unstuck and starting developmental movement once again?

    d.   Consider the three theoretical models in Figure 1. What do they add to your understanding?

Construct 2: Plato and Piaget are both theorists of human development and their organizations are strikingly similar.

   1.   *Learning Objective:* To be able to describe the two developmental frameworks and note their parallels and differences.

   2.   *Cognitive Presentation:* Figures 2 and 3 summarize many important ideas of this construct. The concepts related in the book on these figures are particularly important for understanding the basic conceptions of developmental therapy. These ideas are presented earlier in this chapter.

   3.   *Experiential Exercises or Homework:*

    a.   Think about children and their development. First identify the children's behavior that exemplifies each stage of the Piagetian framework. Then take the Platonic system and determine how children's behavior can be redescribed and considered using Platonic language. Does Piaget extend Plato and does Plato extend Piaget?

    b.   Identify in yourself and your own development specific examples that represent each stage of the four-stage framework. The line between the outer visible world and the more internal world of thinking about the nature of that world is a difficult one to cross. Adolescent anger and frustration often exemplify the difficulty of crossing this line, for it is a troublesome stage in the developing awareness of self.

Construct 3: Intelligence (noesis) and knowledge (episteme) are central aspects of Plato's fourth level. The distinction between truth as knowable and as elusive is critical for the entire argument of this book.

1. *Learning Objective:* To be able to define intelligence and knowledge and to provide examples from one's own personal experience of the interaction between the two.

2. *Cognitive Presentation:* Pages 13–14 and pages 20–22 outline the textual definitions. Knowledge is considered the "lower" state, as no knowledge is ever finally fixed. What we discover is often overturned by new information. Intelligence could be summarized as the awareness that our awareness or knowledge is only temporarily. Even though a belief may last for centuries (such as the belief that the earth is the center of the universe), it may be overturned by the introduction of new data. Yet, knowledge and intelligence seem to exist in a dialectical relationship in which each depends on the other for their ultimate definition.

3. *Experiential Exercises or Homework:*

    a. Identify in yourself a belief you held firmly as a child, only to find by later discovery that your knowledge was based on an inadequate foundation. Apply that same process to a more recent issue in the workplace or the home. What belief have you held personally that has been overturned by new knowledge and experience? How has the interplay or dialectic between knowledge and intelligence played itself out in your own life?

    b. Think of friends, colleagues, or family members who represent the two types of truth. What are their behaviors and thoughts concerning tightly held beliefs? What enables them to hang on? What enables them to let go? Have you known persons so committed to elusive intelligence that they are always changing their minds and never being committed?

    c. Engage in an experiential role play with a client who has the "correct" answer to his or her family difficulty. A common problem of this type is the spouse who blames the other for the problems of the marriage or of the child. Use listening skills to draw out the world view of the client. An alternative topic may be any strongly held belief on the part of the role-played client. The goal in this role play is not to critique the "correctness" of the other person's point of view but to enter in and understand the unique constructions of reality. In this exercise, correctness is interpreted as a metaphor for knowledge and the loosening of the construct system is a metaphor for intelligence.

Construct 4: Dialectics is central to the therapeutic process. It takes two to construct an idea, a concept, or a thing. "Two" can be two constructions in a person's mind. The coconstruction of reality means that we live in dialogue and in relation one to another.

1. *Learning Objectives:* To be able to define dialectics, provide examples of dialectics in action, and to examine one's own dialectic in the interaction of therapy.
2. *Cognitive Presentation:* Pages 17-22 outline the ideas of dialectic in succinct form. Dialectics in therapy at this point are relatively new, and developing a solid understanding of the words and their implications can be difficult. Later material in this book (Chapters Six and Seven) will show that dialectics is simply another way to describe the two-person interaction which is therapy. (Since dialectics will be used frequently in this book, the two major definitions should be kept in mind: (1) dialectics as the process used by the two children described by Piaget or by clients in therapy, and (2) awareness of that process.
3. *Experiential Exercises or Homework:*
   a. It may be useful to read aloud the children's dialogue in this chapter and then to discuss the four-step framework of Piaget. This model of individual comment modified by the next comment modified by the next comment is the movement of the dialectic. It is sometimes hard to see the dialectic, since it

tic. It is sometimes hard to see the dialectic, since it is immediately before us and we experience it so much as part of our being. Developing an awareness of the dialectic requires the individual to become aware of interactions and can lead one to relate with others in a new and deeper fashion.

b.   Observe a child talking to a parent. First observe the causal impact on the child of what the parent says. You may note that the parent "causes" change in the child's behavior and verbalizations.

Next, observe the impact that the child has on the parent. How does the child "cause" the parent's words and behavior to change? How does the parent adapt his or her actions based on what the child does?

Who causes whom to change depends on the perspective of the observer. Dialectics recognizes mutual causation and change and the coevolution of ideas and action. Attempt to observe both at once and note your own difficulties in sorting out the multi-channels of communication that are before you. This experience of personal confusion and difficulty in observation represents your part in the dialectic. Are you causing their behavior or are they causing yours?

c.   Take a moment to consider your own thought processes. Relax and take any two ideas that come to your mind; these ideas need not be related. Consider the two ideas in relation to each other. How are the ideas similar or attached? How are they different or separate? As you contemplate these ideas, you may find yourself creating new ideas out of the *dialectic* of the relationship of the two.

This internal dialogue or dialectic is what Piaget tried to map and outline throughout his career. It is a creative process inherent to the construction of reality in the child and new ideas and thoughts in adult life.

d.   Audiotape, videotape, or role play a discussion with

another person. Ideally, it should be a dialogue around a problem that has not been solved. After five minutes, stop the tape and review each statement, noting the mutual impact you and your partner have on one another. Ask an observer to comment on the constructions of the role play. Then, comment on the construction and impositions on your dialectic made by your observer—observe the observer observing you.

Summary

This chapter has identified a structured approach to the development of consciousness and cognition that may be applied in a variety of situations with a multitude of content dimensions. The structures provided here may be used to describe child development, client change and growth in the interview, and development in therapeutic and counseling theory.

The focus on developmental structure in a unified developmental therapy sphere makes possible the examination of change in consciousness as a superordinate goal of counseling and therapy. Change in consciousness, however, lacks value without concomitant change in behavior in the real world. Although this book focuses on cognitive development, it is important that behavioral development and the generation of behavioral alternatives in ever-increasing dimensions can and must accompany increased cognitive awareness.

This chapter began by stating that development was the aim of counseling and psychotherapy. The developmental therapy model suggests that one important route toward that aim is the systematic development of consciousness. Later chapters will elaborate this idea in greater detail and illustrate how specific counseling and therapy techniques may be used to facilitate cognitive and behavioral development.

The following chapters of this book will focus on both theory and method in counseling and therapy. Specific suggestions will be made for facilitating the developmental movement of clients. Different theories of counseling and therapy may be

more useful with some clients than with others; thus, the assessment of developmental status becomes an important issue. Once
having determined the developmental and cognitive level of a
client, it is possible to systematically plan development with
and for the client.

Chapter Two will examine the concept of dialectics in
more detail and will provide background information that relates these constructions to biological development and research
in counseling and therapy. The Piagetian constructs of assimilation, accommodation, and equilibration will be explored as important ideas relating to the "developmental balance" of clients
and therapists.

∽ 2 ∼

How Person and Environment Shape Each Other

Implications of Therapeutic Context

Consciousness does not develop in a vacuum. It moves and develops in a dialectic with others. The focus of this chapter is on the environment and its impact on individual development. Person-environment transaction can be viewed as perhaps the most familiar form of dialectical relations.

Altman and Gauvain (1981) talk about dialectics as the "interplay of individuality and society." Out of this individual-society or person-environment dialogue comes a unified

> world view or set of assumptions about the functioning of the physical and psychological world. . . .
> [These] oppositional processes function as a unified system . . . [with] a range of possible relationships . . . [and] the relationships are dynamic; changes occur over time and with circumstances. . . . Sequential or cumulative changes involve the Hegelian idea of a thesis and antithesis being resolved by a synthesis that incorporates opposites into a new phenomenon" [p. 286].

In short, the dialogue or dialectic of person and environment suggests that the person impacts the environment and the environment impacts the person. The relationships between person

35

and environment are multitudinous, dynamic, and changing but together are always a unified whole.

The specific aims of this chapter are to present four main concepts that underlie the person-environment dialectic that is therapy. A biological model of evolution as development will be presented as a prototypical model. Assimilation and accommodation are defined and related to the therapeutic process, and information-processing theory is related to assimilation and accommodation. Finally, the developmental therapy position on equilibration will be presented, which is especially important for the eventual development of systematic evaluation instrumentation using the developmental therapy model.

Let us examine the implications of therapeutic person-environment transaction. It is critical to recall that therapy is a relationship in which an environment is provided by the therapist to facilitate growth in the client.

A Very Old Joke

There is an old story about Carl Rogers and a suicidal patient. A client is talking about suicide and Rogers constantly reflects back the client's feelings of depression. The client finally wearies of the session and goes to the window and looks out.

Client: I'm looking out the window and thinking of jumping.

Rogers: You're at the window and feeling like jumping out.

Client: Yes, the situation is impossible and I'm going . . .

Rogers: You feel the situation is impossible and you're climbing out the window.

Client: Yes. I'm going to jump.

Rogers: You're going to jump.

Client: Farewell!

Rogers: You say farewell.

Client: Splat!

Rogers: Splat!

The joke is very unfair to Carl Rogers, but many readers will likely recall individuals from their past who took the joke as reality. I specifically recall two one-hour sessions in graduate school, where I observed a fellow student "work through" two full, consecutive hours of silence—and we admired his work at that time!

The old joke and the exemplification of the joke in real life are cited here because they clearly illustrate that the therapist provides a certain type of environment for a client. It is this environment that makes development possible and facilitates or hinders the movement through the levels of consciousness suggested in Chapter One. Rogers broke with the tradition of therapist control of the interview. He pointed out that the *person* of the therapist strongly affects the change possible for the client. With an emphasis on being and becoming, Rogers moved to a more ontological approach to therapy, one which recognizes the unity of the therapist and client dialectic.

Despite the occasional excesses of his followers, Rogers has, perhaps more than any other person, established the importance of providing an environment for helping in therapy. He stressed the importance of the therapeutic environment, emphasizing the importance of warmth, positive regard, and empathy. If the therapist provides a supportive environment, the client is highly likely to grow and develop. It is this emphasis on environment that is one of Rogers's great contributions to the field of helping.

Other types of therapy provide different environments for their clients, and it is through the person-environment transaction of counseling and therapy that clients are able to move through developmental tasks and developmental stages. Each therapy assists client movement in varying ways, and the varying environments of these therapeutic approaches will be considered later in Chapter Four.

Developmental therapy has sought to unify thinking about change and growth from many differing areas. The following biological model of adaptation is basic to the developmental process.

Evolution as Adaptation:
A Biological and Psychological Model

Evolution is simultaneously a process and an outcome. The outcomes of evolutionary adaptation are apparent in the manifest characteristics of biological organisms. These may appear as varied structures, such as a pheasant's wing structure, size of tail feathers, and genetic capacity for social organization. At the same time, these *present outcomes* are simultaneously *processes* that lead to new outcomes in the future (Ivey and Hurst, 1971).

The analogy in human development is that a developed skill or outcome, such as hand-eye coordination or the ability to reflect feelings in a therapy session, are simultaneously processes that lead to new levels of knowledge and intelligence. Hand-eye coordination, when combined with knowledge about scales and reading music, can lead to the outcome of playing the piano, which in turn can be a process that leads to further outcomes. In clients, the behavioral outcome of passivity later becomes a process that leads to a wide variety of personal outcomes, such as lack of assertiveness, failure to use abilities, and a lack of self-efficacy or self-worth. These skills, of course, are not just biological; they are also the result of the evolution of social-personal history.

The selection of those characteristics that an organism will have and of those organisms that will indeed survive is determined by certain factors. The first of these factors is genetic; genes produce a specific biological structure, and chance variations provide variety within that structure. Which structure will survive, however, is determined by natural selection and environmental feedback. In effect, a chance genetic change in structure works and will become stabilized if the environmental feedback enables the organism to survive and flourish. Negative feedback may result in the loss of the newly attained structure or even in the extinction of the organism itself.

Within this evolutionary model, every activity or physical characteristic of an organism is an adaptation toward maximum survival probability. The biological model of behavior and physiological adaptation of the Argus pheasant described by Lorenz (1966) provides a case in point:

> Wherever we find exaggerated development of colorful feathers, bizarre forms, and so on, in the male, we may suspect that the males no longer fight but that the last word in the choice of a mate is spoken by the female, and that the male has no means of contesting this decision. Birds of Paradise, the Ruff, the Mandarin Duck, and the Argus Pheasant show examples of such behavior. The Argus hen pheasant reacts to the large secondary wing feathers of the cock; they are decorated with beautiful eye spots and the cock spreads them before her during courtship. They are so huge that the cock can scarcely fly, and the bigger they are the more they stimulate the hen. The number of progeny produced by a cock in a certain period of time is in direct proportion to the length of these feathers, and, even if their extreme development is unfavorable in other ways—his unwieldiness may cause him to be eaten by a predator while a rival with less absurdly exaggerated wings may escape— he will nevertheless leave more descendants than will a plainer cock. So the predisposition to huge wing feathers is preserved, quite against the interests of the species. One could well imagine an Argus hen that reacted to a small red spot on the wings of the male, which would disappear when he folded his wings and interfere neither with his flying capacity nor with his protective color, but the evolution of the Argus pheasant has run itself into a blind alley. The males continue to compete in producing the largest possible wing feathers, and these birds will never reach a sensible solution and "decide" to stop this nonsense at once [p. 37].

The environment of the Argus pheasant provides feed-back that both supports and opposes the evolutionary adaptation of secondary wing feathers. Supporting the enlargement of the structures is the ability to attract females and beget more offspring. Negative feedback comes from the predators who may devour the bird, thus preventing progeny. Whether or not the wing-feather structures survive depends on the process of feed-back adaptation.

Similarly, the problems clients present in therapy are outcomes of their past and present environments. Their behavior, thoughts, feelings, and symptoms are structures that were originally developed to achieve future survival, despite their now-obvious ineffectiveness. These psychological structures once served a functional use, but they have become autonomous and useless appendages, much like the overly large wing feathers of the Argus pheasant. Our task as therapists and counselors is to provide a new environment that provides more useful and accurate environmental feedback and thus returns the client to the process of growth and development. It is also important to note that evolutionary biology has no specific definable end, and we find ourselves again facing the Platonic concepts of knowledge (*episteme*, an end) and intelligence (*noesis*, a process of knowing).

Just as in evolutionary biology, the outcome of therapy has no specific definable end. Psychotherapists and counselors enjoy talking about the outcome of their efforts. Did the interview make a positive difference in the life of a patient? It depends. This point may be illustrated by the author's experience of an encounter group at Esalen in Big Sur, California, in the 1960s. The first outcome was good. I enjoyed the process of the group, for their insights immediately changed the way I responded and acted. It is good to walk barefoot at Big Sur and enjoy hot tubs. A week later, back home, I encountered my family and the outcome was a disaster—they did not want an open-shirted, shoeless psychologist for a husband and father. A year later, what I had learned at Esalen facilitated my own group leadership skills and again the experience seemed worth-while—what I learned as an outcome had become a process leading to other things. Two years later, disenchanted with the encounter movement, the whole effort seemed a colossal waste. And so the evaluation of the experience continues to change over the years.

Environments clearly have a powerful impact on our thinking and being. They produce outcomes that are simultaneously processes leading to other outcomes. If we provide the warmth and nonpossessive positive regard of the Rogerian environment, certain outcomes and processes are likely to follow. On the other hand, if we provide a behavioral environment focused on specific objectives, different outcomes and processes may be expected. The nature of the therapeutic environment affects what is likely to follow later.

This integrated view of process and outcome suggests that distinctions typically made in counseling and therapy research may be overly simplistic. Clearly, the separation of process and outcome is not nearly as neat as the research literature would suggest. Again we may relate process and outcome research to the Platonic concepts of knowledge and intelligence. Knowledge may be considered analogous to outcome and intelligence to process. Which is the more important will be in the eye of the beholder.

Biological (the Argus pheasant), psychological (our clients and ourselves), and philosophical (Platonic knowledge and intelligence) constructs may be blended into a unity in which process and outcome distinctions paradoxically become clearer and at the same time more blurred. Process and outcome appear to be a unity in their diversity, both being core aspects of the other.

Assimilation and accommodation, two central constructions of Piagetian theory, carry this unity further and also again illustrate the importance of the therapeutic environment as a person-environment transaction.

Accommodation, Assimilation, and Therapeutic Environments

The task of the therapist is to transform client knowledge and action into more useful formulations. The therapist seeks to provide an environment to facilitate this process. Accommodation and assimilation are two aspects of a single process (or outcome). These constructs may be useful formulations for the understanding and conduct of the therapeutic process.

Piaget ([1952] 1963) considers assimilation the "basic fact of psychic life" that shows at each stage of mental life in "the tendency toward repetition of behavior patterns and toward the utilization of external objects in the framework of such repetition" (p. 42). Assimilation is the cognitive process by which we integrate new data into our lives. We identify a tree as a tree because we have preexisting mental structures that have shown us that this object is indeed a tree. As we encounter life, we use constructs or schemata that enable us to understand and act. Clients have assimilated mental structures that worked for them in the past, but they often continue to use them even after the original utility of the structures is lost. Much like the overly enlarged wing feathers of the Argus pheasant, the assimilated structures may no longer be useful.

In his personal construct psychology, Kelly (1955) talks about tight constructs—those that cannot be changed easily. The task of the therapist is to help the client loosen constructs or ideas. Tight constructs represent overassimilation.

Accommodation occurs constantly when the individual confronts a new stimulus. First, the individual tries to assimilate the new data into existing schemata or constructs. This is not always possible, and accommodation requires that the individual either loosen old assimilations or constructs or build new assimilations or constructs by generating new schemata. This modification or transformation of mental structures is termed accommodation.

Assimilation and accommodation are different ways to describe a single process. In accommodation, the individual receives (and possibly transforms) a stimulus from the environment; in assimilation, the individual acts on and imposes his or her perspectives on the environment. One aspect is impossible without the other. Like yin and yang, they are inseparable, even though one may be prepotent and primarily operative at a particular time of development. Together these constructions represent the adaptative process of development.

The developmental therapy constructions of assimilation and accommodation are a modification and extension of Piaget's original ideas. In an attempt to relate these ideas to the therapeutic process, these constructs are used as metaphors for further exploration. Accommodation, in this context, is a somewhat more passive act than that suggested by Piaget, and assimilation is considered the more active process. In this book I have increased the scope of these distinctions to facilitate clarity of expression and utility for therapeutic action.

In accommodation one takes in or accommodates to the environment. As one gazes out of the window that overlooks a pond, it is possible to take in the total environment all at once. In order to cope with an environment effectively, one must incorporate and adapt to the environment. Failure to adapt represents overly rigid structures and the inability to accommodate to the new. In a psychodynamic or Freudian sense, the failure to adapt to new data represents "repeating without remembering" and the repetition compulsion. (Note also Piaget's comment at the beginning of this section on how assimilation leads to behavioral repetition.)

However, it is possible to overaccommodate, to *become* the environment and lose one's sense of self. This, of course, happens in many meditative exercises—the total experience of what "*is.*" Woody Allen's movie *Zelig* featured a character who accommodated so completely to his environment that he became like the people around him. When talking to physicians, he became (or thought he was) a physician himself and used medical language in his conversation. With fat people, his stomach ballooned; with quiet individuals, he too became quiet.

All of us have a bit of the accommodative Zelig in us; we behave and respond differently in different environmental contexts. At a loud party, many of us tend to behave as others do and may be more noisy and drink more than usual. When abroad, we may try to eat using both knife and fork so as to be more in synchrony with our new environment. The accommodative pose demands that we take the perspective of the other and transform our cognitive structures. If we fail to take in and accommodate to what is around us and distort the world into our own picture of how things should be, we move toward autism and alienation from others. Empathy demands that we as therapists enter the world view of our clients and accommodate to their world views. The Rogerian mirroring of the responses of others and the extensive use of listening skills may be considered a prime example of the accommodative pose in counseling and therapy.

Accommodation is therefore central to our perceptions and our ability to receive the world as it is, to incorporate and transform these data, and to accommodate to reality. The following formal definition is proposed by Furth (1970):

> The outgoing process of an operative action oriented toward some particular reality state. Accommodation applies a general structure to a particular situation; as such, it always contains some element of newness. In a restricted sense, accommodation to a new situation leads to the differentiation of a previous structure and thus the emergence of new structures [p. 157].

The overaccommodation represented by Woody Allen in the film *Zelig* exemplifies how accommodation may turn into something very close to assimilation. To use Kelly's personal construct terms again, the loose cognitive structures represented by overaccommodation have become so permeable and open that they have become a form of tightness or assimilated rigidity. Thus, assimilation and accommodation again appear as two different ways of describing a single process. Furth elaborates and regards assimilation as "the incorporating process of an operative action. A taking in of environmental data, not in a causal, mechanistic sense, but as a function of an internal structure that by its own nature seeks activity through assimilation of potential material from the environment" (p. 158).

Assimilation implies an incorporation of the environment from one's own frame of reference. Zelig's frame of reference was to always accommodate to the world around him. In this somewhat confusing and recursive sense, it may be seen that assimilation and accommodation are closely related yet paradoxically distinct processes. Together their dialectic forms a unity of perception. Accommodation is intimately tied to a parallel process of assimilation.

In assimilation, we take environmental data and filter it through preexisting structures and knowledge. In viewing a pond, for example, people will not just accommodate and take in all of the pond. Instead, they will respond to the pond in individually unique ways. A biologist may focus on the ecosystem of the pond or on the mating habits of Canadian geese. A child may want to go swimming or collect reeds. A psychologist may focus on interpreting and classifying the behaviors of the biologist and the child. In assimilation, we impose our own order on the environment and thus change the environment.

Over-assimilators may devour data and distort everything to their own frame of reference. Witness the psychoanalytic patient in the midst of analysis who interprets the behavior of everyone he or she meets in a Freudian frame of reference. A chat with a member of a religious cult provides another example of individuals who tend to interpret all data from their own perspective. At a conference of psychologists, particularly in a debate between so-called behaviorists and humanists, one will often find individuals assimilating data from the other into their own frame of reference. A problem common to many clients in therapy is constant imposition of their theoretical lens or world view on their family and others. Again, Zelig's constant mode of being was accommodative, which in its extremity becomes assimilative in nature.

Rogerian therapy has been presented as a primarily accommodative approach to helping. A central task of the person-centered counselor or therapist is to understand and accommodate to the world view of the other. Behavioral and psychodynamic methods, in contrast, are primarily assimilative in that they often seek to have the client use their theoretical lens. However, these distinctions are open to serious question.

While relatively clear distinctions between accommodation and assimilation are possible, the two constructs are ultimately inseparable. For example, the old Rogerian joke about the client jumping out of the window appears at first glance to represent the ultimate in accommodation, since the therapist seems to be simply mirroring the words and behavior of the client. Yet, to provide this type of mirroring behavior requires a strong, focused theoretical orientation that allows one to listen to and accommodate to another person. Thus, the ultimate accommodator, who watches the client jump out of the window (or who sits through two full interviews saying nothing), is in fact a very powerful assimilator in that the Rogerian theoretical lens has been directly imposed on the client. The belief that each person can find her or his own way given a supportive therapeutic environment is itself a powerful assimilation. The point here is that accommodative behavior can be defined as assimilative if one wishes to take that particular point of view.

It has been suggested that analytic psychology is a primarily assimilative orientation. Clearly, the goal is often to enable the patient to view the world as the therapist believes Freud described it. This imposition of one's belief on another individual is criticized by some as strongly as is the lack of imposition of action in person-centered therapy. However, analytic psychology is also accommodative if one wishes to view it from another perspective.

Consider classical psychoanalytic free association. The client is encouraged to say whatever comes into his or her mind, with minimal participation on the part of the analyst. As the analyst listens and accommodates to the client's presentation, the client gradually develops a unified picture of the self. The use of free association in analysis can be viewed as an even more accommodative act than the Rogerian act of mirroring, yet it too comes from a powerful set of theoretical laws and assimilations.

Generally speaking, however, therapies which are more action oriented tend to be assimilative in nature. Psychodynamic treatment, rational-emotive therapy, transactional analysis, and behavioral psychology, for example, tend to take data in and label it through their own theoretical lenses. Nonetheless, it is clear that there can be no totally assimilative and no totally accommodative therapy. Assimilation and accommodation work together as part of a unity. Unless behavioral or rational-emotive psychologists can accommodate to new data coming in from their clients, their assimilations will be of little use.

A client may complain about bad treatment and discrimination from an employer. The psychoanalyst may construct the behavior as relating to past difficulties with parents or other significant *objects*. The rational-emotive therapist may see the situation as a result of illogical thinking ("Is it really *that* awful?"). The transactional (TA) therapist may analyze the situation from parent, adult, and child perspectives, while the behavioral psychologist may search for stimulus-response conditions. The person-centered therapist may construct the situation as an example of the need for more self-actualization. Each will behave in accord with their theoretical lens and assimilations, but each will also accommodate to the extent of listening to and hearing the client.

In counseling or therapy, the counselor is the environment of the client, and the client is the environment of the therapist (see Figure 5). The counselor may accommodate to the client through empathic response and assume the client's perspective. Selman (1976) talks about stages of perspective-taking; the more highly developed the individual, the more able one is to accommodate and understand the perspective of the other. Accommodative therapies are good at providing clients with images of how they construct reality. In Rogerian therapy, for example, the therapist takes the perspective of the client and reflects back the client's frame of reference. Associated with accommodative counseling and therapy are the listening skills of paraphrasing, reflection of feeling, the minimal encourage, and the summary (Ivey and Authier, 1978). As therapists strive for empathy with their clients, they seek to accommodate to the perspective of the client's world.

Predominantly assimilative therapists also accommodate to the client by listening carefully. Therapists who assimilate may show warmth and respect and be highly interested in their client's frame of reference. However, their ultimate task is to reframe the client's view of reality from their theoretical perspective. Assimilative therapists seek to enlist the client in their world view so that the client accommodates to them. They may

Figure 5. Person-Environment Interaction in Therapy

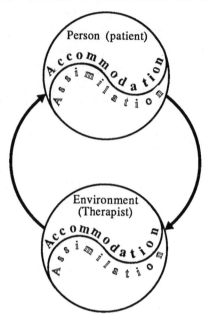

Note: Yet, let us remember that the client is always the therapist's environment.

accomplish this through the use of the influencing skills such as interpretation, directives, logical consequences, feedback, and confrontation (Ivey, 1983a).

Assimilation, Accommodation, and Therapeutic Theory

It may be useful at this point to summarize the concepts of assimilation and accommodation and then to relate them to alternative orientations to therapy and counseling. Greater distinctions have been made here between accommodative therapies and assimilative therapies than would usually be found in practice. As stated earlier, the distinctions in this discussion have gone beyond usual Piagetian formulations. Nonetheless, they are theoretically and practically useful. For example, behavioral theory is discussed as primarily assimilative. However, if one examined a behavioral session, one would be impressed with how carefully many behavioral therapists try to understand and accommodate to the world views of their clients. As such, the distinctions between the two concepts must always be made with care.

The following outline summarizes the basic argument:

1. Clients construct their representations of the world through two key processes:
   a. *Accommodation:* Incorporating the environment, reacting to it, and changing structures. Over-accommodators "become" the environment. Associated with loose personal constructs.
   b. *Assimilation:* Viewing the environment through pre-existing mental structures and making the data fit to them, thus imposing one's point of view on the environment. Over-assimilators may devour data and distort it into their own frame of reference. Associated with tight personal constructs.
   c. *Combinatory Accommodation/Assimilation:* This term has been coined to indicate more clearly that it is not possible to separate the twin processes. A world view that has been assimilated is the result of the past history of accommodations. A client knows or has assimilated the concept of mother through a long history of accommodation. In turn, the assimilations of the past determine how one accommodates to present stimuli. We can only know (accommodate to) a tree and its potentials if past assimilations have taught us about trees. Assimilation and accommodation are twin aspects of a unity. Permeable personal constructs may be associated with this view, although the very nature of the twin processes may also result in overly tight or overly loose construct systems.
2. In therapy, the counselor is the environment. The counselor may *accommodate* to the client through empathic responding (perspective-taking) or may *assimilate* client data through a preexisting theoretical lens (behavioral, Rogerian, psychodynamic). In either case, the therapist

is still involved in *combinatorial assimilation/accommodation.*

3. The client, working with an *accommodating* counselor, will have the opportunity to have his or her past *assimilations* fed back (mirrored) and may develop a new construction of reality with the clarified data. With an *assimilating* therapist, the client may learn to *accommodate* to and to adopt the therapist's hopefully more workable construction of reality.

4. Therapists and counselors all use *combinatorial assimilation/accommodation,* but different skills and theories are most commonly associated with each:

   a. *Accommodation:* The theory most associated with accommodating to the client is Rogerian person-centered therapy. Skills most associated with accommodation are those of encouragement and restatement, paraphrase, reflection of feeling, and summarization.

   b. *Assimilation:* Theories most associated with assimilation include psychodynamic, behavioral, and rational-emotive. Skills associated with assimilation include interpretation, directives, logical consequences, feedback, and advice.

   c. *Combinatory Accommodation/Assimilation:* All theories give some emphasis to listening and thus to accommodation. All theories, including Rogerian theory, have world views and thus impose their perceptions on clients. The skills of questioning and confrontation are perhaps prime examples of combinatorial skills, although all skills, even providing directives, involve some accommodation.

5. Therapy and counseling, then, may be viewed as a person-environment transaction in which two "realities" are met and accommodated and assimilated by the two parties—therapist and client, counselor and counselee.

Clients who engage in therapy or counseling with an accommodating or listening counselor will have the opportunity to have their own constructions and assimilations of data fed back to them. In the process of seeing themselves in a mirror, they may gain a new perspective on themselves and reassimilate their view of themselves or of a situation.

By way of contrast, clients who engage in therapy that has an assimilative orientation are expected to join the perspective of the therapist and eventually accommodate to a systematic world view that is not necessarily their own.

It must not be forgotten, of course, that the client serves as an environment for the therapist. As the therapist receives data from the client, he or she must first hear it accurately, which requires the accommodative process and listening skills. However, some counselors are over-assimilators, who take only a brief time to hear a reality separate from their own. Specific examples of overassimilation of the therapist include the inability to hear the client accurately and distortions of client experience, particularly as manifested in counter-transference phenomena. However, overaccommodation can be equally problematic and occurs when the counselor is too easily seduced to the client's point of view, ends up defending the client unrealistically, and fails to provide alternative views of reality that may be more useful.

Thus, assimilation and accommodation must exist in a cognitive balance, or one of permeable constructs, if client growth is to occur. The therapist must offer an environment that is facilitative to the client in assimilating new data and new representations and constructions of reality.

However, the therapeutic environment involves far more complex elements than just the assimilation and accommodation processes. Information-processing theory perhaps provides a more detailed and accurate explanation of the person-environment transaction that is counseling and therapy.

Attention, Information-Processing Theory, and Person-Environment Transaction

This section extends the concepts of assimilation and accommodation to information-processing theory. During each instant of our existence, we are constantly processing (assimilating and accommodating) information. "Strange to say, a ten-second period of thinking sometimes required as many minutes to re-count to make clear" (Woodworth, 1938, p. 783).

Accommodation and assimilation have a common meet-ing place in the focus of *attention*. The twin processes may be said to be in a constant battle or dialectic for control of *atten-tional processes*. The internal locus of control of attention, of course, is assimilations—the structures preexisting in the indi-vidual client. The external locus of control lies in accommodat-ing to the environmental stimuli surrounding the client.

The construct of attention brings the importance of ac-commodation and assimilation to an even more central position in counseling and psychotherapy. Ivey (1971) has given exten-sive consideration to attention and attending behavior. Attend-ing behavior is the externally observable Watsonian behavioral processes of eye contact, body language, vocal qualities, and verbal following. Attention is a more subtle and introspective quality:

> It is possible . . . for an interviewer to be engaging
> in attending behavior in terms of all physical and
> verbal manifestations while his (or her) attention
> is directed elsewhere. The Skinnerian view of at-
> tention is one that is best observed in the behav-
> ioral relationship of one individual to another. The
> focus of attention as described by William James,
> however, remains a more intuitive, inner-directed
> matter, less subject to direct observation [Ivey,
> 1971, p. 47].

Assimilation may be described as attention directed from with-in and accommodation as attention directed from without. At-tending behavior and the externally observable behavior of the therapist represent the stimuli that the client receives. Atten-tion is the internal, unobservable processes of assimilation and accommodation. Attending and other observable behaviors are the external stimuli to which attention may be drawn.

Attending behavior on the part of the therapist may be considered analogous to the stimulus of the light toward which the infant often attends in early life. Attention is the internal process of the infant (or the client) in response to the stimulus. When the infant notices the light, he or she has no preexisting preverbal assimilation or construct of light. Thus, the infant must first accommodate to that external stimulus. Once that accommodation has been established, it becomes an assimilated structure through which future lights will be viewed. By analogy, the clients meets the therapist with preexisting mental structures. Through the provision of attending behavior and many other directly observable and countable behaviors and theoretical practices, the therapist provides an environment (metaphorically, a "new light") to which the client can accommodate and then generate new cognitive structures and, later, behaviors.

Attention and attending behavior thus form the "window" between introspectionist and cognitive studies and behaviorism. Attending behavior and observables are the stimulus-response conditions between clients and therapists. Attention is the internal process of assimilation and accommodation of both.

Information-processing theory adds a further dimension to the framework. Most information-processing models have been conceptualized in terms of only one person and have failed to consider the person-environment transaction that is the reality. Figure 6 presents a two-person information-processing model that makes possible the integration of both cognitive and behavioral approaches to interpersonal interaction.

The model in Figure 6 is adapted from summary writings by Blumenthal (1977), Anderson (1985), and Ericsson and Simon (1984). All three discussions explore the literature on cognition and information processing and are in general concurrence with the following points. Unique to the developmental therapy model integration is (1) the dialectical portrayal of person-environment transaction—not just one person is processing information; there are two people in therapy; (2) the integration of Piagetian constructs of assimilation and accommodation, which seems to help explain certain key aspects of the attentional and memory process; and (3) the visual diagram that

Figure 6. Information Processing as a Person-Environment Transaction

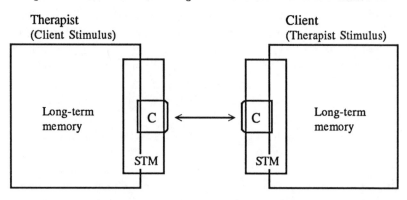

1. *Overview.* Two persons are in a complex interaction in which each serves as the environment and primary stimulus for the other. From the client point of view, the therapist stimulus is observed (accommodated) through sensory modalities (seeing, hearing, feeling). These observations in consciousness (C) may enter short-term memory (STM) and, if sufficiently impactful, may also enter long-term memory (LTM). Information from the therapist stimulus that reaches long-term memory is more likely to result in cognitive and behavioral change.

But, clients are not just passive accommodators. They come to the session with preexisting cognitive structures that they have assimilated from the past and that already exist in long-term memory at both a conscious and unconscious level. The therapist may serve as a trigger and bring up past memory structures (assimilations), which impact short-term memory and consciousness. Thus, the client may appear to be attending to and accommodating to the therapist, but attentional processes may be responding to the therapist as parent, or the client thought or cognitive patterns may be in a very different place from what the therapist observes.

Therapists observe only client observable behavior. They usually come to the interview with a theoretical lens in long-term memory and thus consistently tend to interpret client behavior from their assimilated theoretical world view. When the client provides a stimulus about parents, a Freudian assimilation is very different from a behavioral assimilation. The therapist may be so fully assimilated by theory that there is failure to listen and accommodate to the client stimulus. In such cases, the need for accommodative listening skills, and perhaps a person-centered approach, may be seen. Finally, certain client stimuli trigger key long-term memories of the therapist, and the therapist may respond to these unconscious processes without awareness of the client.

2. *Consciousness* (C) may be defined as the psychological present, which ranges in length from 100 milliseconds (the rapid attentional integration period) to 750 milliseconds (the conscious present or buffer period). Consciousness has access to short-term and long-term memory. Thus, an indi-

Figure 6. Information Processing as a Person-Environment Transaction, Cont'd.

vidual may be attending to (accommodating to) information from external sources (the therapist) or from internal sources (STM or LTM). The conscious present, whether defined as 100 msec or 750 msec, represents the ground on which assimilation and accommodation meet. Past assimilations may determine how the present environment of the therapist is interpreted. The task of the therapist is to enter the consciousness of the other and to facilitate the development of new cognitions and the accommodation of new stimuli. To accomplish this aim, of course, the therapist must simultaneously accommodate to the client stimulus and assimilate data appropriately into new interventions.

3. *Short-term memory* (STM) holds impressions immediately accessible to consciousness for approximately ten seconds. Unless supported by attentional reinforcement from the external stimulus (accommodation) or from past internal stimuli (assimilation), information will rapidly decay after that period. Research indicates that we can hold about 100 items in our short-term memory. Apparently, it is in this period that new data is fully accommodated and assimilated and made ready for entry into long-term storage. Interference from long-term memory through emotion or repression may prohibit some items from entering long-term memory.

4. *Long-term memory* (LTM) is the storehouse of past assimilations and accommodations. It may also be described as the area of the preconscious (to which we have easy and direct access at our cognitive will) and the unconscious (which is both with us and not with us depending on external stimuli and internal emotional states).

5. *Relationship*. It is important to note that the conscious period of 100 to 750 msec has been overlain on both short-term and long-term memory. Most diagrams separate the conscious present, STM, and LTM. More likely, however, the portrayal above illustrates that we *always* have direct and immediate access to LTM. This is illustrated dramatically when our attention redirects away from pleasant conversation to driving when we face a dangerous icy road. The stimulus of the road triggers the LTM to action and directs behavior and thought. In a similar fashion, we always have access to the multitude of assimilated structures and images in our LTM.

allows portrayal of how immediate consciousness has access to long-term memory. (Most diagrams of this type separate long-term memory in a separate "box" from STM and immediate consciousness.) While an overview of the diagram and its central points may be found in Figure 6, it is nonetheless useful to describe the basic model in more detail.

First, if one is to process information in an information-processing model, one must have information to process. At the most basic level, that information comes from the external environment. Consider again the example of the infant who notices the light. The baby comes to the light because it is the brightest stimulus among the many things in the bumbling confusion of the world. The infant first accommodates to the light and then gradually assimilates the experience. The therapist is the brightest and most powerful stimulus in the interview (as is the client for the therapist). But both client and therapist come to the interview with long social-historical backgrounds that will affect the way each accommodates to and assimilates the constructs of the other. Each has a *dual relation* with the other. The therapist, for example, observes the client afresh, allowing accommodation, but assimilated long-term memory may intrude as the second aspect of the relation. Similarly, the client has both immediate perceptions and long-term constructions in memory. Four parts exist in two positions (Lacan, [1966] 1977). By this Lacan means that cultural/social history is very much in the present, even though we may not be consciously aware of its presence. Thus, therapy is a very complex exercise, as is life itself. This Lacanian framework is expanded on pp. 317-322.

Each of the players observe the stimulus of the other through their sense perceptions of seeing and hearing and, potentially, feeling. These sense perceptions themselves may be pure accommodations in which the client, for example, takes in the therapist accurately, since the therapist "is." More likely, however, the therapist represents someone from the client's past history, perhaps a parent or other authority figure. This initial transference from past assimilated history means that client perceptions may be distorted and inaccurate. After all, the therapist is not the client's father or mother, even though the client may respond as such.

Similar processes are occurring in the cognitions of the therapist. He or she may see the client as id, ego, and superego; as parent, adult, or child; or as a set of stimulus-response conditions. Past theoretical assimilations of the therapist may cause him or her to notice and categorize certain behaviors of the client while simultaneously ignoring others. If past assimilations of both client and therapist are strong enough, they may even manage not to see and hear (accommodate to) the distinctive person before them.

The conscious present (C in Figure 6) has been defined as roughly either the 100 milliseconds of the *rapid attentional integration* (Blumenthal, 1977) or the 750 milliseconds of the *conscious present* (Bekesy, 1931), or the *buffer period* (Atkinson and Shiffrin, 1971). Research reveals that the time for taking one item into short-term memory varies from 50 to 250 msec with 100 msec being an approximate average. In this 100-msec glance, we can note one word on this page, the place of four or more objects on a table, the breathtaking view of Mt. Rainier near Seattle, a few notes of a Beethoven symphony, or a client's Freudian slip. Each of these represents an accommodation, or taking in, of what exists. (Yet, paradoxically, we would not know what we are taking in if we had not previously built in or assimilated cognitive structures that allow us to process the data before us—again, the effect of the combinatorial workings of assimilation and accommodation.)

On the other hand, the 100-msec period can be taken over by long-term memory. When seeing, one does not see but rather sees images of the past. The client may appear to be attending to the therapist through good, direct eye contact but be actually thinking of a troublesome sexual problem. Similarly, the therapist may be exerting excellent attending behavior but thinking about a theoretical question represented by the client.

Interestingly, if the exposure to an event is less than 100 msec, research indicates that the individual *constructs* a picture or meaning out of the partial stimulus drawing on short-term and long-term memory and past assimilations (see Smith and Westerlundh, 1980). If the shortened event is intense enough (a quick flash of electricity), it may still impact present consciousness.

The 750-msec conscious present (with a range of from 500 msec to two seconds, depending on the individual) is of interest because researchers find that this is the period in which images may be summated and may enter into short-term or long-term memory. We may hold seven (plus or minus two) bits or chunks of information in our minds during this period. If an individual concentrates for about one second on one thing (for example, a particular itch on your body at this time or a specific thing you may note in the room), that item will enter short-term memory. This buffer delay, or conscious present, works as an information-processing system that can balance the internal stimuli (past assimilations and drives from the body—itches, the need to eliminate or to sneeze) with new stimulus input (the words of the therapist, the sexuality of the therapist, the picture hanging in back of the therapist's head, the siren sounding outside the window). The cognitive struggle in assimilation and accommodation is for space in the conscious present.

In 1900 Freud speculated that the mechanism of consciousness may have two sensory surfaces, one that interfaces with the immediate environment and one that interfaces with memory (cited in Blumenthal, 1977, p. 60). The clarity of Freud's statement now seems to be thoroughly supported by the neo-Piagetian approach suggested here and the extensive background of research in both introspective and cognitive psychology.

The conscious present, whether defined as 100 msec or 750 msec, is the time during which the counselor and therapist have to enter the assimilative world of the client. Short-term memory holds impressions immediately accessible to consciousness for approximately ten seconds. Unless supported by attentional reinforcement from the external stimulus (primarily accommodation) or from past internal stimuli (primarily assimilation), information will decay rapidly. Research indicates that we can hold approximately 100 items in our short-term memory. These items can be repeated bits of information from the outside (a statement from the therapist that demands complete attention) or the inside (a past view of a therapist-perceived error that enables the client to deny or negate external stimuli). It may be hypothesized that the integration and chaining of information in this time period of short-term memory determines what will enter into long-term memory.

Blumenthal (1977) talks about the *absolute judgment*

span in which the individual judges the relationship between internal and external stimuli. What seems to happen is that the person sees an external stimulus and matches it with an internal representation (assimilation), much like computer scanning. If the scan matches, then the judgment is yes; if not, no, and the individual will have to consider accommodating a new piece of information in the long-term storage bank.

Freud's 1925 article (Freud, [1925] 1961) on negation provides an interesting parallel with the above analysis:

> Let us consider where the ego ("I") ... learnt the technique that it now applies to its process of thought. It happened at the sensory end of the mental apparatus, in connection with sense perceptions. For... perception is not a purely passive process. The ego ("I") periodically sends out small amounts of cathexis (emotion) into the perceptual system, by means of which it samples the external stimuli, and then after every such tentative advance it draws back again [p. 239].

The language may be different from that of information-processing theory, but the parallels between Freudian constructs and the view presented here should be apparent.

Freud's 1925 article is particularly relevant here. He points out that we encounter so many stimuli and events in our mental life that we must negate or repress many of these events just to function. In effect, to say yes, we must say no. We must say no to many external stimuli if one stimulus is to enter our consciousness; we must simultaneously say no to a multitude of long-term memory assimilations to allow one bit of new data in. If we attended to everything, we would be attending to nothing and become physiologically and psychologically "jammed." It is necessary that we repress information from both the present and past if we are to function as human beings.

Long-term memory (LTM) may be considered the storehouse of past assimilations and memories. It may be equated roughly with the Freudian preconscious and unconscious. Some items are easily accessible; others are buried deep and may even be totally unaccessible. Some theorists about cognition talk of habit formation. A habit in a Piagetian sense is a set of cognitive assimilations or schemata. There are many habit patterns that we repeat over and over again.

Piagetian schema theory perhaps best describes the process of long-term memory development. The young child develops small schemata, and then these schemata are hierarchically ordered into a larger and larger schema. For example, looking at a light involves at least three schemata: (1) perceptual—the child must notice the light, (2) motor coordination of many muscles of the eye, and (3) cognitive coordination of awareness. Unless all three schemata are in place, the child cannot attend to the light. Until the eye is coordinated with hand movements, eye-hand coordination cannot develop. And hand coordination and voluntary control of the hand require an immense number of schemata and practices. The eye-hand coordination is a transcendent and critical schema and is required for reaching for a rattle, feeding oneself, and eventually, in later life, working on a word processor.

In schema theory, small bits of cognitions are increasingly combined with other small bits into ever-enlarging gestalts. The combination is part and parcel of smaller schemata, but the whole is larger than the parts. The environment that the therapist provides for the client is similarly built from many small schemata. The therapist may have participated in microcounseling skill-training programs. A counselor trainee first learns the importance of attending behavior (which itself consists of four smaller schemata—eye contact, body language, vocal qualities, and verbal following). The schema of attending behavior is then joined with other schemata of listening skills—such as encouraging, paraphrasing, reflection of feeling, and summarization—into a larger schema termed the basic listening sequence. The basic listening sequence is then combined with influencing skills such as directives, advice, interpretation, and confrontation to build ever-enlarging patterns of schemata. Then, these skills are utilized in a systematic five-stage model of the interview (see Ivey, 1983a; Ivey and Matthews, 1984) into a full interview. The interview in turn may be combined with different theories of helping with extremely large combinations of schemata. Finally, the therapist, equipped with skills and theoretical schemata, meets the client, who similarly comes to the session with many highly developed schemata.

In a sense, it can be said that the person-environment transaction of psychotherapy and counseling is the meeting of two long-term memories or two combinations of preconscious and unconscious storehouses. Bringing life to the session is the 100- to 750-msec consciousness in which therapist and client face new data that they must accommodate and assimilate. This interaction is dialectical and mutually influencing and involving. While the prime goal of the session is for the therapist to "change" the client, it should be apparent that the client has some opportunity to "change" the therapist. One place long-term change may be demonstrated as a result of this interaction is in language. Researchers have found that clients often tend to mirror the words of their therapists. Examination of interviews of Rogers, Perls, and Ellis with the same client (Gloria) revealed that the client accommodated to the language system of each therapist in turn (Meara, Shannon, and Pepinsky, 1979; Meara, Pepinsky, Shannon, and Murray, 1981). Some reassurance about these findings is provided by a study in which white counselors tended to imitate their Black clients' language usage rather than using their own words (Fry, Kropf, and Coe, 1980).

Habits, concepts, schemata, and patterns have the quality of *automatization,* that is, they repeat themselves automatically and are very useful. For example, we need automatic patterns to drive a car or dance. We cannot think of all the schemata we have in our minds if we are to function effectively. At the same time, habits tend to be stereotyped and to not sufficiently allow for new input. One can think about how one's ability "falls apart" when following a difficult route in a new city or when learning a new dance step that is somewhat similar to an old one. Habitual patterns can become inappropriate, witness the psychoanalytic construct of repetition. Repetition involves the constant reiteration of *structures* of thought and behavior even though the *content* may be different. Thus, an obsessive personality may repeat the desire to control in many different situations. The assimilated obsessive pattern is habitual. To break this pattern, the obsessive must learn and acknowledge the presence of the analyst and eventually open his or her mind to new accommodations.

Clients often come to therapy with automatizations or patterns of assimilations that require change and loosening. Therapists sometimes also come to therapy with overly automatic behavior and miss "seeing" the client before them. The question of developmental change and growth for both client and therapist may be raised. Parts of the solution can be found in Piaget's equilibration theory.

Equilibration: Changing the Environment and the Cognitive Balance

How does the young child accommodate to the world and assimilate simple ideas and movements into ever-enlarging constructions of the world? How do clients develop their individual and unique patterns of accommodations and assimilations of the world—some of which are useful, others of which are major hindrances? Schema theory and equilibration are important processes that can be used to help explain this complexity. The use of smaller schemata to build larger and larger schemata has been elaborated. Equilibration speaks to the nature of the schemata that have been developed.

A child who primarily accommodates to the world will tend to have many small schemata. If a child or person primarily accommodates, they will see little in the world but differences and distinctions. Groupings and patterns require assimilation, the coordination of related schemata. For example, the word "tree" is a general or universal term that, at first glance, seems highly descriptive. Yet, this universal term actually refers to no particular distinctive tree. All trees are uniquely different one from the other, just as our fingerprints, vocal tone, body type, and life patterns are different one from another. It does little good to have thousands of distinctions for "tree" or "person" or "house." It is critical that the child and adult have the ability to assimilate patterns or groupings. Accommodation is clearly not enough. As Wadsworth (1984) comments:

> When confronted with a new stimulus, a child tries to assimilate it into existing schemata. Sometimes this is not possible. . . . There are no schemata into which it readily fits. . . . What does the child do? Essentially, he (or she) can do one of two things: (1) . . . create a new schema into which he can place the stimulus (new index card in the file). (2) . . . modify an existing schema so that the stimulus will fit into it. Both are forms of accommodation. . . . Both actions result in a change in or development of cognitive structures (schemata) [p. 15].

Given the constructs of assimilation and accommodation, it can be argued that clients and patients must have a balance of the two (a cognitive balance) if they are to adapt and cope with a world of ever-present stability and change. A client who always accommodates and seldom assimilates will have a large number of unintegrated schemata and be unable to notice similarities. Many clients come to therapy with unintegrated schemata, and the task of therapy is to help these clients see repeating patterns in their behavior and thus promote assimilation. At the same time, at an unconscious level, this client already has excessively strong assimilations, which underlie these behavioral patterns. Thus, the therapist must also promote the openness of accommodation, enabling the client to develop unique responses to new people. A client may, for example, be acting in his or her relationship to a superior at work in a fashion similar to his or her relationship with a parent. When the therapist points out the similar pattern in the two schemata, a larger assimilation results as the client sees the similarities of two previously distinct situations. Moreover, the client can accommodate to differences between his or her parent and the boss.

A client with a problem of assimilation might constantly be building large schemata and not noticing important differences. The client might well realize that patterns are repeating

and need help in making distinctions and in learning how to accommodate more effectively. In the recognition of repeating
patterns, we see the inseparable balance of assimilation and accommodation. The client who overassimilates has already accommodated to similarities but has not accommodated to differences. The client who overaccommodates has not assimilated
similarities but has assimilated differences. Once again, we see
that assimilation and accommodation cannot be truly separated.

Equilibration is the cognitive balance between assimilation and accommodation. The child and the adult are constantly seeking a balance between the two. A *positive balance* occurs
when one overemphasizes assimilation without concurrent appropriate accommodation. In therapy this may show up in
transference and counter-transference problems. Or the client
may assimilate the therapist's statements into previously existing cognitive structures. The client engaged in a positive balance
will tend to be difficult to move or change.

A *negative balance* occurs when one overemphasizes accommodation and constantly reacts to new input as new and
different, with multiple schemata. In the negative, accommodating balance, the individual has failed to *conserve* past knowledge. Underaccommodation may result in resistance on the part
of the client—the client may be unable to see parallels suggested by the therapist or may be overly willing to accept therapist suggestions and advice. The client will tend to be open to
experience, but this very openness or spontaneity is part of the
problem.

The obsessional neurotic may be characterized as assimilative in nature, while the varieties of hysteria are primarily accommodative. The obsessive will repeat behavior in an effort to
control, while the hysterical personality is "all over the place"—
seemingly out of control. However, obsessive and hysterical personality styles have more than a passing acquaintance with assimilation and accommodation. Just as assimilation and accommodation are twin processes, each inseparable from the other,
so are obsessive and hysterical personality styles deeply entwined
—"Under every hysteric is an obsessive and under every obsessive is a hysteric."

Breuer's (Breuer and Freud, 1893) work with Anna O. illustrates how assimilation and accommodation may present themselves in the hysteric. At the time her father was dying, Anna O. went into serious hysterical reaction, which included the loss of the ability to speak her native language, suicide attempts, and a variety of physical symptoms. Anna O. would now be diagnosed as having a conversion reaction, major depression, and atypical psychosis (see the *DSM-III Casebook* [Spitzer, Skodol, Gibbon, and Williams, 1981, p. 332]). Anna O.'s symptomatology changed constantly; she reacted to different people in vastly different ways. These reactions represent at a surface level a wide variety of accommodations to constant change. Through hypnosis and the "talking cure," Breuer gradually narrowed the cause of Anna O.'s symptoms; he found that each time she discussed the first appearance of a hysterical symptom, that symptom would disappear.

> She lost the power of speech (1) as a result of fear, after her first hallucination at night, (2) after having suppressed a remark another time (by active inhibition), (3) after having been blamed for something, and (4) on every analogous occasion (when she felt mortified). She began coughing for the first time when once, as she was sitting by her father's bedside, he heard the sound of dance music coming from a neighboring house, felt a sudden wish to be there, and was overcome with self-reproaches. Thereafter, throughout the whole length of her illness, she reacted to any markedly rhythmical music with a *tussis nervosa*. . . . Each symptom disappeared after she described its first occurence [Breuer and Freud, (1893) p. 40].

In an example such as this, we may see the assimilative portion or obsessive nature of Anna O.'s behavior. She is accommodating to a single event, which is new, but is putting it into previously existing assimilated structures. Her accommodative process, like Zelig's, is so extreme that it becomes a form of rigid assimilation. In a similar fashion, it would be possible to analyze the behavior and action of the obsessive personality.

To return to the counseling and therapy process, the client who may over- or underaccommodate or over- or underassimilate may be desirous of a more effective cognitive balance or equilibration. Equilibration represents a kind of homeostasis in which a temporary truce between accommodation and assimilation is secured and the person has a moment of stability. Generally, Piagetian theorists (for instance, Wadsworth, 1984) seem to suggest that equilibration and cognitive balance is a goal. However, homeostasis never seems enough for the seeking, assimilating child or for the developing, curious, adventurous client in therapy and counseling.

Schemata generated from assimilations and accommodations may be transformed into new, larger, and more effective schemata (or less effective ones, as in the case of Anna O.). Developing new, large schemata requires the generation of new constructs, new behaviors, new understandings, and the willingness to enter new experiences. Just as the child has transformed smaller schemata of eye-hand coordination, and grasping into new, larger patterns, so can clients combine interpretations from the therapist with past experiences and, perhaps, a role play and generate a new and larger transformation or understanding of their lives.

Piagetian theory presents four types of solutions to the problem of equilibration or resolution of the balance of accommodation and assimilation:

> Two *alpha* solutions:
>   Negative balance: Overemphasis on assimilation.
>   Positive balance: Overemphasis on accommodation.
> *Beta* solution: Equilibration or balancing between the two alpha solutions.
> *Gamma* solution: A new totality or schema is generated from past assimilations and accommodations.

Viktor Frankl in *Man's Search for Meaning* (1959) offers helpful examples of each of the above. Frankl survived the German concentration camps because he was able to utilize a variety of cognitive procedures to ensure his survival. To survive in the concentration camp environment, one must accommodate to many rules and regulations if one is to adapt and survive at all. Overaccommodation (alpha solution, positive balance) is represented by individuals who totally cooperated with the Nazis to ensure their own survival. In overassimilation (alpha solution, negative balance), the person eliminates present data and substitutes other information as a protection from the currrent environment. Frankl's text provides several examples of this type of adaptation: A man was dying next to him; Frankl, instead of accommodating to the man's death, focused his attention on a dry crust of bread. At another time while cleaning latrines in the cold rain, Frankl thought of his beloved wife. Refusal to accommodate to present reality helped him survive. Examples of the beta solution (or equilibration) were when Frankl helped other prisoners plan their escape (although he himself did not attempt escape) and when he talked with others in intellectually stimulating study groups. All of these techniques together represent a transcendent or gamma solution that enabled Frankl to see a sunset instead of the horror of the camp. His experiences also provided the basis for a way of thinking about therapy that has had an impact on millions.

As might be anticipated, clients come to therapy with varying patterns of cognitive balance of equilibration. With some clients, we as therapists seek to induce more of certain alpha solutions. We might wish to enable a client to accommodate more readily to his or her new surroundings and to be more flexible in accommodating to, for example, the needs of a new baby in the home. With other clients, we may seek to enable them to assimilate new information and ideas about child rearing or about transactional analysis or assertiveness training. In each of these efforts, we are seeking to facilitate a beta solution, or a more adequate homeostasis. When we seek to develop new skills, new behaviors, and new insights in the client, we are searching with them for transcendent solutions, or gamma solutions.

Any client will be utilizing one or more of the cognitive

balance styles. Generally, our goal is to move clients to a beta or gamma solution. With some clients, it may be wise to achieve a delicate balance between an overly assimilative or overly accommodative position. As an extreme example, a client facing death from cancer or on death row in prison may be wise to use an overly assimilative alpha posture to cope with the trauma.

Other clients may benefit from a more accommodative orientation. When one is living in a small space for a period of time (such as a submarine or a space capsule), there is a great need to accommodate to and assimilate this environment. If one brings past cognitions into these situations, they may prove totally unworkable. Anyone who enters the institutional framework of society needs to take an accommodative posture in order to survive. Whether facing the first day of school, learning the rules of basketball, entering a jail or prison, or facing an IRS tax audit, it is most helpful to be able to accommodate successfully to the new data. In each case, however, the individual will be more successful in accommodating if he or she has a solid, preexisting, assimilated structure that is relevant to the new program. Accommodation is generally more stressful than assimilation, since the individual must take in new data rather than comfortably fit it into old, previously existing structures.

The type of environment that a therapist seeks to provide rests on the need for an assimilative-accommodative balance. A client with highly organized patterns of assimilation may benefit from working with an accommodative therapist who reflects back the assimilations so the client can then reorganize them him- or herself. (Interestingly, the process of reorganizing old assimilations into new constructs is a major form of accommodation. Assimilations are primarily moved by new data through the process of accommodation.) Alternatively, the client may need to be challenged by an assimilative theory in which the therapist provides substantial new input that upsets the cognitive balance and provides stimulus for concept reorganization and new assimilations.

The major issue in counseling and therapy, however, is the matter of *transforming* old assimilations or schemata into new and more useful formulations. Chapter Five gives special attention to the generation of new knowledge and the creation of new meanings as represented by the gamma solution.

Theory into Practice

Consciousness grows in a dialectical relationship with the environment. An error frequently made in considering conscious mental functioning is to omit the truth of how the environment determines so much of what and how one thinks and does. Whereas Chapter One focuses on the internal nature of conscious development, this chapter emphasizes the point that it is the environment that nurtures and heavily determines cognition and behavior.

A therapeutic reinterpretation of the Piagetian constructs of assimilation and accommodation is central to this chapter, and these two processes are the means by which the data of development are generated. The following outline can help the therapist apply theory to actual situations.

Construct 1: The environment is the context within which development occurs. The task of the therapist is presented as providing an environment for the client that permits and facilitates natural growth from within the client.

1. *Learning Objective:* To be able to define the person-environment dialectic that is therapy and life and to understand that each outcome of the process leads to further outcomes and processes in a constant dialectic interaction.

2. *Cognitive Presentation:* Pages 35–41 contain a complex array of data, but two basic points are made: (1) The commonly used terms "person-environment" and "individual society" are themselves dialectical in nature—it is important to remember that the environment determines the nature of the person, but that the person also shapes the environment; (2) the evolutionary process of an Argus pheasant is heavily determined by the environment. Each adaptation of the pheasant creates a response in the environment, which determines the survival of the

organism. Each adaptation (wing feathers) is an *out-come* that is simultaneously a process leading to something else. Similarly, the dichotomy in psychotherapy between process and outcome is itself somewhat arbitrary and false.

3. *Experiential Exercises or Homework:*
   a. Examine biological organism/environment interaction and consider how flowers grow in relation to environmental stimulation, deer in relationship to wolves on an island, and what happens to a landscape when it is strip-mined. Each process is an outcome leading to yet another process or outcome.
   b. In a role-played interview, draw out from another person the following data concerning personal developmental progressions. (1) Ask your client to identify a developmental step that was important to him or her (such as graduation from high school, learning to play the piano, making a place on the school team, winning an event). Draw out of the individual the facts and feelings surrounding that event, using basic listening skills. (2) Ask your client how that developmental step or *outcome* became a process leading to other outcomes later in life. For example, how did high school graduation lead to new problems and opportunities? How did this developmental step/outcome become part of the life process? How did you impact your parents and friends and how did they impact you?

Construct 2: Assimilation and accommodation are twin motors of development, and therapist and client play out this dialectic in their own environmental relationship.

1. *Learning Objectives:* To be able to define assimilation and accommodation, to relate them to Kelly's concepts of tight, loose, and permeable construct systems, and to identify therapeutic theories as they may exemplify assimilation and accommodation.
2. *Cognitive Presentation:* Pages 41–51 present this infor-

mation. The summary on pages 48–50 may be useful to illustrate the key ideas of this chapter. Most important is the idea that client and therapist perceptions change through a mutual exercise of assimilation and accommodation.

3. *Experiential Exercises or Homework:*

   a. View a film of Carl Rogers (or any other therapist) in action. This may be useful to help explore the nature of the therapeutic environment and to determine whether it is primarily assimilative or accommodative in nature. What happens to the client's personal construct system as a result of the therapeutic interaction? Note specific instances of therapist assimilations that the client uses to transform thinking and accommodate to a new way of thinking or being. How does the therapist change through the twin processes? In this process we may see the client gradually adopting the personal constructs of the therapist.

   b. List popular theories of therapy and consider the degree to which each is accommodative and assimilative in nature. How do all work toward Kelly-type permeable constructs?

   c. Examine one of your own personal constructions of reality and introspect on your own assimilative and accommodative processes. Consider an idea you hold especially important to you (religion, a theory, a vital belief about the nature of humankind). This may be an assimilated idea. Think back on how this idea was constructed in the first place through accommodation and assimilation dialectics. Then consider how this assimilated idea both facilitates and works against new accommodations to the environment.

Construct 3: A dialectic view of information-processing theory provides a useful formulation for bringing experimental psychology, ideas of assimilation and accommodation, and therapy together in a useful synthesis. The central idea is that experimental research on perception and integration of ideas appears to support the conceptual formulations of this chapter.

1. *Learning Objectives:* To be able to define several key terms or ideas: attention, the relationship of research to information processing in terms of time to assimilate and accommodate, consciousness, short-term memory, long-term memory, rapid attentional integration, conscious present, buffer period, absolute judgment span, schema theory, and automatization.

    All these terms and their related ideas lead to the central learning objective of conceptualizing and identifying the dual relation that is the counselor-client interaction and determining how this dual relation may be constructed in learning theory formulations.

2. *Cognitive Presentation:* Pages 51-62 present the ideas of this construct in detail. The summary Figure 6 may be described as central to the presentation.

    It is important to note the extensions of these concepts to Freud's work in 1900 and in 1925, particularly the need to negate much of what is there in order to take in new data into internal structures. Without negation, overaccommodation (such as was the case for Zelig) is a likely outcome. On the other hand, when there is too much negation of external reality through assimilated past structures, no accommodation is possible as new data are not allowed.

    Schema theory is also summarized and an example of skill acquisition in counseling is provided. Just as a counselor or therapist acquires (assimilates and accommodates) new skills, so do clients acquire skills through their dual relationship with the therapist.

3. *Experiential Exercises or Homework:*
    a. A variety of perceptual exercises focusing on one's own attentional processes may be helpful. For example, stop for a moment and view the scene before you. Think about the "eye of consciousness," the 100- to 750-msec period in which perceptions are

formed. Then think about the ten-second period of short-term memory. Finally, allow yourself to drift in long-term memory and note the many associations that develop. Focus on one object (thus negating other perceptions), then focus or attend to the whole scene before you.

The presentation of rapid attentional integrations and other such terms tends to be intellectualized and too easily forgotten. You will find it helpful if you continue generating perceptual and memory exercises to obtain a more experiential understanding of these concepts.

b.   Experiment with the relationship of what is observed to Freudian constructs of unconscious thought. Focus on one object in your visual field. Note an emotion or affect associated with that object. Allow yourself to free associate and flow back to other objects and memories. As you move to exploration of the long-term memory, consider how associations in the mind are connected by affect and emotion. A wide variety of psychodynamic free association exercises are possible using these methods. Notice that a meditative or light hypnotic state may be produced at will. You may find that your sense of linear time changes as your perceptions and thoughts change.

c.   Piagetian schema theory can provide a useful theoretical and conceptual basis for the practice of therapy. Review the material on microskills development and then examine how you bring together small bits of information into ever-enlarging schemata. One example might be something you have done in sports or music. Think through the specific, small cognitions and behaviors that are integrated into ever-enlarging gestalts of understanding and action. It is this integration of information that is often lacking in clients who present themselves for therapy. Our task as therapists is to help rearrange

long-term memory and schemata into more facilitative patterns. This transformational process represents the gamma solution (described in the final section of the chapter) in which assimilation and
accommodation work together to produce change
and development.

*Construct 4: The cognitive balance or style of equilibration
often repeats itself again and again in the individual; it may represent a strength or it may represent a deficit of cognition in
need of remediation.* Equilibration is the balance of assimilative
and accommodative styles. It is this balanace that the therapist
seeks to impact.

1. *Learning Objectives:* To be able to identify equilibrative
   styles of assimilation and accommodation and to suggest
   therapeutic alternatives to meet client needs.
2. *Cognitive Presentation:* Pages 62–69 summarize the four
   possible solutions to the problem of equilibration. Of
   special importance is Breuer's case of Anna O. and how
   her behavior as a hysteric may be interpreted using this
   framework. From this example, the central issue of potential value for the therapist appears to be to (1) identify the cognitive style of the client, particularly those
   clients that represent "stuck," alpha solutions; and (2)
   facilitate client movement to beta or gamma solutions
   through dialectical intervention. Frankl's experience in
   the concentration camp was used as an example of a
   transcendent gamma solution.
3. *Experiential Exercises or Homework:*
   a. Identify times in which you produced difficulties
       for yourself through either negative or positive alpha
       solutions, through overaccommodating or overassi-
       milating. How did you transcend the alpha solution
       and move to a beta or gamma solution? What were
       the dimensions of the transformation?
   b. Creativity may be described as a gamma solution as
       it is often represented by the generation of a new
       totality or schema. As such, virtually all creativity

exercises have at least metaphorical relevance to this problem. A client in therapy must create a new solution. Discuss and describe your own personal experience with creativity or that of another person you have observed. Apply these concepts to the therapeutic process.

c. Describe past clients you have worked with using the framework of the four solutions for balancing assimilation and accommodation. Be specific and outline identifiable dimensions so that others examining your clients can understand your frame of reference and reasoning. Later in this text, a scale for evaluating therapeutic impact is built on this idea. Can you anticipate the scale or develop one of your own to assess client cognitive change and development?

d. Review the case of Anna O., which was described *both* as a positive and negative alpha solution. Can you describe how she could be viewed from both perspectives of alpha solutions? How is she an over-accommodator? An over-assimilator? Given these analyses, what is the nature of the therapeutic environment that might be most helpful?

Summary

Whereas Chapter One focused on the development of consciousness, this chapter has described the environments that help promote the development of consciousness. Therapists provide varying types of environments for their clients, and these environments provide the context for client growth.

Vital to the concept of growth is awareness of the basic biological models of evolution and the manner in which environments shape individuals and individuals shape environments. The "end" of evolutionary adaptation is simultaneously a "process" leading toward new, future "ends." The distinction between process and outcome in terms of counseling and therapy research and practice may be arbitrary and incorrect.

Assimilation and accommodation, twin Piagetian constructs, have been central concepts in this chapter. Each is simultaneously an end and a process within itself. Furthermore, they are in a dialectical relationship and represent a unity. Assimilation perhaps is the more basic structure, for it seems that people are born behaving—it is part of a person's inborn "wiring." Yet, as we are born behaving, it is our accommodation to and of our environment that shapes our behavior and eventual assimilations. A child cannot know a light bulb or a parent unless they are there in the environment. The cultural environment of Japan is clearly different from the environment of North America. Each environment demands accommodations from the individual that over time add up to large differences in assimilated patterns among different people.

In therapy we find that most theories are basically assimilative in nature, with the possible exception of Rogerian person-centered methods. The old nondirective school of Rogers appears to be close to a truly accommodative orientation to helping. In therapy the environment provided by the therapist may heavily impact the direction of change, growth, and development. Nonetheless, these distinctions are somewhat arbitrary, and the suggested construct of combinatory assimilation/accommodation reminds us that the two are inseparable.

Information-processing theory was presented in the context of person-environment transaction. Research on attentional factors and cognitive processes suggests that the *conscious present* may be defined as existing within a period of between 100 and 750 milliseconds. In this conscious present and short-term memory exists a struggle between person and environment in which a judgment is made whether or not to accommodate to new data or to use old assimilations to organize the same data into previously existing patterns. Information-processing theory can be related to an array of constructs, ranging from behaviorism through Freudian ideas of the unconscious.

This chapter brings these diverse data together in the review of Piaget's equilibration theory. The concepts of equilibration are highly useful in establishing the goals of therapy and in planning useful matches of therapeutic environment for clients' different cognitive styles.

Chapter Three will examine Piagetian developmental theory in more detail and will briefly explore issues of environment. It also includes highly specific methodological suggestions for moving individuals through specific developmental stages of consciousness.

Chapter Four will again bring back environmental constructs and further explore the issue of "which therapy for which individual at what time under what conditions." Chapter Five will return to the critical issue of therapeutic transformation and how one can use theory to produce developmental change and growth.

ৡ 3 ৡ

Therapy as Development

Facilitating
Cognitive-Developmental
Change

Becoming an independent, formal operational adult is the theme of this chapter. We usually think of Piaget's theories as primarily relating to the child, yet they serve as helpful metaphors for the construction of therapeutic theory and method that enables us to examine adult change and development. After a consideration of how Piaget's theories relate to adolescents and adults, highly specific techniques will be presented as a suggested system for leading clients to alternative and more effective ways of framing and interpreting their experience.

But, Won't Granny Need Her Socks?

Piaget's developmental framework is simply and beautifully summarized by Knowles and Reeves, who observe how the stages manifest themselves in children's dealings with the issues of death and dying. Jill, a five-year-old preoperational child, is worried about her father, whose own mother has just died. Jill brings in Granny's socks, and her father asks her what she has in mind. She says: "Well, Daddy, I've been worried about Granny. When she was at home, she liked to keep her feet warm in those big gray socks. . . . Now that she's gone dead, she didn't have a chance to get those socks before she went away. Isn't she going to be cold without them?" (Knowles and Reeves, 1983, p. 1).

78

Death is too abstract a concept for a child in the sensori-motor or preoperational stage. Given more complexity than she could understand, Jill constructed a magical, irrational meaning so she could cope with the world around her. It is this magical (and ofttimes marvelous) world in which the child brings puzzling and incongruous events to a beginning level of cognitive understanding.

At the concrete operations stage (ages six through twelve), children tend to see death in highly concrete terms. A dead rat may be pushed with a stick to see if it moves. At a funeral, the child may visit and revisit the coffin studying the body carefully. At the early stages of concrete operations, death may be seen simply as the absence of movement; hence, the frequent confusion between death and sleeping. Knowles and Reeves point out that children may not fully realize that death is irreversible until eight or nine years of age. At this same point, children begin to understand causes of death (at first weapons and later illness). The idea of one's own death is quite remote.

During adolescence, with the beginning of formal operational thinking, death may be actively denied. The here and now, peer-group orientation of teenagers often leads them to deny death despite its reality. The negation of death represents an important transformation in the development of an independent self. At a funeral, the adolescent may stay in the back, refuse to cry, and appear isolated and alone. Underlying much of this behavior is a deep personal egocentricity and a search for personal identity: "I'd rather die than go to school with my hair looking so awful." This denial and egocentric stage, present to a greater or lesser extent in all young people, later yields to personal awareness of death and the many complexities of its meanings. It is also a part of becoming a fully independent, formal, operational adult.

Piaget, Psychotherapy, and Development

Adult development in therapy and counseling follows a sequence similar to that of children working through the Piagetian stages. Furthermore, specific therapeutic interventions may be used to promote change and movement through this cycle. Adults may work through the stages in just a few sessions or even statements, or it may take a long, slow process to unfold and facilitate personal growth through the interaction of client and therapist. Adults take in sensori-motor data, organize information into schemata or patterns, which may be sensori-motor experience, irrational, preoperational ideas, or concrete linear rational thought. They then may think about their thoughts and actions in a formal operational manner. Therapists and counselors take clients through these developmental processes through the interview and in short-term and long-term psychotherapy. The dialectic or dialogue that occurs between therapist and client may reopen the client who is fixated at any developmental level and result in further future development.

Each of us is constantly and humanly engaged in sensori-motor learning, preoperational thinking, and concrete and formal operational thought. Earlier stages of development do not disappear with childhood, but continue as active processes within us as new developmental tasks and stages confront us. Development does not end until death.

Clients often come to therapy with preoperational thinking patterns very similar to those of five-year-old Jill. We may call these adult preoperational thoughts "irrational ideas," "transference," "obsessions," or any of a variety of labels that indicate thinking or behavior which does not meet cultural norms. The thinking patterns (consciousness levels) and behaviors of some clients are often much like those of a young child. These clients may misinterpret the phenomenology of sensory data. They may put together irrational, magical explanations of what happens around them from what they see, hear, and feel. The reality of what they see is misinformed by ideas or cognitions that preexist in their minds and distort their organization of sense impressions. Their assimilations in long-term memory may preclude their changing and adapting through accommodative processes.

Through skilled questioning and listening, therapists may move clients to concreteness in identifying what is happening in their lives. Through this effort aimed at concrete understanding of the client's perspective, we as therapists often learn the rationale or blockage that has led to ineffective thinking and behavior. Later, we may assist clients to understand linear thinking and the causes and effects underlying their difficulties. The behavioral psychotherapist, for example, may be particularly effective in helping clients to operate concretely on their environment and to use specific and predictable laws of cause and effect. Assertiveness training is a good example of a method that is helpful in assisting clients to act predictably on their environment.

Many therapists and counselors are not satisfied with concrete action and predictability. They seek to move clients to a richer affective and cognitive understanding of themselves and their situations. Here the epistemology, or way of thinking about the situation, moves from embeddedness in the situation to thinking about thinking and involves formal operational thinking. Cognitive-behavior modification, the reframing of irrational ideas, and the examination of self in Rogerian and existential theories are illustrations of formal operational therapeutic activities.

Chapter One (Figures 3 and 4) extensively examines the distinction and dialectic between knowledge (*episteme*) and intelligence (*noesis*) and presents a fourth level of cognition. Piagetian theory does not ordinarily separate formal operational thinking into a fourth level, since one of its premises is that formal operations establish the basic framework for further reflections or thinking about thinking about thinking. Furth's (1981) useful chapter summarizes Piaget's new theory of equilibration in a hierarchical model of increasing complexity in which self observes self observing self, and the end result is close to the dialectic framework suggested here. Others (for example, Kegan, 1982) discuss a post-formal operational level and dialectical development. (Because there is some disagreement as to whether or not Piaget truly discusses dialectics, this complex area will be reserved for discussion in more depth at the conclusion of this chapter.)

Piaget's Four Major Levels of Development

Adult development follows a sequence of events closely allied with those identified with Piaget and the Platonic levels of consciousness. The relation of Platonic and Piagetian conceptions is an important basis for the theory and method of this book. There are impressive parallels between the two frameworks (which are separated by 2,000 years). In this chapter, I hope to integrate ancient and current theorizing about human development with that of constructive, empirical practice in counseling and psychotherapy.

Although Piaget describes four major levels of development (or three, if one prefers to integrate the sensori-motor and preoperational periods), he clearly states that these levels are arbitrary. Development is a flowing process, and the distinctions between the levels are made because they are descriptively useful. It would be possible to delineate five, ten, or eighty-three levels of development, not just four. Although Piaget and his colleagues constantly emphasize the arbitrariness of these stages, Piaget's empirical work and conceptual writings and those of his followers have tended to reify, to specifically make real and concrete, what originally began as abstract ideas. Thus, the stages summarized here may be best considered an admixture of a reality that Piaget himself has produced by presenting his ideas. Once named, described, and researched by a multitude of individuals, arbitrary constructs formed in the world of ideas become a reality that imposes rather directly on our life experiences. What was once Piagetian intelligence has become more fixed knowledge.

The major stages of child and adult development are discussed below in some detail and, more briefly, in Figure 7.

Stage 1. Early Sensori-Motor Learning (birth to two years). The child relies on sensory experience. He or she takes in (accommodates to) data from the environment through the five senses and gradually organizes (assimilates) these data with motoric experience. An early developmental task, discussed previously, is eye-hand coordination. The child may see a rattle in the environment. By initially random movement, the child may hit the rattle. This feedback is first accommodated and then becomes a new assimilation in which the child has "learned" that the hand and arm movements may be planfully directed to obtain desired environmental feedback. Two schemata, or sets of eye and hand movements, have been integrated or coordinated into one larger developmental unit. The basic Piagetian dialogue or dialectic has been: (1) action by the child, (2) environmental feedback adapted to step 1 when the rattle moves, and (3) adaptation by the child through noticing and acting on data from step 2. In Chapter One, this three-step framework is illustrated by two children developing knowledge together, but the structure of this relationship repeats itself in the "communication as adaptation" between the child and the rattle in the environment. The child is engaged in coconstruction of reality with objects in the environment. In the child's mind, the coconstruction continues in a relation of self with self.

The child begins the sensori-motor stage with an immensely egocentric approach ("I am the world," "My mommy is me," "I am the nipple") but gradually differentiates self from objects in the world. Elementary causation and "if/then" relationships are noted ("If I hit the rattle, then it moves") even without verbal constructs. From eighteen to twenty-four months, simple representation occurs and the child is able to generate images of toys that are not immediately seen.

New knowledge and awareness follow a parallel pattern in adults, although the movement through developmental stages may be instantaneous. Knowledge or development starts with sensory-based experience—the images or shadows of the world described in Plato's "Allegory of the Cave" (see the Epilogue). Whether adult or child, we take in data through the five senses; these data sometimes overpower us. It is possible to overaccommodate to sensory simuli and find oneself in a sort of self-hypnosis or immobility. Thus, it is critical that we assimilate and organize sensory stimuli into schemata or patterns. The individual may organize or assimilate these images of sense-based data into useful patterns, or the schemata or patterns may be illusory and ineffective. Development can start only in sense-based experience. Clients come to counseling sessions describing

Figure 7. Four Stages of Development:
The Relationship of Adult and Child Patterns

1. Sensori-Motor

The "child" receives an immense amount of sense impressions (see-ing, hearing, feeling, tasting, smelling) and must learn to coordinate or organize this experience. Adults also accommodate to the world of senses, but often approach it through fixed assimilated structures that determine the way they process and coordinate sensori-motor data. Affect may be summarized in the statement "I am my feelings" in which there is limited distinction made between what is seen, heard, and felt and emotions. Sensori-motor experience may also be manifested by the client whose life is figuratively (and sometimes literally) in pieces. A troubled client or pa-tient may have difficulty in coordinating the "bumbling confusion" of the world. Emotionally, this individual may be close to that of infant experi-ence.

Therapies associated with the sensori-motor period focus on body sensations (Rolfing, relaxation training, dance therapy, bioenergetics) or may use these same sensations as building blocks without conscious aware-ness in the theory (Gestalt, Rogerian, psychodynamic). Both adults and children may fail to recognize themselves as separate from their sensory input. This may be termed the integration of self with object.

2. Preoperational

The child has separated self from object, but often magically (ego-centrically) believes that others see and construct the world as he or she does.

The adult comes to therapy with assimilated defense mechanisms, such as projection, believing that the way he or she perceives the world is universal. This also manifests itself in irrational or illogical thinking or stuck, repetitive behavior that is ineffective.

Affect begins to be separated from cognition. The child may over-react or underreact to an event. The emotion may be inappropriate to the situation. Most therapies seek to understand client preoperational think-ing and move to higher, more sophisticated levels of consciousness and behavior.

3. Concrete Operations

The child first learns to name and describe the world, but full con-crete operations come later as linear causality and predictability are learned. The child is able to act on (operate on) the world with predictable effect and impact. Conservation is particularly important.

Affective development begins to show personal control and reversi-bility and a basic understanding of feelings is shown.

The adult in therapy becomes able to act on the world with some degree of prediction: "I do or think this, then this happens." The self is more clearly separated from object, and the individual is able to think about his or her actions and their impact.

Concrete operational therapies include many behavioral approaches, particularly assertiveness training and much of vocational counseling and planning.

Figure 7. Four Stages of Development:
The Relationship of Adult and Child Patterns, Cont'd.

4. Formal Operational

The adolescent may first realize the self by egocentric denial ("I am not a child") but gradually comes to a full awareness of self and is able to think about thinking and think about feelings. The adolescent can take data and integrate it into multiple perspectives—combine information from different areas.

The basis for idealistic thinking or thoughts about thinking and knowledge is established. Fully functioning adults represent this stage. However, the thoughts one has about oneself may be inaccurate or biased and in and of themselves preoperational.

Therapies associated primarily with this stage include Rogerian, existentialist, cognitive, and psychodynamic—those therapies that focus on thinking.

what they see, hear, and feel. Many theories of counseling and therapy discuss the importance of helping clients *see* situations and themselves more clearly, *hearing* others accurately, and "getting in touch" with *feelings*. The raw stuff of counseling is sensory based. Experimental perceptual psychology examines many of these issues, as does phenomenologically oriented therapeutic psychology.

The child concretizes affect in the body and does not separate self from emotion. The emotion may dominate the child completely and dictate its reaction to the world. This is most obvious in a child crying for a bottle or a two-year-old overwhelmed by a tantrum. The sense impressions precede behavior and thought.

The affective dimensions of this stage may be summed up in the words: I am my feelings. In the older child or adult facing a crisis situation, the individual may regress to earlier stages. When facing an accident, there is often no separation of self from the situation. When frustrated, many adults and children briefly blow up and in the process "become their feelings." Needless to say, individuals may develop a life-style in which they are led by their affect and emotions.

The construct of attending behavior in counselor training may be viewed as critical if one is to engage in an effective interview. The therapist must supply individually and culturally appropriate eye contact and facilitative body language and vocal tone for the client. Without this foundation skill of sensory-based attending, even the most effective therapist is at risk.

In a similar fashion, client observation skills provide a useful framework for how clients experience the world. There is some thought that people may have "primary lead systems," that is, specific perceptual systems for accommodating to the world. Some clients may "see" a family member while others may "hear" or "feel" them. This system of noting clients' sensory styles was originated by Bandler and Grinder (1975) and extended by Lankton (1980) and resulted in much interest and research. The data of this research, however, were not as promising as hoped: The matter was revealed to be much more complex than was originally believed. Ridings (1986) reviews over twenty studies with varying results. The concept of "primary sensory" processing has not held up under scrutiny.

However, consider the process of hypnotherapists, who focus on sensory input and elementary sensory experience and tend to use multiple sensory input systems. Witness the following trance induction for "preoperative preparation" for anesthesiology described by Rodger (1973). (It is interesting and somewhat amusing to note the words "preoperational preparation," as indeed sensori-motor data are required preparation for later preoperational thinking and later concrete operational work. Later, the therapist or surgeon can think about the concrete operation just completed.)

Hypnotic Preoperative Preparation

1. From the time you are given your prenarcosis until you are back in your room again—and even after that—you need pay attention only to the voice that speaks directly to you. All other sounds can seem very far away—a soothing, lulling, background sound.

2. As you are being given your medication, you can start a pleasant daydream going . . . and give it your full attention. As you allow your eyes to close, you shut out all visual stimulation . . . and your medication takes its full effect . . . so you can

enjoy that drowsy, dreamy, sleepy feeling . . . a lovely lassitude.

3. You listen to the voice that speaks directly to you . . . and respond appropriately. Simple instructions will be given you to make it easier for you.

4. You can set your mind right now to keep all the muscles in the operative area soft, limp, and comfortable during the operation and afterward. Any time they tighten up, you make them soft and comfortable again.

5. Your breathing stays calm and deep and easy. Your heartbeat stays calm, strong, and regular.

6. Your body functions return rapidly to normal as the anesthesia wears off.

7. As the time for your operation approaches, you can find an interesting sense of anticipation that replaces apprehension.

8. Afterward, as you look back on this experience, you can be pleasantly surprised to find how much easier it was than you thought it would be! [Rodger, 1973, p. 29, used by permission].

Hypnotherapists are not the only ones who use sensorimotor experiencing. Fritz Perls (1969) is a master of bodily oriented data and "here and now, notice what is happening" focus. For example:

Perls: Let this develop. Allow yourself to tremble, get your feelings. . . . (*Her whole body begins to move a little.*) Yah, let it happen. Can you dance it? Get up and dance it. Let your eyes open, just so that you stay in touch with your body, with what you want to express physically . . . yah. (*She walks trembling and jerkily, almost staggering.*) Now, dance rattlesnake. (*She moves, slowly and sinuously graceful.*) . . . How does it feel to be a rattlesnake now? [p. 163].

Once a person was in touch with bodily experience, "working through" could proceed.

Carl Rogers (1961) focuses almost totally on the feeling aspects of processing, which many argue are the most central for enhancing client development. This method is apparent in the fifth interview with his client Mrs. Oak, for example:

> *Therapist:* (*Softly and with an empathic tenderness toward the hurt she is experiencing.*) You feel that here at the basis of it as you experience it is a feeling of real tears for yourself. But *that* you can't show, mustn't show, so that's been covered by bitterness that you don't like, that you'd like to be rid of. You almost feel you'd rather absorb the hurt—than to feel the bitterness. (*Pause.*) And what you seem to be saying quite strongly is, I do *hurt,* and I've tried to cover it up [p. 94].

In this example, the primary effort on Rogers's part is to think about feelings in a clear formal operational manner. However, before that stage can be reached, the basis of mutual understanding of feelings must be understood.

In a videotape demonstration by Ivey (1983a) of a psychodynamic dream analysis, note the following leads on the part of the therapist:

> Umm . . . O.K. I get the pattern of the dream, the coming comfortably with your friends Pat and Charles. I hear the waves going down on a lovely day. I see a lot of bright colors and I assume good feeling; then there's the dark green, the emergency, and then the wave coming up and getting the book. . . .
>
> What do you see as the clearest image of the dream? . . . What are the clearest feelings associated [with the dream image] ? [pp. 7-8].

Thus, sensori-motor data provide the foundation for client experiencing. Transcripts of many therapeutic sessions reveal that words, images, and constructs are used that relate to sensory experience. Given this pattern, it may be that the sensori-motor therapies of bioenergetics (Lowen, 1967), the Feldenkrais movement system (1972), and other therapeutic philosophies have more relevance than has been granted them. Relaxation training, of course, is a common sensori-motor therapy. It seems likely that the constructs of Bandler and Grinder (1975) are important but may have been presented in an overly simplistic fashion and not adequately tied to a theoretical foundation.

Structured behavioral approaches, which organize the environment for clients, are also characteristic of this approach to helping. Just as parents must structure the environment of the child carefully so he or she can grow, so do some behavioral psychotherapists structure the environment, particularly with the disturbed patient. In a similar fashion, therapists structure the environment for inpatients in a psychiatric hospital.

Relationships between people are ultimately based on sensory data. We often know in the first fifteen seconds whether or not we want to continue a relationship. Many people speak of clear, visual images of their first love—the way the lover's voice sounded, the feelings that were engendered, the environment. Sensori-motor data provide the basis for contact.

Stage 2. Preoperational Thinking (two to seven years). Although the child's motoric development is rapid, the preoperational child's world is often irrational and magical. As the child's vocabulary increases, he or she becomes less egocentric and more aware of others, yet descriptions of causality and action are quite restricted and limited. During these ages, the foundation for logic and rationality is most firmly established.

The Piagetian construct of *conservation* is particularly important in explaining the nature of preoperational thought patterns. To conserve knowledge, the child must learn that a situation or an object, even though transformed or changed in part, remains the same. For example, if a child's parent puts on a Santa Claus suit without a beard or mask, the child may fail to recognize the parent and cry. This lack of conservation is to be expected at ages fifteen to twenty-eight months but not at three or four years of age. The following is a good example of how a child early on masters many logical operations.

Conservation is often discussed in relation to Piaget's famous illustration of the water glasses. A child observes a quantity of water being poured into a tall, thin glass. The water is then poured into a short, broad glass that is capable of holding the same quantity of water. If conservation of knowledge has been attained, the child will recognize that the amount of water in each glass is the same. If not, the child may exclaim with surprise, "Some of the water gone!" and view the situation magically. The word "magic" is a useful construct to describe preoperational, childish thinking. The use of such "nonlogical" connections between events or things is a necessary preoperational step before the child undertakes the difficult task of concrete thinking. Consider the metaphor of employing a preoperational hypnotic procedure before a surgical operation. Before the operation, nurses and staff must complete preoperational work. Just as in surgery, it is often not easy, without preparation, to conduct any concrete operation that will help a client improve his or her situation.

This is not to say that the preoperational, sensori-motor child exists totally in a world of irrationality and magic. Rather, the child is busy making meaning and sense out of a confusing world and from ages two to seven is engaging in immense progress toward Piagetian operational stages. The difficulty in identifying definite developmental stages may be apparent. The young child has many areas where he or she is able to think concretely and predictably about the world. These may range from kicking a ball to finding a friend to learning letters and numerals and to perhaps even reading. Just because a child is magical in one area of thinking does not mean that he or she operates totally in a preoperational world.

Preoperational (irrational, magical) thinking is evident in most counseling clients and is often the reason the client seeks help. These clients are typically unable to operate on their environment in terms of behavioral adaptation, and their lack of both skills and knowledge can prevent effective action in the world. There are many parallels between the preoperational child discussed by Piaget and the clients seen in counseling and psychotherapy.

Among clients in therapy, magical, preoperational thinking may be evident in statements such as "My mother made me
do it" (error of causation); "All men are awful," "I can never
get an erection" (error of overgeneralization); "My children
hate me" (overgeneralization and deletion of relevant data); and
"He makes me mad" (distortion—the person is attributing responsibility—and error of causation). The parenthetical comments refer to logical errors often made in the thinking process
by children and adults.

Preoperational patterns are also manifest in behavior. The
person may lack skills and be unable to accomplish something.
Equally likely, the person may have the skills but be unable to
transfer the skills to a new situation. For example, the person
may talk well with a friend and listen effectively but be verbally
inept in a group. Preoperational behavioral patterns are manifested in the lower-level Freudian defense mechanisms. Denial
illustrates, for example, the inability to transfer or conserve
knowledge. Just as the young child denies that the shorter water
glass contains the same volume of water, the patient may deny
the reality of a spouse's deep caring and love because of one single instance of failure. This inability to conserve past knowledge
is parallel to the example of the young child who fails to recognize a parent in a Santa Claus suit.

The sentences of preoperational clients tend to be seman-
tically ill formed. Clients may be able to describe elements of
their sensory experience but have not organized this experience
into meaningful, logical, and useful patterns. They may, for example, have "logic-tight" thinking (they have thought themselves into a corner) such as: "I can't go into a department store
because once someone was rude to me. Now I am too fright-
ened to try it." Such individuals may have wondrously complex and sophisticated explanations, but the fact remains that
they are unable to operate in their environment. All therapies
must deal with the issue of how clients organize and make sense
of their sensori-motor experiences, and at another level, all therapies must cope with the issue of how clients organize and
make sense of their concrete operational, formal operational,
and even higher levels of experience. Thus, a person can be pre-

operational in spite of highly sophisticated thought patterns. It is possible to be preoperational in thinking about thinking about thinking. Sophistication and knowledge are not sufficient in themselves to enable a person to think logically and live effectively.

There are several ways in which therapy can address preoperational thought and action. One is through skills training and psychoeducation, which focus directly on teaching patients how to operate more effectively in their environment. Goldstein's (1973) structured learning therapy is a good example of how patients can be taught to cope effectively and to operate on their world. The transformation from preoperational thinking to concrete operations was also demonstrated by Ivey (1973) when he taught specific sensori-motor skills such as eye contact, appropriate body language, and vocal tone to psychiatric inpatients. He followed this instruction with concrete operational training in communication skills and then moved to help patients think about thinking and to anticipate difficulties in transferring their newly learned skills to the world outside the hospital. Two useful references on skill training are Larson's *Teaching Psychological Skills* (1984) and Marshall, Kurtz, and Associates' *Interpersonal Helping Skills* (1982).

Albert Ellis's (1971) rational-emotive therapy and the work of cognitive behaviorists such as Beck (1976) and Meichenbaum (1977) also clearly illustrate the transformational process that moves the client from preoperational thinking to higher levels of operative thought. These and other therapists directly address the magical thinking process and help clarify irrational ideas, overgeneralization, deletion of significant facts, and other errors of illogical thinking.

Most preoperational clients (whether at the "lowest" childlike level or the "highest" sophisticated adult level) are able to describe elements or aspects of their experience. Often, they are not able to describe the experience fully or rationally. The task of the counselor or therapist is to assist the client in moving toward enlightenment (even if "only" re-enlightenment).

For therapists, the move to concrete operations is handled most effectively and efficiently by posing the specific concrete questions: "Could you give me a specific example?" "Could you describe concretely what happened?" Counselors and therapists have known for years that concreteness is a highly useful foundation for effective helping. Questions such as "What specifically did your mother say? What did you say? What did you do? Then what happened next?" provide systematic descriptions of what actually happened that has been subsequently distorted into illogic or the inability to act.

The search for concrete specifics leads the client to concrete operational thinking and, hopefully, to later concrete action. At this point a developmental sequence of counseling and interviewing skills is becoming manifest. (This developmental sequence is summarized later in this chapter.) First, the client must be grounded in sensori-motor experience through contact with the therapist. Second, the elements of experience can be identified and named and magical, preoperational thought patterns can be ignored. Third, through special questioning and support, concrete thought and behavioral sequences can be encouraged. Later, the client may be able to examine linear causality (late concrete operations) and repetitive patterns of behavior (early formal operations) and to eventually approach and possibly change patterns of thought and action in late formal operational thinking. It may be sufficient, of course, for many clients simply to stop therapy after they have gained concrete alternatives that they can use to operate more effectively on the world.

An all-too-common error can occur when the therapist attends directly to preoperational thought. For example, some therapists reinforce their depressed clients who talk about their depression. Therapists often make the mistake of listening to the depressive and asking questions that only focus on and increase the depression. When talking with schizophrenics who manifest flight of ideas in their conversational patterns, it is preferable to find the logic in their thinking and ignore the illogic. Otherwise, the confused talk patterns will continue. This, of course, does not deny the critical importance of hearing (accommodating to) the client's perceptions, but rather emphasizes the importance of helping truly disturbed clients accommodate to and eventually assimilate the therapist's interpretation of reality.

The process of development has usually been thought of as occurring only within the client. The spiraling process of increasingly complex thought patterns for an individual is typical of development. However, development is better discussed in terms of the mutual cogeneration of "reality" by both client and therapist. If the therapist is to facilitate the client's progress out of the "cave" of her or his existence, the therapist must also take in sensori-motor data, organize it systematically (and not assume that a single theoretical orientation works with all clients), and test it out with the client. The dialectic pattern of the dialogue follows the basic Piagetian three-step formula of: (1) remark by client, (2) remark by therapist in reaction to 1, and (3) remark by client in reaction to 2. Counseling and therapy represent this person-environment dialectic in action. Unfortunately, if this dialectic is ineffective, clients may sink to lower levels of functioning. Every interaction between a client and therapist acts to make things better or worse.

Stage 3. Concrete Operations (seven through eleven and thirteen years). The child moves in this stage to logical thought patterns and demonstrates the ability to apply more sophisticated logic to concrete problems and concerns. In earlier stages of concrete operational thinking, the child is dominated by external reality and his or her own unique perceptions. Although children experience difficulty at this stage, they later learn how to assume the viewpoints of others, anticipate and explain cause and effect, and make linear explanations of reality that are similar to the concepts of belief about the visible world as described by Plato.

The child now is able to conserve ideas rather effectively. The question of which glass has the most water is now answered correctly, although more complex issues of conservation and relationship remain unknown. The acquisition of the concept of conservation of numbers illustrates this point. The examiner may line up a row of eight black pebbles and place immediately above it a row of eight white pebbles. The child may count and say that each row has the same number, thus illustrating elementary conservation. The examiner may then spread out the eight white pebbles so that the white line is now longer than the black line. Many children still believe that the white line has more pebbles than the black line even though they have counted the pebbles.

The pebble example is a very important illustration of the complexity of conservation and the fact that preoperational thought patterns remain even though the child (or adult) is clearly working most of the time at the concrete operations level. We do not ever truly leave earlier developmental stages. We are always relying on our sense impressions, identifying the elements of experience, and organizing these elements. Inevitably, no one child or even the most sophisticated adult can organize everything perfectly—human preoperational thought and magical organization of data remain a part of us. Sensory data from our environment are constantly bombarding us, and their complexity is such that organization for "final meaning" is impossible.*

In affective development, this stage brings with it awareness of the reversibility of and linear causality in feelings. In the early stages, the child may say, "I love Teddy." Later, this is followed by, "I love Teddy and Teddy loves me." At a point late in concrete operations, the child may say, "I love Teddy because . . ." At the concrete operations level, it should be apparent that the child has separated from affect and uses affect for concrete operations and actions on the world. Affect may lead behavior, but it is more under control of the child or actor.

It could be argued that many (perhaps most) adults operate at the concrete level emotionally. This, of course, is more likely true of men than women. Through childrearing practices in this society, men are often taught to disregard their emotions —"don't cry; be a man." Owing to this, men may split the self from emotion, and the result is the very concretizing of emo-

*The paradox of "final meaning" is used here deliberately. Consider the old logical puzzle stated by the Cretan sage: "All Cretans lie." Is the sage telling "the truth" or not? Is the statement that "final meaning" is impossible a truth or itself a falsehood? Language, our main mode of communication, often fails to tell the full story of truth.

tion that may lead to more controlling rather than emotionally expressive behavior. These individuals tend to act in an instrumental, purposive manner, with relatively little thought for the perspectives and feelings of other people. Feelings are often simplified and seen as "good" or "bad." Further development of affect leads children and adults to linear, straightforward, holistic feelings, where the complexity and reality of mixed or ambivalent feelings is absent.

In contrast, women in our culture are often encouraged and allowed to experience their emotions. Thus, they may be more sensitive to their own bodies and feelings from an early age. They also may be better equipped to move more rapidly through concrete operational feelings to relational formal operational thinking. However, let us keep in mind the many individual and cultural variations on this theme. No one individual follows a predefined pattern.

In the later period of concrete operations, the child moves more to a deeper understanding of causality: "If you do X, then Y occurs." Experiences are not seen so much as isolated events but rather as related sequences. At this age, the child moves from unconnected pieces to an ordered sequence of life and living. Despite newly found sophistication and understanding, the child often has real difficulty with patterns and abstract questions. A child of twelve years may be expert at naming and listing all the state capitals but totally unable to discuss abstract notions such as government or the nature of laws. The child may draw up a social studies time line on Indian and U.S. battles but miss the abstract point that the land originally was owned by Indians.

The implications of concrete operations for counseling and therapy have already been outlined in some detail in the preceding section on preoperational thinking. Therapists constantly engage clients in the search for concrete specifics of their situations. Through drawing out the elements of experience and then giving them concrete form, therapists can assist clients in seeing the logic of their situations. Once the internal logic is seen, causality may be broached: "If you do that to your child, then what is likely to happen?" "If you continue to procrastinate, what may you anticipate as a result?"

The Piagetian dialectic three-step model again may be helpful. For example, in an assertiveness training exercise, a client may learn how to speak up and not let the spouse override him or her constantly. This learning represents step one. Step two occurs when the client actually applies this learning to the situation with his or her spouse. If it works and the spouse changes, the dialectic has been successfully moved to step three, and a twin spiral of development between client and spouse has been initiated. If the assertiveness training is not effective, development remains arrested, and the client can return to the therapist, who can take the data into account and revise treatment plans on the basis of the environmental feedback.

Conservation is an important concept for counseling and therapy. Object relations theorists talk about object constancy and its importance to the child (for example, see Fairbairn, 1952; Mahler, 1971; Masterson, 1985; and Winnicott, 1958). Even at the sensori-motor level, the child requires a constancy in the mother (and father) in order to conserve and develop a knowledge of relationships with others. The child accommodates (takes in) and assimilates (acts on) the mother. The mother, in turn, does the same with the child. Each is person and each is environment, both assimilating and accommodating, cogenerating in the sense of dialectical, mutual development to higher levels of the spiral. However, the mother may have experienced a difficult childhood herself and perhaps has assimilated an image of a mother who is rough and does not care for a child and thus passes these same messages on to the child. The child takes in these messages and in turn assimilates and acts on the mother from this perspective. The mother and child produce each other.

Alternatively, the relationship between mother and child may become so close that no one else, including the father, is allowed psychologically into the environment. Mother and child cogenerate a close spiraling world that may work for them but fails to account for the world beyond. Similarly, a young couple in love may cogenerate a perfect environment that is effective until the birth of a child disturbs their tight little world.

Object relations theorists argue that this cogenerated relationship between a child and early objects prepares the way for the child as adult. The elements of experience that are central—certain preoperational thought patterns and concrete modes of operating in the world—may be carried throughout life resulting in an adult who always remains, in some ways, a very young child.

Masterson's (1981) developmental object relations approach is a useful practical extension of this theory. Drawing from Mahler (1971) and Bowlby (1969, 1973b), Masterson suggests three major phases in infancy, each of which needs to be worked through successfully in relation to the mother. Below is a summary of his major constructions with a comparison of Piagetian stages of development.

Piaget	*Masterson*
0-2 yrs. Sensori-motor	
0-1 month. Reflex and spontaneous movements	0-3 mo. *Autistic*
1-4 mo. First habits and primary circular reaction	3-18 mo. *Symbiotic*
	(3-8 mo. Separation-Individuation subphase of differention)
4-8 mo. Secondary circular reaction	
8-12 mo. Coordination of means and ends	(8-15 mo. Sep.-Ind. subphase of practicing)
12-18 mo. Tertiary circular reaction	(15-22 mo. Sep.-Ind. subphase of rapproachement)
18-24 mo. Invention through sudden comprehension	18-36 mo. *Separation-Individuation* with earlier subphases (see above)
2-7 yrs. Preoperational stage of representation	36+ mo. On-the-way-to-object-constancy

Piaget describes here what he has observed of the workings of the child's mind, whereas Masterson seems to be describing the key developmental tasks of the growing infant, particularly in dialectical relationship with the mother. Psychosis may grow out of an overly close or rejecting maternal-child relationship in the autistic period, for example. At each developmental level, the child must work through issues of separation from the mother if he or she is to individuate and become a whole object and be capable of whole object relations. The borderline personality, for example, experiences an engulfing close maternal relationship during the autistic period. But, as the child seeks to individuate at later stages, the mother may reward clinging behavior (overattachment) and punish attempts at separation. Masterson, thus, suggests rather specific ways in which early childhood patterns impact later life-style. The adult borderline personality is considered an extension of the early maternal relationship.

The comparison of Masterson to Piaget is useful, since we can see what the child is capable of in terms of cognitive development. And, as Piaget suggests, the child must complete early tasks solidly before moving to the next stage.

In object relations theory, the important fact is that we conserve our relationships with significant others and carry them on in the future. The very concrete being of the counselor or therapist serves as a new stimulus, making possible the generation of new thoughts, behaviors, and actions. In the object relations point of view, the adult child may transfer (conserve) a past history of relationships to the therapist. The task of the therapist is to enter into the world of this adult child and transform experience and experiencing. The therapist becomes a new concrete other and provides a new opportunity for a new system or way of being to evolve. Transference as demonstrated in therapy thus can be described as a form of past overaccommodation that has now become a rigid assimilation. The task of the therapist is to enable the client to accommodate to and eventually assimilate the fact of the difference of the therapist. Again, Masterson is helpful here. He points out that the narcissistic, or borderline, patient repeats past learnings (transference) with the therapist. The therapist, to avoid counter-transference, must interpret the narcissistic behavior and confront the borderline behavior. Due to the personal uniqueness of the therapist-patient relationship, the client may rework old, immobilized forms of developmental arrest.

In therapy, we will encounter clients who have learned to

overaccommodate to their environment. They conserve their past. They try to do what they are told—to be good, keep out of the way, and act as they "should." Such clients in therapy will readily adapt to the frame of reference of the therapist, and it is their very embeddedness that needs to be attacked. Overassimilators, on the other hand, are busy trying to act on the world from their frame of reference. They may have trouble hearing others and alternative points of view unless the alternatives can be framed in their own perspective.

We should, of course, remember that the defense mechanisms of projection, reaction formation, denial, and others vastly complicate this picture. What appears as overaccommodation may in fact be overassimilation. The cognitive balance of accommodation and assimilation is closely related to Piagetian constructs of conservation and reversibility. The manner in which a child or adult conserves may itself be an example of preoperational magical thinking. Conservation, primarily located in the concrete operational period, is not limited to one age group or cognitive style.

The transformation from concrete operations to formal operations is critical to becoming a mature adult. It is considered parallel to crossing "the line" in Plato's distinction between the world of appearance and the world of intelligibility (see Figure 3). It is a move from behavior and action to the abstract world of thought that requires the individual to make a transition from behavior and thinking to the abstraction of thinking about thinking. Counselors and therapists often move clients to this next level with the simple question "Is that a pattern?" Variations of transformational questions include: "Has that happened before?" "Free associate to a similar feeling in a different situation," and "Sounds as if you have had that feeling in other settings too. I recall you used the same words when talking about your husband as you are now when you are talking about your father." Critical to this transformational process is an increased awareness of feeling and affect. These dimensions will be mentioned only briefly in the section on formal operations and will be dealt with more specifically later in this chapter.

Once a client starts thinking about self and her or his actions, the transition to formal operational thinking is initiated. Whereas the transformation to concrete operations occurs in some variation of the question "Could you give me a specific example?" the transformation to more complex thought requires some questioning or prompting in which the client learns to reflect on actions. It may be as simple as the therapist saying, "You just said such and such. Now, would you stop for moment and think about what you just said and what it may imply about yourself and your situation?" And just as early teenagers seek to deny this self-reflectiveness, so will many clients and patients resist this effort on the part of their counselor or therapist. The transition or transformation is as important or more important than what occurs in the cognitive stage itself. (The transformational process will be reviewed in more detail in Chapter Five.)

Stage 4. Formal Operations (eleven through fifteen years). The adolescent can take data and view a situation abstractly, often from several perspectives, and can combine ideas from several areas. The adolescent thinks more about feelings and about thinking itself. Piaget suggests that the process of development culminates in adolescence for it is here that the structures of cognition are fully established. Development continues throughout life but is based on these critical early structures.

Formal operations also involves dimensions of scientific reasoning and hypothesis testing. Adolescent formal thinking, however, is often impeded by egocentricism and extreme concern over physical appearance and how things appear or look. At times, the adolescent actually seems very sensori-motor oriented and preoperational. Some adolescents, for example, become involved in idealistic thinking about a more perfect family or world ("If only you/they would do . . . , then . . ."). However, they often fail to think through the concrete operations required to reach this idealistic state or to consider the multidimensional aspects and full complexity of a problem. In a sense, the "flower children" of San Francisco in the mid-sixties practiced this incomplete type of formal operational thinking. They had logical and complex ideas about reforming the world but did not take dimensions of concrete reality into account; as a result, they eventually became disillusioned and drifted away.

Similarly, many clients in therapy manifest incomplete formal operational thinking and can even be described as pre-operational formal thinkers. Such individuals may have solid, logical structures that are "correct" and "logically tight," but that do not work in reality. One cannot help but think of the dominating husband who demands much from his family ("If only they . . . , then . . ."). He works hard, his logic is correct, but he may not consider more complex reality any more than an egocentric teenager who embarks on early formal opera-tions and needs space for self-discovery. The husband's require-ments might work if all accommodated to his assimilations, but his logic is incomplete and magical in orientation. The world is more complex and multidimensional than he recognizes. This type of problem may have led to the current interest in cogni-tive-behavioral theory and practice (Beck, 1976; Ellis, 1972; and Meichenbaum, 1977). This orientation suggests the need for *both* formal operational thought *and* concrete action in the world. The Platonic worlds of intelligibility and appearances seek unification.

At this level, it is not really possible to separate young people from adults in terms of affect. Feelings are complex, mixed, and can be used in many different ways. In early formal operations, feelings may be denied due to this complexity. Crit-ical to the move to formal operational affect is thinking about feelings per se. Noting that an adolescent or adult gets angry in certain situations, the therapist may ask, "Is that a pattern for you to get angry in situations where people tease you?" or "Why don't you think about this feeling and what it means." Awareness of patterns and thinking about feelings is critical in affective development.

"I like Teddy, but she doesn't do anything but sit there, and that makes me sad. I'd be happy if she were alive." This ex-pression of complex emotions illustrates what happens at the formal operational level. Emotions are complex, rather than "good" or "bad," and one can have many conflicting feelings. Out of this awareness comes the realization that feelings can be validly experienced in multiple ways. A classic problem for adolescents and many clients in counseling is how to come to the awareness that it is valid to have and to become aware of mixed, ambivalent feelings toward others. A goal of therapy can be simply to develop this awareness.

The task of the therapist with formal operational clients varies. One alternative is to work on the formal operations level immediately. This is the task in Rogers's person-centered therapy, Frankl's logotherapy, psychoanalysis, the reframing therapies, and Kelly's personal construct psychology. The aim in these therapies is to focus clients on reframing or reinterpreting reality from a new, broader, and hopefully more effective frame of reference. These theories may provide new ways of thinking and coping with old patterns. All tend to operate somewhat egocentrically in that they do not examine their own assumptions about reality. In their failure to examine their assumptions, these therapies themselves represent a type of formal operational thinking that contrasts sharply with some evolving therapies, which do question their own assumptions and which represent the fourth level of Figure 4.

For example, Fritz Perls has come under attack for ahistoricism:

> None of the modern psychotherapies makes use of a historical approach in dealing with problems of individuals. . . . A historical approach is that one in which clients are seen as changing human beings along a dialectical materialist process of change. . . .
>
> Gestalt therapy [is] a good example of an ahistorical approach, where the politics of therapy . . . along with other historical realities are not taken into consideration. . . . The ahistoricity of modern counseling theories reduces their effectiveness, since the individual's problems are separated from their context. Clear examples are sexism and racism, which have become struggles reflected and mediated by the minds of people. These problems have affected human action over history, determin-

> ing the historical forms of those struggles. Therapy
> cannot claim success in dealing with them [Rivera,
> 1980, pp. 27-28].

However, therapies that focus on the here and now can produce change and this change may be useful. Partially due to their failure to relate pattern recognition to coping with real problems of everyday life (specifically, the absence of transfer of training or generalization procedures), research does not suggest that ahistorical, nonempirical approaches such as those of Rogers and Perls are fully effective (Glass and Kliegl, 1983). It is also important to recall that cognitive-behavioral approaches such as that of Beck (1976) have been indicated by Glass and Kliegl to be more effective. Such therapies make the specifics of patterns more concrete and real than do more global therapies such as those employed by Rogers and Perls. This dialogue between thinking about reality and interpreting reality in more concrete ways may explain the current promise and effectiveness of cognitive-behavioral modification. It seems possible that realism has been brought to bear on ideas, whereas Rogers and Perls focus more on ideas and thought, preferring not to deal with empirical reality.

Once a repeating pattern is discovered and verified, it may be possible to discover that the problem is rooted in earlier history, such as childhood and teenage relationships with significant others. The dynamic therapies of psychoanalysis, object relations theory, and Adler strengthen awareness of patterns and actually start the process of thinking about patterns of patterns. The dynamic therapies, in this way, move to a higher level of abstraction or thinking about thinking about thinking, which is characteristic of the highest formal operational levels.

It is at this point that formal operational thinking as usually defined by Piaget and Piagetians begins to fail, since the theory does not adequately account for the complexity of the thinking that starts to occur. All will be indicated in the final section of this chapter, which considers post-formal thought, dialectics, and person-environment issues, there may be indeed another type or level of consciousness beyond what Piaget has suggested.

Another possibility for working with formal operational clients is afforded by the developmental paradigm. After listening to the formulations of the client, the therapist may help formal operational thinkers get grounded in sensori-motor experience. How does the client see, hear, and feel the phenomena of the world? Based on these sensory data, what elements can the client specify in the situation? In a similar fashion, the complex dynamic therapies can benefit from learnings available at the concrete operational and early formal operational levels.

Specific Techniques for Helping Clients Move Through Developmental Stages

The following steps are designed to illustrate specific therapy and counseling techniques that can be used to assist clients to change their mode of processing concerns in therapy. The techniques, however, may be used as well in informal relationships. The structure provided by these sequencing steps helps others organize their thinking and increase the complexity of thinking, while simultaneously moving toward "higher" conceptual levels.

The following guidelines work empirically but are themselves open to criticism. Some clients will move very easily through the stages, while others will shift, jump, or even drop stages in the process of interviewing. Not everyone moves "upward" in the smooth progression suggested here. The utility of these developmental concepts for facilitating client understanding is fascinating to observe, and this section will be most helpful if you take a friend or willing client through the steps in a real or role-played interview or series of sessions.

There are two types of progression through these stages. It is possible to take one person through the cognitive levels rather quickly if you follow the specific techniques and questions precisely and if you have a willing and verbally able client. On the other hand, clients may not be capable of moving rapidly through the developmental levels. With these clients, who are perhaps the majority, more time seems to be spent at each stage before moving to the next-higher stage. Piaget often complained of the American tendency to rush children through the developmental stages without allowing each individual to experience *horizontal décalage,* the slow and natural unfolding from within. Piaget is correct; unless children and clients have a sufficient level of experience at each cognitive level, they will move to the next with distortion and limited ability. (Chapter Six will explore the issue of horizontal development and therapy in more detail.) Thus, one must be adequately grounded in each stage before further advancement is truly possible and capable of being maintained.

The empirical guidelines presented here should prove useful in conceptualizing and researching client movement and progression. At the same time, individual differences will require a wide range of alternatives to the basic model. Again, reading the following steps is not enough. The concepts will become more meaningful and lasting if you take a real or role-played client through each step. You will note that the cognitive level of the client changes with your varying interventions.

As the material is somewhat complex, it is presented in outline form in Exhibit 1 to clarify and simplify the developmental progressions.

Implicit in all these questions is a return to the sensorimotor stage. We have gone through several alternative perspectives or epistemologies of reality and ideas about reality and now are returning full circle to the beginning. But, paradoxically, we return to the beginning with some level of awareness of the never-ending, ever-changing complexity of life. We have moved from sensori-motor data through an almost infinite abstraction of mirrors as we have thought about our thinking. Data from cognitive and perceptual psychology (see Chapter Two) and our own experience suggest that we do not even own our own sense impressions.

Given this shifting sand, on which rock shall we stand? Or is the rock simply shifting sand itself? At this point, issues of spirituality and faith may become especially important, although such issues may appear at any stage in the developmental and

Exhibit 1. Developmental Therapy: Summary of Techniques

To facilitate the transformation to the next stage of development, consider some strengths that are identified in the client. Recognition of these strengths by the therapist may assist the client in approaching the developmental tasks of the next stage. It will be difficult to make the transformation to the next stage unless the client has some awareness of personal strengths within the present stage. Furthermore, some minimal understanding or competence is needed at each level before the client can move to the next level.

1. Preparation—Identify the Problem
   a. Goal: To obtain a general picture of the problem or concern and search for magical thinking, irrational thought or behavior, discrepancy between the real and ideal, or a *conflict* faced by client.
   b. Basic Techniques: "Could you tell me what you'd like to talk about?" Listening skills to draw out facts, feelings, and possibly underlying meanings of client concerns.
   c. Theoretical Options: Range from free association and discussing a new dream to identifying behavioral problems.
2. Sensori-Motor Issues
   a. Goal: To ground the client in sensory reality and to note basic elements of the situation.
   b. Basic Techniques: "What did you see?" "Hear?" "Feel?" Perhaps give some special emphasis to how the body felt. Offer solid attending skills (culturally appropriate eye contact, body language, vocal tone, and verbal following).
   c. Theoretical Options: Relaxation training exercises, Gestalt excitation techniques, neurolinguistic programming (R), overlapping techniques of seeing, hearing, and feeling, or simply ask: "What behavior did you see? What did you hear? How did you feel?" A careful functional analysis as conducted by a skilled behavioral therapist to search out stimulus-response conditions is also representative of this sensori-motor grouping. Through functional analysis, it is possible to lead to later specific concrete operations and linear cause-and-effect explanations of the problem.
   d. Transformational Question: "How do you organize the things you see, hear, feel?" "What sense do you make of these elements?"
3. Preoperational Issues
   a. Goal: To clarify the preoperational, magical, or irrational ideas or behavior. At issue is for the therapist to hear the client's frame of reference as it is brought to the interview. As such, this phase is often tied with phase 1.
   b. Basic Techniques: Listening to the client's description of the

(continued on next page)

Exhibit 1. Developmental Therapy: Summary of Techniques, Cont'd.

        situation. Directly restating key words or constructs of the client may help access his or her unique constructions of the event. Attempt to draw out specific facts, feelings, and interpretations of the event.

  c. Theoretical Options: Infinite (as always). For cognitive processing, the search for irrational ideas will be important. In behavioral therapy, the distinction between present behavior and desired behavior may represent the preoperational issue. In psychodynamic therapy, the issue may be the desire to understand as compared with present lack of understanding. Each theoretical school has its own constructions of the important irrational or preoperational dimensions that should be addressed in therapy.

  d. Transformational Question: "Could you give me a specific example of your concern?" The client may already have presented an example. The goal is to move the client away from repeating the preoperational idea to a discussion of either sensori-motor elements or concrete details.

4. Concrete Operations

  a. Goal: To draw out in linear, sequential form the concrete specifics of the client's concern. We are not interested in interpretation; rather we want to know specific things that happened in the most concrete form possible. Avoid subjective and evaluative language.

  b. Basic Techniques: Questions and listening skills oriented to drawing out concrete aspects of the situation. A major emphasis on facts. "What happened specifically? What did you say? What did the other person say? What did you *do*? What did he or she *do*?" Distinguished from preoperational in that there the client's interpretation of data may be encouraged to discover irrational dimensions. Here, the emphasis is on mutually agreed on facts, with a limited emphasis on feelings.

  c. Theoretical Options: Mainly behavioral. Even if working in a psychoanalytic orientation, the goal is still to obtain the concrete specifics of a trauma, a dream, or a "triggered" reaction.

  d. Transformational Question: "Given these facts, what causes what?" This question may lead to a return to the preoperational, irrational level of functioning but introduces the late concrete operational issue of causation into the discussion.

5. Late Concrete Operations

  a. Goal: To arrive at a mutually satisfactory system explaining a situation, usually with an "if/then" dimension. The client should be able to operate predictably in thought and action in the environment.

  b. Basic Techniques: Drawing out what happens before and after the occurrence of the problem, concern, conflict, or irrational idea. "What happened just before?" "Then, what happened?"

Exhibit 1. Developmental Therapy: Summary of Techniques, Cont'd.

"What was the result?" This can be represented by an antecedent—behavior—consequent in terms of behavior or as the ABCs of rational-emotive therapy.

    c.   Theoretical Options: Behavioral and RET options seem to be clearest, but their systematic formulations may be used in psychodynamic therapy, family therapy, or another framework.

    d.   Transformational Question: "Is this a repeating pattern?" "Are there other situations where you act out this sequence?"

6.   Early Formal Operational Thinking

    a.   Goal: To identify and think about behavior and thoughts, particularly repeating patterns of behavior.

    b.   Basic Techniques: "You seem to have a tendency to repeat that particular behavior, thought, or interpretation. How do you feel or think about this pattern?" "What does this pattern of behavior or thought *mean* to you?" "What function does this particular pattern serve for you?" The focus of these techniques will tend to be on the client and the client's constructions or interpretations of the situation.

    c.   Theoretical Options: Rogerian client-centered therapy with its emphasis on thinking about feelings and, to some extent, meanings is a framework often effective at this level. Frankl's logotherapy and much of humanistic psychology seem to operate at this self-analytical level.

    d.   Transformational Question: "How is this pattern related to other patterns that may be undergirding your thinking and behavior?"

7.   Late Formal Operational Issues

    a.   Goal: To assist the client to see larger, consistently repeating patterns in his or her life. In effect, we started at the sensorimotor level with many small fragments of thought or behavior, organized them at the preoperational level into sometimes useful (but nonetheless magical) thinking, moved then to concrete descriptions of behaviors and thoughts, then to still larger patterns of thoughts and behaviors, and, at this level, to examining patterns of patterns.

    b.   Basic Techniques: "We see the pattern of behavior you had with your children and the pattern you use with your employees. How might these two patterns relate? Do these two patterns form a still larger pattern?" "What is the feeling you have connected with this (these) patterns? Free associate from that feeling to an earlier period of life."

    c.   Theoretical Options: The psychodynamic therapies of Freud, Jung, and Adler are often characteristic of this level of cognition. Any therapy that deals with reframing reality, particularly from an unconscious orientation, follows this general

(continued on next page)

Exhibit 1. Developmental Therapy: Summary of Techniques, Cont'd.

model. Note that all these orientations still come from a "self-oriented" model in that the client is constructing reality.

    d. Transformational Question: "We've constructed a comprehensive picture that seems to repeat itself—there are positives and negatives in that pattern. How is or was that pattern developed or constructed in a family, social, or historical context?" This transformational question moves to dialectical awareness that personal constructions and meanings are cogenerated in a context of relationship.

8. Dialectical Thinking

    a. Goal: To develop awareness that "reality" is constructed in a dialectical or dialogic relationship with one's family, one's history, one's gender—a host of relational issues. The distinction between knowledge (*episteme*) and intelligence (*noesis*) is not critical at this stage, but awareness that either may be a co-constructed view may be useful.

    b. Basic Techniques: A major change occurs in that the client is encouraged to move beyond his or her own history and think about history is codeveloped or cogenerated with others. As such, questions that bring out awareness of the impact of one's family, ethnic background, race, gender, and so on all help the client see that his or her constructions were developed in the context of a network of relationships.

    c. Theoretical Options: Family therapy, feminist therapy, and Lacanian conceptions all seem to emphasize the dialectic. However, the analysis of transference phenomena in analytic frameworks can lead to dialectic awareness, as can some orientations to object relations theory. All these systems in various ways lead the client to see him- or herself in a coconstructed, codeveloped context.

    d. Transformational Question: "We've seen that your original problem or conflict can be viewed from many perspectives. Identify the flaws in the reasoning or logic behind each of those perspectives." At issue here is developing awareness that *all* perspectives in a deconstructionist framework have fatal illogical, preoperational flaws. We have traveled all this distance to find ourselves again at the beginning.

9. Deconstruction

    a. Goal: To encounter Platonic *noesis* (intelligence) that each piece of hard-won knowledge has inherent flaws. We may find a perfect form, but it soon slips away from us. This may require a willingness to live with the unknowable and to accept the logic of our illogic.

    b. Basic Techniques: "Each of our constructions, ideas, or behaviors contains internal contradictions. Let us seek out and challenge those contradictions. Confront the contradiction!" Even concepts taken for granted such as gender, race, or a specific

Exhibit 1. Developmental Therapy: Summary of Techniques, Cont'd.

pattern of life are all open for reinterpretation and systematic deconstruction as one examines their meaning.

c. Theoretical Options: Derrida and deconstruction theory, post-feminist and post-structural theory, some orientations to literary criticism, some modern feminist approaches. The implications of these new philosophic trends are only now beginning to be dimly sensed by the therapeutic field.

d. Transformational Question: "Is there a unity within this diversity?" This question for some deconstructs deconstructivism and leads us back to the unity of sensori-motor experience and the unity we can experience with others. It suggests that what we originally defined as a "problem" may in truth have been an opportunity.

Which is the higher consciousness?

Sensori-motor	Setting and experiencing a flower
Concrete operational	Putting the flower in an arrangement
Formal operational	Writing a poem about the flower
Dialectical	Analyzing the poem about the flower (or analyzing the analysis of the poem about the flower)

Have we arrived at the "end" only to begin again?

therapeutic process. It would be possible, for example, to work through this same developmental sequence using spiritual dimensions. Whether one wishes to attach a strongly religious flavor to this developmental paradigm or take an intellectualized approach to the issue of deconstruction of reality and ideas, it does seem that we have gone full circle and yet somehow remain a unity.

The presentation in this section is highly specific and action oriented, yet it is derived from an integration of Piagetian and Platonic thought and involves dimensions of information-processing theory. You will find that if you take clients through the specific questions and conceptualizations, the specific techniques work both to identify developmental levels of clients as well as methods that can be used to facilitate immobilized or stuck clients.

The discussion here has not yet considered the equally complex and important area of dialectical affective development, which follows a roughly similar pattern to those identified already.

The Dialectics of Affect

Developing an awareness that feelings shift and change in relation to context is critical to generating an awareness of dialectics and person-environment issues, whether cognitive or affective. The difficult developmental task for transformation involves thinking about thinking about feelings. With this comes the realization that life is even more complex than mixed, ambivalent feelings, that feelings are relative to their context. One may, for example, feel sad about a parent dying, but glad that a difficult year of pain and sickness is over. Furthermore, one may feel personal relief at the end but anger at God for the result. This awareness, however, is the beginning, for as one thinks about thoughts about feelings, one becomes aware of the transitoriness and relativism of emotion. What is "sad" in one context or relation is "joyful and liberating" in another. Thinking about this paradox and its meaning is a clear illustration of "higher-level" cognitive processing of emotion.

Emotion from this perspective, however, becomes very far removed from the sensori-motor or concrete reality of emotion. The reality of feeling has been so far separated that separation itself can become a problem. The "truth" of thinking about thinking about feeling represents *episteme,* or knowledge, an absolute idea of feeling that somehow intuitively "feels" inappropriate. This returns us to the awareness of the depth of sadness surrounding death, and this *noesis,* or intelligence, leads us back to sensori-motor experiencing of death and the possible recapturing of the experience with still more tears.

Paradoxically, affect may be defined as a special type of cognition in which the individual progressively becomes separated from emotion. The task of the therapist may be to return the client to sensori-motor functioning if the affect has become too intellectual. On the other hand, if the affect is contextually out of control, the move to "higher" levels of consciousness may be appropriate. At question, of course, is what is the "correct" cognitive balance.

An adult can work through the four developmental levels in a time span as brief as a minute or less. For example, an important letter may be delayed in the mail. After discovering this, the mother may explode and yell irrationally at her small child. Immediately accommodating to the child's terrified countenance, the mother may say, "I'm not angry," but her tight facial muscles belie her statement and frighten the child. Noting the child's still-fearful face, she may then bend down and tell the child reassuringly, "I'm not angry at you. I'm just frustrated that the letter didn't come." At this point verbal and nonverbal behaviors are synchronized and the child senses something is different. The mother then engages in formal operations and thinks to herself, "Whoops, I blew it. I let my feelings get the best of me. That check will come soon. I'm worried, but somehow we'll survive. *But,* what about the impact of my blow-up on Sally? I'm concerned. I'll have to give her extra attention for awhile if I am going to feel good about myself." The mother follows those thoughts with action to calm the child and herself. In less time than it takes to read this paragraph, the mother has gone through the first three stages of affective development and has shown some thought about the fourth stage.

For counseling and psychotherapy, it may be helpful to identify the emotional as well as the cognitive stage of the client. While cognitive development closely parallels affective development, the two are not necessarily synchronous. Common "wisdom" is that women have more advanced affective development than men and that men are more advanced cognitively. Whether or not this is true is open to speculation and value judgment. If one examines the theories of development of Gilligan (1982) and Kohlberg (1981), one finds differing value systems about affect. In essence, Kohlberg's theory of moral development was generated from studies with men, because women's developmental patterns did not fit the data. Gilligan suggests if we view women from a perspective different than Kohlberg's, women may be found to have more complexity in development than men.

Rogers's client-centered therapy is an excellent example of an affectively oriented approach. A review of Rogers's treatment of Mrs. Oak in *Becoming a Person* (1961) illustrates the progression of feelings in therapy. The following portion is from the eighth interview, in which Mrs. Oak is finally able to look behind the surface of her socially controlled behavior.

> *Mrs. O:*   I have the feeling it isn't guilt. (*Pause, she weeps.*) Of course, I mean, I can't verbalize it yet. (*Then with a rush of emotion.*) It's just being *terribly hurt.*
> [*Comment: Here Mrs. Oak is her feelings. There is no separation of self from emotion, no separation of subject from object.*]
>
> *Rogers:*   M-hm. It isn't guilt except in the sense of being very much wounded somehow.
>
> *Mrs. O:*   (*Weeping.*) It's—you know—often I've been guilty of it myself, but in later years when I've heard parents say to their children, "stop crying," I've had a feeling, a hurt as though, well, why should they tell them to stop crying?
> [*Comment: Mrs. Oak's transfer of her own feelings to the children is an example of preoperational magical feelings. Her thoughts may indeed be correct, but she is demonstrating somewhat inappropriate affect. We also see the beginnings of concrete operations when Mrs. Oak says, "I've had a feeling . . ."*]
> They feeling [*sic*] sorry for themselves, and who can feel more adequately sorry for himself than the child. Well, that is sort of what—I mean, as though I mean, I thought that they should let them cry. And—feel sorry for him too, maybe. In a rather objective kind of way. Well, that's—that's something of the kind of thing I've been experiencing. I mean, now—just right now. And in—in—
> [*Comment: Mrs. Oak is now thinking about her feelings and exhibiting formal operations on them by thinking about them.*]
>
> *Rogers:*   That catches a little more the flavor of the feeling that it's almost as if you're really weeping for yourself.

[*Comment: Rogers supports the formal operational thinking and clarifies it with a reflection of meaning.*]

Mrs. O: Yeah, and again, you see there's conflict. Our culture is such that—I mean, one doesn't indulge in self-pity. But this isn't—I mean, I feel it doesn't quite have that connotation. It may have [p. 93].

[*Comment: Here we see a highly intellectualized, formal operational analysis of emotions that approaches the fourth level of post-formal thinking. Nonetheless, the intellectual analysis remains rooted in sensori-motor experience. The client is still weeping. This is a particularly beautiful example of simultaneously working at several cognitive levels, which is possible in effective psychotherapy. Some clients have the problem that all they are able to do is think about feelings. Stuck in the epistemology of* episteme, *or knowledge, they are unable to experience* noesis *and the transformation back to sensori-motor experiencing.*]

Different theories of therapy give different amounts of emphasis to various stages of emotional development. Lowen's (1967) bioenergetics is one example of a sensori-motor therapy that strongly emphasizes affect. Perls's (1969) demonstrations of Gestalt therapy were wonderfully effective in moving preoperational feelings to concrete levels (for example, "Become that clenched fist; now have it talk to your gut."). While analytic therapies give extensive lip service to affect, some of these therapists work exclusively at the formal operational level and thus avoid experiencing affect. In analysis clients talk about and reflect on their emotions. In effective analytic treatment, affect is at the core of therapy. Cognitive change and intellectualization may be possible without affect, but emotion is necessary for lasting change. While Rogers gives primary attention to affective development, we can also note cognitive changes in Mrs. Oak. Affect and cognition must become a unity for developmental progression.

Some therapies are more thinking oriented; rational-emotive therapy and cognitive-behavior modification have been suggested as two examples of this type. Yet, special techniques within each promote affective as well as cognitive development. Decision-making approaches to counseling, such as that of Janis (1983), focus on what seem to be the most cognitive aspects of counseling. However, even Janis gives great attention to the "emotional role play" as critical to helping some clients work through difficult decisions. The emotional role play is a technique quite similar to that of Kelly's fixed-role therapy.

Thus, most, perhaps all, therapies deal with emotion, although they may give it different emphases. A major question that remains is the relationship of affective theory to cognition.

Assimilation, Accommodation, Affect, and Cognition

Feelings or emotions have been identified as special forms of cognition, and like cognition, they are constructed through the dialectic of person-environment interaction. Feelings are constructed via schemata, which are also intellectual. These special "affective cognitions" are themselves constructed via assimilation and accommodation.

The child, thrown into the world, must accommodate to a cruel or loving mother (or, most likely, some combination of the two such as the "good breast" and the "bad breast" described by Klein [1975]). The data of the mother-child interaction are taken in by the child and accommodated into a general picture (assimilation) of the mother and other objects in the form of father, visitors, and others in the environment. If the relationship with the mother is insufficiently stable or too stable, problems in development inevitably occur. Given the difficulty of maintaining a "correct" balance in a complex and confusing world, it may be anticipated that the child of even the most caring parents will be unprepared for all the difficulties that are to be faced throughout life.

We come to our interactions with new people and new situations with previously established (or conserved) expectations that are both affective and cognitive. We learned these cognitions, affects, and behaviors in our relationship with our family, particularly the mother. As noted earlier, Masterson points out clearly the pathologies that can develop if the interactions with the mother and the father are inappropriate. Splitting between affect and cognition is possible, which can result in a variety of developmental disorders or pathologies. Cognitively, the client may be at an advanced level, but emotionally immature. Affect modifies cognition and cognition modifies affect: There is no affect without cognition, no cognition without affect. The work of Osgood, Suci, and Tannenbaum (1957) illustrates this point. In their semantic differential conceptions, they point out that any object (person or thing) is associated with *affective meaning*. These meanings include evaluation (good/bad), activity (active/passive), and potency (strong/weak).

Osgood, Suci, and Tannenbaum develop their measuring instrument—the semantic differential—by arranging a variety of words, usually adjectives, in polar opposites. Through factor analytic techniques, it has been learned that certain words cluster together in forming evaluation, activity, and potency groupings. What is important about the semantic differential instrument and its conceptual foundations is that words have been systematically identified and related to significant ideas, behaviors, and constructs. The semantic differential is a systematic format for measuring affective meaning and, potentially, affective development.

In counseling and therapy, we wish to clarify affective meaning and ultimately help clients find more satisfactory emotions, particularly as these relate to objects. Each object of a child or adult, be it person, thought, or concrete object, has affective meaning attached to it. In the early stages of development, the affective meaning and the object are intertwined (for example, "I am my feelings"; "If I lose my doll, I have lost me"; "If I am divorced, life is meaningless"). In later stages of life, we gradually separate these feelings from the object, yet they remain attached (separation and attachment) (see Bowlby, 1969, 1973b). Even at the highest levels, where one experiences mixed feelings toward the object and distantly considers the mixed feelings, affect and object remain attached. What has occurred is simply a change in point of view.

The concepts of the semantic differential are useful in clarifying the distinctions of feelings from objects. In the early stages of therapy, the client may have a significant relationship with the mother, certainly an important object in the individual's life. The affective meaning of the mother and self in semantic differential terms may be: "My mother is *dominating, weak,* and *angry* and I *don't like* me much."

Through successful therapy, the objects of mother and myself remain constant or the same. However, the client may describe the object relationship in different terms: "My mother is a *strong* person, but now I am *strong* too. I realize I have mixed feelings of *anger* and *love* toward her, but so does she toward me and that's OK. I'm *able* to take charge of my own life and do things on my own. I feel *much better* about myself and Mother." It may be seen that the first set of semantic descriptors gave the potency and activity to the mother and resulted in a negative self-evaluation. Following therapy, the situation has been mainly reversed; feelings have been clarified and the client ends with a positive, active, and potent self-description. Affect and cognition have changed in their relationship.

In essence, what is being suggested here is that affect only exists in relation to cognition. We may become aware of a fact, a thing, or an event. The meaning of that event, however, is determined by affect in that emotions clarify the distinctions of feelings from cognition about the object. One may have a "good" friend or a "bad" friend. The object friend remains the same, but the meaning of the friend changes in the context of the affective word. Thus, again, we return to Epictetus: "It is not things but our view of things that determines how we feel." Objects and the world remain essentially the same, but our perspective toward these things can change as our cognitions and affect move toward different frames of reference.

The process of movement is ultimately the result of an internal or external dialogue or dialectic. Thus, it seems appropriate to close this chapter on Piagetian development with an extension of his theory, based on Platonic thought, to the world of dialectics, dialogue, and post-formal thought.

Dialectics, Dialogue, and Post-Formal Operations

The discussion of the fourth stage of affect has already summarized some important aspects of the constructivist or dialectical approach to thinking. Important in that definition was that affect changes in relationship to context. Specifically, what is joyful in one context may be sad in another. This contextual approach to affect illustrates the fact that higher-level thinking shows awareness of complexity and context and is changing according to new realities. This point is also illustrated in brief form in the earlier section on technique, which demonstrates specific therapeutic and counseling approaches in coping with post-formal or dialectical issues.

This post-formal dimension in therapy is implicit in some approaches to counseling and therapy and explicit in newer approaches, such as feminist therapy, or, in a sense, in any contextually oriented approach, such as family therapy or organizational development. Therapies that operate from this frame of reference include some of the following dimensions: (1) they use methods from other frames of reference, but their theoretical orientation is "metatheoretical" in that it examines theory and uses theory and method contextually to meet specific ends; (2) they are outcome and process oriented in that specific verifiable truths (*episteme* or knowledge) are sought and used but recognize that truth may be overturned by new data and concepts (*noesis* or intelligence); and (3) they realize that the distinction between realism and idealism, thought and action, and appearance and intelligibility are useful fictions or descriptors but are not necessarily truth. Again, spiritual counseling and therapy offer alternative perspectives to these issues.

Jacques Lacan, the French psychoanalyst, once said, "I do not speak the truth, but I am the truth." Lacan here is referring to the paradoxical nature of reality. Once spoken, history is an enduring truth, although the nature and meaning of that truth will vary with the interpretation of the reader or observer. Lacan as person or as written or spoken text is a form of truth. However, he cannot and does not speak *the* truth from this point of view.

Pablo Picasso, perhaps the greatest artist since Leonardo,

when asked the secret of his work replied, "I do not seek, I find." Lacan elaborates this example when he states about himself, "I am not a poet, I am a poem" (Lacan, [1973] 1978). In these paradoxical and somewhat mystical words, we find the interconnectedness that is human experience. Picasso and Lacan (and ourselves and our clients) can only exist and can only find truth because of their social, historical, and cultural heritage.

For therapeutic purposes, at the level of dialectic, the therapist and client may examine the ever-changing nature of truth and their sociohistorical roots; they may jointly discover new and separate realities, and they may discover new connections between these realities and ideas of realities. Yet, this exercise will but lead them back to new developmental tasks, all of which are firmly rooted in sensori-motor experience. And, the question must be asked, "Did they ever leave sensory-based experience?"

Family therapy theory (Gurman and Kniskern, 1981) and feminist therapy (Ballou and Gabalac, 1984) both are highly contextual systems that examine not only the family and the client but also the total context that produces the client. The examination of the individual in context is a specific example of a dialectical theory in action. Both systems of therapy are expert at examining and questioning their own assumptions about themselves.

Lawler (1975) criticizes Piagetian theory as being somewhat static, despite its developmental orientation. Even though the child is in movement, the goal seems to be "static, metaphysical thought processes." Although Piaget clearly indicates that his stages are abstractions and can be changed, his whole research thrust and that of his followers has been to reify and make real these very abstractions. Although Piagetian theory is complete only through formal operations, some have posited a fourth post-formal, dialectic stage of interaction (Basseches, 1980; Kegan, 1982). The emphasis of these approaches has been to examine relationships between and among things and objects, awareness of motion and change in development, inclusion of issues of context that change meaning, an open-system orientation, and an actual effort to seek out contradiction. The latter is especially important, since it contributes to an awareness of life as it is lived; most counseling and therapy seek to resolve incongruity and contradiction. The dialectic, constructivist approach seeks to encounter this complexity. In the middle of this obtuse and sometimes confusing language, one can identify the theme of person-environment interaction again and again—the importance of context.

Dialectic has already been defined as a dialogue or search for truth. Dialectics requires more than one truth or point of view if development is to occur. Dialectics can be thought of as two individuals cogenerating reality together. However, as noted repeatedly in this book, one individual may construct ideas or reality in his or her head. The illustration of the baby striking the rattle, noting the environmental feedback, and changing action on the basis of data is an example of the dialectical process. Dialectics can occur between and among two or more people or it can occur within a single individual. Interestingly, Piaget, who did not use the word "dialectics" extensively in his writing, presents perhaps the clearest example of the dialectic in the mutual accommodative patterns of personal development.

Another issue that makes the fourth level of consciousness distinct from others is that in this level one thinks about the dialogue that produces thinking and questions previous assumptions concerning the nature of truth. In a sense, we are always in the dialectic, whether at sensori-motor, concrete, or other levels. Dialectic and dialogue describe what *is*. Specific awareness of the nature and importance of the dialectic itself is characteristic of the fourth stage. A seemingly never-ending discussion may occur between therapist and client as they construct many alternative realities. But it is not just construction of alternatives that is important, it is also the examination of these alternatives for their lasting truth value. It is here that the basic issues of *episteme* and knowledge (as a more stable absolute) come into play, as contrasted with *noesis* and the changing, sometimes more mystical view of truth. Here, two views of theology may be similarly constructed: God as permanent and stable and God as evolving change.

Thus, awareness and consideration of the dialectic that is always present may be considered a definition of post-formal thinking. To contemplate the dialectic is to examine the nature of the permanency of assumptions arrived at jointly (either with another person or within the self).

And, it is here that the work of the idealist philosopher Hegel becomes important. In his search for the "absolute ideal," the never-ending "truth," Hegel came upon the dialectic. And, preceding dialectic awareness, his *Phenomenology of Mind* (also translated as *Phenomenology of Spirit,* [1807] 1977) mentions necessary predialectical stages of the mind. The first of these is "sense-certainty," or knowing the world through sense impressions. Following the failure of sense-certainty to provide truth, society and individuals move through perception and understanding of appearances to self-consciousness and to the truth of self-certainty. Again, this truth breaks down as one observes reason, eventually discovering the dialectic. The parallels between Platonic and Piagetian thinking may be apparent through the similarity of key words and descriptors.

Particularly important in the above paragraph is the recognition that "higher" stages of development depend on "lower" stages, and in each higher stage, the lower stages are maintained and transformed (conserved). One does not ever leave the origins of development but remains solidly rooted in the descriptors and experiences of personal and cultural history. Hegel, therefore, brings to development an awareness of history and culture accumulated over the centuries. The Platonic and Piagetian forms of development, while not ahistorical, do not fully account for the power of history in developmental dialectics. This is an issue that the therapeutic profession will likely explore in more detail in ensuing years and is considered in preliminary fashion in this book.

Hegel is recognized as the master of the dialectical method. Truth and knowledge arise through opposites. One first learns of the world through the truth of sense impressions. But all knowledge is not gained through the senses, and one cannot sense one's self as a whole except through what one is not. One is specifically *not* the other object, be it person or thing. The self, then, is born of separation. Consciousness requires a separation of self from object. Higher stages of consciousness move through the same dialectic of (1) gaining a truth; (2) noting a failure of that truth through a contradiction from within or from without; and (3) reconstituting a new truth through a dialectic of thesis, antithesis, and synthesis. The "1-2-3" pattern of Hegelian dialectics, of course, closely approximates the cogeneration of reality by the two children so clearly described by Piaget in 1926.*

The spherical visual model (see Figure 4) is helpful in thinking about the dialectic, whether in Hegelian, Piagetian, or Platonic terms. Each of us represents spheres that affect the direction of other spheres in our universe. The spheres may join and spin together for a while, or they may touch briefly, be put off center, and move into new orbits. Nonetheless, each sphere has been affected by the other.

Therapy itself is a dialectic. There are two people cogenerating reality. But like Piaget, counseling and therapy theorists have been embedded in linear concrete operational thinking and formal operations and have failed to see the inherent dialectic of the process. Counseling and therapy are, by their very nature, already dialectic. Clients affect their therapists—they change methods, write papers, and learn from their clients. Similarly, clients often learn from and are impacted by their therapists. Neither therapist nor client is often aware of the impact and what is important in their interaction.

Given the multidimensional interaction of counseling and therapy and its extreme complexity, it is small wonder that we have been thankful for theories that help simplify this complexity. However, it now becomes clear that useful simplifications such as those of Freud, Skinner, Rogers, and others are

---

*This view of Hegel is certainly not common among philosophers and his many critics. The position taken here toward what is sometimes termed "Hegelian absolutism" is that the closest we can come to an "absolute" in that this concept is simultaneously static and changing, *noesis* and *episteme* in a mutual dialectic of change and development. The more static post-Hegelian philosophy of Fichte, however, may be considered an extension, perhaps mistaken, of Hegel's toward the absolutist position.

best considered useful fictions. But these fictions, much like literature, tell us an important part of the story of history. Authorial intention and literary theory (see, for example, the testimony of the author at the beginning of this book) offer us a comprehensive approach to realizing that reality and idealism still lay beyond our finite grasp. Perhaps we should take comfort in the comment of scientists: "It behaves as though it works; why worry?"

Why worry? "What, me worry?" Alfred E. Neuman of *Mad* magazine has said it well. What is there to worry about? Knowing the world and how we know the world relate to issues of epistemology. Ethics, correct action in the world, is closely related to epistemology. Ethics is usually thought of as a part of moral development. However, moral development cannot be separated from ethical action any more than affective development can be separated from cognitive development. Our epistemology, or way of knowing, impacts and directs our ethical practices. The vectors of thought and action of ethical practice are a result of our intentionality. Again, looking forward, the issue of the good and what is of value (axiology) must inform our actions.

And so it is with all of us at sensori-motor, preoperational, concrete operational, and formal operational systems of epistemology or thinking. We are so immersed and embedded in our thought processes that we fail to see the most simple things before us and within us—namely, how we generate knowledge and being, the very foundation of how we are constituted as individuals and groups. But as we move to more abstract issues of ethics and epistemology, dialectics and correct action, we once again find ourselves mired in the abyss of sense experience. After all, it is the only game in town.

The therapy process has been presented as a complex dialectical process in which counselor and client coconstruct reality. Running through all constructions of development is this dialectic. We cannot know sense experience except in relation; we cannot act operationally (concrete or formal) without an object on which to act; and we cannot know the underlying dialectic process abstractly without the vagaries of sense experience. The circle and the spiral continue, but perhaps we have added the register of truth to the psychological process that is now beginning to become apparent as philosophy in action.

Theory into Practice

The specifics of developmental therapy strongly suggest the importance of using neo-Piagetian and neo-Platonic conceptions in actual work with clients and developing these concepts in terms of general action skills for therapeutic practice. The goal here is to diagnose developmental level, intervene with a variety of specific questions and techniques designed to move developmental cognitions, and note and assess developmental movement.

Construct 1: Metaphors of Piagetian sensori-motor, preoperational, concrete operational, and formal operational thinking and functioning exist in adult functioning and may be considered useful theoretical diagnostic and treatment formulations.

1. *Learning Objectives:* To be able to define examples of adult thought and action at sensori-motor, preoperational, concrete, and formal levels and to identify them in the practice of therapy.

2. *Cognitive Presentation:* The ideas underlying this chapter are formulated on pages 78–105. Although they are presented with a variety of complex interpretations, the basic idea should remain clear: adults present themselves in therapy with varying types of cognitions that contain important correspondences to basic Piagetian formulations.

3. *Experiential Exercises or Homework:*
   a. Think of an event from your own childhood in which you engaged in preoperational, magical thinking. Outline how your thinking was preoperational in nature. Then outline the specific sensori-motor sense impressions that led to that thinking. What did you see, hear, feel? Point out how your own preoperational thinking may have led to incorrect concrete operations on the environment.
   b. Go through the above exercise again, but from an

adult frame of reference. Identify a present or past irrational belief or an ineffective piece of behavior or thought as metaphorically analogous to a child's preoperational patterns. Through reflection, experience sensori-motor foundations of this experience and examine the way the thought, belief, or behavior led you to act in the concrete world.

c.   As you experience the above two exercises, you are engaging in formal operational thinking; you are "thinking about thinking." Now add to the two prior exercises a consideration of affect as well as cognition. In summary form, sensori-motor affect is described as "I am my feelings," preoperational as a form of splitting affect from appropriate feelings, and concrete operational affect as being more under the control of the individual and leading or modifying cognitions. Formal operational affect involves a distancing from feelings in which one meditates and thinks about those feelings and often experiences and changes those feeling states in the process. (The formal operational thinking about feelings often leads to new sensori-motor experiences of affect and new states of affective being.)

Apply these brief summaries of affect to both your childhood and your adult experience.

d.   Identify a client and outline how this client represents preoperational, sensori-motor, concrete operational, and formal operational modes of being. Define and discuss the affective dimensions of this client.

Construct 2: It is possible to take a verbal individual in step-by-step fashion systematically through specific techniques that enable us to see verbal change in constructs and thinking patterns. Furthermore, any client may be assisted in exploring a specific phase of developmental cognition in a planful manner.

1.   *Learning Objectives:* To be able to take a verbal client through the nine specific developmental cognitive stages.

To be able to facilitate a client to explore one specific cognitive stage in more depth before moving on.

2. *Cognitive Presentation:* Highly specific questions have been suggested for nine specific developmental stages of cognition on pages 105-111. The presentation states that the first task is to identify a problem, which ordinarily can be expected to be presented in some form of pre-operational, illogical thinking. This is followed by the grounding of the client in sensory experience, and there then ensues a gradual set of questions and transformations, which ultimately enables the verbal client to examine the same problem from a wide variety of cognitive points of view.

The emphasis in the presentation is on change and movement. This is *not* to suggest that therapy and counseling operate as quickly as the model might suggest is possible. What is sought here is conceptual awareness of how the therapist's actions can relate to and help facilitate the development of alternative modes of cognition.

In assisting a client to explore a single type of cognition in more depth, the questions at each stage are designed to provide the therapist with a way of opening an issue or the session with the client. Rapid movement through cognitive levels is not therapy; it is an exercise. For a client to move to new and more complex levels of cognition will require time. Furthermore, it appears that different types of theoretical conceptions are more effective at one type of cognitive level than at another (for instance, relaxation training and sensory-oriented therapy seem to be more appropriate at the sensori-motor level, although typical thought approaches to counseling, such as cognitive or Rogerian therapy, may be best represented at the formal operations level).

3. *Experiential Exercises or Homework:*
   a. Think of an event in your own life that is of some importance to you (a specific difficulty you had with a loved one, a friend, or a parent) and, using the guidelines on pages 105-111, write down your own

answers to the cognitive-developmental questions.
Note particularly what happens as you approach the
dialectical stage.

b.   Take a volunteer client through the same exercise.
Ideally, videotape or audiotape your work. In your
first attempt, keep the specific words of the exercise before you rather than trying to work through
the entire series by memory. Your goal is mastery—
the ability to facilitate another person's cognitive
development.

c.   Go through the same two exercises as above, but
this time, focus on single cognitive stages and seek
to explore each stage in more depth. For example,
start with the concrete operational questions and
then follow these with questions of increased speci-
ficity so that the cognitions associated with that
stage become increasingly clear. As each developmental stage is approached, move into more depth
of experience and understanding.

d.   Apply the concepts of the above exercises to your
own actual practice of therapy and counseling.

*Construct 3: Through meaningful interaction with a therapist,
the affect associated with a cognitive topic can and will change
from passive, weak, and negative evaluation to active, strong,
and positive evaluation.*

1.   *Cognitive Presentation:* A few brief pages (112-118) outline important outcomes of successful therapy, the
change in movement from less positive and effective adjective descriptors to more positive. The theory is that
affect modifies cognition, much as in the statement "I
am a sad individual." If therapy is effective, the cognitive "individual" remains the same, but the affective
meaning around that cognition changes: for example, "I
am a glad individual." By using affective descriptors of
their conditions, clients suggest to us what needs to be
changed. The presentation suggests that much of what is
important to our clients is more accessible to us than we
often recognize.

2. *Learning Objectives:* To be able to note and list semantic differential-type descriptors in the client language system and by effective interaction move the client to more positive evaluative, potent, and active descriptors.
3. *Experiential Exercises or Homework:*
   a. Examine the typescript of Carl Rogers with Mrs. Oak included earlier and note the change in self-descriptors during his brief interchange with her. Are the descriptors more positive in evaluation, more potent, and more active?
   b. Engage in a role-played interview. The client should attempt to use negative self-descriptors. You, as therapist, should focus on these negative descriptors and treat them as preoperational ideas. Specifically, take the negative descriptor back to sensori-motor experience and then work through concrete operations and formal operations. Through this exercise, the client may be expected to change these self-descriptors to a new frame of reference.
   c. Evaluate your own work as a therapist by considering the changes your clients make in their self-descriptors. Are your clients talking about themselves and their world in more active, potent, and positive evaluative statements?

Construct 4: Dialectical frames of reference of therapy suggest new constructions of affect and of the therapeutic process itself.
   1. *Learning Objectives:* To be able to describe affect in dialectical terms and to enter the task of constructing methods of therapeutic change that are more consciously dialectical in nature.
   2. *Cognitive Presentation:* More dialectical issues are presented on pages 119–125 and examine how context changes the meaning of the event by providing another frame of reference for the search for elusive truth.
   3. *Experiential Exercises or Homework:*
      a. Consider a single important event in your life that originally had a strong positive or negative meaning

associated with it. Get "in touch" with that emotion. Now, change the context of how you think
about the emotion. For example, you may have
thought about the joy of high school graduation; a
change in context perhaps enables you to become
aware of the sadness you may have felt toward the
same event because it meant leaving home. Emotions are too often taken as a given of experience
without the awareness that the contextual dialectic
often determines the meaning of the event and of
the emotion one attaches to it.

b. Identify a present concern in your life, change the
context of the concern, and note how your emotion
changes.

c. Apply this experience to a client. Many clients come
to therapy stuck with only one apparent emotion.
The dialectic contextualization of emotion will help
bring a relativism to emotion that can be facilitative
in helping a client work through an experience that
was previously immobilized. The changing of cognitive environments can be an important part of reframing or reinterpreting life experience. Rogers's
work with Mrs. Oak is illustrative of how her changing context changed her emotional experience of an
event.

d. The final section of this chapter discusses dialectics
as a search for elusive truth. Most people in this culture operate in concrete operations or formal operations and do not engage in the more complex aspects
of dialectical reasoning. What are your personal reactions to these dialectical formulations? What feelings or thoughts do they bring to mind? Even though
it is argued that we act and grow in dialectics, we
find it difficult to think and conceptualize in this
same frame of reference.

Summary

The power of neo-Piagetian thought for reconstructing
our view of the therapeutic interview and client change over

time seems large. This chapter has suggested that it is possible to assess the developmental level of a client and then to apply rather specific interventions to facilitate the individual's developmental movement. Moreover, these constructs are relevant to therapies that are as different as Rogerian person-centered therapy, Gestalt therapy, and psychoanalysis.

Given the conceptual leap of this chapter, perhaps some cautions are in order. First, it is vital to recall once again Piaget's injunction against the American tendency to move children through developmental phases too rapidly. Movement without an adequate foundation is not developmental progression, but more the client's learning of a "trick," much as a dog will learn to jump through a hoop. Moving a client through the nine steps suggested in this chapter can be accomplished rather easily through the suggested dialectical formulations. However, for this progression to be meaningful and lasting, much more than this exercise is needed.

The importance of a solid foundation for development is perhaps best illustrated by the object relations theorists, particularly the work of Masterson discussed in this chapter. There are interesting parallels between his developmental object relations theory and Piaget. Masterson, interestingly, seems more a dialectician than Piaget. Masterson emphasizes the importance of solid foundations in infancy for cognitive and emotional development, and he stresses the importance of the mother-child interaction (and later the father as well). Cognitive and emotional development do not occur in a vacuum; they occur in a mother-child relationship, in the family, the community, and the culture.

The next chapter will explore in some depth the environment that the therapist offers the client. Masterson might point out that the therapist becomes a new object of relationship for the client. Very likely that client will bring old patterns of interpersonal relationship to the interview. It is the environment the therapist provides that determines the future growth and development of the client. The client may attempt to trick the therapist into continuing old patterns, and thus a problematic therapeutic relationship of transference and counter-transference may cloud the matter.

A consideration of the environment provided by the therapist gives us an opportunity to reconsider issues of old accommodations and assimilations, and this may open the way for a new equilibration or cognitive-affective balance.

✌ 4 ✍

Matching Therapeutic Style with Client's Developmental Level

This chapter presents the therapist as detective—one who must enter the world and world view of another. By doing so, the therapist can adapt style and theory and provide a suitable environment for meeting the client's unique needs. A conceptual framework for adapting alternative therapeutic theories to clients is presented in this chapter, along with specific suggestions for assessing the developmental level of the client.

The Purloined Consciousness

Nil sapiente odiosius acumine nimio.
(Nothing is more odious than too much acumen.)

Seneca

At Paris, just after dark one gusty evening in the autumn of 18——, I was enjoying the twofold luxury of meditation and a meerschaum, in company with my friend C. Auguste Dupin, in his little black library, or bookcloset, *au troisième,* No. 33 Rue Dunot, Faubourg, St. Germain. For one hour at least we had maintained a profound silence; while each, to any casual observer, might have seemed intently and exclusively occupied with the curling eddies of smoke that oppressed the atmosphere of the chamber . . . when the door of our apartment was thrown open and admitted our old acquaintance, Monsieur G——, the Prefect of the Paris police [Poe, (1845) 1946, p. 125].

Thus begins what is perhaps the most famous and influential detective story in literary history, "The Purloined Letter." Edgar Allan Poe created the "thinking" detective—clearly the forerunner of Sherlock Holmes—thus casting the mold for the entire genre of detective stories.

Psychotherapy and counseling are analogous to a detective story. There is a detective as well as a complex, confusing situation to be unraveled. Those who think most highly and complexly—the brilliant detectives such as Dupin—are the analysts and skilled therapists. And there are also those effective plodders like the Paris Prefect G——. There is, of course, a third party to the situation—the silent observer, that is, ourselves, as we read and involve ourselves in the story. The threesome in *au troisième* at No. 33 on a street we do not know thus includes us immediately in the story.

Many of us reading detective stories are surprised and delighted when we find out who the "crook" is (someone who was there all the time, before our eyes) and discover how we missed the clues. This "coming together" with the author impells us to a stage of higher consciousness and awareness. And, we often find friends who recognized the killer or thief early to be odious nuisances. As observers of the story, we often prefer not to see what is occurring before our very eyes.

In "The Purloined Letter," Prefect G—— talks to Dupin about a minister who has stolen an incriminating letter from the queen, under her very eyes, while conversing with her and the king about state affairs. The queen, worried that the king will learn of the letter, wants it back and has enlisted the prefect and the Paris police to find it. The police fail, and Dupin takes on the task (which has become that of the typical fictional detective) of outthinking the traditional police and the criminal.

Before Dupin starts his rapid and simple resolution of the crime, he tells the observer about his thinking process. He first describes the naive efforts of the Paris police.

"The measures, then," he continued, "were good in their kind, and well executed; their defect lay in their being inapplicable to the case, and to the man. A certain set of highly ingenious resources are, with the Prefect, a sort of Procrustean bed, to which he forcibly adapts his designs. But he perpetually errs by being too deep or too shallow, for the matter in hand; and many a schoolboy is a better reasoner than he. I knew one about eight years of age, whose success at guessing in the game of 'even and odd' attracted universal admiration. The game is simple, and is played with marbles. One player holds in his hand a number of these toys, and demands of another whether that number is even or odd. If the guess is right, the guesser wins one; if wrong, he loses one. The boy to whom I allude won all the marbles of the school. Of course he had some principle of guessing; and this lay in mere observation and admeasurement of his opponents. For example, an arrant simpleton is his opponent, and, holding up his closed hand asks, 'Are they even or odd?' Our schoolboy replies, 'Odd,' and loses; but upon the second trial he wins, for he then says to himself, 'The simpleton had them even upon the first trial, and his amount of cunning is just sufficient to make him have them odd upon the second; I will therefore guess odd';—and he guesses odd, and wins. Now, with a simpleton a degree above the first, he would have reasoned thus: 'This fellow finds that in the first instance I guess odd, and, in the second, he will propose himself upon the first impulse a simple variation from even to odd, as did the first simpleton; but then a second thought will suggest that this is too simple a variation, and finally he will decide upon putting it even as before. I will therefore guess even'; —he guesses even, and wins. Now this mode of reasoning in the schoolboy, whom his fellows termed 'lucky'—what, in its last analysis, is it?"

"It is merely," said I, "an identification of the reasoner's intellect with that of his opponent."

"It is," said Dupin; "and, upon inquiring of the boy by what means he effected the *thorough* identification in which his success consisted, I received answer as follows: 'When I wish to find out how wise, or how stupid, or how good, or how wicked is any one, or what are his thoughts at the moment, I fashion the expression of my face, as accurately as possible in accordance with the expression of his, and then wait to see what thoughts or sentiments arise in my mind or heart, as if to match or correspond with the expression.' This response of the schoolboy lies at the bottom of all the spurious profundity which has been attributed to Rochefoucauld, to La Bougive, to Machiavelli, and to Campanella."

"And the identification," I said, "of the reasoner's intellect with that of his opponent, depends, if I understand you aright, upon the accuracy with which the opponent's intellect is admeasured."

"For its practical value it depends upon this," replied Dupin; "and the Prefect and his cohort fail so frequently, first by default of this identification, and secondly, by ill-admeasurement, or rather through non-admeasurement, of the intellect with which they are engaged. They consider only their own ideas of ingenuity; and in searching for anything hidden, advert only to the modes in which *they* would have hidden it. They are right in this much—that their own ingenuity is a faithful representative of the *mass*; but when the cunning of the individual felon is diverse in character from their own, the felon foils them, of course. This always happens when it is above their own, and very usually when it is below. They have no variation of principle in their investigations; at best, when urged by some unusual emergency—by some extraordinary reward they extend or exaggerate their

old modes of *practice,* without touching their principles" [Poe, (1845) 1966, pp. 131-133].

Dupin has told us his method. He then visits the minister's hotel and rooms and, while chatting with the minister socially, finds the purloined letter, as expected, conspicuously
displayed in a card rack just below the mantlepiece. Through
simple duplicity, the minister is directed to look out the window, and Dupin substitutes his own "letter" for that of the
queen. He returns the letter to the mystified prefect and claims
the reward, but the story does not end there.

Dupin leaves his own mark with a blank sheet of paper
saying: *"Un dessein si funeste, S'il n'est digne d'Attree, est
digne de Thyeste* (Such a fatal scheme, if not worthy of Atreus,
is worthy of Thyestes"). Thus, the cycle of deception continues.

A Theoretical Reading of the Purloined Consciousness

"The Purloined Letter" has been the object of analysis of
innumerable literary critiques. Notable among these has been
the psychoanalytic interpretation of Bonaparte (1971), who
does much with the triadic structure of observer, observed, and
observer observing the observed in terms of classical psychoanalytic Oedipal interpretations. In oversimplified form, it may
be useful to recall that Poe draws the reader into the mystery
as passive observer of a variety of seductions and mysteries.
Lacan (1975) made a classic interpretation of Poe's story in a
complex and diffuse piece that, in turn, has been criticized
roundly by Derrida (1975). Over three hundred pieces of literary criticism exist that analyze this one pivotal detective story
(see Muller and Richardson, 1987). This extensive literature on
"The Purloined Letter," in turn, has led to extensive analysis of
why this story is so influential.

Whether one accepts the semiotic, modern Freudian interpretations of Lacan, the classical work of Bonaparte, or Derrida's deconstruction theory, it can be seen that underlying the
text is an epistemological consistency that is in accord with the
orientation of this book. "The Purloined Letter" could be said

to be an allegory of knowing that is somewhat parallel but very different from Plato's and Piaget's levels of knowing. The basic metaphor for the "allegory of the purloined letter" may be described in the person of the eight-year-old marble champion. The child's success lies in entering the thinking world of the other, anticipating how the other thinks and constructs events in the world. In this sense, Poe's eight-year-old boy is analogous to the enlightened person of higher consciousness who enters the thinking world of another. If one is to understand others, one must understand their epistemology, or way of knowing the world.

Specifically, the marble champion recognizes likely consistencies in his companions' behavior. The simpleton is analogous to the late preoperational or early concrete operational individual; he moves the marble from hand to hand without any understanding of the competition. The simpleton is embedded in his construction of reality. The slightly more advanced competitor is aware of the eight-year-old champion and keeps the marble in the same hand; but the champion anticipates the change through "identification of the reasoner's intellect with that of his opponent." The second, more advanced simpleton represents concrete operations—an individual who is actively thinking about the environment and anticipating results. The champion, of course, represents a type of formal operational thinking that illustrates awareness of self in relation to others— the contemplation of patterns of behavior and the ability to cope with multiple realities.

The Paris prefect and the detective Dupin represent different cognitive levels. The prefect is more embedded in the situation. He, like the simpleton, assumes that the other person thinks as he does, and he projects his thoughts on the minister. He and his staff search the minister's apartment and go to unusual effort to find the letter but are always limited by their own cognitions. The prefect and his staff fail to think about the thinking of the other.

The minister, a "higher-level simpleton," anticipates the prefect and hides the letter in plain sight. Dupin, the master thinker, is able to empathize and put himself in the place of both the minister and the prefect. By a simple ruse, Dupin is able to misdirect the minister's attention and take the purloined letter.

This is the allegory of the purloined consciousness: One must enter the way of knowing the world of the other—the other's epistemology—if one is to produce impact and change.

To be an effective detective, guide, or therapist, one must read and interpret the thinking of others. If we are to enter the world view, epistemology, and consciousness level of our clients, we must adjust our thinking processes and methods to be consonant with their cognitive processes. It does little good to offer a formal operational therapy to a client who is unable to operate concretely on the world.

The distinction between a detective story and psychotherapy, however, lies in what is the purpose of the detection. Detectives want to dupe and capture the other, whereas therapists seek to enter the world of the other to promote growth. While the processes of understanding the other may be parallel, the goal of mastery is radically different. Therapy and counseling seek to raise the consciousness of the client, whereas detectives simply seek to master the consciousness of the other. It is this very act of active mastery that requires even the best detectives such as Dupin back to repeat their tasks over and over again. At the conclusion of the story Dupin himself remains entrapped by the process of mastery over another. Dupin's somewhat smug self-satisfaction suggests a lack of awareness of self in relation to others and the dialectic. It can be suggested by analogy that despite our apparent effectiveness as therapists, we can become entrapped by our own thinking processes and lose sight of our clients as coevolving human beings. (This problem can show itself as counter-transference.)

Therapy is concerned with liberating individuals and their consciousness. The liberation process that constitutes effective therapy and counseling involves understanding the client and bringing him or her to an equivalent level of consciousness with the therapist. However, many therapeutic orientations (like Dupin) deem it satisfactory to correct the client without effecting a change in consciousness. Different therapeutic theories have different goals. This chapter relates therapeutic styles and environments by using a quadrant model derived from the sphere in Figure 3.

The goal of matching therapeutic environment with the consciousness level (world view or epistemology) of the client may provide a partial answer to Gordon Paul's (1967) classic question: "*What* treatment, by *whom,* is most effective for *this* individual with *that* specific problem, under *which* set of circumstances, and *how* does it come about?" Missing from Paul's statement, of course, is the question of goal, value, and axiology: *All* of the above issues plus "for *what* goal or direction?" For what purpose are we conducting counseling and psychotherapy? For duping and deception, purposeless change, or studied development? This chapter presents a partial response to this question, which is explored further in later chapters.

Style-Shift Counseling

"Style-shift counseling" is the highly persuasive term used by Anderson (1982), and it describes in a few words the thrust of this chapter: If your present style of counseling and therapy does not work, shift your style to meet the developmental needs of your client. Furthermore, as your client develops increased cognitive complexity and moves through developmental stages, shift your style to remain with the client. From his working experience in the Canadian prison system, and in consultation with Ivey (1983a, pp. 213–219), Anderson has evolved a practical system for integrating developmental theory with counseling methods.

Anderson's prime thrust is to classify interviewing or counseling styles. He stresses that there is no wrong style, and that it is helpful if the counselor is competent in more than one theory or method. He suggests five basic steps in the style-shift counseling process: (1) assess the readiness level of the client (where is he or she developmentally?), (2) choose a counseling approach that matches the developmental level, (3) try the approach, (4) evaluate its effectiveness, and (5) shift style to another approach if the intervention is ineffective.

Four basic types of counseling style are suggested. The first focuses on providing a structured environment for the client, and Anderson suggests behavior modification and the "environmental engineering" approach as suitable at this level. The effort is to provide the client with a structured environment in which certain choices are the ones most likely to be reinforced or allowed. (In his choice of therapeutic models, it is possible to see the influence of his work with a particular prison population.)

The second counseling style is termed *thinking* and is exemplified by reality therapy and rational-emotive therapy. This approach is considered to be most effective with those clients who are cognitively at the concrete operational stage of development. The third style is *feeling* and is represented by person-centered and existential/humanistic approaches. Here, of course, the client is able to think about thinking and about feelings. This level corresponds to the marble champion in Poe's story.

The fourth style is termed the *learning level,* and here Anderson emphasizes psychoeducation and workshop training as a way to increase human potential. Examples of learning models include encounter groups, structured skills training, and a variety of individual and group human relations learning programs. At this point, the Anderson model diverges from the dialectic model presented in this book, but there remains a parallel in that both emphasize the search for movement and new developmental tasks.

The above summary should illustrate that there are parallel counseling approaches to the neo-Piagetian and Platonic conceptions of client development outlined in this book. For each client, the therapist or counselor provides an environment for developmental growth. Providing an appropriate therapeutic environment that is matched to the current developmental level of the client may be useful in facilitating growth and change. Most therapies cover several phases of the client's development. For example, although psychodynamic approaches focus on late formal operations, they also emphasize sensori-motor experience, the recognition of preoperational thinking patterns, and other topics in the search for higher understanding. Any client can be a mixture of several developmental levels; there are no purely formal operational or concrete operational clients.

Four Therapeutic Styles and Their Relation
to Developmental Level

Four therapeutic environments are summarized in Figure 8: environmental structuring, coaching, consulting, and dialectic. These four styles are designed to match clients who may be operating in the sensori-motor, concrete operations, formal operations, and dialectical modes of cognitive functioning. However, matching therapeutic style to client need is more complex than the figure indicates. A special danger of models and figures is that they may oversimplify an immensely complex relationship.

Nonetheless, this model of environmental style provides a useful reminder that therapists provide environments for their clients. Therapists all too often simply provide the same environment for every client in the expectation that the client will eventually match their style. Such an approach to therapy and counseling represents an oversimplification of human complexity that can verge on naive psychological imperialism. The thrust of this book is to explore complex dimensions and to emphasize that simple process and outcome distinctions and arguments about the "best" therapy are ways of thinking that are no longer satisfactory for professional practice or research.

Before turning to the separate aspects of the model with examples of representative theories, it is important to use one sample theoretical approach to illustrate how the several dimensions of the therapeutic environment might also be demonstrated by a single theory. For example, a reality therapist might immediately emphasize contact and relationship with a delinquent youth. Much might be done in a sensori-motor and concrete operational manner to develop the relationship. The client may play Ping-Pong, take the youth on trips, and just "pal around" for months before undertaking examination of irrational, irresponsible behavior. Success in reality therapy begins to show when the youth learns concrete causality—what is to be expected or anticipated as a result of action. As the youth grows in the therapeutic process, the therapeutic environment provided by the therapist changes. The structured early environment becomes more open and challenging as the youth is encouraged to think about his or her condition. Patterns of behavior and thinking may be identified, and the youth is challenged to consider thinking things through in a formal operational manner. Reality therapy is fully successful when the child learns about self and is able to make independent, self-conscious decisions. Finally, it should be remembered that throughout this process, the delinquent youth is never fixated totally at any one developmental level; the therapist has to remain flexible and move through many different therapeutic environments with the youth.

There is a danger in classifying clients and therapies, because each is actually more complex that what can be accounted for in any classification system. We should recall Piaget's injunction that developmental levels such as sensori-motor and others can be infinitely divided. However, each therapy has special strengths for coping with various aspects of client development, as the following discussion reveals.

Style 1. Environmental Structuring. The therapeutic milieu provides solid personal contact, a relationship, and warmth (as needed by the individual) and is grounded in sensori-motor reality. There is an emphasis on providing sufficient structure and direction so that the client can make a complex world more manageable. A baby is not able to cope with the confusion of the world, nor is a deeply troubled client. The complex must be made simple. At the same time, the therapist must lead the way toward more complex later understandings. All therapy needs to be grounded in sensory experience at various points in the therapeutic process in order to enhance client development. This basic dimension of sensori-motor experience forms a foundation for later growth.

It is not the purpose of this book to review alternative therapies in detail. Rather it is suggested that the direct emphasis on body experience in therapy is more important than usually

Figure 8. Four Therapeutic Environmental Styles and Their Relationship to Developmental Therapy

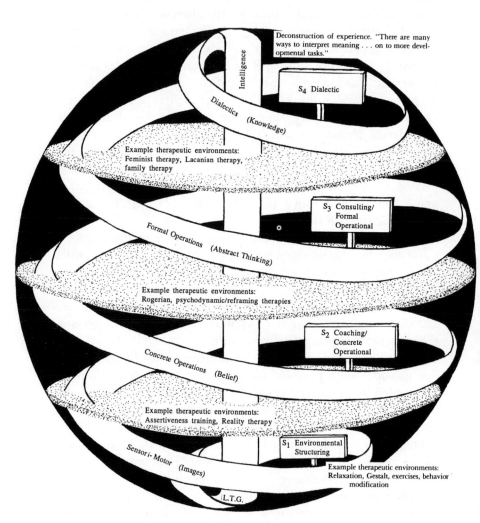

The developmental theory of psychotherapy is based on the paradox of development: to arrive where we started and to know the place for the first time. Life is simultaneously a journey, a destination, and a state of being.

Note: This diagram was first drawn by Lois T. Grady and is used here with her permission.

Figure 8. Four Therapeutic Environmental Styles and Their Relationship to Developmental Therapy, Cont'd.

Further illustrations of the four fundamental environmental styles:

Style 1. Environmental Structuring. The therapeutic environment is warm, structured, and relatively directive. Bioenergetics, relaxation training, Reichian-based therapies that focus on the body are examples. Structured behavioral approaches for in-hospital psychiatric treatment are also examples of this style. The behavior of the therapist often focuses on telling the client what to do. Influencing skills are used to a high degree.

This level is developmentally appropriate for clients with problems in sensori-motor functioning or to ground clients in sensory-based data. A client may come in blaming the parent. The therapist seeks to obtain sensory data and the facts about the preoperational conceptual problem. Transformation involves the concretizing of preoperational thought.

Style 2. Coaching/Concrete Operational. The therapeutic environment seeks to provide considerable structure for individual development, but the client participates more in the generation of ideas and structures. Examples of therapies include assertiveness training, reality therapy, decisional counseling. There is a balance of listening and interpersonal influence skills.

This level is developmentally appropriate for individuals who have difficulty in concretely impacting their environment. For example, weight control programs or smoking cessation programs from a decisional or behavioral point of view exemplify this approach. The goal is to move toward clearer definition of linear causality and the ability to act predictably on the environment.

Style 3: Consulting/Formal Operational. In the early stages, warmth and support are particularly important to facilitate the development of an individual self-awareness. At this stage, resistance may be particularly strong to directions and influence, and so listening skills may be most appropriate. Rogerian therapy and logotherapy are characteristic of therapies useful in the early stages of this quadrant, whereas reframing therapies such as psychodynamic or transactional analysis may be more appropriate at a later stage. At the later stages, more action on the part of the therapist again becomes appropriate. Cognitive behavior modification may join style 3 with coaching style 2 as well.

This stage is appropriate for those who are entering or working at the formal operations level. The goal is first to obtain a clear sense of self or direction but later to encourage the generation of alternative frames of reference.

Style 4: Dialectics. The dialectical approach to therapy may be characterized by an egalitarian search for truth. Depending on the theoretical orientation, there may be a fair amount of self-disclosure (feminist therapy) or very little (Lacanian). There is a tendency to discount "final" truths and a willingness to encounter new questions and developmental tasks. Contradiction may be actively sought, as opposed to the tendency in other quadrants to resolve and synthesize contradiction.

(continued on next page)

Figure 8. Four Therapeutic Environmental Styles and Their Relationship
to Developmental Therapy, Cont'd.

Although the nature of the dialectic may make the techniques of
therapies of this orientation suitable for those of "lower" developmental
levels, full participation in the dialectic of therapy will eventually require
the client to reach new levels of consciousness. Common to those experiencing this level of personal search will be awareness of the tension between *noesis* and *episteme*, between permanent and elusive truth.

Dialectical deconstruction of experience occurs when awareness
that "truth" as discovered in context requires a movement or shift, often
involving a "return to the beginning" for a new developmental task.

"It seems wise to join the client in his or her cognitive constructions of the world and then to move with the client, shifting therapeutic
style as appropriate to client needs and wishes."

admitted. Exercises and methods such as Gestalt therapy activities, relaxation training, dance therapy, and massage may not
totally solve a client's problems but may help overly intellectualized clients, who have lost their sense of body, to become
grounded in physical reality.

The directiveness provided by certain forms of behavior
modification and environmental structuring help the client organize and conceptualize the world. Moreover, when a therapist asks the client to mention what was seen, heard, and felt
in a dream or traumatic experience, the client learns to examine
sensory reality.

Style 2: Coaching or Concrete Operational. As the client
develops a more concrete organization of experience, magical
thinking disappears and linear causality begins to emerge. At
this stage the therapist continues to provide a highly structured
environment but invites the client to operate more fully on the
environment and be increasingly aware of what happens as a result of his or her actions.

The metaphor of the therapist as coach is appropriate for
this developmental level. The effective coach provides an atmosphere of direction and structure and notices the unique talents
of the athlete. A dialogue or dialectic is directed by the coach in
an attempt to facilitate individual achievement and self-manage-
ment.

Assertiveness training is a particularly clear example of the coaching style in therapy. Assertiveness training often includes role play, which concretizes abstract talk into real behavior. Behavioral goals are established, and the client is coached and directed toward acting to attain specific anticipated results.

For example, a client may say, "I can't do anything with my son. He's hopeless." This preoperational statement can be converted to concrete thinking via questioning techniques ("What did your son specifically do?" "What did you do or say?"). Once preoperational thinking has been transformed by the environment provided by the therapist, it is possible to correct irrational thinking, develop a systematic plan of action, or role play a more assertive and appropriate response.

The emphasis in this concrete or coaching approach to personal growth and development is on thinking and action. While feelings may be present, they are not stressed extensively, often because the individual is not able to cope effectively with feelings. In these cases, a detached, formal operational environment is more effective in dealing with emotions (although some would argue that the body therapies, which excite and impel emotional expression, may be effective). Nonetheless, emotions are present at the concrete operational level and must be dealt with, most often through simple reflection and acknowledgment. Recognizing that a client feels a certain way may be sufficient at this stage.

Therapists employing style 3 formal operations also take their clients through concrete operations. The examination of defense mechanisms in terms of concrete behaviors, the discussion of specifics of a dream or a childhood traumatic event, and the role playing of transactional analysis "parent" scripts all require concrete discussion of what happens and in what sequence. No free association in psychoanalysis is without concrete elements of experience. In later stages, thus, the boundaries between concrete and early formal thinking will not be fully distinct.

As the client matures in concrete operations with the help of a facilitative coach, the environment of therapy may transform itself and the client-therapist relation. This can be brought about by asking clients to reflect on their past behavior or experiences. One effective approach is to ask the client, "Could you stop for a moment and reflect on what you just said and how you feel and think about it?" Asking the clients to identify repeating patterns is another way to help them think about themselves in a more formal operational manner.

Style 3. Consulting or Formal Operational. The consultant metaphor is helpful in describing this approach. In a consultant relationship, the focus is on the individual and what the individual thinks and feels about him- or herself and the situation. The management consultant often asks the manager-client about actions in the organization and seeks to help the client think about him- or herself and, perhaps, to transform the self and the organization through this thought process.

The environment provided by Rogerian and psychodynamic orientations represents the consultation model in that these therapies force the individual to think about the self as self. Needless to say, these therapeutic styles are likely to be more effective with full, formal operational clients. In the early stages of formal operations, the client may be highly egocentric (similar to an early teenager), and one of the best ways to avoid resistance is to employ Rogers's (1957) "necessary and sufficient conditions" for therapy. These conditions offer important dimensions that are necessary in helping the egocentric client make the full transformation to formal operations. The process is as follows: Two persons are in contact, the client is vulnerable and anxious, the therapist experiences unconditional positive regard for the client, the therapist experiences empathic understanding, and the client receives regard and empathy, at least to a minimal degree. Given such a supportive environment, the client may generate his or her own new ways of reframing the world.

The reframing therapies of psychoanalysis, Jungian, and Adlerian therapies are more assimilative in nature, whereas the task of the Rogerian therapist is to accommodate to the client's struggle. Therapists of the former orientation do not hesitate to share their world view and may even directly seek to bring clients to their interpretation of reality. Since many analytic patients are at the formal operations stage and are also high assimilators, issues of resistance and transference may become important.

A special case of formal operational therapy is represented by cognitive-behavior modification (Beck, 1976; Beck and others, 1979; Meichenbaum, 1977) and rational-emotive therapy (Ellis, 1971). These types of therapy appear to move between and among concrete operations and formal operations rather freely. Moreover, most of these approaches rely heavily on sense-based data and seek to provide solid contact and warmth for clients. It can be argued that the effectiveness of the cognitive-behavioral approaches lies in a mix of techniques, where several things happen at once. Ultimately, these approaches seem to be formal operational in nature. Whereas assertiveness training tends to focus on how the person behaves and acts, cognitive-behavioral therapy considers in addition how the person thinks and feels about the behavioral world. These therapies do not stop with cognitive ideas (idealism) but constantly seek to transform and act on their approaches in the real world (empiricism or realism).

Formal operational therapies assume that clients can take a look at themselves. Many patients and clients are embedded in their own construction of the world. A major task of formal operational therapies is to remove the client from the concrete world to the world of ideas—thinking and reflecting about thought and action. Certain types of formal operational theories closely resemble the dialectical model. Beck (in Diffily, 1984), for example, suggests a three-step model for producing change in a client's thinking patterns: One, recognize what the client is thinking. Through the use of listening skills, identify specifically what a client is thinking and how he or she thinks. Two, enable the client to recognize faulty or ineffective thinking patterns (such as preoperational or contradictory statements). Through cognitive reframes and feedback, the client learns to reflect on thinking patterns. This thinking about thinking is very typical of formal operational thinking. Three, obtain feedback to see if the changes have developed and if the reasoning is correct. This step requires that the client take the thought back to the "real" world (the therapy hour is the world of "idealism") and see if change can be effected.

Beck's approach is structurally somewhat similar to Piaget's 1926 ([1930] 1955) illustration of children coconstructing reality via the dialectic. Beck assumes that a client can look at him- or herself. An examination of a typescript of Beck's work, however, reveals that he often follows a systematic progression of verbal steps not unlike that presented in the preceding chapter, where it was suggested that specific questions and statements on the part of the therapist can lead to specific results in client cognitive development. For example, Beck (1979) was working with a depressed patient who had failed to leave his bedside for a period of time. Beck asked him if he could walk to the door of his room. The man said he would collapse. Beck said, "I'll catch you." Through successive steps, the man was shortly able to walk all over the hospital and in one month was discharged. In this approach, the therapist starts with sensori-motor experience, transforms the preoperational idea to concrete motor behavior, and in the later stages of therapy, starts (if necessary) the reflective process of thinking about thinking. Cognitive-behavior therapy appears to offer much in the way of combining the several levels of developmental therapy. This itself may explain why Glass and Kliegl (1983) found cognitive-behavioral approaches to therapy the most effective.

The objective of therapies in the formal operational or consulting environment is to generate alternative frames of reference. Things do not change so much as the ways clients think about things change. However, it seems very clear from any systematic examination of research literature that unless changes in thinking or ideas are accompanied by action in the real world, therapy is often only partially effective. Thought without action is often empty.

Frankl's logotherapy (Frankl, [1946] 1952, 1959; Lukas, 1984) is another reframing approach that has some things in common with consulting therapies but that provides a more dialectical view of helping, as does the work of the hypnotherapist Milton Erickson (Erickson, Rossi, and Rossi, 1976; Haley, 1973).

Style 4. Dialectics. Dialectical therapy and counseling are best summarized in the phrase "confront the contradiction." Whereas the task of the other three levels of therapy is to resolve contradiction, the assumption at the dialectical level is that contradiction, incongruity, and discrepancy are facts of life and must be sought actively and lived with. Although resolution may be sought after, contradiction must be recognized as a very real part of life experience.

In addition, therapy that can be categorized as dialectical examines the basis of truth on which theory rests. It is, of course, somewhat risky to say that complex and important theories, such as Rogers's person-centered therapy or American ego psychology, are nondialectical and fail to examine their own frames of reference. However, when these theories are contrasted with the constant self-examination of therapeutic systems such as that of feminist therapy, family therapy, or that of the psychoanalyst Jacques Lacan, one finds a marked difference in the degree of the "search for elusive truth." Nonetheless, *all* meaningful therapy is to some extent dialectical; dialectics are necessary for the change process to occur.

For purposes of this discussion, dialectical therapies will be considered to be those that self-consciously recognize and study their own approaches to the truth. In Plato's sense, they examine the underlying assumptions and goals of their practice. Beck's cognitive work is a particularly clear example of a system of thinking that closely approximates most of the aspects of a self-consciously dialectical framework.

Dialectics has been too often described in the thesis/ antithesis terms of Marxism. This leads one to think that only one major contradiction must be resolved before proceeding. At this point, Cornford's ([1941] 1982) translation of Plato's *Republic* again becomes useful. "The higher method is called dialectic, a word which since Hegel has acquired misleading associations. In the *Republic* it simply means the technique of philosophical conversation (dialogue) carried on by question and answer and seeking to render an 'account' of some Form" (p. 223). The question-and-answer structure of Platonic dialogue does not ordinarily result in simple resolution of thesis and antithesis, such as is often assumed in Hegelian and Marxist theory. Thus, dialectical therapy is not only self-conscious, it is always aware of an underlying process that searches for truth.

The early work of Piaget also defines a dialectical approach. Somewhat like Beck, Piaget did not always contemplate the assumptions on which he was operating (although this point may be arguable). Indeed, the open-systems goals of Ellis or Rogers are in accord with much of dialectical thinking. The Piagetian therapeutic method similar to that of Beck's follows this pattern: (1) remark by client (thesis), (2) remark by therapist (antithesis), (3) remark by client building on 2 (synthesis leading to new antithesis). When considered over the full range of development, it can be seen that dialectics is an inescapable aspect of serious person-environment or person-situation construction of therapy or development. When this pattern is more understandably (and less ideologically) termed "dialogue," one can understand that growth, therapy, and development are the inevitable result of dialectics.

The prominent Russian theorist Luria (1929) utilizes Piagetian thinking to clarify the nature of dialectics, and his comments are not far from the sometimes more easily understood dialogue of person-environment construction.

> A keen regard for the real, the ability to take into account all sorts of changing conditions, so as to be able not only to adapt to the real world but also to predict its dynamics and to adapt it to oneself; a considerable plasticity and flexibility of behavior that enable one to use different devices and different means, depending on the situation; and, finally, the rejection of all pat, ossified forms of behavior— these are the traits of behavior that best reflect a dialectical method of thinking [p. 99].

Løve (1982), a Norwegian therapist and theorist, interestingly, also uses a Piagetian example to describe dialectics.

> I will illustrate this concept with the way a child handles his bottle. This example is more Piaget

(1968) than Hegel, but it does illustrate that dialectic principle as I shall use it. A child's actions toward a bottle (for example, touching it) would be thesis—the bottle's reaction (answer) antithesis, and the way in which he learns to hold it (discovering its holdiness qualities) synthesis. In the synthesis, the touching, the response of the bottle, and the holding are contained. In the next action a new synthesis and thesis evolve and in turn are integrated into a new synthesis. This model can be applied to more complicated interpersonal situations, for example the clinician-patient relationship. The patient acts with aggression (thesis); the clinician responds with understanding (antithesis). The patient then has to integrate "my aggression—the therapist's response" into a synthesis. This could mean the patient has the opportunity to live aggression in a new way [p. 22].

Løve adds an important dimension missing from the discussion thus far. Nothing is destroyed in the synthesis or production of knowledge in the dialogue. However, data are transformed into new ways of thinking, feeling, and action. The object or structure has been preserved in a transformational change. Put in a simple analogy, the client's "deck of cards" has been shuffled into a new order. The "cards" are the same, but the meaning (and potentially the action) is different. The shuffling of the dialectic is a transformation of knowing. (This transformational process will be considered in depth in the following chapter.)

At this point, the question may be asked, "What has this to do with therapy and the so-called highest stage of awareness?" The dialectical stage for the client involves awareness of the dialectic and the active seeking of contradiction and the continuous search for truth. The therapist must provide an environment that supports the development and awareness of life as process—life as dialectic: "We have to think pure change, or *think antithesis within the antithesis itself*, or *contradiction*" (Hegel, [1807] 1977, p. 99). This means that the goal of therapy becomes not realization, but actualization; not resolution, but revolution; not stability and homeostasis, but change and development.

Three types of therapeutic environments are provided here as examples of dialectic awareness—feminist therapy, Lacanian psychoanalysis, and some family therapy. A fourth approach to seeking contradiction and pure change is suggested by the developmental orientation of psychoeducation (for example, Ivey and Alschuler, 1973; Larson, 1984; and Mosher and Sprinthall, 1971).

Ballou and Gabalac (1984) propose that feminist therapy involves the following primary dimensions: (1) egalitarian and equal relationship between therapist and client; (2) an active, participative counseling style that seeks to confront the client with the need for growth and resolution (contradiction may be actively sought); and (3) the attempt to take newly discovered contradictions into the community to seek active solutions. Women do not truly "end" feminist therapy; they encounter the contradictions of society and start working on these new, ever-changing contradictions. Much as described by Hegel, the feminist movement is interested in "pure change." A definition of health is awareness of and living with incongruency and contradiction. The following interview conducted by therapist Mary Ballou (1984) illustrates the above points:

> *Counselor:* In our first meeting last session, you gave me information about your history, current life, focus of concerns and your world view. We clarified your feminist values orientation and your wish to explore your career and family conflicts as well as the options open to you and your perceptions and feelings about them. I shared with you some information about my orientation to counseling and my feminist world views. We also agreed to work together for six sessions and then reevaluate. I am wondering what kind of reactions you have had to our first session in the intervening time?
>
> *Client:* Well, there, my reactions are complex and

many. I felt easy with you and your explanation of why you needed particular information or why you were suggesting certain things, like the contract, made sense and I relaxed. It was easy to tell you of my history, development, and current confusion. I felt relief that you did not see me as sick or incompetent. It helped when you suggested that many women face similar issues and can resolve them and in different ways. I felt supported, understood, and not trivialized, as I often have when I have raised these issues before. Also, I felt hopeful that I was not alone but at the same time the options would be mine, not standard sexist or feminist ideology about what women should do.

Counselor: Those reactions are certainly complex and well thought out as well as positive. Were there any other reactions that were less clear or troublesome?

Client: There's one but it is a bit vague. It's, well, I don't know—aha—well, how to think about our interaction. This is not like the counseling I had years ago, which was more removed and professionally distant, but it is not like my friends in the feminist support group either.

Counselor: Is there a context or relationship that it is similar to for you?

Client: Perhaps it is like my colleagues with whom I do joint work in the research grant, but in our sessions there seems more room for me and my needs. And it is sort of like the feelings I had with the licensed nurse practitioner who worked with me in the home birth of my last child, but not so focused. But there really is no other model that fits this experience very closely.

Counselor: So our interaction does not fit with your past experiences very well. How is that for you?

Client: Well, I am unsure about how to relate with you. Like, do I invite you to lunch, ask personal questions, or treat you like an expert or boss?

Counselor: So the role and boundaries are unclear and, am I right, unsettling? [Mary Ballou, Northeastern University. Used by permission.]

In the above example, the therapist (Ballou) is involved in many critical processes simultaneously. You may first note the Piagetian three-step process in which the therapist adapts and changes in relation to the client. The client also adapts and changes in each interaction, and this seems to exemplify the egalitarian aspect of feminist therapy. There is clearly a search for cultural and historical truth as a background for the individual therapy ("It was easy to tell you of my history, development, and current confusion. . . . It helped when you suggested that many women face similar issues"). Context is also critical as shown in the counselor's statement: "Is there a context or relationship that it is similar to for you?" Through this process, the female client comes to the awareness that the truth or her "problem" is also a societal and cultural problem. The therapeutic dialectic or dialogue has sharpened and redefined the nature of truth.

Successful feminist therapy helps women see contradictions in their lives and moves its clients to a new consciousness level. With that new consciousness level comes a puzzling and confusing array of decisions—a new set of developmental tasks. Successful therapy has returned the client to the first stage of development—sensori-motor awareness and the fullness of possibility. With this return to the beginning, coupled with the awareness of having returned to the starting point, developmental tasks of relationship and work can be approached anew.

Another self-consciously dialectical approach to therapy is that of Jacques Lacan, who smiles cynically at the U.S. psychoanalytic establishment's "ego psychology," which assumes that an individual is free and capable of making a decision outside the dialectic of social conditions and personal-cultural history. Much like feminist therapists, Lacan seeks to help clients become aware that life is more complex and contradictory than it appears. Although Lacan's writing and thinking are often obtuse and difficult, his philosophy of treatment is dialectic and has some practical value. For example, in his statement "The Direction of the Treatment and the Principles of Its Power" (Lacan, [1966] 1977), he suggests specific dialectic principles of therapeutic action. Lacan points out that theory cannot stand outside the immediate relationship of therapist and patient and cultural, historical, and social conditions.

Lacan states that the place of interpretation in therapy is "motivated by no topographical priority. It is also that in Freud this rectification is dialectical and set out from the subject's own words, which means that an interpretation can be right only by being . . . an interpretation" (p. 240). Thus, Lacan suggests that a person conducts therapy by making almost any kind of interpretation or reframing of reality. Lacan then points out that pattern dominates therapy and that clients may replay old patterns within the therapy hour. Since the client is only with the therapist for this hour, the client will replay or act out old patterns (transference) with the analyst.

As the client acts out past patterns, the therapist assumes the role of "transitional object" and thus enables the client to first act out old stereotyped patterns and then develop new transitional patterns in relationship to the therapist. The parallels in this interpretation of Lacan and feminist therapy should be apparent. Ballou served as a transitional object for her client by providing immediate support for the client's difficult period of transition to a new truth, a new form of being. Classical object relations theory (Winnicott, 1958) tends to consider transitional objects as souvenirs of the past and fails to note that people, particularly therapists, can also act as transitional objects for future growth. The example of feminist therapy above represents the dialectic of transition, as does this interpretation of Lacanian theory. The feminist therapist, by establishing an equal relationship with the client, serves as a useful transitional object for new and further growth. The Lacanian therapist is more distant, somewhat like the classical psychoanalyst, but, nevertheless, serves the same purpose. Lacan calls for a "return to Freud," and his interpretation of psychodynamic theory is more complex and dialectical than that ordinarily practiced in North America.

Lacan also considers the issue of "how to act with one's being" in the therapy session. The answer is simple: "There is no other way out of the transference neurosis than to make the patient sit down by the window and show him all the pleasant aspects of nature, adding: 'Go out there. Now you're a good child' " (p. 256). The answer to the dialectic is somewhat different than that of feminist therapy and focuses on acceptance of duality and contradiction, whereas feminist therapy more actively seeks to cope with and change reality. Lacan in other writings deals with this issue more directly and discusses the concept of "correct distance," meaning the correct distance between people—the recognition of interdependence rather than a false independence or false dependence. The concept of interdependence itself represents the dialectic in action—people learning from and with each other. In both the feminist and Lacanian models, client and therapist exist in a dialectical relationship.

Family therapy, particularly as exemplified by the epistemological orientation of Keeney (1983), is also a rich source of dialectical thinking. Family therapy is deeply aware of the contextual aspects of therapy and of the fact that the therapist and the family have an inevitably embedded relationship. Keeney builds on Bateson's (1979) dialectic of form and process. The first category (*order of recursion*) represents behavior in which the process is the description of simple action. In family therapy, the first task often is simply to describe what is seen. In turn, what is seen may be abstracted into a classification of form, which in the early stages represents categories of action. The dialectic of behavior occurs in the interplay between description of family action and categorization of that same action. Different family therapy theories may describe the same action using similar words but may classify that action differently.

For example, consider the behavior of a husband and wife who are sexually incompatible. The behavior of each may be described and then categorized into such items as the eye-contact patterns and the specific vocalizations and behaviors each employs as they approach the sex act. Each type of family therapy describes the same behaviors but might categorize them differently.

The dialectic of context takes the analysis to a higher level. Here descriptions of interactions among family members may be made and then classified into categories of interaction. Family therapists often criticize individually oriented therapy as being too focused on action and on categorizing action and as missing the more complex interactional nature of being. The couple with a sexual difficulty can also be described contextually. Their interactions may be described as a sequence of behaviors. For instance, the wife may touch the husband naturally and warmly, and he may instantly react with a demand for sexual contact. The wife may then become angry at his lack of sensitivity, and he may leave the house. This can happen in the context of a recent argument with their teenaged daughter, who shows incipient signs of bulimia, or in the context of the husband, who has had a bad day at work. These descriptions of interaction may then be variously categorized according to the family therapy theory employed. A behavioral family therapist, for example, might describe the patterns as stimulus-response, while a strategic-systemic therapist might describe the interaction as embedded and repeating. A psychodynamically oriented family therapist may describe the interchange as a pattern of mutual dependency with simultaneous fear of overattachment.

The metacontext dialectic moves to further levels of abstraction in which descriptions of family "choreography" may be made. Here the analysis is of "patterns of patterns" of interaction. How is the family "choreographed" to play out their family script of repeating interactions? What is the nature of the social, historical, and contextual play? In turn, these descriptions may be categorized into systems and types of plays.

It is at the metacontext level that theoretical differences become most apparent. Bowen's (1978) intergenerational family therapy might search for an ongoing family choreography that applies to several generations of family members and would question how the present family in therapy is reenacting the old patterns of previous generations. McGoldrick, Pearce, and Giordano (1982) have fully documented how cultural patterns are choreographed in the daily behavior of countless families. Thus, they would add detailed information to the Bowen model on how Italian, Jewish, Irish, or Black culture might influence the interaction of the sexually incompatible couple.

As one moves to the more complex orders of recursion and analysis, the therapist further departs from the actual behavior that ultimately must be changed. A major question for family therapy is how to determine the level at which the intervention should occur—at the behavioral, contextual, or meta-contextual level? Each intervention affects the total system. If the decision is made to change behavior and if this change is effective, the total interaction of the family changes. Alternatively, a culturally oriented intervention at the most abstract level may also be expected to influence changes in behavior.

Family therapy theory has effectively raised the question of which level of intervention is most appropriate and has pointed out that interconnections exist between and among the several levels of analysis. The awareness of the process and the fact that the family therapist is part of that process makes family therapy dialectical. The ability to examine oneself and one's place in the therapeutic process is an example of dialectics.

Most family therapists, however, seem to prefer to keep this awareness to themselves and not pass on dialectical awareness of the process directly to their clients. This is done in the belief that consciousness of the change process may result in remission and return to old behavior. Family therapists who operate from this framework, of course, are quite different from those who operate in the egalitarian or dialectical frameworks of the feminist and Lacanian models. This tendency to place the therapist above the client can be considered a dialectic of knowledge (*episteme*) as compared to the more elusive dialectic of intelligence (*noesis*).

The enriching techniques of feminist therapy, Lacan, and family therapy are also evident in the psychoeducational movement. Psychoeducation is concerned with teaching new skills and ideas to clients at any developmental stage (be it sensori-motor, concrete operational, or formal operational). However, a contradiction is encountered in that skills are taught in the belief that "learning how to fish for tomorrow is more important than eating fish today." Skill training has already been discussed, in the section on Anderson's style-shift theory. Skill training is oriented to a world that is believed to constantly provide individuals with new developmental tasks and challenges. And, of course, all therapy, be it Rolfing or depth psychoanalysis, primal scream or rational-emotive, person-centered or family therapy, is oriented to some degree to the goal of helping people find their own unique directions in the world. In this sense, *all* therapy is self-consciously dialectical.

Regardless of how one defines the "highest stage," it is apparent that individuals and aggregates of individuals are capable of generating multiple realities. But, morally speaking and for practical purposes, the concept of a highest stage may be an error. The concept of *noesis* and intelligence become manifestly important as we realize that knowledge is transitory and changing. As Piaget once said, "For every problem solved, new questions arise." The approaches to therapy and psychoeducation discussed here are representative of methods that provide individuals with an orientation to life that is more process oriented and less attentive to "final" outcome.

Each developmental task solved presents an opportunity for more external growth and also provides an opportunity for richer internal growth and the learning of new developmental tasks. As such, each person who continues on to higher levels of development is also, paradoxically, forced to return to basic sensori-motor and preoperational experience if growth is not to stultify in closed-ended knowledge (*episteme*).

The skilled individual who decides to learn a foreign language so that she or he can relate more effectively with another group must enter language training at the lowest level and work through sensori-motor, preoperational, and concrete experience before being able to engage in formal operations with the new language. This recycling to continually new developmental tasks may be the most important dimension of Figure 8.

Given that development has no definable end from this point of view, it is useful to consider the practical process of assessing the client's developmental level in order to provide an appropriate environment for growth. One good entry point for work with a client is that the therapist assess his or her own general as well as specific developmental functioning in the problem area and then provide a therapeutic environment that matches the constructs and developmental level of the client.

Assessing Client Developmental Level

The model presented here would be easy to distort. Developmental counseling requires more than simply inserting stage-relevant counseling methods into the therapeutic process. First and foremost, all clients will be a mixture of several different developmental levels and will most likely present a variety of developmental tasks that need completing. These tasks will themselves represent varying sensori-motor, preoperational, concrete, and formal operational sequences. A client may be magical and preoperational on one level, concrete operational on another, formal operational on another, and dialectical on still another. Contrary to the all-too-common belief, development is not a forward-moving, linear process. Due to the many differing developmental tasks, we are all mixtures of many, many developmental levels.

Thus, in a single interview, the therapist may have to provide several therapeutic environments at multiple levels in order to accommodate to client experiencing. Most likely, one mode of thinking and feeling will be predominant in the session, but this is not necessarily so. Therefore, the therapist must accurately assess the client's developmental level and then match counseling interventions with client needs. There are several alternatives for assessing client developmental levels.

First, one might assume that a new adult client is at the concrete operations level. (Making this assumption means that even if it is necessary to shift treatment style, the change process is less abrupt.) Typically, after establishing rapport, the therapist usually asks some variation of the question "Could you tell me what you'd like to talk about?" This open-ended question will often not only provide an overview of the client's concern but might also indicate how the client is conceptualizing the concern.

In response to the open invitation to talk, the concrete operational client will fairly readily describe the issue in action terminology. One may expect concrete data: "I just flunked my exam because I didn't study" or "I am depressed because my wife left me for another man" or "I was just assaulted. Here is what happened to me."

As might be expected, most clients in such situations will be more preoperational than operational. Instead of concrete data, the therapist may expect illogical constructions of the preoperational type. These individuals would not ordinarily be seeking counseling if they could at least act concretely on their environment. One might hear: "I flunked my exam. I don't understand why" or "I feel vaguely anxious about work . . . oh yes, you're right, my wife did leave, but that's not important, I can take it" or "I don't know what happened . . . I was walking along the street and then I found myself lying on the ground." Each of these statements more closely represents what typically may be expected in client illogic. The predominant mode of thinking may be formal operational or concrete, but the therapist is likely to find distortions, deletions, and overgeneralizations in the client's discussion. These errors of thinking (or behavior) represent preoperational states.

Clients tell us in their natural language how they conceptualize their world and organize it, and we as therapists must learn the underlying constructions of the thinking process as manifested in language.

"Rooting" preoperational issues in sense certainty, to use Hegel's term, is not as easy as it sounds, particularly if the problem is convoluted in preoperational thinking. Simply getting clients to *see, hear,* and *feel* their sensory world may be a time-consuming and complex task in itself. In this instance, the shift to a more sensori-motor–based therapy may be needed, especially if the therapist is to obtain a more accurate picture of what has happened. Too often, therapy and counseling proceed without the benefits of sensori-motor reality, which provides a foundation for later development.

Formal operational thinking can be observed in the client who analyzes a problem from a distance and who also may have certain preoperational dimensions to the formal operational thought patterns. For example: "I've been thinking about how guilty I have been about not studying for the examinations. I'm not worried about the examination, but I want to talk with you a little more about my pattern of guilt" or "What is there in me that needs to change? I think I'm a good person, but somehow she didn't think so and left me. How can I improve?" or "I know it is terrible to be assaulted like I was, but I don't have any feeling about it. I need to understand why that is so." Even though these clients are basically approaching their problems with formal operational language (thinking about thinking and separating self from object), there is a tendency for preoperational logic to appear in their verbalizations. In such cases, therapists must approach the client and assess cognition on several dimensions. They must (1) concretize the event; (2) obtain some sense of how the event is perceived by the client; and (3) help the client find more adaptable, flexible, and less egocentric and dependent thought patterns.

Dialectical thinking is less likely to be observed, but with the advent of systems thinking and family therapy, therapists may need to anticipate this form of distorted thinking. Needless to say, distortions may also occur in dialectical or relational thinkers: "The teacher didn't present material clearly; I know that I have to cope with a system, but somehow, I still don't want to" or "What went on between my wife and me . . . it almost seems a repeat of the pattern I had with my first wife" (thinking of patterns of patterns) or "This is a sexist world. I should be able to walk the street without being beaten. So what if I went out at 3:00 A.M. in the morning in a rough part of the city. It's a free world." The individuals here have more complex thought patterns than those operating in earlier stages, but their complexity has closed in on itself with non-effective cybernetic closed loops—*episteme* or "true knowledge" in action, which, although complex, still misses important dimensions of multipotentiality. Paradoxically, these cognitively complex thinkers have oversimplified their environments—they have a choreography of metacontext that is not working.

Clients' nonverbal behaviors supplement their verbalizations. If the therapist overassimilates data and provides an environment that seems too low-level, one may expect the client to be offended and to indicate this by raised eyes (perhaps to the ceiling), frowning, increased speech rate and volume, body shifts (back in the chair, with arms or legs crossed, or sitting forward aggressively), or jiggling legs or playing with objects.

On the other hand, if the client finds that the therapist is offering therapeutic conditions at too high a developmental level, one may expect the client to listen very intently, with eyes lowered in a seemingly pleading aspect as if seeking information and with the body slumped, perhaps in a supplicating position. Hand gestures may be "asking" for more information and clarity.

In effect, the client's verbal and nonverbal behavior indicates clearly that appropriate environmental matching has not occurred. With the more aggressive client, it is apparent that a higher-level environment is appropriate, at least for the moment (client perceptions of what they need may not always be totally accurate). At this point, the therapist can listen closely to the client and, with better rapport, help the client move toward "lower," more useful frames of reference for coping with the problem. On the other hand, the supplicating client may at first need more structure and direction before the therapist can move to a more advanced level of relationship.

The following chart shows general behaviors that may be helpful in identifying client developmental level. These dimensions may also be useful in identifying specific factors that can be used to measure progress and change through counseling and psychotherapy. The following list provides a general guide to the effectiveness of therapeutic interventions:

Lower Developmental Levels	*Higher Developmental Levels*
Incongruous verbal and non-verbal behaviors with obvious contradictions	Congruent verbal and nonverbal behavior
Negative "I" statements ("I can't," "I won't," "I'm not able.")	Positive "I" statements ("I can," "I will," "I am able.")
Negative, confused, and inappropriate emotions	Positive emotions appropriate to context; acceptance of appropriate "negative" feelings, ability to deal with mixed emotions toward significant objects
Passive, impotent, and negative adjectives modifying significant objects	Active, potent, positive descriptors
External locus of control	Internal locus of control
Dependence/Excessive independence	Interdependent/Dialectic

(The above dimensions of locus of control and dependence/independence are culturally varying items. Some may point out that all of the above are culturally dependent variables [Ivey, 1983a, p. 218].)

In this culture, one who ends therapy with congruent behavior, positive self-statements, and appropriate emotionality plus independence and an internal locus of control is a healthy individual. This goal is culturally dependent. For instance, in Japan, the goal of Japanese therapy may be the elimination of excessive independence with the goal of bringing the client toward a more interdependent or dependent relationship. Furthermore, some of the items above will be manifested differently by men and women. For example, some male therapists may actively seek to "cure" assertive females to help them become more passive accommodators.

Given the likelihood of individual and cultural differences, it seems clear that one framework for determining advanced development may not be enough. Cultural and sexual differences may modify the meaning of development.

Weinstein and Alschuler (1985) have developed a theory of self-knowledge that addresses this issue. Self-knowledge is the way a person describes, predicts, and manages inner experience. Self-knowledge theory has arrived at specific questions, which may be asked of individuals to determine their cognitive and affective level of development. A summary of specific questions that Weinstein and Alschuler use in assessment of clients follows. They have identified the individual's stage of development as that point at which the client finds it impossible to answer the assessment questions in a fully logical and correct manner.

The language of Weinstein and Alschuler's model closely approximates that of developmental therapy. They first discuss *elemental self-knowledge,* which is roughly parallel to preoperational thought. This is followed by *situational self-knowledge,* which closely approximates concrete operations. *Pattern self-knowledge* is the transition point to formal operations, and *transformational self-knowledge* means the reflection on patterns of patterns and is similar to early dialectical levels of thought.

The following questions are adaptations of Weinstein and Alschuler's procedures that may be used to assess cognitive functioning of the individual on a particular issue.

1. At the elemental (or preoperational stage), ask: Where did it happen? When? What were you doing when it happened? Who was there? What did you do? How did people look? What did you say? What happened right after that? What did you want? How did you look? How did your body feel? What did you like or dislike about it?

These questions are similar to those proposed for moving people through developmental stages, but their use is different in that the purpose in this instance is assessment rather than developmental change. If a client finds it difficult to identify the elements of experience concretely, it is a clear indication that the therapist should stay at this developmental stage for a longer period of time. The question "Could you give me a specific example?" requires that individuals call on elements of their own experience and thus requires a somewhat higher level of cognitive functioning.

2. At the situational (or middle concrete operations) level, ask: What were some of the things you were saying to yourself during the time? What were the feelings you were experiencing? What made you think that? What did you think would happen? How did it affect the rest of the day? What did you want more (less) of?

The search here is for descriptions of situations. Some causality may be demonstrated by the client's answers to the questions. Generalization and patterned thinking are not shown. Prompting may be necessary to help the client develop connections.

3. At the internal pattern (early formal operations) stage, ask: How did your response to this remind you of other situations? Is that a pattern? Do you feel the same way in other situations? Is that typical of your thoughts and feelings?

It may be observed that this framework includes a more central emphasis on feelings. The questions are abstract and require one to think about thinking and behavior. The questions will not be understood or answered effectively by someone at the concrete operations level.

4. At the transformational (late formal operations or early dialectic) stage, ask: When you are feeling that way, do or could you do anything about that? When you find yourself having those kinds of thoughts, can you do anything about it? What things do or could you say to yourself that would change, alter, or interrupt what you are feeling and thinking? How do your beliefs about that affect your attitude?

These are action-oriented questions that assume that the client can act on his or her internal or external environment. The individual is thinking about thinking and is thinking about specific actions that he or she may or may not engage in.

Questions such as the above may be used by the therapist, counselor, or researcher to more precisely assess developmental level and to provide meaningful helping environments appropriate to that assessment. It also must be remembered that any client is a mixture of several levels of cognitive and affective development and that it is unwise to impose a single view of the appropriate environment for the client. Thus, a client can answer questions on one topic at the highest level but respond at the lowest level on the next topic. Development is a task-specific activity.

With skillful questioning and prompting, a client may move very quickly through several developmental levels. In a five-minute period, the full developmental cycle may move from sensori-motor to full formal operations and dialectics and back again. The therapist may use several theories in tandem or use a single theory and employ alternative perspectives.

Three types of assessment procedures for identifying client developmental level are (1) direct observation of the client's nonverbal behavior (whether indicators of interventions are at too high or too low a level; client nonverbals are assertive and direct if too low and supplicating and asking if too high); (2) evaluation based on the six dimensions—*all culturally related*—including the degree of verbal and nonverbal contradictions, negative "I" statements, emotional expressions, adjective descriptors, and locus of control; and (3) the Weinstein-Alschuler frame of reference. The first procedure gives the developmental therapist a rough indication of the congruence of the interview, the six dimensions provide a combination of clinical and researchable dimensions for identifying specific client developmental functioning, and the Weinstein-Alschuler framework provides specific assessment questions that can be asked.

Once having assessed developmental functioning, the therapist may then introduce developmentally appropriate therapeutic interventions.

Theory into Practice

Central to this chapter is the idea that the therapist is a detective who seeks to enter into the cognitive world of the client. Therapy demands that we consider the perspective of others—this is called empathy. Each therapeutic school attempts to provide a systematic construction of the world of the client and a "map" that can help practitioners make sense of and understand the client's unique individual constructions.

This chapter suggests that although all theories cover all aspects of the developmental sphere, certain theories have claimed certain portions of the sphere. That is, some therapies operate mostly at the concrete operational level, others at the formal operational level, while others, such as cognitive behavioral, appear to function at multiple levels.

Anderson's conception of style-shift counseling perhaps best catches the thrust of this chapter in a few words: "If your client does not respond to your therapeutic intervention, *shift your style* to another approach." The failure to move and develop with your client may result in your being left behind or in your retarding the client's developmental growth. The following outline presents some techniques for incorporating these concepts into practice.

Construct 1: If your present style of counseling and therapy does not work, shift your style to meet the developmental needs of your client. Furthermore, as your client develops increased cognitive complexity and moves through developmental stages, shift your style to remain with the client.

1. *Learning Objectives:* To be able to define four specific developmental styles of therapy and their corresponding developmental levels. To be able to identify those therapies that represent predominant styles. To identify within single dimensions of therapeutic schools how these therapies relate to all four levels of developmental functioning.

2. *Cognitive Presentation:* Figure 8 and the accompanying narrative briefly summarize the major concepts of this framework, and pages 133–162 provide further discussion and illustration of these concepts.

3. *Experiential Exercises or Homework:*
    a. There are perhaps 250 types of therapy that compete for prominence and acceptance. List as many theories as possible and classify each theory into the

four suggested levels. Note particularly that cognitive-behavioral systems, such as those of Beck, Ellis, and Meichenbaum, defy easy categorization. The term "cognitive-behavioral" specifically implies the effort of the theory to cover more than one aspect of the spherical model. Beck's model, for example, appears to be more in the style 3, formal operational category, although Meichenbaum's conceptions rely slightly more on style 2. Ellis seems to represent styles 1, 2, and 3, with a predominance of style 2. You may not agree with this interpretation; what is important is that you develop an awareness that different theories have predominant and different cognitive styles.

b. Find specific examples of how each therapy in the above listing and categorization relates to other areas of the developmental sphere. The implications of this exercise have already been partially suggested in the discussion of cognitive-behavioral frames of reference in item a above. A classic psychoanalytic model, for example, represents an advanced formal operations frame of reference. Yet, when a dream is discussed, the patient will describe the sense experience and feelings of the dream. The lack of understanding of the dream represents preoperational functioning. The description of the dream in concrete terms may be considered a form of concrete operations. As the client free associates and discovers patterns in the dream (how the feelings and sequence of the dream relate to a current problem in daily life), the client moves toward formal operational thinking. Finally, as the client applies classical analytic theory to the dream, the client is thinking about thinking, or conducting advanced formal operations on the nature of the dream and its interpretation. Dialectical thinking begins to appear when the client moves to transference issues and begins to realize that the manner in which the dream was constructed is partially determined by the presence of the analyst. Deconstruction and awareness of context may follow.

The task in this exercise is to apply similar reasoning to specific therapies so that the workings of the therapy are not restricted to just one aspect of the spherical model. Awareness of the complexities of all theories should result from this exercise. Relaxation training, for example, seems a simple and clear representation of sensori-motor therapy. How is it concrete operational, formal operational, or dialectical?

c. Obtain typescripts, audiotapes, and videotapes of therapeutic sessions. Find specific examples of the therapist's style that represent each of the four levels of therapeutic environment. How does the client respond to each style presentation? Can you find examples of the therapist failing to shift his or her style, with resultant discomfort for the client and slowing of the therapeutic process?

Construct 2: The goal of therapy becomes not realization but actualization, not resolution but revolution, not stability and homeostasis but change and development.

1. *Learning Objectives:* To be able to define the goals of dialectically oriented therapy as the active search for contradiction; to realize that movement, not stability, is the goal.

2. *Cognitive Presentation:* Pages 151–162 focus on dialectical therapy, with several examples of the model in practice. The words "confront the contradiction" are emphasized here. Whereas in most therapeutic models the aim is resolution of contradiction, the aim of dialectical therapy is awareness of and living with the fact of the continuous contradictions that one faces in life. In a sense, the dialectic model is a rigorous challenge to the concepts of homeostasis that have ruled the medical and psychotherapeutic professions for years.

The presentation is based on the simple statement: "There is no cure for life." Rather, like Don Quixote, one must seek "the impossible dream" or, like Saint Francis, recognize the dialectic one has with the universe. (Luria perhaps best summarizes this approach.)

3. *Experiential Exercises or Homework:*

a. Feminist therapy has been presented as an important and developing dialectical framework for therapy. Study the brief interview typescript and note specific examples of "confronting the contradiction" that illustrate the ability to move beyond problem resolution and into a less certain form of knowledge or being.

Build on these observations by further examination of feminist therapy and its basic principles. How are the concepts of dialectics manifested? Can you identify concrete examples of Luria's definition of dialectics?

Finally, specify some concrete behavioral specifics of feminist therapy and design a training or research program that compares them with traditional modes of helping.

b. An interpretation of Lacan's treatment theory has been presented in this chapter. Apply Lacan's five principles, as interpreted here, to your own work in therapy:

(1) How does your practice and theory currently relate to cultural, historical, or social conditions? What part of your practice is uniquely you (if any)? How are interpretations affected by these three conditions? Lacan suggests that therapy begins from a cultural base, not from the unique individual basis so often preferred by North American therapists.

(2) "An interpretation can be right only by being ... an interpretation." Decode this somewhat paradoxical statement by Lacan. Does it mean that there is no correct and final interpretation

and that our goal in therapy is simply movement and change?

(3) The client will play out past patterns with us
in the therapy hour. This act of transferring
behavior from the past to the present is characteristic of much of analytically oriented
theory. How do clients play out with you their
cultural, historical, and social past?

(4) The person of the therapist serves as the transitional object. What does this mean in your
own practice? From a Lacanian point of view,
you serve as a possible transitional person for
the client from the stuckness and immobility
of the past to the freedom and dialectic of
the future. The way in which you conduct
your dialectical relationship with clients can
enable them to work through their past his-
tories and to embark on the transition to new
states of being. How might you conceptualize
your own personal role as a transitional object?

(5) "There is no other way out of the transference
neurosis than to make the patient sit down by
the window and show him all the pleasant aspects of nature, adding: 'Go out there. Now
you're a good child' " (Lacan, [1966] 1977, p.
256). Reframing of the world as positive and
containing opportunities is important in helping the client act with his or her being. In this
way, Lacan offers a more optimistic reading of
Freudian thinking than does the more pessi-
mistic Freud himself. One can focus on positives or negatives. The search for the good may
also be interpreted as Don Quixote's search for
the impossible dream—once one finds it, it
often slips away.

Important in Lacan's concept of effective
treatment is the idea of "correct distance" and

the recognition of interdependence. Independence is seen by Lacan as American and very egocentric. What implications does his alternative construction of the purpose of therapy have for you? What does it say about the social and historical conditions underlying much of nondialectical therapy in North America?

c. Using the constructs of family therapy as described in Bateson's dialectic of form and process, construct a systematic formulation of alternative modes of family therapy. Although much of family therapy is dialectical in nature, some models may be more linear and concrete operational than others.

Give special attention to the question of types of intervention in family therapy. At what level should the intervention occur—should it be at the behavioral, contextual, or metacontextual level?

d. Taking a very different direction, provide specific examples from several approaches to therapy as they consider or fail to consider the issue of knowledge (*episteme*) as contrasted with intelligence (*noesis*). How do various therapies account for the "return to the beginning" and the need to engage in new developmental tasks?

Construct 3: It is possible to assess client developmental level using a variety of relatively specific means. However, it is important to recall that each and every client is a mixture of many developmental levels. To say that one client is totally at one level of development at a point in time would be a serious error.

1. *Learning Objectives:* To be able to assess client developmental level from four frames of reference: (1) sensorimotor or preoperational, concrete, formal, and dialectic; (2) observation of client attending behaviors; (3) observation of client verbal and nonverbal behavior; and (4) a model of cognitive assessment questioning suggested by Weinstein and Alschuler. Also, to be able to recognize that these assessments are all, to some extent, unidimen-

sional and do not describe the full complexity of the human being before us.

2. *Cognitive Presentation:* Pages 162–169 present the four models of developmental level assessment. Again, clients function on many levels, and thus developmental assessment is to be considered only a part of the client's total developmental framework.

   In assessing development, one must start somewhere, and it is useful to consider the client as at the concrete operations level. The value in this assumption is that it is possible to move to sensori-motor or formal operational style with a minimum of effort. The task of the therapist is to note the preoperational statement—whether it is an irrational idea, an ineffective behavior, or a highly complex thought—that seems to keep the client immobilized and unable to encounter the dialectic.

3. *Experiential Exercises or Homework:*

   a. Using the concepts in this chapter (and your experience with these concepts throughout this book), develop a list of specific behaviors characteristic of sensori-motor or preoperational, concrete, formal, and dialectical frames of reference. Then, classify client behavior using typescripts and videotapes of counseling and therapy. As a final step, observe your own clients in the therapy hour. What specific examples of these levels of thinking do you find?

   b. If the therapist overassimilates data and provides an environment that seems too low-level, one may expect the client to be offended and to indicate this by raised eyes (perhaps to the ceiling), frowning, increased speech rate and volume, body shifts, . . . or jiggling legs and playing with objects.

      If the client finds that the therapist is offering therapeutic conditions at too high a developmental level, one may expect the client to listen very intently, with eyes lowered in a seemingly pleading aspect as if seeking information, and with the body slumped, perhaps in a supplicating position. Hand gestures may be "asking" for more information and clarity.

These two statements summarize key nonverbal behaviors that may indicate that you have not adequately matched your client's developmental level. Observe videotapes and interviews of your own for these dimensions. Note how you may have automatically changed your therapeutic environment in response to such nonverbal signals.

c.   Specific verbal and nonverbal behaviors for further assessing developmental level are suggested earlier in the chapter. Apply these to your observations of videotapes and audiotapes of therapy. The possibilities for research on these dimensions as possible outcome variables for therapy should be apparent. Use this list to expand the attending behavior nonverbals from item b above and apply the concepts in your own therapeutic practice.

d.   Weinstein and Alschuler (1985) have developed a helpful set of assessment questions to facilitate determination of the developmental level of an individual on a specific topic. Use those questions in a real or role-played client situation. Note how client verbalizations change as a result of your developmental assessment. This change in client thinking is a specific result of your personal dialectical relationship with the client. Note that your questioning process changes both you and the client.

Summary

Four therapeutic environments have been identified in this chapter. Each style provides a different environment for clients as they move through various developmental levels in therapy and counseling. Figure 8 summarizes this model.

It is critical to recall that therapy is a person-environment

transaction. Different therapies offer varying types of environments for clients; matching therapy with defined developmental
levels of the client is most useful.

Piaget's concept of horizontal and vertical *décalage* is valuable, and the predominant theme of this chapter has been
vertical *décalage*—the relatively rapid movement through developmental levels. At this point it is vital to remember Piaget's
insistent and constant criticisms of Americans who use his
framework. He stressed that development can be rushed using
this type of model, but if it is, development will be only temporary and the individual will regress because insufficient background and foundation will have been developed and mastered.
Thus, it is not enough to move clients rapidly through several
developmental stages. It is also important to take time to ensure
that sufficient horizontal foundations at each level are laid before progressing to higher, more complex levels of functioning.

Moving to higher levels of functioning requires an understanding of transition points and the complexities of the dialectical formulations. The next chapter examines how movement
occurs in the sphere. How does a client transform reality and
move to a new stage of consciousness? And how can that movement be reinforced and maintained? Important in this process is
an understanding of the paradox of dialectics, which is simultaneously the "highest" and the "lowest" form of cognition.

Chapter Six explores horizontal and holistic development. How can we build a solid foundation of client cognitive
style and concurrently move clients to broader understandings
at other levels of development?

❧ 5 ❧

How Clients Move to
New Developmental Levels

The Process of Transformation

Piaget has described the source of creativity as a mystery. Piagetian theory is concerned with the development and creation of new knowledge, so this mystery of creation is central to the discovery of how the child, adolescent, or adult creates new knowledge and moves to a new mode of being or thinking.

The intent of this chapter is to demystify the transformational process and examine how change and stage development may occur. Key to this chapter is the idea that the creative and transformational process of Piagetian theory is analogous to the change or developmental process that occurs in counseling and psychotherapy. Creativity, whether in children or in clients in therapy, is the transformation of previously existing structures into something new.

The words "creativity," "change," "growth," "development," and "transformation" are all closely related. Each involves a synthesis of disparate parts into a new whole. All of these terms suggest movement toward a new relationship with the environment.

Confrontation of discrepancy and incongruity is basic to therapeutic transformation in clients. Several examples of change processes in therapy will be presented and related to the underlying transformational model. However, change or transformation that is not adequately established on a firm foundation is likely to disappear over time. Thus, this chapter on transforma-

179

tion and creativity closes with concepts and techniques designed to prevent relapse and unwanted return to prior stages.

Basic to creativity is the confrontation of discrepancies, the awareness of difference. The result of confrontation is a possible synthesis of the past into a new gestalt. A five-point scale for the measurement of the creative process in therapy will be presented as an indicator of the degree of synthesis that has been achieved by a therapeutic intervention.

Certain preconditions in the environment seem essential if the individual is to develop. Transformation and creation do not just occur in dramatic sudden jumps. They also occur in continually assembled bits and pieces that are gradually brought together into what appears magically as innovation. This is beautifully evident in one of the creative master magicians— Piaget.

The Creative Piaget

Piaget ([1972] 1981) has described his own approach to the creation of new knowledge as follows:

> A few more words on the source or origin of creativity. In the course of my life, it has happened that I have come upon one or two little ideas, and when I reflect upon the origin of these, I find there are three conditions. The first condition is to work alone, to ignore everybody else, and to mistrust every influence from the outside.
>
> When I was a student, I had a professor of physics who said: "Every time you start to work on a new problem, do not read anything. Instead, go as far as you can go on your own. After you have gone as far as you can on your own and you come to your solution, then read what has been said about it and take that into account and make any corrections that you might think justified." I am afraid I may have followed this precept too completely; that is, I may have read too little. But

to console myself or to take away any feelings of guilt I may have had, I like to think of Freud's dictum that the greatest punishment that divinity sends to him who writes is to have to read the works of others.

The second condition that I think is necessary is to read a great deal in other disciplines, not in one's own discipline. For a psychologist, for instance, it is important to read in biology, epistemology, and logic, so as to develop an interdisciplinary outlook. Reading a lot in the related and surrounding fields, but not in one's own precise field, is necessary.

And a third aspect I think in my case has been that I have always had in my head an adversary—that is, a school of thought whose ideas one considers to be wrong. Maybe one will do them injustice and deform them by taking them as adversary. But nonetheless, one's own ideas are always there as a contrast.

My own personal whipping boy is the logical positivists or empiricists in general. This has been my adversary all through my life. For instance, the activity of the subject, the knowing subject, is minimized in logical positivism, whereas in my own thinking the activity of the subject is at the very center of the development of intelligence.

Knowledge in my view is a structuration of reality and not just a copy. The development of intelligence is not just a matter of empirical associations, but it is a construction on the part of the subject. So throughout all my work, the adversary has been empiricism, logical positivism. As I say, I may not always be just to my adversary, but it serves a useful role for me [p. 222].

In this description, Piaget clearly points out that the origin of knowledge is within the person and that transformation or creation of new knowledge is ultimately a lonely process. Yet, before Piaget undertook this lonely process of transformation, he read widely and took in considerable new information; in effect, he almost randomly accommodated to new data from the environment. Needless to say, these (and other) accommodations later were assimilated into new constructions of knowledge. If new data from the environment were smoothly combined or assimilated into preexisting structures, no significant stage transformation would have occurred. He could have established an equilibration (beta solution) in which homeostasis or cognitive balance would have been maintained.

Piaget chose imbalance. He allowed his internal system to be perturbed by the inconsistencies in what he read as he compared these with his present state of assimilated knowledge. He actively regarded the logical positivists and empiricists as his own whipping boy. Perturbation, the engagement of discrepancies or incongruities, is a Piagetian construct that is regarded as necessary for growth.

A system of knowledge must be perturbed, disturbed, or confronted (to use the language of therapy) if that system is to change, grow, and develop. A Piaget, a child, an adolescent, or a client in therapy must see contradictions between constructions of reality before it is possible for them to open their cognitive balance to new constructions of reality. One must accommodate to contradiction itself before new assimilations (creations) are possible. Although Piaget stresses the aloneness of his constructivist activity, it is clear that he is not alone at the writing table—he brings with him an environment of extensive reading as well as an active adversary—logical positivism and empiricism. In the process of assimilating his adversary, he accommodates to new data and thus changes past assimilated structures; this results in new knowledge and structures.

In a parallel fashion, clients and patients construct new realities alone, but the perturbations or confrontations of the therapist heighten the probability of development and change. Creativity may appear to occur alone and within one individual, but it ultimately involves a dialectic of some sort with the environment, even if that environment is an internalized part of the creator.

Piaget's Mechanism of Creativity

One of the most basic examples of Piagetian development is the primary circular reaction, the active repeating of results first achieved by chance. Piaget ([1952] 1963) describes his four-month-old daughter, Lucienne, as she grasps a rattle. Lucienne sees the rattle and her hands make random grasping movements. Piaget puts the rattle within reach of one hand, and when she touches it by chance, she immediately grasps it. In this case, Lucienne has in a beginning sense coordinated eye and hand movements. Although full intentional control is not yet possible, the child does demonstrate intention—she seeks the rattle. She is also apparently aware that movement of her hand may reach the rattle. And, although the movements are not directly, specifically, and intentionally in the direction of the rattle, the environment (her father) moves the rattle closer and eventually she grasps it. In turn, the environment (the rattle and perhaps Piaget's smile) provides feedback that indicates the movement was successful.

Lucienne constructed new knowledge by the feedback generated by her grasping. Structurally, this primary circular reaction follows an analogous dialectic process to that of the two children described in Chapter One, specifically:

Two Children's *Coconstruction Dialectic*	*Lucienne's* *Coconstruction Dialectic*
1. Remark by A	1. Random reaching
2. Remark by B adapted to 1	2. Rattle (environment) adapted to 1
3. Remark by A adapted to 2	3. Semirandom reaching adapted to 2

Lucienne brought prior assimilations or knowledge (looking and hand movements) and accommodated new data into the old schema; this, over time, will result in the creation of new knowledge, that of full eye-hand coordination.

Piaget describes this process of creation as *reflexive abstraction*, in which the individual derives knowledge from his or her own actions and the coordination of actions. In a most beginning way, Lucienne has demonstrated the dialectic of reflexive abstraction. Piaget also talks about secondary and tertiary circular reactions in which the level of complexity and thinking increases, self becomes increasingly separated from object, and the individual eventually begins to think about thinking. For illustrative purposes, the example of Lucienne should be sufficient for drawing analogies of higher levels of development.

Piaget's process of creativity is not that dissimilar from his daughter's. He describes himself as working alone to generate new knowledge; Lucienne generates the intelligence of eye-hand coordination by herself. However, both had some relation to the environment that perturbed their internal systems. Piaget read widely to accommodate to a complex environment; Lucienne studied her environment as closely as Piaget in order to accommodate to it and to take in new data. Perturbation and system disruption factors for Piaget were his quest for the answer to a complex problem and his antagonism toward logical positivism and empiricism. The perturbation in Lucienne's environment was the appearance of the interesting rattle. Both Piaget and Lucienne constructed and integrated new knowledge by assimilations that acted on the environment—the dialectic of person and environment.

The mechanism of creativity, and ultimately of stage transformation, is reflected in the simple model of person-environment interaction and the primary circular reaction. Creativity is not generated from nothing; rather it is the synthesis of disparate parts into a new, whole, reflexive abstraction. Piaget suggests that all acts of intellectual activity are reflexive abstractions.*

---

*In a particularly interesting aside to his discussion of creativity, Piaget comments that the Greek discoveries of geometry and early mathematics were based on a very realistic, almost sensori-motor view. The Greeks did not allow algebra into their scheme of mathematics. In the seventeenth century, the development of algebra inspired society to consider its actions and mathematics. Later, Descartes outlined the patterns that brought together the fields of algebra and geometry. Finally, Newton brought together mathematical operations to infinity in calculus. Interestingly, Piaget does not talk about Einstein's and Heisenberg's conceptions of relativity, in which even concepts of infinity can be questioned as final

More apropos, however, is how perturbation relates to the concepts of confrontation and creativity in psychotherapy and counseling.

Perturbation, Confrontation, and Dialectics

To be creative, Piaget required an incongruity in his system, which perturbed him and drove him toward a more creative synthesis. This perturbation resulted from his confrontation with the empiricists and logical positivists in his environment. Lucienne was perturbed by the rattle in her environment and the difficulty of reaching it. Perturbation, the awareness of contradiction and incongruity in the environment, seems at the heart of the creative, transforming process. Change and development in psychotherapy and counseling require confrontation of discrepancies, the perturbation of existing cognitive structures. The creative process of psychotherapeutic change is analogous to the learning process of Piaget and Lucienne.

The dialectical process also involves perturbation, but the word "antithesis" is substituted for perturbation and discrepancy. The movement of the dialectic—the confrontation of thesis and antithesis to synthesis—has been well described by the philosopher Ver Eecke (1984a, 1985). Ver Eecke states that each synthesis (position, idea, act, behavior, and so on) inevitably breaks down due to some form of internal incongruity, contradiction, or conflict. The antithesis often comes from internal contradictions of the original synthesis. A mistake often made in interpretation of dialectics is that the antithesis is "pure" opposition. Antithesis as pure opposition is possible, but it is more usual that internal contradiction breaks down the homeostasis of the synthesis. Again, an antithesis may develop from contradictions internal to the organism or to the problem's solution.

A synthesis is a new gestalt that results from the reshuffling and reorganization of the "opposition" of thesis and

---

solutions. Thus, the creation of major thought periods in society may coincide at least by analogy with the concepts of Piagetian creativity and stage development discussed here.

antithesis. Something "new" has been created out of the formerly existing pieces. Ver Eecke describes the constant change and development in the dialectic as "existential movement." An adaptation of his concepts is represented in Figure 9.*

For instance, in therapy the client might present as a problem worry over masturbation (original synthesis of prob-

Figure 9. Ver Eecke's Model of Existential Movement

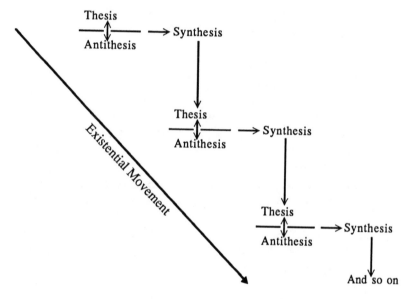

*Figure 9 is a mixture of Ver Eecke's, John Muller's (1985), and the author's constructions of their ideas. Ver Eecke first presented a diagram visually quite similar to this in a lecture at the University of Massachusetts in 1985. Later John Muller presented the idea of a gap in the dialectic. He pointed out that the gap (or eye of consciousness in Figure 6 of Chapter Two) between oppositions must be open for the movement of the dialectic:

Thesis
——— ———
Antithesis

If the gap is closed, no new data can be accommodated and the client's old assimilations will predominate. If the gap is "blown," or too open, too much accommodation and new data may come in. In "worst-case scenarios" the client may fail to distinguish between the inner and the outer world in psychosis, and a pulsation of the gap seems necessary.

lem); new data from the therapist might illustrate the contradictory view (antithesis) that masturbation is considered by many to be healthy. A new synthesis emerges that at first has no contradiction ("masturbation is healthy"). This new synthesis itself may soon break down into thesis ("masturbation is healthy") and antithesis ("yes, but sex with another human being might be more enjoyable"). The client can explore this contradiction with the therapist, and a new synthesis may evolve—masturbation should be stopped even though it is healthy and sexual activity with a human being should be substituted. The new synthesis, itself, may break down into thesis (the belief that sexual activity with another is better than masturbation) as the inevitable contradiction that sex is not always available is discovered (antithesis). Out of this contradiction may evolve a position (third synthesis) that permits both masturbation and sexual activity.

It can be seen that the third synthesis itself contains the seeds of further contradiction and more struggle between thesis and antithesis, including some or all of the following possibilities: With what sex should activity occur? How often and in what place? Is birth control an issue? Should condoms or related means be used to prevent AIDS? Each answer (synthesis) to these contradictions—the relationships with a possible child, lover, or so on—all lead to further contradictions.

This constant movement of the dialectic Ver Eecke terms existential movement, the slide toward elusive truth. The short existence of a new synthesis may be considered analogous to the Platonic concept of *episteme,* or knowledge, and the movement toward truth represents *noesis,* or more elusive, changing truth.

The dialectical process, then, may be considered closely related to the primary circular reaction of creativity as represented by the examples of Piaget and his daughter, Lucienne. Dialectics, which examines the confrontation of discrepancies and incongruity, is a constantly moving, creative process in which each synthesis leads to a new synthesis.

Perturbation, dialectics, and creativity are useful in generating client movement and change in therapy.

Therapy, Confrontation, and Creativity

To return to Piagetian thinking, one key aspect of pre-operational thought is Piaget's construct of *centration,* the tendency to focus on one key aspect of a stimulus while at the same time failing to notice other relevant aspects. It is necessary that the individual "decenter" and view the situation more complexly or holistically. The decentering process may be considered analogous to loosening tight client constructs around a topic, which thus enables the client to view a life situation or problem from a more cognitively complex point of view.

The client enters therapy overly centered, overly fixed in one way of framing the world. Our task as therapists is to enable the client to decenter, to see his or her whole situation more completely and, through the process of the dialectical confrontation, to move to a new synthesis.

Kelly (1955) has a different way of framing a closely related situation. Clients come to therapy with overly tight and constricting (or overly loose) cognitive construct systems. The goal of therapy is to help the client form permeable constructs that allow input of data and permit change and adaptation to environmental contingencies. Permeable construct systems are required for creativity and meaningful change. One may observe the gaps in the adaptation of Ver Eecke's model of dialectics through which the creative movement of new knowledge leading toward synthesis escapes. These gaps are a visual portrayal of Kelly's permeable constructs. Overly tight construct systems close the gaps to further knowledge, but overly open systems permit constant dialectical movement and change to become constant.

Pointing out contradictions is critical to the dialectical process. Unless clients can experience contradictions in their own lives, it will be difficult for them to move to a new synthesis or to even attempt a synthesis. Confrontation can be encouraged by how one person frames questions and presents contradictions to another individual. How the therapist frames the situation can help the client find a new, creative synthesis.

The tendency of those reading Piaget has been to focus on his observations of children. However, the questions Piaget asks of children are perhaps as interesting as his observations. Each question inevitably perturbs the synthesis that is in the subject. Questioning represents a form of antithesis to the child's synthesis (and in therapy performs the same function for the client). Consider the questions asked by Piaget (and simultaneously remember the counseling and therapy axiom that "behind every question there is a statement"). The following questions are selected from Piaget's *The Child's Conception of Physical Causality* ([1960] 1972):

> "When you go for a walk in the evening, does the moon stand still?"
> "What makes the clouds move?"
> "What is the wind?"
> "What has happened?" (A child has been given a deflated ball.)
> "Why is a shadow here?"
> "How does this bicycle work?"

Each of these questions draws the child's attention to a contradiction, of which the child is not necessarily aware. When the contradiction is pointed out by Piaget, the child attempts an after-the-fact explanation or synthesis. The nature of the child's resolution (synthesis) of that discrepancy indicates the nature of the child's thinking on a particular topic. In some cases, the contradiction is clear (for example, the ball is not round), but in other cases, the experimenter has perturbed (or confronted) the child with a contradiction. In such cases, it seems clear that Piaget's questions disrupt the cognitive balance or current equilibration of the child.

Sometimes it seems that the questions Piaget asks lead the child to a specific answer. If the child has not thought about the moon standing still, Piaget himself has supplied the perturbation that requires the child to find some sort of synthesis. Through skilled questioning, it is possible to lead children (and clients in therapy) to "perform" beyond their usual cognitive levels. In this sense, the questioning procedures designed to move people through cognitive levels suggested in Chapter Three are also somewhat suspect. It does little good to "move developmental progressions'' if that movement is caused by the therapist. (Given Piaget's leading questioning strategy, it is somewhat amusing that Piaget often criticizes North American interpretations of his point of view as unduly influencing the child's thinking process.)

Plato's *Meno* (see Rouse, 1956) presents Socrates drawing out a complex geometrical theory from a slave boy through skilled questioning and illustrates the impact of skilled questioning and the movement of the dialectic toward elusive truth.

> *Socrates:* Is this a four-cornered space having all these lines equal, all four?
>
> *Boy:* Surely.
>
> *Socrates:* And these across the middle, are they not equal too?
>
> *Boy:* Yes.
>
> . . .
>
> *Socrates:* Are not these four lines equal, and don't they contain this space within them?
>
> *Boy:* Yes, that is right.
>
> *Socrates:* Just consider: How big is this space?
>
> *Boy:* I don't understand.
>
> *Socrates:* Does not each of these lines cut each of these spaces, four spaces in half? Is that right?
>
> *Boy:* Yes.
>
> *Socrates:* How many spaces as big as that are in this middle space?
>
> *Boy:* Four.
>
> *Socrates:* How many in this one (A)?
>
> *Boy:* Two.
>
> *Socrates:* How many times two is four?
>
> *Boy:* Twice.
>
> *Socrates:* Then how many (square) feet big is this middle space?
>
> *Boy:* Eight (square) feet [pp. 43–49].

Socrates uses this discourse to suggest that knowledge exists in the slave boy even without instruction. Another view of this is, of course, possible. Given the elements of knowledge, anyone can construct the facts. The *Meno,* however, fails to adequately account for the influence of the extensive and skilled questioning of Socrates and the coconstruction of knowledge that occurred. Despite the sophistication and obvious utility of Plato's philosophy, he seems not to have been fully aware of the dialectics of coconstruction of reality. He fails to note his part in the construction developed by the slave boy.

Although critical of empirical studies, Piaget, like Plato, does not seem to give adequate recognition to his own skilled questioning and observation. The question perhaps shall always remain: Are we seeing the child's reasoning or that of Piaget and Socrates? Whatever one's viewpoint, it nonetheless remains true that knowledge gained through skilled questioning and minimal participation on the part of the subject is not likely to be retained over time.

To return to the question of children's creativity—in response to a question, the child may provide Piaget with an alpha solution in which the cognitive balance is skewed negatively or positively. The child, in such cases, comes up with a preoperational or magical type of answer that relatively ineffectively reflects reality ("That isn't a ball"). A child may have a firmer cognitive balance and generate a beta solution ("The ball is broke" or "Somehow it got busted"). Some children will stop, think, realize that a fully accurate answer is not readily possible, and then will transcend available data, make new connections, and create a new answer in a gamma (transcendent) solution ("Someone let the air out" or "It might have been run over by a truck" or "It hasn't been blown up yet"). The cognitive sophistication of the child in these examples falls roughly in a measurable scale of cognition, which will shortly be explored in more depth.

Psychotherapy could be defined as the art of effective perturbation—the act of confronting client discrepancies and contradictions wisely and accurately and in a timely fashion. Effective confrontation of client behavior is a major precursor to growth, development, and later integration of new knowledge and skills. If a client successfully integrates or synthesizes a confrontation in a gamma solution, he or she has moved to a higher level of understanding or assimilation.

A paraphrase of Piaget's questioning of the child in his famous water glass experiment might be: "In this hand I have a glass of water—note the water in the glass [a tall tumbler of water]. Now I am going to pour it into the glass [a short, wide glass] in my other hand. How is this possible?" This, of course, is not how Piaget formed the question, but any review of his questioning style reveals a constant pattern of clarifying contradictions that the child is asked to explain or synthesize. Piaget did not supply the answers nearly so completely as Socrates, but he was nonetheless involved in the cocreation of knowledge.

The formula "on one hand/but on the other hand" is a basic semantic format for the confrontation statement in psychotherapy that opens the way for the dialectic and dialogue between therapist and client. In this manner the therapist may deliberately seek to cocreate new knowledge and ways of thinking with a client. It is not necessary to think of oneself as separate and just an "observer" of the child (or client) as Piaget and Socrates did. This verbal paradigm of coconstruction is used in a multitude of ways when therapists confront discrepancies in their clients. Through the clarifying process of listening carefully and of detailed observation, therapists are able to mirror back to clients their contradictions, thus perturbing their cognitive systems and promoting the possibility of growth and development. Ideally, that perturbation created by such confrontation should be cognitively appropriate at the developmental level of the client. Clients can present several types of discrepancies in the interview, and these discrepancies may be confronted and perturbed from a variety of theoretical orientations. Just as Piaget and Socrates influence the direction of thought of the child, so do different therapists change the flow of client thought.

Confrontation, the active perturbation of clients, is a force that can promote change and development in client cognition and, later, in their behavioral action. For example, consider the following list of confrontation statements that therapists of varying orientations might employ. Each confrontation statement represents an antithesis to the present client thesis and promotes movement and change.

1. Discrepancies between nonverbal behaviors:
    Gestalt: I see you smiling, but what about that closed fist held tightly over your stomach? Have your fist talk to your smile.
2. Discrepancies between two statements:
    Psychodynamic: You just said that your boss's controlling style bothered you. On the other hand, earlier you said that his clear organization of your job for you reminded you of the way your father helped you with schoolwork. How do you put those ideas together?
3. Discrepancies between what one says and what one does:
    Behavioral: On one hand, you say you'd like to be more assertive, but on the other, you found this week that speaking up in class was even more fearful than before and you preferred being quiet. Tell me specifically what you thought and felt in that situation.
4. Discrepancies between people (between client and a loved one, between a client and a supervisor or colleague):
    Marital therapist: On one hand your spouse says "Be free and do your own thing," but on the other hand, you're afraid of what is really meant by that statement.
5. Between a client and a situation (cannot find a job, experiencing racism, sexism, harassment, and so on):
    Vocational counselor: You'd really like to obtain work in management and you feel very competent, but on the other hand, you feel that employers are discriminating against you. You never seem to get that second interview that gets you the job. Have I heard you correctly?
6. Discrepancies between real and ideal self:
    Person-centered therapist: Sounds as if you're saying you feel angry at yourself for not reaching your goals ... and then you feel frustrated with yourself, since you also believe that the goals shouldn't be that important. It somehow just doesn't square with the easygoing, relaxed person you'd like to be.
7. Discrepancies between present and desired behavior:

Behavioral therapist: You're presently unable to walk through a department store without heavy anxiety. Your goal is to learn how to relax and handle public situations.

8. Discrepancies between conscious and unconscious wishes: *Psychodynamic therapist:* You've said a number of times that you'd like to have a better sexual relationship with your spouse. Now, your analysis of this new dream is that you might indeed prefer things as they are as it provides you with a safer distance.

These questions obviously provide only a beginning, but the alert counselor or therapist will identify and feed back these contradictions clearly and accurately and will thus support and facilitate client understanding and a new dialectical synthesis. Needless to say, an extensive array of confrontation statements to the above situations could be made from many differing theoretical viewpoints.

In this type of perturbation, the counselor basically accommodates to the client as the client presents him- or herself through listening skills and then feeds back observations, words, and constructs through paraphrasing, reflection of feeling or meaning, and summarization. In none of the cases above did the therapist offer a direct interpretation or suggest a specific resolution of the contradiction. But the therapist is involved and is not separate from that process. Missing from most readings of both Plato and Piaget is the manner in which they were involved with and participating in the development of the individuals they described. Without the therapist to note and clarify contradictions, client growth and development would move more slowly, if at all.

However, reflecting back what contradictions one has observed may not be sufficient to promote and produce development in the client. When a confrontation is not resolved via listening skills, then influencing skills (directives, logical consequences, advice, and interpretation) may be more effective in helping the client move from the stuck preoperational mode of being to a more active intentionality mode (see Ivey, 1983a; Ivey and Gluckstern, 1983). Thus, although the emphasis to this point has been on clarifying the contradiction through careful listening and structuring (the predominantly accommodative mode of therapy), the use of the assimilative influencing skills and techniques may often be necessary.

The therapist or counselor who uses the predominantly influencing mode presents theoretical conceptions, ideas, and behaviors, which represent therapist assimilations that the therapist would like to see the client first accommodate to and then assimilate as part of her or his own reality. Using listening skills, the therapist accommodates to the client and feeds back client assimilations through the client's words and ideas. As a result of this interchange, the client will often change her or his previous assimilated structures. In contrast, the therapist who uses influencing skills seeks to have the client accommodate to and internalize the therapist's constructions, ideas, and interpretations.

The imposition of a theoretical perspective on the client, whether it is psychodynamic, primal scream, or Rogerian person-centered is an assimilative process in which the client learns to accommodate to the therapist's world view. Even in the most nondirective orientation (if it has an impact on the client), certain accommodations to the therapist will be made and ultimately assimilated into the client's thinking.

The interconnections of assimilation and accommodation should be noted in the process of therapy. For example, the listening therapist who primarily attempts to accommodate to the client must simultaneously assimilate the client's world view. The client who hears that world view fed back by the therapist must accommodate and hear that world view before a new, reconstructed assimilation may occur. In the influencing style, the therapist must accommodate adequately to the client before presenting theoretical or methodological assimilations. Complete separation of the twin Piagetian constructs is not possible.

What is the client's response to therapist or counselor interventions? Does the client indeed first accommodate to and later assimilate the ideas presented? What are the impact and effectiveness of therapeutic interventions?

Assessing Immediate Client Reaction
to Therapeutic Interventions

The theory presented above can be practically useful in the therapeutic interview. It is possible to know immediately how well the client has responded to statements of the therapist by using a five-point scale based on Piagetian constructs of equilibration.

When a child is faced with the Piagetian question of the water glass, the child may respond by:

1. Denying any difference: The child fails to note and observe any distinctions at all. The child may not even respond to the question, but look elsewhere or pick up a new toy. Nothing has been overtly accommodated or assimilated.
2. Examining only a part of the contradiction: "The water has moved." "Now there is less water" (in the move from the tall to the short, wide tumbler). This exemplifies preoperational thinking and an alpha solution. Only a partial perturbation has occurred. There is a partial accommodation, but no real change in the larger pattern of assimilation.
3. Acknowledging that a discrepancy or change exists but not providing any real data on what or why the change has occurred: "The water has moved from one glass to the other." This would indicate that the beginnings of conservation, an early beta solution, or a form of homeostasis has been developed. Accommodation is apparent, but no important new assimilation or construction has occurred.
4. Generating a linear, correct, casual explanation: "The water has been moved from the tall glass to the short glass, and the amount of water is the same regardless of the size of the glass." This is an early gamma solution, typical of logical thinking in concrete operations. The data have been fully accommodated, and a beginning assimilation is apparent.
5. Evidencing multiple operations on the data: "The water may be considered a metaphor for life. As we move water from one glass to another, there are traces of water left in the first glass, so some is lost in the process, although they

might appear equal. As we move to different stages in life, we, too, leave traces, and these traces may last or evaporate over time." This is a transcendent gamma solution, characteristic of full formal operations in that the individual is now thinking about thinking. Here we have an advanced example of assimilation.

These five types of solutions to problems serve as helpful metaphors for the development of a scale to measure client cognitive complexity and how effectively an individual responds to a therapeutic intervention or confrontation. For example:

Therapist: On one hand, you say you love your wife, but on the other hand, she says that your verbal abuse is driving her to distraction.

Level 1 Response: That's not so, I love my wife. (*The old cognitive balance is maintained through denial and magical thinking. Old client constructions or assimilations are so strong that new data are not accommodated or taken in.*)

Level 2 Response: I'm trying to do better. I sent her flowers last week. (*The client is working on only a part of the contradiction, an alpha solution. There is some accommodation to the therapist, but no new assimilation or change in internal construction in the client.*)

Level 3 Response: I can sense what you're saying. I do love her, but my yelling at her doesn't convey that feeling. (*This interchangeable beta solution tends to maintain the status quo. The client has accommodated, but no new assimilation is apparent except perhaps an increased awareness of the issue.*)

Level 4 Response: I guess I yell at her because I care for her so much and because I have pressure on the job. (*This represents an early gamma solution, since logic is concretely correct. More is in this statement than was in the summary of the counselor. The confrontation has been accommodated and a new assimilation is apparent.*)

Level 5 Response: Now, I understand, I have feelings of both love and anger. I feel dependent on her, and to be that close to anyone frightens me. I'm going to let go some of my controls and let her know I want her to be herself. Changing my behavior will be more difficult though, but I am going to do it. (*In this formal operational, transcendent gamma solution the client is clearly in the assimilative mode but has also accommodated to the intervention and moved to a new level.*)

Each of the above client responses indicates increasing cognitive complexity. At the highest level, the client must transcend present behavior and move to new constructs and ways of being in the world. Generation of new knowledge generally seems to occur only at levels 4 and 5. In the example above, the "success" of the therapist's perturbation or confrontation depends on what happens to the client's cognitions or actions, *not* on therapist action, as is commonly assumed in research on "facilitative conditions" (Carkhuff, 1969; Parloff, Waskow, and Wolfe, 1978).

At issue in therapy and counseling research is the impact of the therapist's intervention on the client. The discussion here focuses on cognition and does not take behavioral action into account. It could be validly argued that cognitions without accompanying actions are magical and preoperational in themselves, no matter how sophisticated and complex. Given this problem, the final sections of this chapter will explore how the generalization of new cognitions learned in therapy can apply to the client's real world. In the scale discussed here and in the Piagetian constructs of assimilation and accommodation, we are dealing with the world of ideas about reality rather than with reality itself.

However, the issue becomes philosophically dense when we recognize that ideas once conceived take on a reality of their own. True separation of cognition from action may be theoretically useful and practical but may be considered an artificial splitting of conceptual error and perhaps not as necessary as we think.

Thus, it is critical that the five-point scale presented in Figure 10 be related rather directly to therapy and its aims. At one level, it is possible to assess the client's cognitions in response to a single intervention on the part of the therapist; it is also possible to map out patterns of responses, determine general cognitive styles of individuals, and, perhaps more impor-

Figure 10. Developmental Level Scale

The client response to a therapist's intervention may be rated on a five-point developmental level scale. The framework for the scale is based on: (1) Piagetian alpha, beta, and gamma solutions; (2) a descriptive list of psychodynamic defense mechanisms believed to be illustrative of each level; and (3) an emphasis on confrontation, the engagement of discrepancies.

Level 1: The Negative Alpha Solution
In this response, the client tends to be under the control of past assimilations and seems unable to take in and accommodate new data from the therapist. Or, accommodation to therapist interventions is so complete and the accommodative style is so rigid that it represents basic assimilation.

Related defense mechanisms: denial of external reality, major distortion, or frankly delusionary or incorrect perceptions or statements. The rigid accommodative style might be represented by flight of ideas or extreme superficial agreement with the therapist.

Score as level 1 if the client fails to recognize or deal with the contradiction or conflict, makes an abrupt topic shift, or exhibits clear indications of defense mechanisms of denial or distortion. Example:

Therapist: You appear to be very angry toward your spouse.

Client: I'm not sorry. I love him. (*level 1*)

Level 2: The More Mature Alpha Solution
This response shows up in most preoperational statements, where one finds irrational ideas or ineffective behavioral patterns. Most clients will present their problems at this level. Usually, portions of clients' statements will be in accord with reality, but they will often be blind to some of their illogical thinking.

Related defense mechanisms: immature defense mechanisms such as projection, partial repression, passive-aggressive thoughts or actions, acting out, immature fantasy, reaction formation, displacement, mild regression, simple conversion, provocative behavior.

Score as level 2 if the client deals with only a portion of the discrepancy or problem or overgeneralizes, deletes, or mildly distorts the verbalizations of the other. The thinking process will be in some way clearly preoperational in that the client cannot operate effectively on the environment or work effectively with others. Examples:

Therapist: You appear to be very angry toward your spouse.

Client 1:   Yes, sometimes I find myself a little bit annoyed. (*level 2*)

Client 2:   Sometimes I find myself daydreaming about how I'd like to yell, but I never say anything. (*level 2*)

(continued on next page)

Figure 10. Developmental Level Scale, Cont'd.

Level 3: The Beta Solution
    This response represents homeostasis—the client seeks to maintain the situation as it is. A beta solution represents a description of reality that often corresponds to that presented by the therapist, but nothing new is added by the client.
    Related defense mechanisms: intellectualization, rationalization, identification, failure to bring actions into concert with ideas and feelings. In using these defense mechanisms, the client recognizes the contradictions in the present synthesis but does not move on to a new position.
    Score as level 3 if the individual describes a situation relatively accurately and tends to leave it there. The statement "There it is again," with the hands thrown up in mock inability to do anything, may be characteristic of a person at this level. Concrete operational, if/then descriptions may be expected. Examples:

Therapist: You appear to be very angry with your spouse.
Client 1:   Yes, I am very angry—very angry. (*level 3*)
Client 2:   Uh-huh, that's right; for example, last night she wouldn't sleep with me. It made me very angry. (*level 3. Nothing new has been added except another example of the angry situation. The new situation could be said to be interchangeable with other situations, but the client does not observe the pattern of repetition.*)

Level 4: The Early Gamma Solution
    In this response, the client moves beyond homeostasis to the creation of something new. The client has added something new to her or his cognitive-behavioral frame of reference, something that was not there before. This transformation may represent an accommodation to the therapist's intervention.
    Related defense mechanisms: altruism, humor, suppression, anticipation of the future, and sublimation. These more mature defense mechanisms, often considered healthy, help the client live with the situation more effectively. The client recognizes the contradiction and moves toward a partial synthesis or new solution.
    Score as level 4 if the client or therapist adds something new to the discussion and the client reflects this new idea in his or her verbalizations or behavior. At times, the underlying conflict will remain as an underlying contradiction. A sublimation, for example, may represent a "good" resolution, but the underlying conflict remains. Generally speaking, there will be some evidence of formal operational thinking and self thinking about self, including some awareness and acceptance of the fact that one cannot "have it all." Examples:

Therapist: You appear to be very angry with your spouse.
Client 1:   Yes, but that's part of life. I have to accept the fact that she won't behave as I want all the time. I've learned to involve myself in my work and as a Scoutmaster. It helps. (*level 4. This response represents awareness and partial action.*)

Figure 10. Developmental Level Scale, Cont'd.

Client 2:   You bet, he really ticks me off, sometimes almost constantly. I'm beginning to see a pattern in it, however. He seems to get angry when I'm working hard. He yells, then I yell, then we make up, even make love as a way of getting along. Just a game, but I'm getting tired of it. (*level 4. This response shows awareness of formal operational thinking and self thinking about self or situation. No transcendent solution is apparent.*)

Level 5: The Transcendent Gamma Solution

At this point there are no defense mechanisms that are immediately apparent. The client has arrived at a new synthesis, often of both thought and action. This synthesis itself will shortly break down into new contradictions, but for the moment, a transcendent or transforming solution has been achieved.

Scores of level 5 will be rare and, most likely, temporary and will only appear in a few client responses in an interview. The client has confronted contradiction in the context and seen beyond the confines of present-day reality for a short time. Examples:

Therapist: You appear to be very angry with your spouse.

Client 1:   I didn't know that it showed. I guess I've been angry for a long time . . . whew . . . (*Pause.*) It gives me a whole new way to look at things. (*level 5. A transcendent way of looking at things has been developed. Although it may be momentary, the client is able to confront internal and external contradiction. This client is rated 5 because a new awareness has been integrated. If the client had heretofore been denying anger, this would be a clear example of a newly integrated piece of knowledge. It is also apparent that this new data almost immediately returns the client to a level 2 or 3 response as the client learns about contradictions in the newly learned synthesis. The next client example is similar. New insights and new behaviors lead to new issues within the therapy dialectic.*)

Client 2:   Yes, and it's time I did something about it. She played the pattern several times now, and I haven't said anything. Could you help me deal with it? (*level 5. Again, new information is being revealed, and the client is ready to attempt to bring thought and action together to deal with the spouse.*)

tant, relate these data to practical implications for cognitive growth and behavioral change.

An Illustration of Cognitive Progression

The progression of cognitive complexity and transformation in a client can be illustrated using the developmental task of coping with one's father. Note that it is important *both* to think about reality and to act on that reality. "It's Dad's fault that I'm a failure on the job" may be the opening pre-operational statement and can be considered an alpha solution. Employing listening skills, the therapist indicates that the client's point of view has been heard and asks the transformational question "Could you give me a concrete example?" This may move the client toward an early beta solution ("Dad did this and I did that"). Later, issues of concrete causality may be explored and a beta solution discovered ("Oh, I failed on the job because I thought I should respond to customers as my father did"). If therapy continues, the therapist may add assertiveness training, and the client may learn new answers to old problems, which thus results in a gamma solution and a new answer to an old issue. In this case, the true effectiveness of therapy is demonstrated in the area of action.

As illustrated in the above paragraph, the movement from sense awareness (level 1) to preoperational thought (level 2) to concrete operations (level 3) to formal operations (level 4) to dialectical awareness and action (level 5) can be described in Piagetian language or in a five-step model that has utility for clinical practice and research.

Throughout this book, what can happen in therapy or counseling is described as a continuation up the cognitive ladder. The therapist may ask "Is that a pattern with you?" The client may learn that he or she is responding to superiors and customers as to the absent father. This insight may be very helpful in gaining more comfort with oneself. However, if thinking about thinking about thinking continues, a sort of sophisticated nonaction may result, with no client change occurring, despite extensive cognitive awareness. The old issue of insight without action may become a therapeutic problem. In this case, despite considerable cognitive movement, the client remains behaviorally preoperational.

Finally, the cognitive process discussed above may happen with some clients in less time than it takes to read these pages, but with others the same process may take months. Each change in client development is a step toward increasingly cognitive complexity. A client must have an adequate foundation at each level before the next task can be attempted. (Chapter Six presents more of the complexities of therapy and illustrates how the process may be expected to occur over a series of treatment sessions.)

Returning to the example of the client working through a relationship with the father, let us assume that the client's father has passed away some ten years previously. Nothing can be done about this reality. However, how the client thinks about his or her father is important and is amenable to therapy. In this case, cognition and change in consciousness may be the only route to psychological comfort. No overt behavior changes, but the thinking behind that behavior may change markedly. Again, the distinction between the world of reality and the world of ideas can easily and validly become blurred. If the client continues to talk to colleagues and family members as if he or she were relating to the absent father, then further reflection of unconscious processing or more extensive dialectic formulations may be required.

Mention must again be made of the distinction between changes within a stage and changes or movement from one stage to another. This discussion has used the two types of movement interchangeably. Most teenage and adult clients are at the formal operations stage. The issue they present in therapy may indicate preoperational thought processes, but the rapid change that can occur on issues and in the way the client thinks about them demonstrates that the client is capable of functioning at the formal operations level and that the problem is perhaps ultimately a "within-stage" issue. The issue of between- and within-stage development can be even more complex. Clearly, some individuals function on some topics primarily at the concrete level of thinking, but on other topics, they may be formal operational. Is this individual operating at a concrete or formal stage? The definition of stage is, of course, dependent on the view one takes of stages. From one point of view, the individual is basically formal operational and simply needs some help to function more fully within that stage. Yet, from another point of view, insufficient evidence is available that the individual has indeed made a full transformation to formal operational thinking, and therefore, he or she is truly still basically a concrete thinker. Given these alternative definitions, it seems again that clear distinctions are not easily made between phases and stages or within- and between-stage development.

The post-formal or dialectical stage is one that many adults do not reach, because it requires an ability to abstract and think about thinking about thinking that exceeds the intellectual capacities of many individuals and because it is not a characteristic of what is necessary for survival in this culture. As suggested in an earlier footnote on Piaget, cultural frameworks themselves may be concrete operational. Thus, the client may feel discomfort because he or she is cognitively higher than the cultural mean. Dialectical awareness, feminist therapy, and family therapy have been proposed as examples of therapeutic methods that allow clients to explore the relationship between themselves and the culture. At this point, things again become complex. Feminists and those with dialectical awareness might suggest that more awareness of this consciousness level is necessary if society, culture, and the world are to survive the threats of racism, sexism, war, and nuclear holocaust. A dialectical awareness necessarily requires the ability to cope with the ultimate complexity of our interactional world.

Given all these possibilities, it nonetheless seems clear that children as well as our clients have relatively definable stages of cognition. In an analogous fashion, larger qualitative changes in thinking occur in psychotherapy and counseling. While some life structures are amenable to immediate and rapid growth through identifiable stages, more complex problems will require substantial time and effort before major change occurs. The movement from preoperational to concrete thinking may prove to be a mammoth undertaking, particularly if rigid defense mechanisms are in place. Describing the process of creating stage movement and transformation is perhaps easier than inducing the process.

The Process of Transformation in Therapy

Perturbation of client systems of thinking through confrontation has been presented as the core method of advancing developmental transformation. Each therapeutic school, be it person-centered, cognitive-behavioral, or psychodynamic, has unique approaches that confront varying types of client discrepancies. Each of these methods, in addition, has its own conceptions of developmental growth and change. However, it may be argued that underlying the varying conceptions of change are methodological consistencies that may be identified and taught within a larger metatheoretical developmental frame.

Critical to this process of growth and transformation are four ingredients: knowledge of the change process itself, structuring of the environment for change, use of developmentally appropriate interventions and theories to produce change, and the prevention of relapse or loss of the insight or change. (This last will be discussed in a separate section concluding this chapter.)

The Change Process. A metamodel of developmental change is presented in this chapter, and it is argued that therapeutic change can be considered parallel to the creative process of Piaget and his daughter, Lucienne. Let us first review briefly the parallels between creative transformations in therapy and those of Piaget and Lucienne.

1. The client, Piaget, and Lucienne all must make their creative discoveries alone. No intervention on the part of a therapist makes any difference unless it is internalized in the client.
2. Each searches "randomly" (yet, paradoxically, systematically) in her or his environment. Lucienne seems to search randomly, but there is an underlying purpose in her randomness—to get at the rattle. Piaget stated that he read randomly, but he had the ultimate intent to write on a particular topic. Clients may appear to be acting randomly in their search for answers and this search is often less effective than true randomness would be. There is usually an underlying purpose or intent to client action and thinking.
3. Each finds help in the environment. Piaget places the rattle closer to Lucienne so she can reach it herself. Piaget obtains assistance from his adversary, logical positivism, and his reading. The client has a therapist to help organize data and keep on track.
4. All three (Piaget, Lucienne, the client) have been made

aware of discrepancies (perturbations) in their thinking or action. All seek to resolve those discrepancies.

The individuals and the content are very different, their experience and affect totally distinct and unique, yet the development of each occurs in a person-environment transaction or dialectic.

The therapeutic model, of course, is directly parallel to Piaget's and Lucienne's creativity. The environment provides the basic structure within which the individual operates. The individual, an active assimilating being, acts within that environment and incorporates what it has to offer. Finally, the environment must offer some sort of reinforcement if change is to be maintained. Again, we see the basic workings of the dialectical person-environment model of the individual, who is growing in a challenging (but appropriately structured) environment.

It is this environment, which is provided by the therapist and counselor, that supplies the dialectical framework so important to client growth and development. This environment may be the confrontation of the Rogerian real and ideal selves, the engagement of a gestalt "split," the examination of an analytic polarity or of Ellis's "irrational idea," or the behavioral analysis of present behavior versus desired behavior. All these methods are concerned with the resolution of incongruity and the synthesis of new knowledge. The environments may differ, but they have in common the desire to promote growth. And, just as family environments in different cultures produce different but effective individuals, so, too, may therapeutic environments differ. Clients will develop differently in different therapeutic environments, but they may be expected to develop and change if the environment makes an impact on them.

Structuring the Environment for Change. Individuals do not change or develop in a vacuum. They grow in appropriate environments for their particular needs and developmental stage. Chapter Four presents therapy and counseling as environment building. The discussion of style-shift counseling points up the need to change style throughout the therapeutic process as the client's cognitive and developmental levels change.

A useful addition to the transformational concepts thus

far presented is the management-training model of Hersey and Blanchard (1982). Their model, termed "situational leadership," focuses on how business managers must change management styles when working with employees of varying developmental levels. Hersey and Blanchard emphasize that environmental structuring is basic to effective management, and they discuss the need to assess employee developmental level and use stage-appropriate interventions in the management process.

Particularly interesting in the Hersey-Blanchard model is the description of the movement of an employee from a lower stage on a developmental task to a higher level. To move an employee to higher-task performance, they suggest providing an appropriate management style that is matched to the developmental level of the employee. Lower-developmental-level employees need more carefully articulated structure. A beginning bank clerk, for example, may need to be told precisely what to do. At a more advanced level, perhaps after three months' experience, the same clerk may no longer respond well to being told what to do and will need an environment that allows for more individual direction of the task. The manager must note the developmental level of the employee on each developmental task (bookkeeping, customer relations, typing) and structure the environment to meet task-specific needs of the employee. Thus, a single employee may need highly specific structuring at one time (learning a new bookkeeping procedure) but may need only general suggestions (how to handle a difficult but important customer) when the employee "naturally" functions at a higher level. Another employee may need just the reverse treatment—highly specific suggestions and directives for handling customer complaints but almost total independence in bookkeeping. Different employees are at different levels for the multiple tasks in business.

Hersey and Blanchard's model is somewhat parallel to the constructs presented in this book. Figure 11 presents an adaptation of their concepts. The manager must provide clear structure and direction if the employee is to move to a higher level. The model then states that the individual should complete the task and, in effect, construct her or his own new management knowledge. This construction of knowledge must take place

Figure 11. A Three-Step Process of Development: Helping a Client or
Employee Move from Preoperational to Concrete Operational Functioning

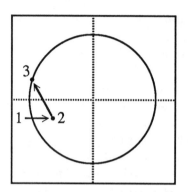

Step 1: Therapist provides
structure and direction. The
environment is structured
for change.

Step 2: The individual does
task or work, with therapist
intervention. This represents
horizontal learning and the
building of an adequate
foundation for the creative
movement to the next level.

Step 3: Reinforcement. The
environment must support the
new learning or it will be lost.

within the employee (or the client). Finally, the manager (or
therapist) should provide feedback and environmental support
to help maintain the new behavior.

Whether it is growth in management skills, coconstruction of language in a five-year-old child, development of creativity in Lucienne and Piaget, or change in clients, the dialectical
model (Figure 12) can explain this process. The model follows
the steps of action (or thesis), notation of reaction (or anithe-
sis), and then a reformulation (or synthesis). This synthesis will
again break down into another "1-2-3" cycle.

When applied to the therapeutic interview, this model
suggests the importance of therapist structuring. By punctuating
the session with questions, confrontations ("on the one hand,
your problem is . . . but on the other hand, your goal is . . ."),
or other therapeutic interventions, the therapist structures the
session and makes client change and development possible. But
this change is not effected unless the client takes in and accommodates to what the therapist has structured and later integrates these new data with previously assimilated structures.
This process of structuring to aid the client in finding her or his
own answers is analogous to Piaget placing the rattle closer to

Figure 12. The Dialectics of Stage Transformation

To facilitate movement of a client through the complexities of transitioning from one stage to another (for instance, from sensori-motor to concrete operations) will require multiple steps, multiple tasks, and allowance for possible regression in the process. This figure is a representation of a portion of that process and illustrates the smaller steps that may be required to effect stage transformation.

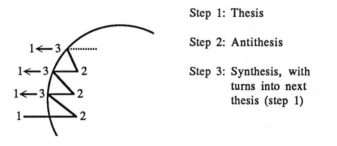

Step 1: Thesis

Step 2: Antithesis

Step 3: Synthesis, with turns into next thesis (step 1)

Lucienne so that she could grasp it herself. Environmental structures make it possible for the individual to act, develop, and grow. Whether the environment is overstructured or understructured will depend on the developmental level and experience of the client.

Developmentally Appropriate Interventions. Chapter Four presented in some detail the concept that different theories may be appropriate for developmentally different clients. Each therapy has at least some methods and techniques for coping with the varying developmental levels of clients. Again, the essential idea is to assess the client's developmental level and provide a therapeutic environment that matches the client's needs.

Since the next chapter will outline the process of therapy and its assessment in detail, only a few brief comments and examples are needed here. Ivey (1983b), for example, provides a videotape demonstration in which he works with the same client using three different therapeutic systems: psychodynamic dream analysis, logotherapy reframing, and behavioral assertiveness training. In each session, the dream is the focal point. The dream is reexperienced (see-hear-feel) and its elements are organized in a linear fashion, which represents the sensori-motor and concrete operations of the three sessions. The dream is not reflected on but is simply used as an operational basis for further exploration. It would have been possible to stay within the psychodynamic model and move to higher levels of cognitive abstraction.

The reframing session, which follows the presentation of the dream, focuses on one pattern in the dream that is recalled from childhood and also operates in the present. In both the dream and in real life, the client fails to speak out for her own wishes. The identification of the pattern represents early formal operational thinking, and the reframing of the pattern (thinking about the pattern or thinking about thinking) into an alternative interpretation represents late formal operations. In reframing, the client is helped by the therapist to see that her childhood behavior was more effective than she had believed *and* that the repeating pattern in her adult life has positive aspects and strengths as well. The dialectic process is bypassed, but it could have been explored through examining the reframing process itself and the cultural implications underlying the entire process.

The final segment of the demonstration is an assertiveness training session in which the client works on her pattern of failing to speak for herself. Clear, behavioral elements of the pattern are sought. The identification of elements of a specific situation where the client has been insufficiently assertive represents the sensori-motor and preoperational dimensions. The actual assertiveness training exemplifies concrete operations and action on the world. In this demonstration, the therapy cycle has moved through the spherical or quadrant model one full cycle and started once again. It would be possible to add reflections on the assertiveness training model and move again to formal operations.

Alternative therapeutic techniques, such as those from cognitive-behavioral orientations (thought stopping, assertiveness training, cognitive reframing, relaxation training), person-centered counseling (listening, focusing on the real self and the ideal self, encounter groups), and psychodynamic orientations (dream analysis, Lowen exercises, gestalt exercises), all provide environments for growth and development. Each therapy and theory in its own way provides different environments to stimulate and promote the growth of the unique person—the client. In turn, the client may respond to those techniques and theories that provide the most effective and useful environment for development according to her or his unique developmental phase.

As stated previously, change in the interview is not necessarily change in the client's daily life. The issue of maintaining the gains of the therapeutic hour may be as important or more important than what occurs inside the interview itself.

Maintaining What Has Been Created in the Interview

The process of change, creativity, and transformation has been described as the result of a person-environment dialectic. However, the question of maintaining the change remains. Will what has been created remain part of the client once he or she is faced with the ongoing dialectic with the external environment outside the interview? Will the client be able to maintain new assimilations or will the larger external environment extinguish new learnings? There are numerous instances of insights gained and behaviors mastered in the interview that are then lost when the client is confronted with an unaccommodating environment.

Piagetians, therapists, and counselors may talk about the importance of person-environment interaction, but they then go on to discuss what happens in the child's, patient's, or client's mind. They thus fail to change the external environment or even to make the individual aware of the dangers of that environment to new behaviors and thoughts. Thus, as the person is accommodating to the environment and assimilating internal structures provided by that environment, the person is also acting on the environment, causing environmental change, and forcing that environment to respond to and accommodate to the individual. But the environment tends to be larger than the person and is, by and large, more effective at assimilating the individual than the person is at assimilating the environment.

An alcoholic may learn in therapy or in Alcoholics

Anonymous why he or she drinks and may generate behaviors that result in new actions on the environment. But, when the individual returns to the home environment where advertisements for drink abound in the media, where there are bars on every block, and where friends say that "one drink won't hurt," the environment is often victorious over the most valiant efforts of the alcoholic. Similarly, the effects of therapy disappear when the individual is confronted with outside reality—a pattern of drug abuse repeats itself, a client suffers through a third divorce, a child runs away from home the second time, the workaholic returns early Saturday morning to the office. In each of these cases, it is not necessarily that the transformation has failed, but rather that the environment has assimilated change so actively that even the most determined effort at maintaining new behaviors, thoughts, or attitudes learned in therapy becomes almost impossible.

Glass and Kliegl's (1983) most recent meta-analysis of the effects of 475 different pieces of research on the effectiveness of psychotherapy reveals that psychotherapy does seem to produce change. However, in the same article the authors note that much of the effect of psychotherapeutic and counseling change appears to disappear after six months. Change is far easier to produce than it is to maintain. The impact of the environment shows most dramatically in the word "assimilation" as it is often used in the United States. The United States historically has expected immigrants to assimilate to a normative standard of what is American. The impact of the culture is so strong that those who come to our country have little choice but to assimilate. The United States, as an assimilating culture, does not accommodate to the demands and needs of a diverse population. This statement, of course, represents an oversimplification, since recent trends toward bilingual education, the increased interest in and support of ethnicity, and the Black and women's movements suggest that the United States is making a more concentrated effort to accommodate its diverse populations. Nonetheless, the power of an environment to shape and direct behavior in the largest sense should be evident. Given such forces in the environment, it sometimes seems miraculous that any change is maintained at all—that there is any trace left of the psychotherapeutic process.

Given the power of the environment, be it the United States, a family, or the neighborhood ecology of an alcoholic, it can be seen that the newly learned skills of the client will be readily extinguished unless the client is well prepared to cope with life after therapy. Works by Marlatt (1980), Marlatt and Gordon (1985), Marx (1982, 1984), and Janis (1983) present interesting and important approaches to the problem of maintaining new behaviors and thoughts learned in therapy. The process of maintaining change can be considered somewhat analogous to that of large-stage transformations in Piagetian theory. Theory states that the child, in moving from preoperational to concrete thought, has several requirements. First, the child needs a solid foundation of preoperational skills and thoughts. Piaget terms this adequate horizontal *décalage*. It is not possible to move ahead more rapidly than the individual is able. Thus, what is too early learned is often thought of as an artifact rather than as real. Second, the individual must integrate the change solidly into his or her own conceptual framework. This change may be piecemeal and achieved slowly over time. Third, the environment must recognize and support the new learning or the individual must be strong enough internally to carry on despite limited reinforcement.

For an alcoholic, it can be seen that newly learned nondrinking skills will be readily extinguished unless the client is well prepared to cope with life after therapy. The same applies to clients who face problems of weight loss, who wish to cease spousal abuse, or who suffer from depression. Therapy results too often disappear. Programs such as those of Janis and Marlatt and Marx speak to these issues.

Janis terms his method *decisional counseling*. It is a system oriented to style 2 (coaching oriented to those with concrete operational problems). Janis's work at Yale University has emphasized short-term counseling that is oriented toward weight loss and smoking cessation. His research group (Janis, 1983) found that a single interview can be effective in producing behavioral transformations if certain critical ingredients are present in the interview. These ingredients are presented in Figure 13 and are all oriented toward producing change from the first phase of helping to the last.

Figure 13. The Janis Model of Decision Counseling

Critical phases and key variables that determine the motivating power of counselors as change agents

Phase 1: Building up motivating power	1. Encouraging clients to make self-disclosures *versus* not doing so
	2. Giving positive feedback (acceptance and understanding) *versus* giving neutral or negative feedback in response to self-disclosure
	3. Using self-disclosures to give insight and cognitive restructuring *versus* giving little insight or cognitive restructuring
Phase 2: Using motivating power	4. Making directive statements or endorsing specific recommendations regarding actions the client should carry out *versus* abstaining from any directive statements or endorsements
	5. Eliciting commitment to the recommended course of action *versus* not eliciting commitment
	6. Attributing the norms being endorsed to a respected secondary group *versus* not doing so
	7. Giving selective positive feedback *versus* giving noncontingent acceptance or predominantly neutral or negative feedback
	8. Giving communications and training procedures that build up a sense of personal responsibility *versus* giving no such communications or training
Phase 3: Retaining motivating power after contact ends and promoting internalization	9. Giving reassurances that the counselor will continue to maintain an attitude of positive regard *versus* giving no such reassurances
	10. Making arrangements for phone calls, exchange of letters, or other forms of communication that foster hope for future contact, real or symbolic, at the time of terminating face-to-face meetings *versus* making no such arrangements
	11. Giving reminders that continue to foster a sense of personal responsibility *versus* giving no such reminders
	12. Building up the client's self-confidence about succeeding without the aid of the counselor *versus* not doing so

Source: Janis, 1983, p. 26.

The Yale group first builds up "motivating power" in clients by encouraging moderate amounts of self-disclosure, most often through modeling of appropriate self-disclosure on the part of the counselor. As the client shares past experience with weight loss or smoking, the counselor provides positive rather than neutral or negative feedback. (For example: "It's good that you are aware of the difficulty of stopping smoking.") As the session develops, cognitive reframing or interpretation helps provide insight. Rapport, problem definition, and goal setting are important in this portion of the interview.

Janis gives exceptional attention to generalization and maintenance of new thoughts and behaviors in the final two phases of decision counseling. Clients are given directive suggestions for action, and an attempt is made to encourage clients to accept and affirm the positive action statements. Skills for maintaining behavioral changes are taught, and positive feedback is given, contingent only on client change indicators. Unconditional positive regard, as usually conceptualized, is not part of the decisional model. Janis's research findings increasingly suggest that individuals will respond to and learn best in an environment in which certain choices are reinforced and others extinguished. Given these choices on the part of the counselor, it may be seen that the counseling environment itself more closely corresponds to the real-life environment that clients will eventually face.

However, in Janis's third phase, the distinctions between his and traditional approaches to helping become most clear. The counselor seeks to establish a new environment for the client to return to after the interview is completed. The counselor makes plans to stay in contact and follow up with the client, may provide counseling "partners" or a peer group for support of the client's new behavior, and helps the client learn how to succeed without the physical presence of the counselor.

Note that Janis's interview is highly structured toward specific ends and is representative of environmental structuring as represented in the first and second developmental levels of Figure 13. The environment provided by Janis is highly assimilative and acts deliberately on the client to produce accommodation to a new construction of reality, which the client will ultimately assimilate as part of new cognitive and behavioral structures. Janis (1983) describes this as a coaching approach: "When the client regards the health-care practitioner as Olympic coach, she conveys the idea that in some sense she thinks of the coach as treating her like an Olympic star" (p. 41). If clients are regarded by their counselors and therapists as stars, performance is more likely to reach Olympian heights.

The conceptualizations of the Yale group are particularly important because they clearly show that maintaining behavioral change is perhaps not as difficult as many therapists suggest. This seems logical, since most clients in therapy are capable of formal operational thinking. The goal is to use the skills and cognitive capacities the client obviously has and to facilitate return to maximum cognitive and behavioral functioning.

Marlatt (1980), Marlatt and Gordon (1985), and Marx (1982, 1984) have worked with alcohol addiction, weight loss, and the maintenance of new behaviors in business managers. Their work is termed "relapse prevention" and is based on the assumption that the environment a client or manager lives in is quite unpredictable and that engaging in new thoughts or behaviors will be difficult. The task of the counselor, therapist, or management trainer is to inoculate the client against the environment and to help the client assimilate and act on rather than accommodate to the environment. In this sense, both relapse prevention and the Janis model emphasize the importance of environment in helping clients find lasting change.

Clients are taught three main things in relapse prevention. First, they are advised to expect rather than fear temporary errors. Development is not always the automatic, forward movement depicted in flowcharts; rather it is often a jagged set of attempts to put new concepts in place. Second, strategies are taught to heighten awareness of trouble spots, and skills are provided to help the client cope with anticipated difficulties. Third, clients are taught to examine the ways that they con themselves into self-blame for failure. This is particularly critical, because self-blame represents the first step of being assimilated by the environment and the return to old habits.

The relapse prevention process involves two phases. First, the client chooses a skill to be maintained that is voluntary, learnable, and can be operationally defined in terms of specific behaviors (weight loss, alcoholism, a management skill such as stress management). Second, the client is taught specific strategies for change, including awareness of the relapse process itself, distinctions between the environment of the counseling interview and the work environment, identification of high-risk situations (situations where one might want to eat or drink or stressful work problems), analysis of available coping responses and teaching of coping skills where necessary, recognition of emotions attendant on failure, development of self-efficacy (internalization of feelings of competence), and how to reward oneself for gains in maintenance of behavior. An interesting part of the relapse prevention process is the "programmed relapse," in which the client is encouraged, for example, to engage in a planned eating binge. Most clients indeed will relapse at some stage before a newly created behavior is fixed. This paradoxical instruction proves helpful in avoiding self-blame and aids clients in coping with the environmental system.

Both the Janis and the Marlatt and Marx approaches involve a great deal of attention to the individual's relationship with the environment and may be contrasted with many approaches to therapy and counseling that seem to focus totally on the individual. The systems appear to use a variety of fairly typical behavioral and affective techniques, which are used to facilitate individual self-control in the environment. In short, these two important systems of generalization and behavior transfer ensure continuity of therapy with the planned environment change. This is something that most psychotherapy and counseling strategies fail to emphasize.

Therapy and counseling take place in the relatively safe and supportive environment of the therapist. Outside, it is indeed a "cold, cruel world." What the Janis and Marlatt and the Marx models have done is to illustrate clearly that change outside the office cannot be left to chance. Most psychotherapy focuses on providing an environment for change in the office and helps facilitate that change; however, they only provide a modicum of support or reinforcement for that change after the client returns to the family, work, or neighborhood environment. To return to Lucienne and her rattle: If she is allowed only to touch the rattle and grasp it once and does not have a supportive environment that allows and encourages her to grasp, the behavior of grasping will be lost. Like Lucienne (and her father, Piaget), clients need environmental support for new behavior or change will be more likely lamented than cemented.

Theory into Practice

Creativity, development, change, growth, transformation —these words may be used interchangeably to represent the outcome of effective intervention in therapy. The process of creativity involves confrontation of discrepancies in one's environment and the generation of new alternatives for thinking and acting.

This chapter provides examples of the creative process, discusses the importance of confrontation and perturbation in producing creativity, and provides a five-point scale for the assessment of the creative process in terms of client cognitive outcome. Suggestions for implementing these ideas follow.

Construct 1: The creative process involves an existential movement, which results from dialectical confrontation with discrepancies in one's internal or external environment.

  1. *Learning Objective:* To be able to describe the dialectics of the creative process as analogous, whether one is discussing the creativity of Piaget, his daughter Lucienne, or that which occurs in client growth and change.
  2. *Cognitive Presentation:* Pages 179–195 outline several parallels in the creative process. Important among these are that Piaget's and his daughter Lucienne's creative processes occur alone but in reaction or opposition to specific perturbations from the environment. The perturbations are related to the therapeutic use of confrontation—therapy skills, which are designed to perturb the cognitive balance of clients. The visual portrayal of dialectics illustrates the constant generation of creative solu-

tions as represented by existential movement. This visual representation could describe the therapy process, the growth process of Lucienne, or the creation of knowledge by the slave boy in Plato's *Meno*.

3. *Experiential Exercises or Homework:*

a. Using the visual presentation of the dialectic, describe Piaget's creative process, Lucienne's primary circular reaction, and the movement of therapy. In each case, define what are the thesis and antithesis and how they become one in a new, creative synthesis. Then describe and illustrate how the synthesis breaks down once again into thesis and antithesis, thus continuing the process.

Then, describe one of your own experiences as a therapist from this frame of reference. Describe client movement as the exercise of the dialectic. Give special attention to the role of confrontation and perturbation in this process. It may be helpful to take any of a number of therapy typescripts and outline existential movement in this fashion.

b. Give special attention to the gap between thesis and antithesis, which gives rise to change and the evolving new synthesis. Return to Figure 6, which illustrates a conception of two-person information processing. Consider the gap as analogous to the "eye of consciousness." Long-term memory may close or open the gap, or eye.

Using the constructs of dialectics, outline what happens when dialectics is described in terms of information-processing theory.

c. The confrontation skill, that which focuses on discrepancies and incongruities within the client, appears to be particularly important in facilitating the client's dialectical movement due to the perturbation of the client's existing state of being. Note that in the confrontation examples presented, the therapist accommodated to the client's picture of reality but fed back to the client the existing discrepancies.

Piaget seemed to have a special gift for pointing

out discrepancies to children and thus provides us with useful insights into their thinking process.

Examine your own interviews for the use of confrontations; note how clients respond to your perturbations to their systems and how different clients respond differently to the varying types of contradictions. It may prove useful to engage in role plays to practice identifying and confronting contradictions.

d. Search your own immediate environment for examples of the illogical, magical thinking so often represented by irrational statements. Listen to your own interactions with others and note how many irrational statements they make in the course of an ordinary day. As the spirit moves, confront and perturb your friends' and colleagues' irrational, magical thinking (with care and consideration for both yourself and others). If this exercise is successful, you may be indeed startled to realize how much of our interpersonal interaction contains elements of discrepancy and incongruity that we choose to ignore.

Construct 2: It is possible to classify client reactions to therapeutic interventions using a five-point developmental level scale.

1. *Learning Objective:* To be able to classify client statements on the developmental level scale.
2. *Cognitive Presentation:* Pages 196–204 summarize the scale and the background behind it. Figure 10 presents the scale itself.
3. *Experiential Exercises or Homework:*
   a. Classify the following client responses to therapist confrontation statements:

   1. *Therapist:* On one hand, you say you want to retire, but on the other hand, I don't see you taking any steps in that direction.

      Client 1a: I don't see where you got the idea that I want to retire.

Client 1b: That's your opinion. I've done a lot. For example, I'm talking to you.

Client 1c: Yeah, I see what you're saying. I've done a lot of talking, but not much acting.

Client 1d: Well, that settles it. Tomorrow, I'll meet with my insurance agent and get started.

Client 1e: Yes, there is some very real conflict. I like what I'm doing, but it's time to let the young folks come in. Guess that is why I just sit. I think I'll start, though, by seeing my insurance agent and seeing just how much money I do have. That's a start, at least, to a decision.

2.   *Therapist:*   On one hand, Susan, it sounds as if you are really ready to call it a day with your marriage, but I hear some hesitancy in your tone of voice.

Client 2a: That clarifies it for me. I am not as certain as I thought. Certainly, it's been a hassle with Tom, but we've had some good times too. I guess I need to hold my decision and explore it some more. I'm not as certain as I thought.

Client 2b: No, I'm certain I want a divorce. Just tell me about a good lawyer.

Client 2c: You seem to be telling me that I don't come across to you as certain as I thought as I was . . .

Client 2d: Wow. That really hits it! I've been so caught up with his affair and how it hurt that I haven't taken stock. You're right, I am hesitant, but I wasn't aware of it.

Client 2e: You're the one who's hesitant. Can't you hear what I'm saying?

1a = Level 1	2a = Level 4 (new solution, limited insight)
1b = Level 2	2b = Level 2 (partial recognition)

1c = Level 3   2c = Level 3 (interchangeable)

1d = Level 4   2d = Level 5 (develops insight into
                ambivalence)

1e = Level 5   2e = Level 1 (denial)

b. Select your own typescript, audiotape, or videotape
    and rate client behavior on this scale. Give special
    attention to therapist leads that seem to "produce"
    client lower- and higher-level responses. Also, give
    some attention the constructs of Freudian defense
    mechanisms. Can you identify these mechanisms
    operating in the verbalizations of the client (and per-
    haps the counter-transference of the therapist)?

c. Review the above analysis and note that the "mo-
    ments" of movement of the dialectic (levels 4 and 5)
    tend to be relatively rare. Our human functioning
    operates mainly at levels 2 and 3, where we partially
    deny or "hold the contradiction." One of our diffi-
    culties in measuring therapeutic outcome is that it
    comes so quickly and briefly that we may miss the
    fact that it happened. And once it has happened, the
    client's new synthesis so rapidly breaks down into
    another thesis and antithesis. (Distinctions between
    levels 4 and 5 of the scale may be expected to be
    particularly difficult to make.)

    This is not a flaw in the person, the therapist, the
    theory, or even the culture. The concept of synthe-
    sis is closely allied with that of Platonic knowledge
    (*episteme*), and the breakdown of knowledge into
    intelligence (*noesis*) represents the formation of the
    contradiction of synthesis and antithesis. From this
    practical and philosophical point of view, it is sim-
    ply another way of saying that knowledge and
    truth are always elusive and changing. Small wonder
    that we can observe so many irrational, magical
    statements among our colleagues and ourselves in our
    natural environments!

Construct 3: Once new knowledge is grasped through the dialectic, the maintenance of this knowledge is often at risk. Techniques of relapse prevention and generalization of knowledge and behavior are important for maintaining development and encouraging future growth.

There are two key dimensions in this construct. The first is that special effort must be taken to see that new knowledge, whether cognitive or behavioral, is maintained and becomes part of the individual.

The second dimension is more complex. The fixing of new knowledge and behavior brings with it new problems. Let us recall that knowledge is considered elusive and transitory and the fact of having new knowledge firmly implanted makes it difficult for us to return to exactly the same point at which we were before we developed our new syntheses. The effective imparting of new knowledge opens the way for this new knowledge to break down into intelligence (*noesis*), the facing of new contradictions of thesis and antithesis, and the need to face new developmental tasks. (Level 5 insights almost immediately "break down" into level 4.)

1. *Learning Objective:* To be able to describe the process of relapse prevention and utilize methods by which learning from the interview may be maintained and generalized to the daily life of the client.

2. *Cognitive Presentation:* Pages 204-218 outline aspects of change between stages and the maintenance of stage changes. Note that change can be represented by cognitive change and by behavioral change. The issue of unconscious change has not yet been discussed and is reserved for a later chapter.

3. *Experiential Exercises or Homework:*
   a. Examine the description of the change process earlier in this chapter. Using the four-point model, describe how therapeutic process provides help in the environment to make change possible. Then, examine typescripts or your interviews for specific examples of the immediate change process described here. Note, once again, that confrontation provided by

the therapist appears to be the perturbing factor that makes change possible.

b.   Practice structuring the environment for change using the framework adapted from Hersey and Blanchard in management. Take a specific task that you have mastered and describe or teach it to another person. This task may range from a task or skill you engage in on your job (a therapy skill, a system for keeping records of your therapy, a means of handling a difficult colleague) to a home repair task. The issue is to teach or share what you know with another person. In this sharing, work through the three Hersey-Blanchard steps of (1) providing structure and direction, (2) letting the individual *do* the task, and (3) reinforcing or rewarding positive change. This simple framework is comparable to the structure for dialectical movement.

c.   Change and significant movement from one stage or phase to the next usually are not accomplished in the simple model above. More often, a planned series of interactions such as those presented in Figure 12 are necessary to effect and hold the change of stages. Work through the tasks above again, but this time break them down into more manageable and teachable units so that the individual more gradually learns the integration.

d.   Drawing from the concepts of Marlatt and Gordon, Marx, and Janis, plan systematic interventions to ensure that cognitions and behavior learned from your transformational experiences above are maintained in the natural environment. To paraphrase a statement often attributed to Gordon Paul, generalization and maintenance that are not planned are likely to be lamented.

Summary

The concepts of creativity, change, growth, transformation, and development have been used interchangeably in this chapter. In each case, what already exists in the individual is used as a basis for facilitating future movement, usually toward more complexity and broader understanding, with more potential for action, be it behavior, thought, or feeling.

Creation does not occur alone. It occurs in relationship with the environment. As creation occurs, the environment must also change. However, environments, be they family, the workplace, or the ecology of a nation, do not change as easily as individuals. Thus, the first two major steps of change—getting the individual's attention and somehow initiating change—will be of little avail unless the environment provides some support for this change.

Therapy is a person-environment dialectic. It is a developmental process that is seldom self-sustaining. If we are to maintain developmental transformations from our work, more attention to the environment beyond our immediate efforts in the interview seems essential.

Most critical is that the conditions of change provided by many differing types of therapies supply (1) a structured environment for change; (2) some permission and encouragement for change and creativity, which the client must ultimately undertake alone; and (3) some form of reinforcement and support for the client following the change process. This essentially dialectical person-environment approach is, of course, one of reflexive abstraction and is essentially similar to that of Piaget and his daughter, Lucienne, described at the beginning of this chapter.

The importance and process of transformation have been described in this chapter. If theory is truly to be integrated with practice, the transformational process must be examined in the context of the therapeutic process. That is the task of the next chapter—can transformational change occur in a client as a result of the developmental therapy process?

✤ 6 ✤

The Practice of
Developmental Therapy

Case Examples

The purpose of this chapter is to consider two specific examples of therapeutic change in client cognitive development. The first example presents a detailed analysis of a portion of a single interview; the second examines client progression over seven interviews. Together, the sessions reveal that the process and outcome of cognitive change in counseling and therapy can be assessed fairly specifically and can thus provide an opportunity to (1) illustrate that the developmental therapy conceptions do manifest themselves in empirical reality, (2) demonstrate that useful measuring instruments for the assessment of these effects are possible, (3) discuss more specifically the movement of the dialectic in therapeutic process, and (4) consider the cross-cultural validity of the concepts (the second case presented is of a Japanese client in Tokyo).

Before we examine an interview typescript in detail, the following description of the complexity of dialectical development may be useful.

The Multiple Dialectics of Therapy

Dialectics, it can be generally agreed, is a complex and somewhat obtuse approach to interaction. Thus far, the discussion in this book has been content to illustrate several types of dialectical formulations without differentiating among them. Before we consider a therapy typescript, it seems critical that

226

we examine some of the complex ways dialectics may operate in the process of therapy. The following are some key dialectics always present in the therapeutic interview.

The Dialectics of Two-Person Interaction. The first, and perhaps most important, formulation is that of Piaget's ([1930] 1955) description of children coconstructing reality in relationship one to another:

1. Remark by A.
2. Remark by B adapted to 1.
3. Remark by A adapted to 2 (p. 71).

This same description may, of course, be applied to the interaction of the therapist with the client. The client makes a statement, and the therapist's remark must first be adapted to the statement if the dialectic is to move. Then, in turn, the client adapts his or her next remark to the therapist's.

For existential movement to occur, adaptation communication must occur. If the therapist does not adapt his or her remarks to the client or if the client does not adapt his or her remarks to the therapist's intervention, the dialectic remains stuck and immobile—there is no movement.

Either the client or the therapist in this model can restart the movement of the dialectic. The client in a predominantly assimilative therapy (such as classical U.S. ego-analytic psychology) may eventually accommodate to the therapist's remark, thus reopening existential movement. In a more accommodative, listening style of therapy, the therapist may readapt his or her remark or intervention to meet the unique needs of the client.

If the dialectical interaction is working smoothly, the interview follows the pattern portrayed in Figure 14: The therapist provides an antithesis to the client's synthesis. This is done most often and effectively through confrontation, but listening, interpretation, and other skills can also facilitate the movement of the dialectic. The client's thesis breaks down due to the perturbation of the therapist and continues to move. In assimilation and accommodation terminology, the client accommodates

Figure 14. Smooth Dialectical Interaction Between Therapist and Client

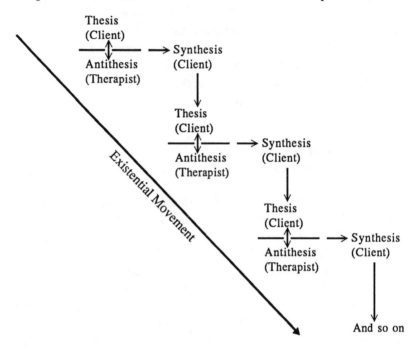

to the therapist, transforms thought and action, and gradually assimilates a new way of being.

The same dual dialectic could be constructed using the therapist's comments as thesis and the client's as antithesis, with the therapist evolving to a new synthesis. In this case, we would see the therapist's remark adapted to the client's remark and the need for continual adaptation on his or her part to facilitate continual movement.

Both dialectical models are occurring simultaneously. Which you attend to, describe, or conduct research on will be your own dialectical impact on the dyad, because the observer impacts the observation through the process of simple observation.

The complexities of therapeutic interaction only begin to appear with this observation. When the constructs of assimilation and accommodation and the dialectic of information-processing theory are superimposed on this model, one begins to sense the need for more simple, linear models of punctuation and description, such as those exemplified by most counseling and therapy theory and by the current state of research in the field.

This particular dialectic could be termed a behavioral dialectic, since what occurs in terms of action can be seen, heard, and often counted. Missing, obviously, are other critical internal cognitive dialectics of the client and the therapist.

Internal Dialectics of Client and Therapist. Two more critical dialectics are occurring between the participants—one within the client and one within the therapist. The client may present an idea (synthesis or thesis). Then, through internal cognitions of that idea (perhaps with help from the therapist), the client begins to sense contradictions (antitheses) in the original idea, and internal cognitive movement has begun.

The therapist, in turn, may have an idea (synthesis or thesis) about a client. External and internal observations may lead the therapist to see contradictions (antitheses) in the original thesis about the client, and a new synthesis about the client will emerge.

The two primarily internal cognitive processes are occurring within the client. These internal processes lead to intentions at the cognitive level that may or may not be acted out on the observable behavioral level.

How client internal cognitions may be changing together with or independent of the therapist and client dialectic are illustrated in Figure 15.

A similar model could be constructed for the internal workings of the mind of the therapist. The distinction between internal and external, of course, can become blurred because cognitions will lead behavior and often become externalized in the process.

Thus, many dialectics are working simultaneously in the process of therapy. What seems to us as therapists the most important and critical is the one we can see, hear, and feel in our relationship with the client. We sense that more is going on than we see and hear and tend to call that dimension the internal

Figure 15. Changing Internal Cognitions Accompanying Therapist
and Client Dialectic

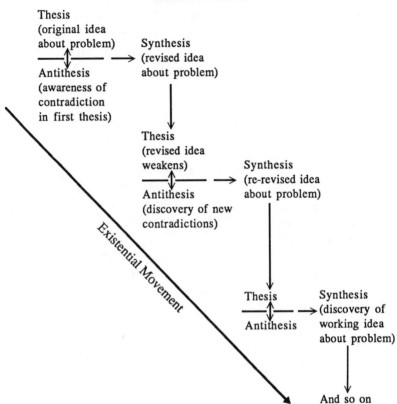

cognitive dialogue of the client. Recent efforts in cognitive
therapy seek to address that important dimension of client
functioning. But there is still more to the dialectical interactions.

   The "True" Complexity of Complexity in Therapy. There
are many other dialectics in operation, some in our conscious
awareness (such as the ones described), some that we are only
dimly aware of (such as the impact of our office or work setting on the client, issues such as our ability to communicate
trustworthiness and status, and factors of culture and gender).
Beyond that we are most likely unaware (unconscious) that our

smile may remind our client of his or her father or mother or that the words "abortion," "separation," or "admission to Westwood University" mean something very different to the client than they do to us. This process of uncovering the meaning of key words and constructs is another important part of the dialectics of therapy.

Currently, the field of therapy is undergoing what is termed the "cognitive unconscious revolution" (see Mahoney, 1984, 1985; Van Den Bergh and Eelen, 1984; Meichenbaum and Gilmore, 1984; Gelso and Carter, 1985). The growing consensus is that "unconscious" means "that of which we are presently unaware." This definition, of course, is in accord with the constructs of long-term memory discussed in Chapter Two. Long-term memory impacts and affects our perceptual processes (through the "eye of consciousness"), cognitions, and behaviors. While we can bring "unconscious" functioning to our attention, there is always something going on beyond our awareness.

What is going on beyond our awareness could be described as the operation of the dialectics of the unconscious or long-term memory. Data are taken in through counseling and therapy, but how they are taken in and how they are processed depends on the preexisting structures in long-term memory. These structures react and interreact with new data in a dialectical relationship. We do not just impact behavior and cognitions with our actions; we are also impacting something beyond our awareness and that of our client. This "something beyond" is the dialectic that occurs in long-term memory or the unconscious.

For example, consider the overt behavior of the therapist in relationship to the client. At the first level, we have observable dialectics, as each remark is adapted to the next remark through communication adaptation. At the second level, the remarks are processed internally by the therapist and the client in terms of cognitions that are relatively accessible. Finally, the perceptions and cognitions are impacting and impacted by the preexisting assimilated structures in long-term memory. Whether or not new data will be accommodated into long-term memory will depend on how open the "eye of consciousness" is. It is

possible that strongly assimilated information in long-term
memory will stop the movement of the dialectic, even though
to outward appearances change is occurring. It is this closing of
the unconscious gap that is represented by the lower-level defense mechanisms of Freud. The dialectics of internal long-term
memory processing are represented greatly oversimplified in
Figure 16.

Figure 16. The Dialectics of Internal Long-Term Memory Processing,
Simplified

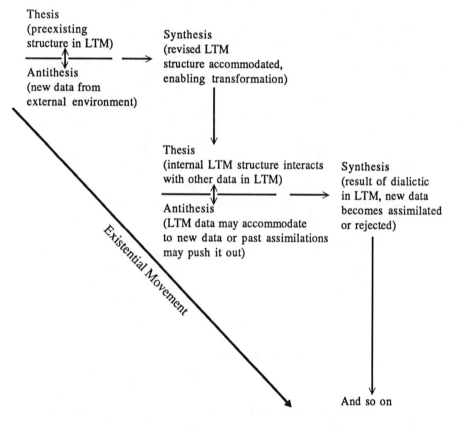

Needless to say, the number of dialectical interactions in
long-term memory or the unconscious are multitudinous. External data from the therapist or one's own internal cognitions can

bring about a vast host of interactions. Given the vast array of variables, it seems indeed remarkable that therapy does any good or has any impact on the client at all. The portrayal above suggests that it is extremely important that the therapist make contact—specifically, to obtain and maintain a relationship so that it becomes possible for the client to accommodate to new data.

The Multitude of Dialectical Relations. It should be apparent at this point that the therapist-client relationship has many separate, distinct, and yet interrelating and interacting dialectics that are occurring simultaneously. The person-environment dialectic of counseling and psychotherapy includes many dimensions for possible growth and change.*

It would appear that any effort to measure holistic change is bound to fail. After all, empirical measures only touch on a part of the total interaction of developmental therapy. An answer to this question of measurement lies in the concept of *punctuation* from systems theory. A punctuation is a "slice of life," a small piece that is cut off and separated from the attached whole. The punctuation is artificial and often linear, but punctuations "work." For example, the world is round; theoretically, a tennis court, football field, or desert cannot be truly flat because of the curvature of the earth and other physical fac-

---

*It seems appropriate at this point to repeat the basic definition of the dialectic presented earlier, since this concept is used in so many related ways.

The word dialectic is used in several different contexts in different ways. Two major formulations underlie these distinctions: (1) the dialectic is a constant process that is always present and active, as in the example of the young children described by Piaget. In such cases the dialectic occurs without conscious awareness on the part of the participants. This same lack of awareness of process may occur between client and therapist and also seems to be part of our general way of being; (2) one may become conscious of the dialectical process. This awareness shows up particularly in therapies such as family therapy and feminist therapy, which attempt to examine the interview process as a person-environment interaction.

In summary, the dialectic is always present even though we may be unaware of it. The words "person-environment" interaction, more familiar to the counseling and therapy professions, may often be used as substitute wording.

tors. Nonetheless, it is possible, for practical purposes, to measure off ("punctuate") a tennis court.

In a similar fashion, it is possible to separate out small pieces of development in therapy. This measurement may also work for our purposes. Clients may show change or even a "cure." But the fact remains that we have only measured a small part of holistic development. This measurement may be useful, but it is incomplete. In addition, we must not forget that the act of measuring impacts what is measured in some way, usually unknown to us. The researcher is embedded in the text of research, not separate from the process as Descartes and the early scientific theorists would have us believe. (The scale for assessing developmental level in Figure 10 is, of necessity, incomplete.)

Systems and interactional notions, however, also point out that any action in one part of the system impacts the total network. Thus, the punctuation afforded by one slice of research reveals change. While the nature of change throughout the system (and its side effects) are not measured, a snapshot may be provided suggesting that some sort of change has occurred. And if the client feels better, perhaps the snapshot of research is a useful, practical piece of work, much like our tennis court. What is not measured and not observed could be described as the unseen "side effects." (These aspects of developmental therapy represent unconscious development and will be explored in more detail at a later point.) Another way to consider the multitude of side effects that occur throughout the therapeutic process is through the operation of multiple dialectics.

Armed with awareness of the limited punctuations we must use for description, let us turn a bit more humbly to what might be termed "developmental microanalysis in the interview."

Developmental Microanalysis in the Interview

This section examines portions of a single interview and illustrates how the developmental dialectic may be examined and at least partially measured from moment to moment in the verbal exchange that goes on between client and therapist.

The following case example places a white middle-class female therapist with a white middle-class male client. The evaluative model discussed below is presented in the context of a common client concern—that of getting along with one's children. This client starts with a discussion of preoperational anger in relation to his children. The therapist at 3 immediately grounds his thinking in affective dimensions and at 4 the client moves to concrete thinking. At 5 the therapist moves to a late concrete operational style followed by a patterned intervention at the formal operational level at 7. This concludes the first phase of the interview. It should be noted that the interpretation at 7 was intended as a negative example in the demonstration, but nonetheless does impact the client's thinking.

In later portions of the interview, the therapist helps the client see that his patterns of behavior with his children repeat themselves in other situations as well. This portion of the interview takes place mostly in an environment of formal operations.

The text of the interview will be rated in several major categories.* The therapist's statements will be rated for (1) the developmental environment provided by her statement, (2) the verbal microskills used, and (3) the nature of the confrontation (if any) present. Client statements will be rated on the developmental level scale. Both therapist and client statements will be discussed as to *some* of their dialectical implications.

1. *Mary:* Would you like to talk a little about the concern that you have to share today, George?
   Developmental environment: Coaching/concrete operational.

---

*This interview, which has been slightly edited, is taken from the videotape "Interpretation" (M. Ivey, 1983), which presents Mary Bradford Ivey demonstrating the microskill of interpretation or reframing. The transcript is also discussed in another frame of reference by Ivey, Ivey, and Simek-Downing (1987). The transcript is copyrighted © by Microtraining Associates, Box 641, North Amherst, Mass. 01059, and is used by permission.

Microskill: Open question.

Confrontation: The therapist invites the client to talk about discrepancy, which perturbs his present state of being—"the concern." The discrepancy implicitly addresses the distinction between the present situation and the ideal situation. We can usually assume that an incongruity between the present and desired situation brings a client to therapy.

Dialectical status: The therapist seeks to facilitate client talk about his concern.

2. *George:*   Well, yes, there's something that even happened this morning, and that is . . . ah . . . the house was a mess. And we had some stuff to do before we went out. So, I knew the kids were busy, so I started to pick up for them. And as I picked up—I didn't have any feelings, I guess, as I began. But, I began to get more tired and really began to feel angry.

Client developmental level: 2, alpha solution. The client is working on only part of the contradiction. He is pre-operational because he is not able to operate predictably on the environment.

Dialectical status: The client presents his thesis, which begins to deconstruct into its own inconsistent antithesis.

3. *Mary:*   Tired and angry?

Developmental environment: Environmental, structuring/sensori-motor, represents moving back a level to ground in sensory experience. As the client is obviously capable of formal operations, he is also being asked to think and to reflect his feelings. This lead is a good example of how a response could be interpreted from one vantage point as sensori-motor but from another as a substage of formal operational thinking.

Microskill: Minimal encouragement designed to facilitate client exploration of meaning of key constructs in more detail.

Confrontation: By putting the weight on the underlying emotions, the present client thesis is being attacked by the therapist antithesis.

Dialectical status: The emotions "tired and angry" provide a foundation for the client's thesis. Exploring these emotions may be anticipated to result in a new synthesis within the client.

4. *George:* Yeah, ah, you see, I've got a lot to do myself. What am I doing picking up this stuff for the kids? . . . So I just went ahead, but I ended up yelling, and it ended up one of those horrible scenes, Mary.

Developmental level: 3, beta solution. The client is presenting data that are interchangeable with the situation. The client is able to describe the concrete operations that occurred in a sequential fashion. There is some ability at the end to discuss the event in late concrete or early formal operational terms (". . . it ended up one of those horrible scenes"). (Behaviorally, the client is most likely still preoperational. This rating only concerns cognitions.)

Dialectical status: The client is now describing his synthesis of existing data in clear fashion. Many beta solutions represent a cognitive equilibration of homeostasis.

5. *Mary:* So you were tired and pushed and you ended up picking up for the kids and doing something you really didn't want to do?

Developmental environment: Coaching/concrete operational.

Microskills: Reflection of feeling, paraphrase.

Confrontation: A clear confrontation of the discrepancy in the client between what he is doing and what he does not want to do. "On one hand, you didn't need to do . . . but you did . . ."

Dialectical status: The therapist has reflected the client's synthesis of data. The synthesis summarizes obvious contradictions in the client's thinking, which should cause dialectical movement in the near future.

6. *George:*   Yeah ...

    Developmental level: 3, interchangeable beta response.
    Dialectical status: The contradiction is being held and
    observed; the homeostasis of the beta solution seems
    clear. Yet this very observation of one's own internal
    behavioral and cognitive contradictions often paves the
    way for developmental change.

7. *Mary:*   You know, it goes back to, it seems to me, you
    know, we talked about some things like this before. . . .
    You're very much like your father. . . . You know, he
    likes to have everything organized and he likes to take
    charge of things, a little bit compulsive about things.

    Developmental environment: Consulting/formal opera-
    tions. Patterns of thinking and behavior are being exam-
    ined. The client is being encouraged to think about
    thinking and behavior.
    Microskill: Interpretation. A new frame of reference is
    being supplied. Interpretations that provide alternative
    frames of reference tend to be at the formal operations
    level.
    Confrontation: The confrontation in this case places
    the client's personal thesis about self alongside an
    antithesis about the father offered by the therapist.
    "On the one hand, you behave ... but on the other
    hand, we see your father behaving ..."
    Dialectical status: An antithesis has been presented in
    opposition to the client's precariously balanced thesis.
    The therapist's antithesis enters into the consciousness
    of the client, and the process of client accommodation
    to a new perception is possible. Old assimilations of the
    client are being challenged. It may be anticipated that
    the client is also being impacted at the level of other
    unconscious dialectic formulations.

8. *George:*   (*somewhat defensively*) You feel I'm too com-
    pulsive?

    Developmental level: 3+. The client is struggling with a
    late beta or early gamma solution.

Dialectical status: His thesis about himself is changing through the confrontation. His defensive tone of voice and nervous gestures indicate perturbation, but he still has not accommodated these new perceptions into his long-term memory.

9. *Mary:* I would think so in this situation. You didn't need to do all these things, but you just went ahead and did them anyway.

   Developmental environment: Consulting/formal operational. The therapist is encouraging the client to think about his behaviors.

   Microskill: Feedback.

   Confrontation: "On the one hand, you didn't need . . . but on the other, you went ahead and . . ."

   Dialectical status: This intervention supports and helps fix the client's new cognitive synthesis through focusing on contradictions in the client's actions.

10. *George:* (*more acceptingly*) Ah, I hadn't thought of it that way.

    Developmental level: 4, an early gamma solution. The client is internalizing a new way to conceptualize or think about the situation. His cognitions are shifting.

    Dialectical status: A new synthesis has been or is being evolved. It may be anticipated that the primary change is at the internal cognitive, dialectical level, although it is possible (even probable) that unconscious factors in long-term memory are also being impacted. Very shortly, this newly evolved synthesis also deconstructs into thesis and antithesis through its own internal contradictions and irrationality.

[The video demonstration stops at this point and Mary Bradford Ivey points out that she deliberately planned a negative reframe as a demonstration of how not to do an interpretation. It may be noted, however, that the impact of the negative interpretation was in some ways positive, again illustrating that the "goodness" of a world view or construction lies in the eye of the beholder.]

11. *Mary:*   OK, I, let's summarize where we were after that
     awful negative interpretation that I did. Ummm . . . the
     house was really a mess. And you really were very, very
     tired and you were angry and you did all the work picking
     things up. Ummm, have you ever, can you get into that
     feeling of tired and angry? Have you had that same feeling
     in other situations? Can you get into that feeling? (*The
     client closes his eyes in response to the gestalt-type inter-
     vention and physically seems to move inside his body.*)
          Developmental environment: Multiple: sensori-motor,
     in terms of getting into body feeling; concrete opera-
     tional, in terms of building on the specific concretes of
     the situation; formal operational, in terms of the
     search for patterns ("Have you had that same feeling
     in other situations?"). Generally speaking, the stronger
     therapeutic interventions are those that work on all
     levels of client functioning. If the therapist added di-
     mensions of transference to the intervention, this could
     be considered the examination of the dialectic. Or, if
     she sought to have the client introspect on the nature
     of dialectical interaction, this also would represent a
     dialectical intervention.
          Microskills: Summarization, directive.
          Confrontation: "On the one hand, you have these feel-
     ings and thoughts in this situation; on the other hand,
     do they occur in other situations as well?" Note that
     virtually every lead the therapist offers contains a con-
     frontation and thus continues the existential movement
     of the client.
          Dialectical status: The client's synthesis is being exam-
     ined, particularly for repeating patterns of cognition
     and behavior. This could be considered a request for
     late formal operational thinking in that the client is
     being asked to think about patterns of behavior. It is
     not just examining patterns, but a beginning search for
     "patterns of patterns."

12. *George:*   Oh yeah, I very much can. Ah . . . in fact right
     away it comes to me that my secretary, Georgia . . . and

Georgia is a lovely person. And if I detail everything for Georgia to do, she does a marvelous job. But I often find . . .

Developmental level: 4. The gamma solution is illustrated as the client is generating new knowledge.

Dialectical status: Immediately, as the client finds a new synthesis and new knowledge, he starts recognizing internal contradictions in his past synthesis of behavior with Georgia. ". . . she does a marvelous job, but I often find . . ." He is examining patterns of behavior.

13. *Mary:* You look angry right there. (*The therapist notes a contradiction in the client's facial expression.*)

Developmental environment: Consulting/formal operational. The client is being urged to think about and be aware of feelings. However, the grounding in sensory experience should be noted as well as the immediacy and concreteness of the therapist's feedback of emotional contradictions.

Microskill: Feedback and reflection of feeling.

Confrontation: "On the one hand, you say . . . but on the other hand, you look angry."

Dialectical status: The client is talking about helping the secretary, but the therapist immediately notes a contradiction between his words and nonverbal expression. The frown very possibly in this situation represents the appearance of unconscious dimensions from long-term memory of which the client is presently unaware. Recognizing this, the therapist provides an opportunity for loosening the preassimilated constructs in long-term memory.

14. *George:* Ah . . . that I end up doing Georgia's work and she sits there reading a mgazine. Sometimes it's harder to explain to her what to do, so I just go ahead and do it myself. And I really don't blow up at her. I think sometimes the poor kids get me blowing up because Georgia isn't doing her job.

Developmental level: 5. A transcendent cognitive solution has been demonstrated. The defense mechanism of displacement has been understood as a pattern. This represents a moment of insight, the transformation of old data into a new structure.

Dialectical status: It may be anticipated that this new synthesis will itself soon break down into a new thesis and antithesis. It might be pointed out that true synthesis would require different behaviors in the real world. The cognitions have clearly changed, and one must suspect that unconscious thought processes not immediately accessible have been impacted as well.

15. *Mary:*   Because she's not doing her job, you're doing Georgia's job and getting angry at the kids.

Developmental environment: Consulting/formal operational, examination of patterns. The causation patterns examined here do not include underlying client assumptions and thus represent early formal operations.

Microskill: Interpretation.

Confrontation: "On the one hand, she's not doing her job, so on the other, you are doing it for her. As a result you are getting angry at the kids." In this case the confrontation includes the client's new synthesis.

Dialectical status: This interpretation helps "set" the new synthesis in the client's mind. In the next client response, we will note that he has incorporated this new synthesis in his own mind, but he is already becoming aware of new internal contradictions. This continuous dialectical movement provides the growth dimensions of developmental therapy.

16. *George:*   Yeah, I kinda like Georgia . . . and she comes in and talks about her problems with me and, you know, I kinda like to help her when I can . . . and I know she's having some issues right now. So I . . . nonetheless, it still leaves it right here on my shoulders. (*He touches his shoulders as if to represent the responsibility resting there.*)

Developmental level: 2. The affect is separate from the feelings. In another frame of reference, this could be considered typical of formal operations in that the client is conducting a great deal of thinking about thinking. Further, the client is aware of his groundedness in sensori-motor experience. The ratings, however, are concerned with dialectical movement as much or more than with the status of the client's being.

Dialectical status: A new synthesis is beginning to be examined.

17. *Mary:*   Leaves you tight and angry. Uh-huh . . . (*Pause.*)

Developmental environment: Consulting/formal operational, but grounded in sensory experience.

Microskill: Reflection of feeling (through reading nonverbals).

Confrontation: "On the one hand, you say . . . but on the other hand, your body is tight and angry."

Dialectical status: Focuses on weakness in new synthesis.

18. *George:*   Yes. (*Pause. George seems to be absorbing the contradiction.*)

Developmental level: 4. The client seems to be integrating the ideas into a new synthesis.

Dialectical status: A new synthesis is already emerging at a broader and deeper level than the last synthesis. The client appears to be accommodating to new thinking and creatively transforming old cognitions into new.

19. *Mary:*   Remember how we talked about some transactional analysis concepts, and we talked about the concept of the, ah, critical parent? I sometimes wonder in this situation if you're not playing a parent role with her. You know, you . . .

Developmental environment: Consulting/formal operational. The therapist is reframing the situation for the client. Transactional analysis as a theory contains some aspects of dialectics. The concept of "transaction," for example between parent and child, requires clients to examine the nature of dialectical relationships. Ivey, Ivey, and Simek-Downing (1987) refer to transactional analysis as a systemic therapy, recognizing some of these dialectical dimensions.

Microskill: Interpretation.

Confrontation: "On the one hand, your thesis has been that you're helping Georgia, but on the other hand, perhaps you are serving as a parent."

Dialectical status: An antithesis is currently being offered by the therapist in contrast to the client's weakening thesis. With the abstraction, more and more data are being considered by the therapist and the client. It should be apparent that an underlying thesis of the therapist is that the original overt behavior with the children serves as an underlying metaphor for many issues in the client's life.

20. *George:* In other words, like the kids, I'm playing the parent role with Georgia.

Developmental level: 5. The client is again generating a new and larger pattern or synthesis in his cognitions. Again, this synthesis is not necessarily manifested in behavioral change.

Dialectical status: A new synthesis is emerging.

21. *Mary:* Yeah, the same kind of thing. You know you're doing her work for her and you're letting her get by with not doing it and then you're coming home and, you know, you're taking it out on the kids . . . the same sort of thing with the kids. How does that seem to fit with you?

Developmental environment: Consulting/formal operations, examination of patterns.

Microskills: Interpretation followed by check-out.

Confrontation: "On the one hand, you didn't see this pattern of behavior and thought before, but here it is."

Dialectical status: The therapist is encouraging the generation of a more broadly based, powerful synthesis in which more specific pieces of behavior and thought are gathered into a larger gestalt. We are seeing the repetition of the primary circular reaction that builds to secondary (and perhaps tertiary) circular reactions. As can be seen in the next reactions of the client, the therapist is very likely touching the client at multiple levels: behavioral, cognitive, and unconscious.

22.   *George:*   (*grabs stomach*) . . . I feel my body just sort of react to that. Yeah, I hadn't thought about that really. I do tend to be too critical of people. Ah . . . I . . . but, the thing is . . . they just aren't doing it—that doesn't sound as bad as compulsive, but . . . on the other hand . . . being critical all the time.

> *Developmental level:* 5, but multiple in that the client has responded to the dialectic of the therapist. The moment of feeling (grabbing the stomach) represents the critical moment where cognition and emotion become one. This paradoxically resembles the lowest stage of affect wherein the person *is* his feelings. George in this statement actually begins in sensori-motor experience (grabbing his stomach), then identifies some preoperational elements ("I feel my body just sort of react to that"), discusses them in concrete operational terms ("they just aren't doing the job"), and finally starts again looking at patterns within the self ("It isn't as bad as compulsive, but . . ."). In one client statement may be found all experience. It is this type of simultaneous experience that suggests that the client is indeed reshuffling thought and which may later lead to more effective new actions.
>
> *Dialectical status:* We see the evolution of a new synthesis in the client, but the therapist does not let it end there.

23.   *Mary:*   Yeah, but there are some positives in that situation, George. Can you see some of the positives? I mean, not only are you a critical parent, you're also a nurturing parent, you know.

> *Developmental environment:* Dialectic. The client is being encouraged to examine self in relationship.
>
> *Microskill:* Interpretation.
>
> *Confrontation:* "You see the negatives in this situation as . . . but on the other hand, there are some positives as well."

Dialectical status: Once having discovered a consistent pattern that becomes a newly discovered and accepted synthesis on the part of the client, the therapist introduces still another contradiction in terms of a dialectical reframe (interpretation) of the situation. In this case, the thesis is coming out of the therapist's experience and transactional analysis theory (her own past and present assimilations of client experience). Her task is to incorporate this new synthesis of data into client experiencing.

24. *George:* Positives? How's that? That doesn't make sense.
Developmental level: 2. The client's synthesis is perturbed by the therapist's new confrontation.
Dialectical status: The client has denied the interpretation, but the interpretation remains open because the dialectic has not been closed. If the client had denied the positive reframe ("No way. You're wrong! I'm a bad person to do that.") the developmental level scale would be rated as 1 owing to the client's denial of the comment. A rating of 5 would be possible if the client had immediately integrated that reframe and interpretation into his own view of self. A rating of 2 seems minimal for the progression of effective developmental therapy. Without at least an incomplete preoperational response, the client seems to be inaccessible to developmental change.

25. *Mary:* Well, I think that you're really trying to take care of everybody when you're straightening up the house and you know that people are tired.
George: That's true.

Mary: You know your secretary's under a lot of pressure. You know that the kids have all kinds of work to do, and so in some ways you can almost reframe what you're doing into being a positive, ummm . . . nurturing type parent. Does that fit? (*Here, the therapist explicates her thinking and draws together many facts and feelings for the client. She also provides further data to justify and*

substantiate her positive reframe. Finally, by encouraging
the client to react to her ("Does that fit?"), she opens the
way for dialectic examination of her thesis.)

Developmental environment: Dialectic.

Microskills: Summarization, interpretation, check-out.

Confrontation: "On the one hand, you could define
your hard work and effort as critical parent, but on the
other hand, it could be reframed as positive caring."

Dialectical status: The client's recently absorbed thesis
is being challenged by the antithesis of the therapist.

26. *George:*   Yeah, nurturing comes up, it feels right because
I guess I did say I like the kids . . . you know . . . they're
busy and I like to help them and I know that Georgia is
not really in a great spot. But it sure ends up with me getting angry. . . . Ah! So, in effect, by being nurtur . . . so
nurturing, I end up being . . .

Mary: Very critical.

George: . . . very critical and very angry.

Developmental level: 5. This comment represents again
the moment of insight and is more comprehensive and
complete than earlier insights. What has happened here
is that the client is able to synthesize several contradictions at once under the new term "nurturing."

Dialectic status: The client is simultaneously examining
behavior and cognitions and seems to have absorbed or
accommodated the new antithesis offered by the therapist. The depth of this accommodation is exemplified
by the creative use of the new data (most likely it has
been assimilated quickly into long-term memory) to
solve new problems. The cognitions of the therapist
have very much entered the inner world of the client.

27. *Mary:*   Yeah. And my question to you is, where is the
adult? You know how we've talked about the parent,
adult, and child. Where is the adult in the situation that
takes charge and does something?

Developmental environment: Coaching/concrete operational, in that the client is being urged to move beyond

cognition to action. Having done fairly well at solving a cognitive task, a new problem clearly arises: How can one act with one's being? Unless matched by concrete operations in the environment, the most sophisticated formal and dialectical operations are often of little use. The critical question is again raised: Are "higher" cognitions necessarily "higher"?

Microskill: Open question with an implicit interpretation.

Confrontation: "On the one hand, you have thought well about this situation and have some good ideas, but now, on the other hand, are you going to be able to *do* something differently?"

Dialectical status: The flow of dialectic existential movement continues. Certain behavioral patterns have led to cognitions, and these cognitions have reinforced behavior. At this point, the dialectic of therapist-client interaction has loosened the cognitive dialectic, but the problem of action on the environment still remains.

If we were to examine the next portion of this typescript, we would find that the client, despite excellent cognitive functioning, remained preoperational in that he was unable to do anything differently. In cases such as this, the treatment of choice often becomes some variety of assertiveness training in which the preoperational client is first grounded in sensorimotor reality and then a prescriptive set of behavioral actions is planned for change in the environment. Once that change occurs, it is helpful to reinforce the change with cognitive, and hopefully unconscious, changes as well.

It is important to note that this therapist never was satisfied with the responses of her client. In virtually every response, she emphasizes contradiction and irrationality in the client's statements. She sought ever-enlarging awareness for the client and the taking in and accounting for ever-increasing amounts of data. Clearly, the large cognitive synthesis just evolved by the client is being attacked by the therapist, who again points out the contradictions in the client's behavior.

With the aid of the therapist, George is able to move from

his first response of 2 to a mean response of 3.8 for his first seven responses. At the end, there are some level-5 responses and a mean of 3.4 for the final six client responses. Also note in the first seven client responses a growth pattern of 2, 3, 3, 3, 4, and 4, leading to the 5 at response number 14. In responses 16 through 30 you will find the client moving fairly rapidly from level 2 to level 5. These patterns of data suggest a means by which a therapist could monitor how a client responds to help within a single interview or over a period of therapy.

The developmental level scale is a process scale that is most often related to the immediate confrontation made by the therapist's preceding intervention. As such, the scale is concerned with movement and how well each client response integrates with the preceding client statement. This client, for example, is clearly able to function at the formal operational level. However, much of his thinking is stuck in less effective modes of being. It would be possible to define his responses as substages within a specific developmental task of the formal operational stage. However, when the scale is conceptualized as oriented toward movement, the rationale for the present suggested scoring system should be apparent.

Let us also consider the movement of this client in a single interview on the other possible evaluative dimensions outlined earlier in this book. Specifically, George has:

1. Developed more congruent verbal behavior. He appears to have brought feelings more into accord with cognitions. Critical to the success of therapy, of course, will be the degree to which he can apply these cognitions to the real world.
2. The negative "I" statements (such as in 2. *George:* "I didn't have any feelings . . . I get more tired . . .") represent a person who feels out of control but are replaced with more positive statements ("I like the kids" and "By being so nurturing, I end up being. . . very critical and very angry"). This type of statement represents insight but not action. In terms of active involvement in the real world, the client may still be preoperational.
3. The confused and negative emotions have been clarified

and separated and now indicate a more positive orientation.

4. The adjectives the client used to describe himself in the
    first part of the session (tired and angry) tend to be passive,
    impotent, and negative but later become more active, po-
    tent, and positive ("I like the kids") and more acknowledg-
    ing of nurturing aspects of himself. Examination of such
    descriptors should soon lead to a systematic format for
    classifying client "semantic differentials" based on actual
    client language. Given the portion of a single session, the
    changes are not nearly as large as those that occur in the
    seven interviews conducted by Fukuhara that are discussed
    in the next section, although the principles of change re-
    main the same.

5. The client's locus of control appears to have become some-
    what more internal, and his cognitions seem to be less con-
    trolled by external events.

6. Through interaction with the therapist, George has moved
    to a more interdependent, dialectical view. At the begin-
    ning of the session, he appeared to be seeking to control
    the situation and thus was deeply embedded in it; he has
    made some useful progress in disengaging himself from
    overinvolvement with the family and with his secretary.

Although this client has made progress in this short interview, there remains much ground to cover. The next chapter will
present the holistic developmental notions of Gilligan (1982).
It can be argued that George is very much embedded in a linear,
male model of cognition. Although this client has made progress
in a brief time, it should be apparent that it will be necessary to
untie many knots before he can move to his full formal operational potential and become fully in tune with his emotions.

The Importance of Confrontation

Despite all the systems of analysis, rating, and classification, one fact should be clear from this interview, namely that
there is constant, insistent emphasis on confrontation in vir-

tually every therapist lead. This constant unbalancing of client homeostasis forces the client to explore new areas of cognition and being. Without the persistent emphasis on change and movement, the client would most likely have stayed the same.

Clients usually come to us in a state of equilibration or cognitive balance that somehow is not working for them. Yet, they will hang onto this cognitive balance unless it is effectively challenged. The manner of challenge or confrontation may be very explicit or it may be quite subtle. What is needed is the exploration of alternative frames of reference for examining the same situation. While confrontation is stressed here, we should recall that the style of confrontation should match the culture and personal constructs of the client. Such a direct confrontative approach would obviously be unsuitable for many clients. Work by Masterson (1981), for example, provides highly specific therapeutic suggestions. The borderline patient may benefit from the systematic variation of the confronting and supportive therapist, while the narcissistic individual may benefit from interpretation and a more subdued form of indirect confrontation.

Perhaps we have been using the wrong word when we seek "change" in therapy. It is possible that the more descriptive and accurate word is "movement," the constant ability to confront the endless discrepancy, incongruity, conflict, and confusion that undergird our lives. Perhaps the best we can hope for is existential movement, the ongoing process of the dialectic, which is so representative of life itself: "The moving finger writes; and, having writ, moves on."

As a preliminary test of the cross-cultural relevance of the present model, let us now turn to a detailed examination of a series of seven interviews completed with a college student in Japan.

Seven Sessions in Japan

Fukuhara (1984) presents a case of developmental change and growth over seven sessions with an eighteen-year-old university client who introduces her problem as follows:

I am in love with a freshman boy who likes me.
This spring, I met this boy . . . and thought our
love would last a long time. However, when I returned from summer vacation, he did not even
seem to want to talk to me. This finally made me
so angry that I became aggressive and we had a
fight. Surprisingly, my boyfriend seemed to like
being told off. Still, he doesn't ask me out, and the
only time I see him is at the activity club. . . . I
project into the future and think that if I continue
to love him, we would eventually get married.
What would my life be then? Would I have to make
sacrifices to his will? . . . Would this eventually de-
stroy my love for him? Should I give up on him
now? [p. 3].

The client's text suggests an embeddedness or an overattachment that is preoperational in nature. The general theme of the
first interview focuses on a relationship described essentially as
"He is mine; I am his." This form of reasoning is indeed holistic, but due to the overattachment allows for no balance of
separation and the needed eventual individuation. The therapeutic task, then, is to put the relationship in perspective, to assist
the client in generating a useful separation of self from others.

Table 1 presents the client's perception of her relationship with the young man through the seven sessions. It may be
observed that she moved from almost total integration of self
with other (sessions 1 and 2) to partial, beginning separation of
self from the boyfriend (sessions 3 and 4) to thinking about the
situation (sessions 5 and 6) and finally to thinking about herself
and needed action (session 7). This movement represents a gradual progression through many of the conceptions of developmental therapy.

As a university student, this client is clearly at the formal
operations level of cognitive capacity; yet her thinking is almost
totally embedded in a sensori-motor reality in that she is ruled
or determined by the environment. The second interview reveals preoperational thinking with some elements of magical

Table 1. An Evaluation of Cognitive Change over Seven Interviews

Interview Session	Client Perception of Relationship	Client Reality Testing Rated by Three Observers			Cognitive Level
1	He is mine; I am his.	--	--	--	Sensori-motor
2	His whole existence is for me; my whole existence is for him; I should come up to his expectations.	--	-	o	Preoperational
3	He should be different from me, but I cannot admit it.	-	o	o	Early concrete operations
4	I can keep my identity only when I am away from him.	o	o	+	Concrete operations
5	I have come to understand his behavior, which is different from mine.	o	+	+	Formal operations
6	I am myself; he is himself.	++	++	++	Formal operations, beginning of dialectic, and integration of all levels of development.
7	I have to do something for my own good.	++	++	++	All levels working simultaneously. Ready for new developmental task.

Note: --very poor reality testing; - poor reality testing; o average reality testing; + good reality testing; ++ very good reality testing.

Source: Fukuhara, 1984, used by permission.

thinking, but she has separated out some of the elements accurately. However, in the third session, we begin to see the transition from preoperational to concrete operations, and the client is able to state in the fourth session a linear, true concrete operation: "I can keep my identity only when I am away from him."

The fifth session reveals the formal operations of which the client is capable. Her reality testing improves, and she reflects on the situation and her own behavior and is able to separate self from situation ("I have come to understand his own behavior, which is different from mine").

The sixth session opens the way to the dialectic, and she establishes a truth ("I am myself; he is himself"). This represents a separation from the boyfriend and simultaneously an attachment to the self and individuation. Having deconstructed the relationship, she returns to a new developmental task, stated simultaneously in sensori-motor, concrete operational, and formal operational terms: "I have to do something for my own good."

This client was able to take data in but assimilated it into her own perspective, which was heavily influenced by feeling. She was unable to accommodate new data from her disinterested boyfriend. By the end of therapy, she had creatively transformed much of her thinking. It could be argued that she moved from early to late formal operations through the process of this therapy, although it is also apparent that her behavior and much of her thought was preoperational in nature.

In these seven interviews, the client has moved through the developmental cycle with the assistance of the therapist. The client is, at the conclusion of therapy, ready to begin again on new developmental tasks. The change of cognition (which leads to action) is not startling but represents the desired outcome of therapy, which is simultaneously a process that leads to something else.

Again, it is important to note that the cognitive changes proposed in this book are clearly manifested in a culture different from the United States. As the cognitive process is structural, rather than content oriented, it may be possible to examine cross-cultural similarities and differences in development using this model.

This Japanese student may also be evaluated on the specific behavioral criteria for assessment of development summarized in Chapter Four. Specifically, the student has:

1. Changed from incongrous verbal behavior ("I should come up to his expectations") to congruent verbalizations ("I am myself; he is himself" and "I have to do something for my own good"). We can assume that nonverbal behavior has also become more congruent.
2. Changed negative "I" statements ("I cannot admit it") to positive ("I am myself").
3. Elaborated formerly negative, confused, and inappropriate emotions into positive ("I have to do something for my own good").
4. Moved her adjective descriptors from passive, impotent, and negative ("I can keep my own identity only when I am away from him") to active, potent, and positive ("I have to do something for my own good").
5. Changed the locus of control from external to internal.
6. Moved from excessive dependence to a more interdependent and dialectical formulation of self.

Given that the Japanese culture values dependence more than does the independent North American culture and, in general, is considered quite different, it is interesting that the anticipated structure of change presented in Chapter Four is clearly manifested here. Possibly the client pattern here represents changes in Japanese culture as it moves swiftly to a more Western orientation. How would an older, more traditional Japanese have acted here?

Given these several perspectives on client developmental movement, it becomes confusing as to "where" the client truly "is." The answer to this is in the eye of the beholder. From Gilligan's frame of reference, the client has simply expanded her knowledge of herself and her complex network of relationships. In short, in therapy everything is happening at once. Simultaneous and sequential behaviors, thoughts, feelings, and actions are occurring all together. Put in its simplest metaphorical terms, the client's deck of cards has been reshuffled; the order may be different, but the deck is the same. However, not totally the same, for the client in her relationship to Fukuhara has taken on a trace of the therapist. A part of Fukuhara has entered into the client's thinking, just as the first shuffling of a new deck of cards leaves it a trace more flexible. Similarly, Fukuhara acquires a trace of the client. We, as viewers of Fukuhara's observations of the client's observations about herself and her male friend, may also perhaps acquire a trace of learning from the reshuffling.

Theory into Practice

Three central constructs form the basis of this chapter. The first examines the nature of multiple dialectics, which play themselves out in the interview, and suggests that the true complexity of the interview can never be fully summarized in words, theory, or research. The second provides (despite the seeming impossibility of the task) a detailed analysis of the interview. Finally, a series of seven interviews from Japan are reviewed as a means of evaluating developmental change over time. The following suggestions are presented to aid the therapist in moving from theory to practice.

Construct 1: Multiple dialectics of therapist-client, internal dialectics within therapist and client, and a vast array of person-environment dialectics exist within a single therapy session.

Dialectics are all too often oversimplified as the simple operation of a single thesis-antithesis. Marxist analysis often incorrectly assumes a simple opposition between capitalism and socialism. Added to this important and central distinction should be multiple factors of sociocultural history, the economic resources of a country, family structure, and the unique dialectics of the individual in regard to sociocultural surroundings.

Just as multiple dialectics play themselves out in an economy, so do multiple dialectics manifest themselves in therapy.

1. *Learning Objective:* To be able to examine a therapy interview and describe a minimum of ten separate and distinct dialectical formulations that may be occurring simultaneously in the session.

2. *Cognitive Presentation:* Pages 226-234 detail some of the major dialectics that occur in a single interview examined earlier in this chapter. It may be helpful to sort through the alternative definitions and uses once again so that the concepts as defined here may be examined and perhaps changed through your own personal dialectic with this material.

3. *Experiential Exercises or Homework:*
   a. Using an interview typescript, audiotape, or videotape film, describe a minimum of ten different and specific dialectical interactions that may be observed.
   b. Apply the same type of analysis to your own therapeutic work.
   c. Using the systematic formulations for presenting the dialectic, outline the specific movement of a single dialectic between therapist and client over a significant portion of an interview. If feasible, conduct the exercise again with one of your own tapes. Give special attention to points at which existential movement appears to be stuck and immobilized. What do you or the therapist do to enable the movement to begin again?

Construct 2: It is possible to score many aspects of interview behavior, but due to the complexity of the interview, the punctuation offered by any linguistic or research system is inevitably incomplete.

1. *Learning Objectives:* To be able to score or classify interviewer behavior as to the type of environment offered (environmental structuring or sensori-motor, coaching/concrete operational, consulting/formal operational, and dialectic) and microskill usage. In addition, to be able to identify the underlying implicit or explicit confrontations of the therapist and to consider the underlying dialectical formulations that may be involved.

To be able to score or classify client behavior as to developmental level using the developmental level scale and to consider the underlying dialectical formulations that may be involved.

2. *Cognitive Presentation:* The typescript presented and analyzed on pages 234–251 summarizes and exemplifies suggested methodology.

3. *Experiential Exercises or Homework:*
   a. Classify an interviewing typescript using the several criteria of (1) therapist environment, (2) microskills, (3) confrontation, (4) therapist dialectical interpretation, (5) client developmental level, and (6) client dialectical interpretation.
   b. Using one of your own interviews, apply the same criteria of scoring. Give special attention to your use of confrontation and note the client responses to your work.

Construct 3: It is possible to note and classify developmental change over a longer series of interviews.

1. *Learning Objective:* To be able to use the evaluation mechanisms suggested in the case presented from Japan to examine client cognitive and behavioral change over time.

   To be able to use the systematic evaluation formulations presented in Chapter Four for examining client change.

2. *Cognitive Presentation:* Information on evaluation mechanisms is contained in this chapter and on pages 251–256 of Chapter Four. This construct and its accompanying exercises are extensions of "Theory into Practice" suggestions made previously in Chapter Four.

3. *Experiential Exercises or Homework:*
   a. As you begin therapy with your next client, keep in mind the constructs suggested in this exercise. When making notes after the interview, attempt to summarize each of the evaluation items used in the Fukuhara case. Give special attention to the original

central preoperational idea or cognition presented by the client. Present the central cognition in summary form as suggested by Fukuhara, but also present specific words or sentences used by the client to support your summary. As therapy progresses, note how this central cognition changes and develops.

Use the material as an informal means to evaluate the progress of your client. It is likely that this informal evaluation will prove more useful to you in the long run than will a more complete, statistically satisfactory research study. Client developmental change is right in front of us if we will only take the time to see what is there.

b. Take a typescript series and apply the constructs and scoring systems suggested here so that you can consider their validity as research instrumentation as well as more informal feedback systems to mark the progress of the interviewing series.

Summary

Again, as Teilhard de Chardin (1955) suggests, "the more we pulverize matter, the more it insists on its fundamental unity." The two cases presented here illustrate the essential wholeness of human beings and the wholeness of our relationship one to another. We have made considerable effort in this chapter to divide the wholeness of human beings into bits and pieces. These "bits" of human beings and relationships do exist, but they are mere punctuations of human experience. Each act we make as individuals reverberates throughout our entire personal system, and each act we make as therapists reverberates not only with the client but also with our own and the client's total system.

Dialectics is a way to frame our unity with ourselves and with others. The early portion of this chapter stresses that we exist in an almost infinite number of dialectical relations and that each of these relations is interconnected with each other.

Thus, while we can punctuate development as linear and forward moving and can generate "slice-of-life" scales for evaluation of this movement, more is happening in terms of side effects, behaviors, cognition, and unconscious processes than we can ever discover or understand.

Yet, our lives are punctuated very much by the reality of a short time span on this planet. We seem to be born, grow, reproduce, and die in predictable patterns. It is here that the punctuations and efforts of therapy may be most useful. But perhaps it will be therapy with a difference—therapy that is more aware of process and the importance of movement than of searching for impossible ends and final knowledge. Again, we face the difficult dialectic of elusive intelligence (*noesis*) and more stable knowledge (*episteme*). Research and evaluation oriented to definable ends seem to represent knowledge; our awareness that we have only a "slice of life" perhaps will help us remember that life is more slippery and complex than we would like to believe.

In the following chapter, three holistic models of development will be examined in the light of the empirical presentation in this chapter.

↜ 7 ↝

Therapy and Beyond

Development as a
Holistic Enterprise

In the process of knowing,
you construct your ontology,
which is already there.

Ontology, the philosophic study of being, is concerned with
what *is* and with that which cannot be described. The developmental therapy position is primarily epistemological. To describe the developmental process, it is necessary to "stand outside" what we are observing. As we describe development, we
take an external position. Yet the truth is that as the observer
describes what is *seen,* the *scene* changes. The observer cannot
be truly separate from what is observed, and the process of observation changes what is observed.

The Heisenberg uncertainty principle in physics serves as
the basic metaphor for this position. When we measure one aspect of an object, we cannot accurately measure a related aspect
of it simultaneously—the observer impacts and changes what is
observed. In Plato's *Meno,* Socrates' questioning style changed
the nature of the slave boy. So also did Piaget's inquiry techniques determine much of what children told him about themselves. Our own questioning and confrontation techniques as
therapists involve us inevitably in a dialectical relationship of
coconstruction with our clients.

Development has been presented as a search for knowl-

261

edge and intelligence—the implication sometimes being that "higher is better," although this concept has been consistently criticized. Development, however, can also occur within as the deeper exploration of a stage or state of being. Development can be viewed as expansion or change in the nature of our being over time.

The theologian Paul Tillich (1964) notes that being (ontology) itself is not the "highest class of existent, but it is what makes existents possible to begin with. Consequently, Being cannot be defined but only paraphrased" (pp. 163-164). Tillich adds to his concept of Being a second concept, that of the New: "The New appears in three aspects, as creation, as restoration, as fulfillment" (p. 164). In effect, being renews itself over time. In the process of time, being creates itself, restores itself to what it was originally ("returns to the beginning"), and in fulfillment, proclaims a new reality in historical time.

Movement in therapy is not necessarily change nor is change necessarily movement. Much like Tillich's concepts of Being and the New, therapy is paradoxically changing and stable but fulfilling itself over time.

Consider an analogy. A new deck of cards is presented to an audience. The cards are in a prearranged order; the stage magician first suggests a game of Fifty-two Pickup and a child volunteers for the game. The cards are strewn about the stage and the child learns the rules of the game. The deck, in a very different order, is returned to the magician by the sheepish child.

Has the deck changed? Has it moved? Clearly, the order and structure have changed, but the cards remain the same. Remaining from the game may be a "trace" of the experience both in the child and in the cards. The experience in the cards might be a slightly increased flexibility, or it might be a rumpled edge that will remain forever a trace of the first game of Fifty-two Pickup.

It is possible to take a deck of cards and restructure the content and order in a vast number of ways (and let us remember that we can also build houses of cards or use them for coasters or as wallpaper). However, without an external dialectic of interaction with players and alternating rules, the deck of cards ultimately becomes a closed system. In interaction with one or more players, the deck of cards may become an open loop capable of something approximating infinite change but always facing imminent demise via entropy.

This chapter is about the infinite possibilities within ourselves and our clients, given the "hands" that we have been dealt. As human beings, we have a genetic and cultural inheritance that, like the deck of cards, is an ultimately closed system of being. If we allow the New, we permit ourselves to be touched by others; we can expand our knowledge and our potential and become more open to change. But, like the deck of cards, we ultimately face entropy in the necessarily closed system that we as physical beings are. However, just as the memory of our personal experience with cards may exist as a trace, so may we as persons leave a trace on other people and the culture that formed us. Perhaps our fulfillment and restoration are what we share of our being with others and our culture.

This chapter presents three developmental models, those of Gilligan, Lacan, and Gregorc, all of which illustrate how an individual being returns to the beginning, despite efforts to move to "higher" levels of being and growth. Not only is growth "upwards," it is perhaps most accurately described as horizontal and "sideways," the natural expansion of the potential that is. Yet, we as interdependent beings do encounter and produce the New.

Development as Relational Holism

Implicit in the developmental framework presented thus far is the idea that development and growth lead toward "higher" and more complex stages. In Western civilization's notion of "progress," this ideal of higher stages of knowledge and being is too often considered a given.

The spherical model of development thus far presented in this book has been presented as linear (moving from "lower" to "higher"), circular (development turning back on itself through a repetition of developmental sequences), spiraling (returning to the beginning at the conclusion of a developmental phase), and holistic (in that all the above occur at once).

In the spherical model, there is a holistic presentation of development. Note that true developmental "progression" allows, or may require, the individual to step off the spiral and remain on one or more developmental planes for further exploration and expansion. The exploration of either a single plane (for example, the concrete operations plane) or multiple planes simultaneously requires one to cease the urge upwards and to explore what *is* in one's immediate being. While one developmental plane may be emphasized at any particular time, we are simultaneously developing in other planes as well.

The concept of simultaneous exploration of multiple planes may be illustrated by the pianist who learns a new Beethoven sonata or a quarterback who learns a new play in football. Both the pianist and quarterback must learn to sense and read the elements of the notes before them, whether they are notes of the music or the notes the coach has provided outlining the play. Then, they must simultaneously engage in the concrete operation of moving the notes and the play to the piano or the field. Effective practice demands feedback and thinking about thinking—How well did the play(ing) go? Unless all processes occur simultaneously in the final performance, the concert or the game may be a failure. Each single developmental process is required simultaneously for holistic performance.

Clients in therapy not only need to develop to higher levels of performance and conceptualization, but they also need to explore the territory in depth if they are to maintain what they have learned from the therapeutic process. They have multiple developmental tasks that must be balanced if they are to "perform" as bank clerks, family members, and lovers. Just like the pianist or quarterback, the client must know the elements of a situation, be able to organize them in concrete operations, demonstrate cognitive ability to reflect on these operations, and participate in the dialectic of change.

Figure 17 extends the concepts described above to the level of coconstruction and dialectics. Here we see the spheres of the client and of the therapist. The developmental sphere of

Figure 17. The Coconstruction of Reality:
Our Unity with Others in the Process

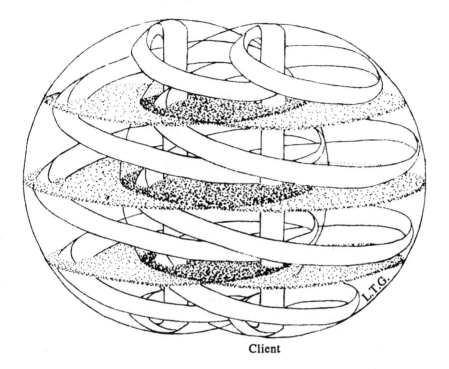

Client

Note: Lois T. Grady first drew this figure, which is used here with her permission.

the therapist intersects with the client. Thus, both client's and therapist's spheres are impacted by the interchange. When the session ends, the client separates and reconstitutes her- or himself. There is a trace of the therapist left with the client and a trace of the client left with the therapist. The being of each has changed through the interaction.

And so it is with personal growth and development. We do not generate ourselves out of a vacuum. Our being comes from our unity with other beings. The child grows in attachments and relations with the mother, the father, the family, and the sociocultural surroundings. We might conceptualize the child as coevolving with many other spheres of influence in the environment. From each, the child takes something of his or her own and becomes unique. Yet, paradoxically, much of this separate uniqueness comes from the developmental path that is so heavily involved with other beings.

Lacan (1973) extends this concept of cogeneration and dialectics in a different direction when he states: "The unconscious is the discourse of the Other" (p. 4). What Lacan is saying is that our very being is so interdependent with others that our unconscious functioning, unknown to us, is determined by our interactions with others with whom we have coevolved. In behavioral terms, this may appear when the child, adolescent, or adult unconsciously mimics the behavior of a parent or family member. The discourse of the Other may show in many culturally approved behaviors and thought patterns. The individual may think he or she is behaving or thinking, but in actuality may be acting out a prearranged script from the family or culture.

A Lacanian view reminds us of our interdependence with others. Although his criticisms of American ego psychology and American individualism are not likely to be well accepted by Americans, his analysis clearly shows that individual, self-actualized behavior is far more directed from the outside than from within, as many would have us believe.

Figure 18 illustrates Lacan's point in more detail. The portrayal is, of necessity, on a flat, two-dimensional plane, but think of the figure as revolving complex spheres (as in Figure 17) that are coevolving together. The infant comes into the world with highly open boundaries and has little sense of self. An overly attached, engulfing mother may lead to development progressions in which the independent self literally does not exist (see, for example, Masterson, 1985). On the other hand, a rejecting or demanding parent may lead to overly tight boundaries in which the child tries to protect the self from the other or Other. The result as shown is an individual with tight construct systems, perhaps obsessive, sociopathic, or even paranoid psychotic. The pathology developed will depend on where the development progression broke down and which defense mechanisms are manifested.

Figure 18. The Dialectics of Development: Possibilities for the Growth of Self and Personal Constructs

	The infant begins with a very open gap for dialectics with the environment.	Through person-environment interaction, the nature of the gap for dialectical change opens or closes.	The result, overly loose, tight, or permeable construct systems, all a result of person-environment dialectics.
Overly attached/ enmeshed	Mother fails to recognize the child as separate.	Without boundaries, the self of the child gradually disappears in multiple interactions.	Overly loose constructs and total "discourse of the Other."
Overly separated/ disengaged	Mother fails to attach to and rejects child.	Child develops increasingly tight boundaries to protect self from others.	Overly tight constructs but still the "discourse of the Other."
Balancing separation and attachment, which leads to individuation	Mother attaches to child but still sees distinctness.	Child encounters many "discourses of the Other" but has internalized the mother's balanced relationship. Child both able to accommodate to new data and use old assimilations to maintain a constantly changing sense of self.	Permeable, open constructs, representing a more positive and flexible "discourse of the Other."

Note: Although this figure synthesizes several ideas about child development, the figure may be best recognized as a simplification of the extreme complexity of interpersonal development, particularly as one might add differing theories to the portrayal. For example, if one were to utilize the Masterson adaptations of developmental object relations theory, specific interpretations of the autistic, symbiotic, and separation/individuation mother-child interactions would require a variety of potential interactions. If one adds the father or extended family to the visualization here, the concepts again would change. Ideas of splitting into self and object representations could complicate the figure even more. Other developmental and object relations theorists might view the key developmental patterns differently. What seems to be valuable in such figures as above is an overview and summary of underlying complex issues.

In normal development, the mother has a more flexible relationship with the child, but with an underlying commitment of love. As necessary, the mother may engulf at times, while at others remove herself and even frustrate the child. Klein (1975) talks about the "good breast" and "bad breast" and the necessity that the child recognize that the mother offers both conditions. Klein also describes the "depressive position," when at six months the child recognizes the mother as a whole object, both rewarding and frustrating. Lacan, more optimistic, terms six months as the "mirror stage," where the child obtains a sense of self as distinct from the Other. Lacan uses the word "jubilation" to describe the child's sense of its own being. Most likely, the child feels basic ambivalence (see Laplanche and Pontalis, [1967] 1973) about this important separation from the mother and the concomitant attachment to the self, which is individuation.

Earlier, Masterson (using the constructs of Mahler and Bowlby) used terms such as the "autistic phase" (birth to three months), in which the child does not truly separate self from others, and the "symbiotic phase" (three to eighteen months), in which the child uses the mother's ego as an umbrella and basic protection, to describe the mother-child relationship.

The second set of diagrams in Figure 18 illustrates the increasingly diffuse or alternatively too rigid boundaries that result for the child with either a rejecting or engulfing parental relationship. In normal development (depicted at the bottom of the second set), we see illustrated the many "discourses of the Other," which the child encounters throughout development. The sum and substance of these many interactions is the child's inculcation into the culture. When one thinks of the many spheres of influence we encounter daily and their influence on our self-perceptions, one has a small understanding of the difficult task the child has to develop a sense of individuation when so heavily pressured by the discourse of the Other.

Given this presentation, Lacan's emphasis on the importance of the Other seems relevant. Furthermore, it is possible to understand his criticism of American ego psychology for its strongly held beliefs in ego, self, and self-actualization. Lacan describes the ego as feeble and small. He stresses our interdependence on others. From his point of view, we are more Other than self.

Figure 18 also may be considered from the standpoint of Kelly's language system. Our goal in childrearing and therapy is to achieve permeable, open constructs in which the "gap" or "eye of consciousness" is open to the dialectic of other individuals.

The larger, single sphere in the same figure illustrates in more detail how these multiple interactions impact the thought, action, and being of the person. The figure illustrates again that we are very much the sum of our interactions with others and that growth is never complete.

The underlying theory of knowledge of developmental therapy has thus far been primarily epistemological in nature. The Piagetian and Platonic models tend to require us to stand apart from ourselves to know and understand. Epistemological orientations imply separation from knowledge and the other. The dialectical orientation of this text is toward interdependence, dialectics, and person-environment awareness. Although much of the description here has been epistemological in nature, there is a theory of knowledge that is perhaps more in accord with the deeper objectives of developmental therapy.

The neo-Platonic philosopher, Plotinus, provides a theory of knowledge that can be considered simultaneously ontological and epistemological. The "One" is the highest principle, the cause, and is omnipresent. Plotinus believed that "every act of cognition, even of self-cognition, presupposes the duality of object and subject" (quoted in Merlan, 1967, p. 353). The multiple acts of cognition suggested in the developmental therapy model tend to follow this Cartesian dualistic frame. Plotinus describes the one as a unity in itself that consists, paradoxically, of "multiplicity in One." This framework allows for a more ontological examination of the developmental process.

Plotinus's realm of the One is followed by the concept of intelligence, which allows exploration of the multiplicity of the One. Intelligence corresponds to the concept of *noesis* (or intelligence) that is stressed repeatedly throughout this book. Intelligence exists within the unity in Plotinus's framework, whereas for Plato, *noesis* appears without and separate. Plato's conceptions, then, are somewhat parallel to the Cartesian split. Yet, paradoxically, it is this very concept of split that enables us to see the One. Unless we separate ourselves from others and the world, we see neither others nor the world.

Ivey and Goncalves (1985) examine the issue of separation and attachment through the lens of the German philosopher Brentano, who was one of Freud's teachers. Brentano considered the issue of intentional existence, the joining of mind and external reality. Brentano suggests that we should concentrate on the study of the "mental act." A mental act may be defined precisely as (1) actions, (2) something of the mind, and (3) an action taken upon objects of the external world. Brentano makes it clear that the separation of thought and action is not possible and that we live in relationship to others—we do not exist alone. Intentionality—thought and action—are a unifying movement in relationship. Brentano reminds us that we are always there in the One through our intentional actions.

It is suggested that the exploration of the One is a difficult search for unity and multiplicity, a stretch toward that elusive *noesis* that slides away from us once it is grasped. Perhaps it is the journey itself we need to explore. In our search for the true end, perhaps we miss both the process and the product of life.

The three conceptual frameworks presented here all challenge the idea that "higher is better." They ultimately suggest that the ontology of being "is" and needs to be recognized as such. Although we may "develop," the question remains similar to that of the playing cards: Is there true change or merely a reshuffling of the deck?

Gilligan's Different Voice

Daly (1973), Gray (1982), and Chesler (1978) all seriously question the male, patriarchal metaphor of "higher is better." Gray describes patriarchy as a "conceptual trap" in which men are more highly valued than women and "in which men's prestige is up and women's prestige is down" (pp. 18-19). The creation legend in Genesis states that "man shall have dominion." Whether it is a pyramid of social class, a management organizational chart, or a spiraling upward developmental framework, success means being at the top. As Gray (1982) describes it: "Ultimately, the problem of patriarchy is conceptual. The problem that patriarchy poses for the human species is not simply that it oppresses women. Patriarchy has erroneously conceptualized and mythed 'Man's Place' in the universe and thus—by the illusion of dominion that it legitimates—it endangers the entire planet" (p. 114).

Since the time of Freud (and before), developmental theorists have assumed and projected a masculine image. Freud's conception of the Oedipal complex was that the male more easily resolves the relationship with the mother and father. The successful Oedipal resolution means that the son gives up his relation with the mother and identifies with the father. Task, work, and independence take precedence over relationship, love, and interdependence.

The daughter, on the other hand, has a close relationship with the mother and continues that relationship, attempting "unsuccessfully" a resolution of the Oedipal situation. Relationships remain central to the girl's life and self-esteem. Work removed from relationships seems strange and unattractive. Yet, if the girl only maintains relationships without developing her own identity, she herself ceases to mature. So, as a woman she must sustain an ongoing and rather precarious cognitive balance. Autonomy in the male sense is considered to be more difficult and dangerous.

These two distinctly culturally different developmental tasks of men and women may result in totally different cultural goals for each. To oversimplify, the task of men is to become separate and autonomous, that of women to maintain attachment and support relationships. Boys must learn separation and autonomy as their prime task of the twin goals of separation and attachment, and girls must learn attachment and relationship (see Bowlby, 1969, 1973a). Although both are essential for full adult development, male and female children experience vastly differing acculturation patterns. The male pattern leads to linear, "upward" development, the female pattern to cyclical, "relational" development.

Which is better, autonomy or relationship, work or love, independence or interdependence? Many feminists have joined the male model in order to gain access to traditionally male domains. The development theories of Kohlberg, Loevinger, and Perry discussed in Chapter One are orientations that reinforce the validity of this approach. Much of the work of developmental theorists represents an unconscious cultural support of the male model, which favors upward movement toward autonomy as the desired form of human growth. Gilligan (1982) suggests a clear alternative for women, which focuses on accepting and encouraging the relational difference as perhaps more useful in today's complex and interdependent world.

Gilligan compares Jake and Amy, both eleven years old, as prime examples of different conceptions of moral development between men and women. Jake and Amy are asked how they would deal with the classic moral dilemma of Heinz (Heinz's wife is dying. He has no money. Does he steal the needed drug?). The two children respond:

Jake: For one thing, a human life is worth more than money and if the druggist only makes a thousand dollars, he is still going to live, but if Heinz doesn't steal the drug, his wife is going to die. (*Why is a life worth more than money?*) Because the druggist can get a thousand dollars later from rich people with cancer, but Heinz can't get his wife again. (*Why not?*) Because people are different and you couldn't get Heinz's wife again (p. 26).

Amy: Well, I don't think so. I think there might be other ways besides stealing it, like if he could borrow the money or make a loan or something, but he really shouldn't steal the drug—but his wife shouldn't die either. (*Why?*) If he stole the drug, he might save his wife then, but if he did, he might have to go to jail, and then his wife might get sicker again, and he couldn't get more of the drug, and it might not be good. So, they should really just talk it out and find some other way to make the money [p. 28].

It could be argued that Jake's point of view is higher and more "principled." He has taken a stand on principle and will act. He is representative of Kohlberg's higher-order thinking, whereas Amy is more at the "good person stage." However, Amy's conception is more cognitively complex, involves the relation of more issues and factors, and does not follow the simple linear reasoning of Jake. Jake accepts the problem as given and seeks to resolve it, whereas Amy reframes the problem in its relational complexity. From the neo-Piagetian view of this book, Jake is at the concrete operations level, and Amy is at the formal operational stage. From one frame of reference, Jake has the "higher" level of conceptualization, but from another, Amy is "higher" and more complex.

Amy is considered by Gilligan (1982) to be representative of a feminine relational construction of reality in which relationships are central and autonomy is secondary:

(*When responsibility to oneself and responsibility to others conflict, how should one choose?*)

Jake: You go about one-fourth to the others and three-fourths to yourself.

Amy: Well, it really depends on the situation. If you have a responsibility with somebody else, then you should keep it to a certain extent, but to the extent that it is really going to hurt you or stop you from doing something that you really, really want, then I think maybe you should put yourself first. But if it is your responsibility to somebody really close to you, you've just got to decide in that situation which is more important, yourself or that person, and like I said, it really depends on what kind of person you are and how you feel about the other person or persons involved.

(*Why?*)

Jake: Because the most important thing in your decision should be yourself. Don't let yourself be totally guided by other people.

Amy: Well, like some people put themselves and things for themselves before they put other people, but some people really care about other people [pp. 35-36].

In summarizing her argument, Gilligan points out that women tend to see moral issues in terms of conflicting responsibilities with "care" and "goodness" being central to a relational orientation. Affect modifies decisions; the pattern is one of formal operations, as compared to thinking and linear causality. Jake is clearly operating from principles and from an autonomous orientation, and he represents the male, hierarchical model.

The expansion of relationships on a decisional plane (or in the even more complex holistic multidimensional plane) is perhaps the best way to summarize development in Gilligan's model. Rather than moving "upward," the individual increasingly becomes aware of complexly interrelated networks and of how each decision ultimately impacts another issue. Although there may be a linear, forward-moving thrust to the decisional process, new issues constantly arise (for every problem solved, a new one emerges), and the developmental cycle must be repeated again and again.

Visually, the hierarchical model is involved in moving to further stages of development and problem solving. The cyclical (or holistic) model involves exploring the horizontal (or multidimensional) plane in full complexity before moving to the next stage.

Figure 8 (p. 144) in Chapter Four summarizes this issue. Jake has taken in the Heinz dilemma, thought about it, and is ready to conduct a concrete operation to solve the problem. On being questioned, he is able to think about it (formal operations) from a principled orientation ("Because the most important thing in the decision should be yourself . . ."). In contrast, Amy is exploring the formal operations plane. She has "stepped off" the developmental spiral or hierarchy and is exploring the territory through formal operational thinking about the problem. With this emphasis on thinking, she is slower to act, since she is more fully aware of the complexity of the problem.

Women who, like Amy, think through the relational implications of the problem may find themselves "left behind" by men, who tend to make decisions and move on. Neither Jake nor Amy is necessarily right or wrong. However, it is clear that Amy explores the territory more carefully and that her thinking is more conceptually "advanced" than Jake's, given the discussion of this book. *But,* from another framework, such as that of Kohlberg (1981), it must be recognized that Jake's framework is the "higher" one.

Relational development, the development of attachments and permanence, is often the task of women. In effect, the love of attachment becomes a task in itself, a special form of complex development. Horizontal exploration in depth may be frequently described as the task of girls and women. Piaget again and again points out that adequate horizontal development is necessary to sustain upward movement on the developmental spiral.

Expansion of the network of relationships as a major form of development is central to Gilligan's thesis. Piaget clearly indicates that this expansion forms a solid foundation on which new stages of conceptual development may be initiated.

Another model of expanded development is offered by Lacan's four discourses.

The Four Discourses of Lacan

Although definitely not conceptualized or presented as a developmental framework, Lacan's four discourses (see Mitchell and Rose, 1982) represent useful conceptual links that provide an opportunity of uniting Gilligan's holistic framework with the four-level model presented in this book. Lacan's concern in his four discourses is with "desire," the underlying motivating factor of human intelligence. Desire might be described as what keeps a person moving over time in a search for Tillich's concept of the New. Lacan has advised us: "Never give up your desire" (quoted in Richardson, 1985).

Lacan's four discourses seem to be talking about the development of a single person, but a close reading suggests that each stage emphasizes the individual's relationship with others. There is no movement in the four discourses without relationship; nothing new develops in ourselves without others. (Lacan's writings are extremely dense, difficult, and obtuse. Lacan deliberately wrote in what he termed "midspeak" in an effort to write in an area between conscious and unconscious experience. As such, reading his material is much like taking a Rorschach test. Lacan forces the reader into a dialectic with the text. This means that interpreting Lacan is an individual and somewhat lonely task. Each person brings his or her own sociocultural history to Lacanian texts. The material that follows is the reading of the author. It is not the definitive "correct" Lacanian reading, nor is it necessarily even a customary reading or interpretation. It is the author's construction based on his own sociocultural history viewed in the context of the developmental therapy model.)

The individual develops in relationship with others. Central to this relationship are the object relations constructions of separation and attachment (see Bowlby, 1969, 1973a; Fairbairn, 1952; Klein, 1975), which play themselves out constantly in the dialectics of development.

The separation of the child from the mother may be described as the most "paradigmatic of all separations" (Clement, 1983, p. 96). Life may be considered as an almost infinite, but nonetheless finite, "set" of separations and attachments. The birth trauma removes the child from the attachment of the womb, and the cutting off of the umbilical cord represents the first rude separation. The way the child is first held represents another attachment. For the girl in Western society, the attachment is shown in a cuddling closeness to the mother or a nurse, whereas the boy may be held out at arm's length, with the exclamation "It's a boy!" In Japanese society, the child is molded to the mother's skin, and the mother adapts her body to the child, thereby first establishing a deeper bond than that which occurs in the Western world. This skin contact with the mother continues for the Japanese child through its early years; another rude separation occurs when the child is expected to be on his or her own and yet to remain dependent on the family.

The child faces a continual set of attachments and separations—the desire for the breast and milk is followed by attachment and then separation. Piaget's daughter, Lucienne, learns through the primary circular reaction how to attach herself to her rattle, but she must also recognize that she is separate from the rattle. Toilet training and the oral stage repeat the basic pattern of separation and attachment. The incredible complexity of the child's life from ages five through seven involves issues of the child's separating into sex-role identification, the fuller discovery of the difference of the sexes, the learning of useful cognitive separations through the movement of preoperational thought into concrete operations, and the major separation in most cultures of the child leaving the home and entering school as an independent being.

The message of separation and attachment continues through life and is repeated with particular emphasis in adolescence. It is also experienced in marriage, the growth and loss of one's children, the loss of one's physical vitality, and then the ultimate separation of death. Death, paradoxically, represents a return to attachment. It has been suggested that the meaning of Freud's ([1928] 1959) death instinct is that "the aim of all life is death" (Appignanesi, 1979, p. 152). When viewed in the context of separation and attachment, the death instinct indeed can be seen as the very healthy desire to separate and individuate and to ultimately to reattach oneself to one's origins.

In *Beyond the Pleasure Principle,* Freud ([1928] 1959) postulates the "Nirvana principle":

> The dominating tendency of mental life, and perhaps of nervous life in general, is the effort to reduce, to keep constant or to remove internal tension due to stimuli (the "Nirvana Principle," to borrow a term from Barbara Low [1920, p. 73])—a tendency which finds expression in the pleasure

> principle; and our recognition of that fact is one
> of our strongest reasons for believing in the exis-
> tence of death instincts [p. 98].

The equilibration or homeostatic desire of a personal balance
between separation and attachment and life and death instincts
may represent our highest desire.

The Lacanian concept of desire, then, may be reinter-
preted as the somewhat illusionary hope for a balance between
separation and attachment, between life and death, between ac-
complishment and being cared for, or between being and doing.
This illusionary desire for stability represents our search for
knowledge (*episteme*). But we also desire intelligence (*noesis*),
movement, and change. In one moment, we want stability, in
the next, change. Our lives are a constant dialectic of desire;
once we achieve our desire, it is no longer our desire. Thus, the
object of our desire, once attained, is satisfying only for a short
time (be it a new stereo, sexual intercourse, or a newly synthe-
sized idea). We shall soon be searching again and moving on
with a new quest. Thus, the importance of the Lacanian caveat
—"Never give up on your desire"—for to do so is death or emotional illness.

Lacan complicates the matter a bit more when he states
that "not wanting to desire" and desiring are one and the same
—a unity within one. However, consider the statement "I no
longer wish to desire." Here is a paradoxical desire not to desire
that also touches on the very nature of being and nonbeing, the
multiplicity within the unity. Put more simply:

Hamlet: To be or not to be? That is the question.

Neitzsche: To do is to be.

Sartre: To be is to do.

Frank Sinatra: Doobie, doobie, doo.

Doing may be said to represent the life instinct, the active assimilation of working on the world (perhaps even in a destructive sense of power). Thus, the doing of life is at times paradox-

ically the enactment of the death instinct. Conversely, being may be said to represent the death instinct, or nirvana principle, in which one accommodates to the organic world as it is; the pleasure of the attachment is also a representation of the death instinct.

It is suggested that Freud's death and life instincts represent a dialectic of desire somewhat parallel to other dialectic formulations that have been either explicitly or implicitly presented earlier, namely:

Attachment
—— ——
Separation

Accommo-dation	Death Instinct	Nirvana Instinct	Uncon-scious
—— ——	—— ——	—— ——	—— ——
Assimila-tion	Life Instinct	Aware-ness	Con-scious

None of the paired concepts can exist without the other. They exist in a dialectical relationship of constant change. Either may be placed above or below the other. They exist in a precarious equilibration or balance, each defining the other through constantly changing syntheses.

Desire may thus be considered a trinity—a desire for balance and homeostasis, a desire for attachment in its variations, and a desire for separation. Given the complexity of desire, it seems small wonder that Lacan constantly talks about the "desire which shall never be filled"—the underpinning root of motivating desire is the impossible dream, a balance that can at best be temporarily fulfilled (the short moment of orgasm, a peak experience, a time of restful meditation). These moments of full attachment may be taken as metaphors in which life and death, separation and attachment, for a short time become "one," but which are shortly overcome by the life instincts of assimilation, separation, and active experience. And each orgasm, peak experience, or meditation requires the simultaneous desire of seeking and letting go—a precarious balancing act of separation and attachment.

Life is about the pursuit of desire, the search for fulfilling one's pleasures. The desire of the sensori-motor infant is to learn the elements of experience and become preoperational, and the preoperational child seeks to become the concrete operational person of the latency period. This is followed by the desire for adolescent formal operational being and, sometimes, by the desire for the discourse of the dialectic. And, when we achieve the adolescent desire of being fully adult, we wish to become a child again. Shakespeare's seven ages of man represent the cycle we desire—in each stage of being, we desire another.

Lacan's four discourses of desire (see Figure 19) represent the fact that we seldom achieve what we desire. This diagram is useful because it indicates clearly that each stage or discourse contains within it aspects of other stages or discourses.

In briefest form, each discourse represents one's total ontology, or being, at the moment (one's feelings, thoughts, *and* actions). In each state of being, the primary desire is for something other than what one is or has. The hysteric ($), out of control, desires mastery. The master (S_1) desires knowledge, which is contained metaphorically in the University. The University (S_2), in turn, desires something beyond knowledge—the ability to know desire itself. The analyst, who has supposedly mastered all the earlier stages, seeks to know the hysterical subject ($). Psychosis or neurosis occurs when any one individual (or family, group, or society) is immobilized or "stuck" (to use Fritz Perls's inelegant but highly descriptive term). There is no end to therapy. Analysis, therapy, or treatment is terminably interminable; there is always a new desire or wish after each cognitive, emotional, or behavioral truce.

The stuckness in neurosis or psychosis, however, may be contrasted with the positivistic orientation of feminist therapy and Gilligan's theories. Being at one place, or many places, for a period of time may represent a choice for expansion and a different type of growth. Nonetheless, it is possible for any person or group to become immobilized in useless repetitions within any position or discourse.

While each state of being is distinctly different from all the others, it is clear that each contains all other dimensions.

Figure 19. The Four Discourses of Lacan

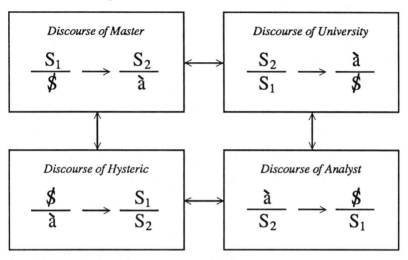

S_1 = master signifier (concrete operations)

S_2 = *savoir*, or knowledge (formal operations, knowledge in the absolute sense without considering underlying assumptions—*episteme*)

$ = split subject (sensori-motor thought in which the child is split or separated and is not aware of the split)

à = *le-plus-de-jour*, or desire (dialectic, the desire for something more than we already have or know—*noesis*)

Note: The references to the four stages as described in this book are *not* those of Lacan, but rather are relations interpreted by the author. It should be noted that desire can flow in either direction, and perhaps even flow to nonadjoining discourses at times.

Specifically, the hysteric (who is equated here with the sensori-motor child or the adult living in a confused and confusing world) gives primacy to the inevitably split subject ($), and thus submerges desire. Yet, paradoxically, desire drives the hysteric and the confused adult. The goal of the hysteric, the child, and the adult is mastery uncomplicated by submerged knowledge.

If the hysteric breaks through sensori-motor and pre-operational thought, concrete operations and the discourse of the master (S_2) become possible. This transformation can come from within or without, but it takes the form of a conceptual leap, as represented by the gap between the four quadrants of the Lacanian model. It may be noted that, within the concrete operational figure, mastery becomes primary and submerges the ultimate split of the sensori-motor subject ("I'm not a baby, I know what I'm doing" or "Don't bother me with another interpretation, send another bomb run to Viet Nam"). Despite the fact that many individuals stay stuck circling in the discourse of the master, they desire knowledge and simultaneously suppress desire. In the discourses of both the hysteric and the master, the action, or doing orientation, takes primacy over the beingness of desire (à).

The movement to the discourse of the University (S_2) gives primacy to knowledge, and the mastery signifier (S_1) of concrete operations and active mastery is suppressed. The classic example of this, of course, is the professor who is interested in knowledge for its own sake and regards practical applications of knowledge with the greatest disdain. The highest prestige in the University is given to those whose work has the least practical significance. (This is perhaps a reflection of Plato's preference for the idea of the table over the table itself—idealism has generally commanded a more respectable philosophical position than realism.) The empirical behavior therapists often work with concrete action and may be regarded with disdain by formal operational theorists, such as psychoanalysts. Partially in response to criticism, behavioral psychology has moved to a more cognitive-behavioral stance (see, for example, Beck, 1976; Meichenbaum, 1977). The philosophies of idealism and empiricism/realism appear to be brought together in the cognitive-behavioral movement, which emphasizes thought, feeling, and action.

The formal operational thought of the University often forgets to examine the assumptions on which it is based and ultimately desires to know desire—the ability to analyze, while simultaneously suppressing the unique subject in the lowest and least-powerful position. The universality of the University too often obscures the particularity of the individual.

Within and without the University, those who analyze and contemplate the nature of knowledge (the analysts [à] who reflect on reflections and assumptions via the dialectic) give supremacy to the study of desire and its movement. In this process knowledge (S_2) and action (S_1) may both be devalued or suppressed as temporary and elusive. The concept of *noesis* and search for elusive truth may become an end in itself. The ultimate desire of the analyst, however, expresses itself in the desire to know the nature of humankind, the split subject ($), and the hysteric. Mastery of reality receives the deepest repression (but it, of course, will resurface as the discourse continues, and continues, and continues).

What has this reading of Lacan achieved? First, it helps remind us that each part contains the whole. Within the hysteric, the young child, and the adult in therapy, there is some ability to act, some knowledge, although the whole process is impelled by suppressed desire. Second, the movement of the patient to concrete operations and mastery of reality requires sufficient time at the sensori-motor plane. Until the developmental tasks of this phase have been satisfactorily concluded, moving to a new stage is likely to be most difficult and perhaps impossible to maintain without regression.

Third, the Lacanian paradigm reminds us, again in a different way, that there is no end to development. We will always return to the beginning, hopefully with a new knowledge that we have returned to the beginning. Yet, there is always more to master, more to know, more to analyze; and the more we achieve these three, the more we can sense our splitness and the need to search and ask further questions. "For each answer we find, three new problems sprout up."

> "You are old, Father William," the young man said,
> And your hair has become very white;
> And yet you incessantly stand on your head.
> Do you think, at your age, it is right?"
> "In my youth," Father William replied to his son,
> "I feared it might injure my brain;
> But now that I'm perfectly sure I have none,
> Why I do it again and again" [Carroll, 1923, p. 50].

The Lacanian model provides a useful complement to that of Gilligan. Gilligan maintains that any action in one part of a human system impacts all other parts. The relational nature of women enables them to be intuitively better able to see multiple realities and the truth that many things happen simultaneously. Even a male linear model, perhaps represented by the discourse of the master, still contains all relational issues simultaneously, but this awareness is suppressed by the central theme of mastery and dominion.

Human development, then, is immensely complex. It appears to be linear and forward moving at first glance, but consider Father William. He is old enough to be aware that bouncing upside down does not make a lot of sense, but he continues, perhaps because it is the only "game in town" he knows. Individuals such as Father William might benefit from the awareness that bouncing upside down is only one alternative and that more time spent on analyzing desire and alternative actions might perhaps be beneficial.

One can develop one aspect of the Lacanian quadrant or the quadrant model of this book in too much detail and end up needlessly repeating oneself. Gilligan indicates the need for expanding all planes and aspects of each plane to achieve something approximating full humanity.

Gregorc provides another useful framework for considering development as a whole. Whereas Lacan emphasizes dialectical development through relations with others and Gilligan stresses the wholeness of development, Gregorc divides development into conceptual styles of adult life. He urges that all aspects of development have relevance and should be respected. He argues militantly against one mode of being as "best."

Gregorc's Model of Adult Styles

Chapter Two, which discusses parallels in evolutionary biology, human development, and the therapeutic process, defines each process as an outcome that leads to further developmental processes and to future outcomes. It seems apparent that each moment of development is at best a temporary "evolutionary truce," or moment of equilibration. During this truce, the Argus pheasant, the developing child, or the client in therapy has the opportunity to consolidate gains and, perhaps, become aware of losses in the new adaptation.

This time of truce may be considered analogous to a single plane of development. The task is to respect and expand the developmental plane of sensori-motor experience, concrete operations, formal operations, or that of dialectical reasoning.

Gregorc (1982a, 1982b) produced an assessment instrument and an accompanying theory that are based on the work of Jung and Ouspensky ([1920] 1970). Interestingly, Gregorc respects each adult style and encourages its further development. An assumption exists in much developmental writing that "higher" is "better." However, Gregorc respects all styles and maintains that each of us are combinations of varying styles.

The first style Gregorc considers is that of the *concrete random* individual. This person's cognitive style is close to the sensori-motor plane. The individual takes in data in a linear, sequential fashion and gives primacy to the senses of seeing, hearing, and feeling. The taking in of data is considered a perceptual style. In effect, the individual absorbs whatever data comes his or her way, and the attention to particular data is heavily determined by the environment. In a Piagetian sense, the perceptual input of the senses represents an accommodative style in that what is "out there" and is most attractive is "taken in." Infants who pay attention to the new noise, color, or sensation in their environment best represent this perceptual orientation. The internal, assimilative organization of the sensori-motor child is random and irregular and gives forth to strange and wonderful plays of the imagination, as represented by Piagetian magical thinking.

Gregorc points out that some adults still give primacy to this cognitive orientation. Our first tendency is to consider that this way of being in the world is "bad," has overly loose construct systems, and is immature. However, the individual whose style is concrete random (or sensori-motor, in the language of this book) has many strengths. Gregorc notes that adult individuals with this style orientation exemplify Einstein's observation that "the most incomprehensible thing about our world is that it is comprehensible." The concrete random or sensori-motor individual is unafraid to take conceptual leaps, is willing to make sense of the world, and is ready to be committed to action. On the other hand, this same individual may be too ready to change behavior (or symptom, if the person is a hysteric) due to his or her ability to take in and accommodate the environment.

The concrete random individual tends to be highly creative and will bring ideas together that no one would ever try to bring together or attempt to make work. This person "is often considered to be a 'gambler' or 'risktaker' by his more conservative friends and co-workers. He is the true 'idea' man who researches, gathers, and produces; he often leaves the detail and completion of his projects to others" (Gregorc, 1982, p. 36). This is the type of person who is ready to generate and consider alternatives, who will not accept the words "don't" and "can't be done," and who tends to be friendly, outgoing, and charming.

This same concrete random individual has less-desirable characteristics as well, and may be unable to stick to a task, changing jobs frequently, forgetting commitments, and jumping too quickly to conclusions. In therapy, this individual tends to present extensions of qualities discussed above. Creativity in this person may deconstruct into semihysterical patterns of symptomatology and magical thinking. Egocentricity may be prominent, as in the young child, and acting-out behavior may be manifest.

Gregorc is quick to point out that there is no individual with a pure cognitive style; each person represents a mixture of many cognitive styles. When a person of a particular cognitive style is in therapy, the therapy issue often surrounds something related to the central cognitive approach. Gregorc suggests that therapists respect each style and encourage individuals to become aware of cognitive style and to develop uniqueness. Gregorc also recommends that therapists broaden and expand cognitive scope. Thus, he both encourages concrete random creativity and also encourages generation and expansion of other style areas.

The *concrete sequential* style is similar to that of the concrete operational frame of reference and the discourse of the master. However, whereas the Lacanian view primarily seems to criticize the discourse of the master, Gregorc is able to see the positives as well. Marc Edmund Jones has stated: "Man must not only see everything through his own eyes, but will always be unable to accept what he cannot examine" (quoted in Gregorc, 1982a, p. 19). The assimilative mode of the master predominates. There is a deliberation in this style, an orderliness; the person is often adverse to change. Whereas the concrete random person is changeable and sometimes too highly impacted by the environment, this individual is described as the "rock of Gibraltar" and prized for dependability. Bank clerks, engineers, and accountants are often examples of this painstaking perfectionistic type of person.

Like the concrete random (sensori-motor) individual, the concrete sequential (concrete operational) individual has both strengths and weaknesses. The "rock," whom we value so highly, may not respond to better alternatives and may cling rigidly to the past. Such individuals may be insensitive to emotional types and overly critical and demanding. In therapy, this orientation may show as obsessiveness and a variety of compulsive behaviors. There may be an inability to reflect on one's actions and an emphasis on reality as the "bottom line."

It is apparent that the concrete operational individual can benefit from the more playful qualities of the sensori-motor or concrete random mode of being, just as the playful person can often benefit from more order and seriousness.

A third cognitive style is termed *abstract random,* which might represent the university, with its random smorgasbord of courses and limited conceptual links that justify the lack of order. Fortunately, the masters of the university, the administration, provide order for the disorderly faculty. The parallels between the abstract random orientation and the discourse of the university, however, are not as clear as in the earlier examples.

The parallels between Gregorc's styles and formal operational thinking are more easily seen. For example, he quotes Antoine de Saint-Exupéry's statement as exemplifying the abstract random individual: "It is only with the heart that one can see rightly; what is essential is invisible to the eye" (quoted in Gregorc, 1982a, p. 29). The adolescent is ruled by emotion (and perhaps the masters of the university would agree that faculty, too, are ruled by passion) and is also engaged in the difficult task of realizing that reality is more than meets the eye.

Adults who represent this cognitive style are described as

living in a world of feeling and imagination. Whereas men tend to represent the concrete operational, concrete sequential orientation, women, by and large, seem to "fit" better with the cognitive description. Thus, Gregorc provides at least indirect evidence that women's cognitive functioning is more advanced than that of men. Rogers's feeling-oriented therapy is often opposed to dogmatic behaviorism and is oriented toward "caring." Gregorc describes this cognitive orientation as primarily feeling and process oriented, whereas the prior orientation tends to be thought and outcome focused. Considerable time may be spent in thinking over the various alternatives (as Amy does in the earlier section on Gilligan's work).

The negative characteristics of the relatively spontaneous, abstract random individual may appear as chronic tardiness, egocentricity, self-doubt or inflated self-image, or any of the many aspects of early adolescent formal operational behavior. Any of these or related characteristics may show up in therapy. Again, such abstract random individuals may benefit by expanding their capacities in the more obsessive mode of concreteness and mastery or by moving to the next developmental plane.

Gregorc's description of the abstract random individual seems to best approximate the early formal operational thought of the adolescent, who is often dominated by emotions. Gregorc does not seem to take the intellective aspects of this form of development fully into account. Neither does he seem to allow for the operation of the dialectic. As such, his fourth stage—*abstract sequential*—is perhaps best conceptualized as late formal operations rather than as dialectical. The dialectic, however, may be implied in Gregorc's work by the fact that he respects and recommends development in all four areas of his framework, each aspect enhancing the other.

The abstract sequential person seems to represent Descartes's cogito and advanced formal operations. Gregorc captures the world of this individual in the words, "as I think, so I am." This statement provides a clear example of idealistic philosophy and the suppression of the split subject ($) in the individual's desire for knowledge. Thus, at this point, Gregorc has recaptured the discourse of the University in its fullest sense.

The abstract sequential or late formal operational individual often relies on intellect rather than passion and feeling. This person is well able to organize and synthesize data to think about thinking about thinking. This individual can separate self from object and study things in a detached fashion but often fails to observe that the observer impacts the observation. Feeling is subordinated, and this individual may be accused of emotional coldness.

The therapeutic stereotype of this orientation is the cold and unfeeling analytic therapist who seeks to impose the "correct" interpretation of Freud. It is this stereotype that Lacan was talking about when he urged a "return to Freud," harshly criticizing U.S. ego-analytic psychology and accusing this movement of obscuring the real meaning of Freud's thought: "Obscurantism is, in particular, the function assumed by psychoanalysis in the propagation of a style that calls itself the *American way of life,* insofar as it is characterized by the revival of notions long since refuted in the field of psychoanalysis, such as the predominance of the functions of the ego" (Lacan, [1973] 1978, p. 127). Lacan calls for a movement to the dialectic and an awareness of relationship and of the fact that "truth," such as firm *episteme,* is an illusion.

Given that dialectical thinking seldom appears in North America, Gregorc should not be faulted for its absence. It could be argued that the fourth quadrant is represented by some of the abstract sequential descriptions. The abstract sequential individual appears to be a person who has permanent, fixed knowledge in the form of Plato's *episteme.* Such individuals will often be difficult patients owing to their intellectual capacities, distrust of feeling, and skepticism. At the same time, their abilities to organize knowledge, conceptualize, and think about the "big picture" make these individuals successful scientists, managers, and even international diplomats. Their intellectual capacity may at times, however, be undermined by their own ability to explain things away.

Gregorc does not use the word dialectic, but his self-study program is dialectical in functioning and representative of the fourth quadrant. As said before, Gregorc points out that society needs each type of individual and is incomplete without each type's varied talents. Furthermore, each individual has some of the other personal styles within him- or herself, and it is this internal "dialectic of personal styles" that gives movement to the process of development.

"When you begin to know yourself, development begins automatically" (Gregorc, 1982, p. 49). Once an individual examines her or his style either alone or with a therapist and notes the contradictions and discrepancies in the homeostatic patterns, development has already begun. Gregorc presents a series of exercises in which individuals are encouraged to respond to sentence completion stems (for instance, "My attitude toward change is . . .") and to compare their free responses with his clinical and research observations. He then introduces discrepancy by asking the subjects to examine these responses and to indicate how they "wish" they were. This provides the opening for the dialectic of the "real self" (how the client responded to his style inventory and the open sentence stems) and the "ideal self" (how the client would like to be). Many of the exercises Gregorc provides are structurally similar to those used in Kelly's (1955) personal construct psychology, in which the goal is to produce permeable cognitive construct systems for viewing the world, rather than overly tight (sequential, concrete) or loose (abstract, random) constructs.

An Attempt at Developmental Synthesis

Gregorc's work and conceptions are clearly very different from those of Gilligan, Lacan, and this book. Yet, his work seems to provide a useful and practical framework for conceptualizing and implementing ideas presented here. The tendency in developmental orientations is to move "forward" to "higher" states of mental being. Gilligan points out most forcefully that our conception that higher is better is seriously in error, but beyond this general point her practical methods for expanding one's being seem remote.

Lacan would seem to add further perspective to Gilligan's thesis in that he clearly demonstrates that all development is interrelated and inseparable. We are related not only to ourselves, but also to others and to our familial and cultural history. His framework shows us how to integrate developmental psychology in a systematic formulation that is still in rough accord with the Piagetian and Platonic orientation of this book. Lacan also provides the clearest link between Freud and the unconscious, and these conceptions will be explored in more depth in the concluding chapter.

Yet, it is Gregorc, more the pragmatist, who provides conceptual links to practice and development. Gregorc, working from the more mystical frameworks of Jung and Ouspensky, has generated a theory and a practical instrument for the assessment of cognitive style. He makes suggestions about how to work on expanding style and simultaneously respects each style with dogged determination. With Gilligan, Lacan, or other developmental conceptions described within this book, it is too easy to assume that one orientation is "better" or most "correct." Gregorc seldom falls into that evaluative trap.

Gregorc's assessment techniques and instrumentation are promising, but they lack full scientific validation. The data on his work in terms of its empirical validity are only beginning to be assembled. There are other cognitive frameworks that may prove more productive than his. Nonetheless, it seems patently clear that the conceptual model is solid and provides a useful philosophic and pragmatic alternative to the perhaps old-fashioned idea that development is linear, hierarchical, and forward moving.

A Brief Venture into Theology

It is not the purpose of this book to become involved in theological exploration, but the relationships among holistic orientations to development and the multiplicity in Plotinus's spiritual orientations are too self-evident to be totally ignored. Rather than answer the question of the relationship of the One to multiplicity, it may be helpful to point out some of the alternative descriptions of this issue.

The Old Testament and the Torah recognize the Oneness of God, yet stress separation of humankind from God. Knowl-

edge is what causes the separation. It is possible that this interpretation claims a continuing ultimate split in the human subject.

The Gnostic tradition at one time presented an important competing mode of thought to the early Jewish and
Pauline conceptions. The Gnostics were killed—"stoned to
death"—for their attempt to reconcile separation. The Gnostic
view is dualistic and regards God as unknowable. But the Gnostic view (Jonas, 1958) of knowledge is different in holding
that by gaining knowledge, the individual can become a "par-
taker in the divine existence . . . which means more than assimilating him to the divine essence" (p. 35). In the Gnostic view,
cognition or knowledge leads one to participate in the One.

"In the many, there are one." This phrase and its many
variations will be found in Christianity, Judaism, and Eastern
religions. The question of the knower (the human) and the "to
be known" (God) is answered in many variations. In each answer, we find a struggle with the paradox of being—that of
being simultaneously separate from the world yet at the same
time deeply attached.

Perhaps the comment of my Aunt Margaret, made in the
sixties at the time of the San Francisco hippies, sums it up:
"Why are they running around trying to find themselves? Can't
they see that they are already there?"

Theory into Practice

This chapter is designed to balance the implied progression of "higher is better," "complexity is better," or the "developmental therapy model is *the* model." Each construction of
the world of appearances or the intelligible world is just that—a
construction, a map, an attempt to describe the indescribable.

Underlying this chapter is ontology, the study of being.
Being is undefinable, but we still attempt to conquer that impossible dream. Our quest is usually in some form of epistemological inquiry in which we separate ourselves artificially
from being; thus, being changes in the process of our description.

Sartre (1956) said that "we must abandon the primacy of

knowledge if we wish to establish that knowledge. Of course, consciousness can know and know itself. But it is in itself something other than a knowledge turned back upon itself" (p. li). He goes on to point out that consciousness is awareness or consciousness of something but that "consciousness is prior to nothingness and 'is derived' from being" (p. lvi).

The task in this chapter has been to restore being to centrality and to increase our awareness that our descriptions have still not described the "is-ness," "being-in-ourselves," or "being-in-becoming" that we all are.

The chapter begins with the metaphor of the deck of cards and illustrates how change comes from interaction with the environment. We are like a deck of cards that changes through interaction with the environment of the New.

Three models of holistic development are presented that compete with and supplement the developmental therapy model. Each model enriches the concept of development and helps us become aware that the definition of developmental therapy is only in the beginning stages. We face a new task in the next decade for the conceptualization and practice of therapy.

Construct 1: Development occurs within the person and in interaction with the environment. Each small developmental change within a single developmental schema reverberates throughout the entire individual system. Furthermore, each change in one person reverberates throughout many, virtually infinite, systems with which we live and act.

1. *Learning Objectives:* To be able to define and discuss development as a holistic process. To be able to criticize the epistemological distinctions of developmental therapy with the awareness that the very process of description has changed what has just been described.

2. *Cognitive Presentation:* In a sense, the entire book has been working toward this point, especially with the constant emphasis on the dialectic between knowledge (*episteme*) and intelligence (*noesis*). Pages 261–270 present the overarching framework of this chapter—development as relational holism.

3. *Experiential Exercises or Homework:*
    a. Take a new deck of cards, break it, shuffle it, play a
        game of solitaire. What has happened to that deck?
        What of the New has been added? What trace of you
        remains in the deck? What trace of the cards remains
        in you? How has your observation of the process
        changed the process? The act of observing changes
        the nature of being.
    b. Observe yourself in the mirror. What happens to you
        as you observe yourself? You may want to set up
        two mirrors angled so that you can observe yourself
        observing yourself observing yourself. What trace of
        this experience remains in you? Has the act of ob-
        serving impacted your development?
    c. Interact with a friend or family member. What hap-
        pens when you talk to the person? Is he or she the
        same? Are you? How has even the briefest interac-
        tion left traces with both of you?
    d. Piano playing and quarterbacking were presented as
        two examples of how action requires one to simul-
        taneously integrate all developmental levels. Using
        these two examples as a basis, think about how bal-
        let, typing, driving, swimming, or learning advanced
        calculus can be described in a similar fashion. How
        are all four developmental planes playing themselves
        out simultaneously in smooth and successful action?
        Consider the act of therapy itself. How do we in
        therapy manifest all developmental levels simultane-
        ously?
    e. Consider Figure 17 and think of yourself as a ther-
        apist interacting with a client. Close your eyes and
        visualize the two spheres coming together. Do you
        and the client move together in synchrony? How
        does your action change the being of the client?
        How does the client change your being? The next
        time you are in a therapeutic session, think of the
        twin spheres and their interactions on each other.
        What do you learn or relearn about the therapeutic
        process?

f. Lacan's "the unconscious is the discourse of the Other" is a difficult concept to grasp, especially for ego-oriented or self-actualization–oriented North Americans. Consider Figure 18; draw a circle representing your own sphere of development. Then draw circles (spheres) representing your mother, father, family members, and other important individuals in your life. You may wish to take time to illustrate how each of these spheres impacts one another as well as you.

Add circles (spheres of influence) that represent your ethnic heritage, your gender, sexual orientation, race, and important reference groups, such as peer groups and membership groups. Add a sphere for your religious heritage and your economic background. Continue to add other important spheres of influence to the circles, always trying to illustrate how each sphere impacts other spheres in your total system.

You may find that adding more spheres of influence produces a sphere of "unity" in that the grouping of all the spheres produces a new and larger sphere with many interlacing parts. At this point, note that the small circles at the top of Figure 18 produce the beginnings of a new "sphere of spheres."

g. Review these several exercises; note that all of them are in varying ways oriented toward identifying and experiencing Plotinus's concept of the multiplicity of the One.

Construct 2: Gilligan's relational model of development offers an important challenge to traditional, male models of linear progressive development.

1. *Learning Objectives:* To be able to describe Gilligan's model, to compare and contrast it with linear models moving toward "higher" levels of development, and to describe the importance of the twin developmental tasks of separation and attachment.

The relational model of Gilligan has had an important

effect on developmental theory and has raised a major question as to "correctness" of traditional theories. Gilligan's work and that of other feminist theorists will likely be increasingly recognized over the years.

2. *Cognitive Presentation:* The concepts are presented on pages 270-275.

3. *Experiential Exercises or Homework:*

    a. The feminist analyses of Daly, Gray, and Chesler are not likely to be accepted easily by all readers. Perhaps the most useful exercise is simply to reread them and consider your own position on the concept of patriarchy. Do you agree that developmental theorists have most often constructed development in a male model of "higher is better"? How would you criticize their positions? What strengths and new ideas do they provide you?

    b. The elementary discussions of the Oedipal development of men and women emphasize that the successful male resolution is separation and autonomy and the successful female resolution is attachment and relationship. Recognizing that this is a simplification of a complex issue, consider the concepts in your own sex role development. If you are a male, did your family push toward separation and autonomous development? If you are female, did they reward and reinforce your attachment and relational behavior? *What specific actions did your family take to lead you in these directions?* What does this model miss in your own development—perhaps your own complexity and many varying forces pulling in different directions?

    c. Read the Jake and Amy dialogue again. Then ask men and women and boys and girls the same question about the Heinz dilemma. What do you observe?

    d. What does Gilligan's framework add to the total idea of developmental therapy as outlined in this book? Does each act we make indeed reverberate throughout the entire system?

Construct 3: The concepts of separation and attachment play themselves out again and again in child and adult development. The desire of the individual is to balance these twin developmental tasks, which resemble issues of stability versus issues of change. The broader implications of this discussion focus on movement and change as a result of this dialectic—separation and attachment, stability and change, and knowledge and intelligence are all needed to sustain life and for us to meet our desire.

1. *Learning Objectives:* To be able to define the dual tasks of separation and attachment, particularly as they relate to issues of male autonomous development and female relational development.

   To be able to define and discuss the dialectics of desire, the search for what we cannot obtain.

2. *Cognitive Presentation:* Pages 276–284 present these data. These concepts are complex and are perhaps best considered as background data supplementing the Gilligan material and further illustrating the complexity of the One.

3. *Experiential Exercises or Homework:*

   a. Outline, from your own life or from the life of a client, the way you or the client faced separation and attachment tasks over several developmental stages. For example, at the age of six, most of us must separate from the home and learn to attach to a teacher and the school. At the time of marriage, we must separate from parents and attach to a spouse and to new in-laws. Each age brings with it special tasks of development. Out of the successful completion of these tasks comes the development of individuation, the conception of self as a separate yet attached individual.

      Use the following outline to define the multiplicity of the repeating tasks of separation and attachment: (1) birth; (2) six months—definition of self as separate from the mother; (3) twelve to eighteen months—separation as one learns to walk; (4) two years—anal control; (5) leaving home for nursery school; (6) the complexities of the period of five to seven, in which sex role identification and Piagetian concrete operations begin to function more fully; (7) leaving for school; (8) attachments to peers as an adolescent; (9) leaving for college or for a job; (10) marriage or the establishment of a new home; (11) the arrival of a child; (12) the child moving to school; (13) the child becoming increasingly separate; (14) changes in life through key "passages," such as the crises at ages thirty, forty, and fifty; (15) the separation of the child from the home; (16) awareness of age and reattachment to one's spouse or lover, while simultaneously detaching from one's job; (17) attachment to new friends and location in retirement, looking forward to or fearing the separation and attachment that occur with death.

b. Meditate on the above outline and consider how each developmental task of separation and attachment relates to the spherical model of this book. The complexity of development in the multiplicity of the One becomes staggering.

c. The Lacanian concept of desire is especially difficult, but it can be approached through the example of our desire for a new automobile, house, piece of clothing, stereo set, and other tangible goods. We seek our desire through efforts to obtain, for example, a new house. But once we obtain that new house, it is no longer our desire; our desire shifts to furniture, and once that desire is met, to perhaps a patio. There seems to be no end to the desires one finds in a home. *But,* once the desire for the dream house is completed, many, many people sell that house and move to another and start the process again.

Identify a similar example in your own life or that of a client. How does the drive of our desire lead us on?

d. "Never give up on your desire." What happens to us and to others if we give up our desire, even though our desire may never be fulfilled?

e. Return to the broad, spherical model of developmental therapy. How do the concepts of separation and attachment and desire relate to the model? How do these concepts relate to the conduct of your own life and that of your clients?

Construct 4: The four discourses of Lacan illustrate some parallels to the four planes of the developmental therapy spherical model. Each of Lacan's discourses contains the other discourses within.

1. *Learning Objective:* To be able to define the four discourses of Lacan and relate them to the developmental therapy model.

2. *Cognitive Presentation:* Figure 19 presents the four discourses in visual form, and supplementary reading follows. What is perhaps most important in the four discourses is that they represent another language frame for considering development. Each language frame is another valuable road map of a piece of the complexity of human interaction and therapy.

3. *Experiential Exercises or Homework:*
   a. Each discourse represents one's total ontology or being at a point in time. Examine Figure 19 and find examples in your past history and behavior that seem representative of that particular mode of being. *Do not read this book's definition and do not attempt to decode Lacan's discussion in his books.* Recall that Lacan is talking to us in "midspeak." Use the discourse as a Rorschach or TAT and project your own thoughts on the text. You may be surprised at how well you understand the four discourses if you stop trying to comprehend them intellectually.
   b. Having identified informal examples of each of the discourses in your own life or that of a client, con-

sider the dialectic relationship each space of the discourse implies. Specifically, if you think of yourself in the discourse of the master, what is your relation with others from this position? If you are in the position of the hysteric, how might you relate to those who are in the position of the master? In a simplified sense, the model is not unlike that of transactional analysis. Your ontology or being starts from a position and the ontology or being of the Other starts from a position. The dialectic is the nature of your interaction with the being or ontology of the Other. The nature of your dialectic and your coconstructions will be determined by your being as you meet.

As an example of the above, a person in the discourse of the master who meets a person in the discourse of the hysteric is likely to be offended by the flightiness of the hysteric and may seek to control the discourse of the Other. What happens when two discourses of the master meet—the search for domination? What about the role of the analyst, whether that of the therapist or that of the person who analyzes in relation to other discourses?

Do you and others have more than one discourse operating at a single point in time?

c. Examine the Lacanian equations repeating within the four discourses. What sense can you make of them?

d. Read the material again. How would you change what is said on those pages? What do your projections on Lacan's midspeak add to the discourse of this book?

e. When you feel ready, read a page of Lacan at random—only one page. Digest it slowly. What is your projection on the text? What is he saying? What do others see? Can you engage in a developmental dialectic with his text?

f. Return to the developmental therapy model. What can you add to the model from these readings and experiences?

Construct 5: Gregorc presents four models of adult style, which have some rough correspondence to aspects of the developmental therapy model. As with Gilligan, Lacan, or any other developmental theorist, the dialectic between or among models may increase the richness and explanatory power of all.

1. *Learning Objective:* To be able to define Gregorc's four models of adult style and to relate these constructs to other holistic models and to that of developmental therapy.

2. *Cognitive Presentation:* Gregorc's concept is presented in this chapter in fairly straightforward terms. You may find it helpful to obtain some of his materials for further reading and to take some of his instruments, particularly the "Gregorc Style Delineator" (Gregorc, 1982a).

3. *Experiential Exercises or Homework:*
   a. On a sheet of paper, write down Gregorc's four modes and adult styles. Then write down the four planes of developmental therapy. Put them together in your own way. Then examine the reading and see whether or not you agree with the interpretations in this book. You will learn more about Gregorc through your own actions than from reading. Through action and thought, you are engaging in a coconstruction with Gregorc and this book. If you simply read this book, you are forcing yourself into the constructions presented here. True dialectics requires movement. A book is static. How can you make the ideas here move in your own direction?
   b. Consider the concepts of Gregorc, the four discourses of Lacan, and the Gilligan model. How might you organize and relate each? How would you have them impact and change developmental therapy? How would the concepts of developmental therapy change those models? What other models of development might you seek to add to this dialectical interchange?
   c. Using the rather immense data from the preceding exercise, develop your own set of concepts that might enrich your own practice of therapy or that

of others. How might you establish psychoeducational programs to teach these alternative constructions? Would you seek to impose your own constructions or would you attempt to engage others in a dialectic with you?

Construct 6: The idea of multiplicity in One and the framework of Plotinus appear to have theological implications.
1. *Experiential Exercise:* How do you respond to this construct? What implications does it have for your own understanding and action? What projections do you make on construct 6?

Summary

The dialectic of developmental therapy seems ever to move to complexity—an evolving awareness of difference, distinctiveness, and interaction. Yet, paradoxically, we find repeating patterns, continuing new connections between and among theories and constructs. The midwestern George Kelly merges with the French intellectual Jacques Lacan, the important work of Carol Gilligan may be related to John Bowlby's attachment theory, and Anthony Gregorc demonstrates how all these ideas may be implemented in practice, although he derives his ideas from the more mystical frameworks of Ouspensky and Jung.

Unity among difference may be described as the central theme of this chapter. Teilhard de Chardin's comment summarizes the chapter in just a few words: "The more we split and pulverize matter artificially, the more insistently it proclaims its fundamental unity." One can only describe by separating oneself from what is described. Epistemologically, to know we must become separate. Yet, paradoxically, as we become increasingly separate, we become more and more conscious of our fundamental unity. We have returned to the beginning, to our ontology and our being with an awareness of the New and the fact that it is not new. In the theory of knowledge of Lacan and Plotinus, we have multiplicity in One.

Epistemology and ontology, from one point of view, may

be described as having an uneasy dialectic one with the other. It is possible to know only if we have something to know. But, as the Heisenberg principle reminds us, our knowing or observation ultimately changes and affects what is observed. The "immaculate perception" (or conception) exists or does not exist in our being and our understanding of being.

For practical purposes, the theory of this chapter offers some guidance, perhaps most clearly in the formulations of Gilligan and Gregorc, who both remind us that developmental theory has important implications for practice. The Lacanian model, more conceptual in nature, describes what is and perhaps serves as an integrating force to remind us of our mutual interdependence one on the Other. Perhaps this concept of interdependence and mutuality may not be fully practical in an individualistic society, but it does offer an interesting alternative and challenge to the nature of our being.

In the concluding pages of this book, the complexity of developmental therapy will increase somewhat. Special attention will be given to development that is beyond our conscious awareness. Is it possible to "develop" the unconscious, if indeed the unconscious does exist?

8

Development over the Life Span

"It seems to me that mankind has wholly failed to perceive the power of Love," begins Aristophanes in Plato's *Symposium* (quoted in Rouse, 1956, p. 85). Aristophanes then tells the complex story of the generation of sexual difference from four-legged, androgynous spherical creatures who were the forerunners of humankind.

> The shape of man was quite round. . . . They walked upright as now, whichever direction they liked; and when they wanted to run fast, they rolled over and over on the ends of eight limbs they had in those days. . . . They had terrible strength and force and great were their ambitions; they attacked the gods. . . . They tried to climb into heaven intending to make war on the gods [p. 86].

Zeus and the other gods held council, because they were concerned about the wild behavior of the creatures, and the decision was made to split them in half. Since that time, humankind has tried to rejoin the two halves, and each side is searching for its lost counterpart. "Then each of us is the tally (half) of a man; he is sliced like a flatfish, and two made of one. So each one seeks his other tally" (p. 87). The two parts were asked what they desired, and oneness was their ultimate wish. If Hephaistos (the god of fire) were to stand near, he might ask, "Is it only that you desire to be together as close as possible, and not to be apart from each other night and day? For if that is what you desire, I am ready to melt you and meld you together. . . . If that were offered, we know that not a single one

304

would object, or be found to wish anything else . . . and so the desire for the whole and the pursuit of it is named Love" (p. 88).

Freud was watching his grandson, aged one-and-a-half, at play. The child was playing with a reel of string and threw it into the crib saying "O-o-o-o" and other sounds of interest and satisfaction. Freud observed that this is the German sound for "gone." Freud also noted that his grandson was reeling the string back and joyfully saying "da," German for "there." "This, then, was the complete game, disappearance and return. As a rule, one only witnessed its first act, which was repeated untiringly as a game in itself, though there was no doubt that the greater pleasure was attached to the second act" (Freud, [1928] 1959, pp. 33–34).

Freud observes that the game represents the child's playing out the leave-taking of his mother and her future return. Freud considers his grandson's play a metaphor for one of humankind's greatest achievements—the ability to acknowledge and accept our separateness from the other and to simultaneously express our desire to return to a union.

Children frequently at this age throw a spoon from their high chair to the floor. They often throw with glee and then cry immediately for its return. Younger children may cry when the mother absents herself from the child's room and then exclaim with joy upon her return. In each of these examples, Piaget might note the principle of object constancy: the child is seeking to learn that the object (reel of string, spoon, or mother) is still there even when not seen. Piaget (1954, p. 51) observes Jacqueline (aged ten months) as he takes a toy parrot from her hands and hides it under a mattress while she watches. When the parrot disappears, she searches for the object where it first was rather than where she saw it hidden. In this case, Jacqueline clearly has a beginning form of object constancy or stability of object but does not yet connect how to search for it.

A major task of life-span development is to separate ourselves from our attachments to others and to individuate. At the same time, we have the equally important task of reattaching ourselves to others in new relationships. We must separate from

parents as we go to school, then attach to friends, but separate
from both friends and parents when we leave home. We must
attach ourselves to a new relationship in adulthood but separate a bit with the arrival of children. Each life stage brings new
challenges of development, of separation and attachment.

This chapter explores development over the life span and
does so within a synthesis of Piagetian stages, Bowlby's attachment theory (1969, 1973a, 1973b) and Haley's (1973) life-cycle
model.

However, life-span development is more than development of the conscious dimensions of experience. The final sections of this chapter will explore the development of the unconscious, the "beyond our awareness."

Splitness, Separation, and Attachment

Freud's grandson and Piaget's daughter represent two
variations of how an individual deals with separation and object
attachment. Object relations theorists (Klein, 1975; Fairbairn,
1952; Guntrip, 1961; Kernberg, 1976; Mahler, 1971; and Winnicott, 1958) interpret in differing ways the theme of children
learning to deal with separation and attachment—the paradox of
becoming a separate human being while remaining suitably in
relationship to other human beings.

The emphasis in object relation theory is primarily on
separation and individuation—on becoming a separate self—and
is perhaps best illustrated by the currently popular work of Masterson (1981, 1985) on the borderline personality. Masterson
deftly and effectively points out how the borderline mother too
often engulfs or rejects the child; in each case, the child fails to
gain a full sense of self. In his "developmental object relations
view," Masterson argues for separation and individuation—the
finding of a uniquely satisfying self—as the goal of therapy.

The concept of separation and individuation is quite persuasive, and the work of object relations theorists will be increasingly recognized and popularized throughout the helping
field over the next decade. The focus on separation, however,
should be considered a peculiarly North American cultural for-

mulation and perhaps an extension of the male, patriarchal model discussed in the preceding chapter as compared to the relational developmental theories of Gilligan.

However, it is Bowlby (1969, 1973a, 1973b) who perhaps best outlines in his attachment theory that we have two tasks of living—to separate ourselves from others and to attach ourselves to others. The equilibration of these twin tasks of development provide much of the focus of therapy and counseling. Perhaps it is an issue of recognizing our interdependence, as Lacan has suggested, rather than one of total separation. Individuation, of course, is often defined as the ability to relate effectively, but the very word "individuation" implies a cultural separateness.

In perhaps oversimplified terms, the basic issue of life is coping with separation and attachment. Our ontology, or nature of being, may be constructed with variations on this theme. Like the spherical creatures of Plato's *Symposium,* we are inevitably split from humankind, yet we remain attached and interdependent despite our very splitness.

What the healthy personality needs is a balance or equilibration between the impossible demands of separation and attachment. This balance is often provided by the movement of the dialectic, for it is in the process of movement that we can simultaneously feel both separation and attachment as one. For the dialectic to be ready to overturn, the therapist must "fill" the vessel of client need and demand. This filling or entering in represents attachment. But once the client is full, he or she will separate into a new and different human being. The duration of the union of separation and attachment is short, but for clients these moments are timeless because they fulfill the desire of the client to have it all, if only for a moment.

One must complete separation and individuation tasks and develop firm constructs of development at each stage before one can detach (decenter) and move to the next developmental stage of life. Development that proceeds too rapidly and is incomplete will result in the repetition of old childhood developmental failures in future relationships. Witness, for example, the individual who divorces, then remarries, and finds him- or herself repeating old developmental patterns, despite the best of intentions.

Unless we fulfill our developmental destiny at each life stage, we seem bound to repeat our past developmental history.

Development over the Life Span

This section examines life-span development from two perspectives. The first is that of separation and attachment, the identification of how issues of individuation and relationship play themselves out over the life span. The second perspective considers how the developmental therapy model relates to life-span development.

Developmental Tasks and the Life Cycle. There are a multitude of models for outlining development over the life span. One of the earliest and most influential has been that of Erikson (1950) outlined in Figure 2. Erikson's eight stages range from infancy with its tasks of trust versus mistrust, to old age with its issues of ego integrity versus despair. The Erikson model is that of individual development, although well contextualized and with an awareness of the importance of relations with others in a cultural setting.

Haley's (1973) life-cycle model provides a more relational picture of human development. Haley points out that we cocreate and coevolve together in the relational setting of the family. Each member of the family has different developmental tasks over the life span. Thus, at one point in time, the father and mother may face the issues of middle marriage, with one daughter about to enter high school and young adulthood, and then also be faced with a surprise second child and the attendant issues of childrearing. The daughter and the new baby have their own unique developmental tasks. But each completes or fails to complete development in the context of the relationship with the family. The complexity of family development, of course, can be extended by considering the family as an intergenerational network—the developmental issues of grandparents, siblings, and perhaps even close relatives and friends. Haley reminds us that development occurs in a network of relationship.

Figure 20 presents the Haley life-cycle model as adapted by Fleming (1986), who has pointed out some of the critical separation and attachment issues in development. At this point, it should be emphasized that Haley's model is of the "normal" family, which is becoming increasingly rare. The model should also be conceptualized as to how it varies with the single-parent family, the lesbian or gay family, and the distinctions that may occur within varying cultural and socioeconomic groups. With this brief summary of life-span development in mind,

Figure 20. Jay Haley's Family Life-Cycle Model in Relation to Issues of Separation and Attachment

Developmental Stage	Developmental Tasks and Issues of Separation and Attachment
1. Young adulthood	Increasing attachment with peers. Separation from parents. "Courtship," selection of mate, choice of career or education.
2. Early marriage	Attachment to mate and new friends. Further separation from parents and reattachment to parents. Attachment to in-laws. Establishing the home, career or job initiated.
3. Childbirth and childrearing	Separate from dyadic spouse relationship and attach to infant. Establish new relations with parents, in-laws, peers. Begin detachment from child as school begins. Career establishment, balancing sex roles and work, establishing economic sufficiency.
4. Middle marriage	Progressive separation from children. Begin reattachment with spouse or further separation or disengagement. Mid-life crises: success or failure of career and other endeavors.
5. Leaving home	Children separate from parents, couple reattaches as dyad or separates. New attachment to child's spouse or lover. Deeper attachment to parents as couple become caregivers. Mid-fifties crises: work, relationship, parents, awareness of one's own vulnerability and approaching old age.
6. Old age and retirement	Separate from careers, attach more as dyad, adult children reattach as caregivers. Use of leisure, health, finances, review of one's life.

Source: Fleming, 1986. p. 1. Used by permission.

let us examine how the developmental therapy framework might relate to these developmental processes and tasks.

Developmental Therapy over the Life Span. Whether one wishes to use the Erikson, Haley, or another model of life-span development, issues of sensori-motor, concrete operations, formal operations, and the play of the dialectic manifest themselves throughout the life span. As just one specific example, young parents have relatively little idea of what it means to be a mother or father until they physically experience the child. The first viewing and holding of the child are memorable sensory events, implanted kinesthetically, visually, and emotionally in the mind of the parents. So too are they implanted in the child, for this "holding environment" (Klein, 1975) forms a basis for the child's conception of self and her or his development throughout life.

The father (and, to some extent, the mother) tends to learn about the child through fragments of information. The father attempts to piece together an idea of how to cope with this new being. Many fathers have little idea of what to do; they are preoperational in their thinking and acting with the child. Their faulty thinking may lead to problems in relationship with the child and with the mother.

As the bits and pieces of being a father or mother come into a gestalt, the young parents learn the concrete operations necessary to work with the child. Concurrently, young fathers and mothers will spend hours conversing with friends and family about problems of childrearing. This processing often relates to late concrete operations, but is close to formal operations as they are seeking patterns of behavior that may be more effective.

The parents may start regarding themselves as father and mother—the thinking about thinking characteristic of formal operations. More often, this would seem to occur in the mother than the father.

If the parents appeared for therapy, one might find that they are repeating the patterns of their own childrearing; such a discussion would be at the late formal operations or early dialectical stage. Issues of men as fathers and traditional versus nontraditional roles for mothers might be examined, with special attention to feminist constructions of the family. The couple may examine how they are replaying the cultural demands of parenting that are imposed on them without their awareness.

Finally, parents might examine the constant search for the "right" form of parenting and realize that right is relative to the culture and to the unique child they have. The parents might eventually realize that their relationship with the child and each other is replaying the dialectic between knowledge ("correct" childrearing) and intelligence (awareness that "correctness" is contextual and hard to define).

For practical purposes, then, the examination of life-span development reveals that the theoretical frame of developmental therapy plays itself out again and again through the developmental tasks and phases of parents and their children. At times, the therapist will work with young parents who are overly separated from one another with the mother perhaps overattached to the child. The overattachment may represent preoperational thinking and behaving, which can be approached through the basic developmental techniques and conceptions suggested by developmental theory *praxis*—the integration of theory and practice.

The therapist may need to help formal operational parents experience their child more at a sensori-motor and play level. Other parents may need education in the concrete operations of being a parent. Owing to the incredible complexity of childrearing, parents may find themselves stuck and immobilized at many sensori-motor, concrete, formal, and dialectical tasks. The important and difficult task of the developmental therapist is to assess and diagnose the specific developmental task within the life framework and then to assist the couple to move forward using an approach that matches theory to client needs.

This one example illustrates the extreme complexity of the therapeutic process. If the therapist works only with the mother, the action nonetheless impacts the father and the child. As multiple developmental tasks and separation and attachment issues are playing themselves out simultaneously, it is not truly possible to be aware of all the many other developmental tasks that may be affected by change in one area.

The example of parental reaction to the developmental tasks surrounding the birth of the child perhaps can serve as a metaphor for other life developmental tasks. The child going to school must work through separation and attachment issues, put together sensori-motor fragments into concrete operations, and eventually learn to think about self. Similarly, the same person at age sixty-five must work through separation and attachment issues surrounding retirement and aging, put together the sensori-motor fragments of this new experience into concrete operations, and learn to think about self effectively.

Whether one is six or sixty, he or she faces a life full of developmental tasks, opportunities, and problems. Undergirding these developmental tasks is the fundamental role of the therapist to smooth the flow through the developmental therapy progressions and to help individuals deal with issues of separation and attachment or individuation and relationship.

Unless the developmental tasks at each level are accomplished, the next level will present problems and old issues will repeat themselves again and again. It is often the task of the therapist to help the client end this aimless, stuck, immobilized repetition, which is the result of incompletion of developmental tasks.

There is more going on in development than meets the eye of consciousness, and development is too complex for us to be aware of it all. Making the issue even more complex are the multitude of cultural factors underlying these developmental stages, developmental tasks, and developmental therapy progressions.

Holistic Life-Span Development. Carol Gilligan's relational theory, the four discourses of Jacques Lacan, and Erik Erikson's developmental concepts all contain one important idea in common—*development occurs holistically, not in strict linear sequence.* The spherical model of developmental therapy illustrates that linear and holistic models may be integrated. Gilligan stresses the importance of relationships, Lacan's discourses remind us that each stage of development contains all the other stages, and Erikson's theory is built on the premise that one must complete each developmental task successfully or problems will occur in later life.

The emphasis on family therapy and the life-cycle model (Figure 20) also is holistic and reminds us of how critical is the person-environment dialectic to personal growth and development. The Gilligan, Lacan, and Erikson models all stress the importance of environment, but the family models and the dialectical models of developmental therapy may be useful in extending these therapists' ideas.

The multispherical model(s) of developmental therapy are an attempt to illustrate that everything, indeed, is happening all at once. The slang phrase "bent out of shape" describes rather well what happens when developmental progressions are out of phase. It is possible to have very solid intellectual and formal operational capacities with very limited concrete operations. As Gregorc suggests, we as individuals are balances of many different styles and ways of being. But would an "ideal person" be balanced in all aspects? Do we seek a society of "roundheads"? Most likely not; variation is the norm and perhaps the wish of humans. Do we really wish to become the four-legged spherical creatures that Plato describes? Indeed, what is the nature of our desire?

Given that everything is happening developmentally at once, it may be helpful to examine the person-environment or dialectical interactions within development in summary form. Figure 21 is a representation of life-span developmental theory, a portrayal of the many issues that occur throughout the life span. This figure may be considered an integration of Bowlby's separation and attachment theories and Haley's life-cycle theory, with developmental progressions as conceptualized by Piaget, Masterson, Freud, and Erikson. A child matures in a family life-cycle context. The family provides the environment for the early stages of dialectical development.

Each theory incorporated in Figure 21 provides a useful perspective on the totality that is development. Piagetian theory seems especially useful to remind us of what is going on in the mind of the child who is experiencing primary object relations

Figure 21. Life-Span Developmental Theory

Age	Piaget	Masterson	Freud	Erikson
0–2 Sensori-motor	0–1 mo. Reflex and spontaneous movements	0–3 mo. Autistic	Oral	Oral Sensory (Basic trust vs. mistrust)
	1–4 mo. First habits and primary circular reaction	3–18 mo. Symbiotic		
		(Separation-individuation 18–36 mo. with subphases as below)		
		3–8 mo. S-I Differentiation	(6 mo. Lacan's "mirror stage" and Klein's depressive position)	
	4–8 mo. Secondary circular reaction	8–15 mo. S-I Practicing		
	8–12 mo. Coordination of means and ends			
	12–18 mo. Tertiary circular reaction			

(In this phase of the family life cycle, the child is completely dependent on the environment for survival. The introduction of a new human being into the family life cycle may be destructive to the family dyad, but certainly the structure of the family changes markedly.)

Age	Piaget	Masterson	Freud	Erikson
	18 mo.–2 yrs. Invention through sudden comprehension	15–22 mo. S-I Rapprochement	18 mo.–3 yrs. Anal	Muscular-Anal (Autonomy vs. shame and doubt)

(The child becomes more aware of environment and develops a beginning sense of control. How the environment responds to the child heavily determines what the child becomes. The family at this phase must simultaneously provide support and encouragement for differentiation and individuation, particularly as represented by Masterson's presentation of the rapprochement stage.)

Age	Piaget	Masterson	Freud	Erikson
2–7 years Preoperational (Many discussions include preoperational dimensions as part of sensori-motor functioning.)	Preoperational stage of representation, early symbolism, language learning	36+ mo. "On-the-way-to-object-constancy"	3–8 Phallic/Oedipal	Locomotor-genital (Initiative vs. guilt)

(During this period, the child has "everything going on at once." Major tasks of separation and individuation are completed further, being built on past object relations. The child works from a framework of preoperational thinking, which is often magical. At this time the child learns to take a cultural role of initiative, learns sex roles, and—hopefully—will learn that people and family are constant objects that are both good and bad. The separation of the child from the home may result in major stress to the parents.)

7–12 years Concrete Operations

		Latency
Conservation, Commutibility, Seriation, Classification, Class inclusion, Contradiction	The way the child and adult develop has already been determined by earlier development. The rest may be considered metaphor on the past. A major task is the development of a sense of self.	Latency (Industry vs. inferiority)

(The child continues the separation/individuation process from the family. There will be an emphasis on concrete problems, listing, and organization, particularly if earlier developmental tasks have been completed successfully in a working family. Divorce in the preoperational/phallic/Oedipal period can be particularly destructive. The child builds a sense of industry on the past. We should note that Erikson's constructs are heavily culturally based, and that different cultures may feature the movement through the developmental stages very differently. At this stage the child develops independent relationships with peers and increasingly generates a sense of self.)

12–19 Formal Operations

	Adolescence
Learning how to identify the unique self and separate self from self thus enabling "thinking about one's self."	Puberty and Adolescence (Identity vs. role confusion)

(The adolescent starts thinking about self as independent in this chapter and finds his or her unique identity. The separation process from the family continues, and the late adolescent may be expected to socialize and date to initiate the approximate beginnings of his or her own family.)

(continued on next page)

Figure 21. Life-Span Developmental Theory, Cont'd.

Age	Developmental Therapy	Masterson	Freud	Erikson
19-30 Young Adulthood	In developmental therapy conceptions, the adult continues to recycle old processes of sensori-motor, concrete, and formal operations. The adult may exhibit pre-operational magical thinking. The individual may become aware of the dialectic.	The mother may repeat old patterns of mothering learned in childhood, thus continuing old problem behaviors. Similarly, the spouses may relate to each other as they would to past parent figures.	Young Adulthood	Young Adulthood (Intimacy vs. isolation)

(Haley would note the importance of forming the family and/or entering the workplace. In these and other developmental tasks of this portion of the life span, we again can see that the foundation of the past will heavily determine the present life of the individual.)

30-45 Middle Adulthood			Adulthood	(30-60) Adulthood (Generativity vs. stagnation)
45-60 Late Adulthood				

(Children grow and develop during this period; the individual defines success in work. The issues of the forties and fifties life crises may occur. Divorce, the entry into a new work situation, the development of new relationships, or the impact of the absent child may cause many individuals to again repeat old childhood patterns—both parents and children.)

60+ Maturity				Maturity (Ego integrity vs. despair)

(As Erikson and Haley both note, the success at maturity heavily depends on the success with which the individual has met past life developmental tasks. Once again, we may find early childhood patterns repeating themselves in daily patterns of behavior, thought, and feeling. The individual must learn to face the most threatening separation of all—death.)

with the mother. Freud and Erikson provide familiar linkages of these two theories to well-known constructs over the life span. Furthermore, Erikson is particularly helpful as he, perhaps better than anyone else, illustrates that development is indeed a life-span issue in which we constantly recycle old developmental tasks as we face new issues and decisions.

Yet, no one theorist provides us with all the answers. Each theory summarized here is helpful in reminding us of a special part of the developmental process. Yet, even these are not complete. Developmental theorists such as Kegan, Loevinger, and Perry, mentioned in Chapter One, also provide alternative perspectives that help us enrich our understanding of the complex process of development.

Developmental therapy is concerned with facilitating development over the life span. It is also concerned with family development and the person-environment dialectics of groups and organizations, although the latter have not been discussed in this book. Families, groups, and organizations may be expected to follow the progressions of the theory and should be amenable to varying adaptations of the theories of therapy and change presented here.

Development in a Cultural Context. Counseling and therapy are usually thought of as two-person relationships because they usually involve a counselor and a client. Historically, it has been believed that all that is necessary is for the therapist (or the teacher, lawyer, or governance structure) to be empathic toward the client. There is now reason to believe that empathy requires a broader understanding (Ivey, Ivey, and Simek-Downing, 1987). It could be said that *four* participants may be found in the interview: the therapist, with her or his cultural and historical background, and the client, with his or her cultural and historical background.

Lacan (see Clement, 1983; Lacan, 1966) suggests that the

Note: Most of the material in this section is taken verbatim from A. Ivey, "The Multicultural Practice of Therapy: Ethics, Empathy, and Dialectics" in a special issue of the *Journal of Social and Clinical Psychology* (forthcoming 1987) on the relationship between clinical, counseling, and social psychology, and is used here by permission of the author.

interview is not just a relationship between the two people who are physically present. In addition, each client brings a special cultural and historical background that impacts powerfully in the session. Details of such differences are outlined with explicit force in McGoldrick, Pearce, and Giordano's *Ethnicity and Family Therapy* (1982). What appears to be individual behavior is more truly described as a cultural artifact. It is pointed out, for example, that British-Americans are often expected to leave home upon completing school, but that Italian-Americans may be expected to live near their parents. Therapy without awareness of such basic cultural differences may result in unethical practices and damage to the client. These differences are even more important given cultural distance between therapist and client.

Counseling and psychotherapy theory historically have considered cultural differences of secondary importance. This is particularly so for the basic triad of therapy—psychodynamic, behavioral, and existential/humanistic. While each theory accounts for cultural and sexual differences, these critical factors tend to become lost in the complexities of the theory. Schneiderman (1983) has stated that "those who attempt to erase (*or forget*) cultural differences, who wish to create a society where Otherness is nonexistent, come to be alienated.... The moral condemnation of Otherness is racist; of this there can be little doubt" (p. 174).

Empathy requires us to be aware of individual uniqueness and "Otherness" (social and historical factors). Clinical and counseling psychology over the years have tended to focus on individual uniqueness. The search for the "best" treatment for each client and the arguments about the "correct" theory all presuppose that "the answer" exists. Traditional definitions of empathy (see Rogers, 1957; Carkhuff, 1969; Ivey and Simek-Downing, 1980) have focused on entering the unique perspective of the individual and have failed to give adequate attention to social and environmental dimensions. This situation is illustrated in Figure 22. Here social forces do impinge on the interview, but the counselor and client tend to ignore them.

Sometimes in cross-cultural counseling the client is aware

Figure 22. Cultural/Historical Dimensions Neglected in the
Therapeutic Relationship

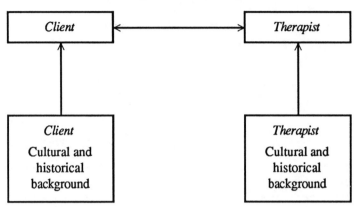

of her or his unique culture, but the therapist is not (see Figure 23). The client, in turn, may respond to the individualistic nature of the therapist's theoretical and practical orientation but fail to see the person of the therapist. Ethical therapy is most difficult under such circumstances.

Obviously, the desired model is for the client and counselor to each be aware of culture and history and to use these elements in an empathic manner. Empathy requires awareness

Figure 23. Client Aware, Therapist Unaware, of
Cultural/Historical Dimensions

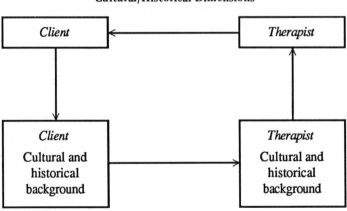

and understanding not only of the unique individual but also of the broad array of cultural and historical factors that may underlie individual experience.

Occasionally, a therapist will discover someone who "triggers" his or her cultural and historical unconscious. In this situation the two individuals may think they are talking to each other but in reality are enacting their own cultural scripts (see Figure 24). In such cases, therapist and counselor "talk past" the person in front of them.

Figure 24. Client and Therapist Enacting Their Own Cultural Scripts

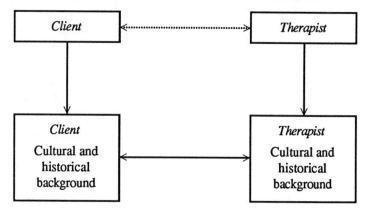

Empathy demands awareness of *both* the individual and the culture. Not only must we be empathic toward the client, we must be equally empathic toward what is cultural in the client and its impact on both the client and on ourselves. A dialectical view of empathy, moreover, suggests that the client needs to be able to understand us as individuals and cultural beings. Figure 25 shows once again that the individual and culture cannot be truly separated. However, the distinction suggested here emphasizes that both social and clinical/counseling psychologists need to be more fully aware of the complexity of the human being.

Lacan's famous "Z diagram" (1977; 1978, p. 193) is presented in modified form in Figure 26. In Lacanian analysis, the therapist focuses on the cultural and historical background

Figure 25. Client and Therapist Empathic Toward Each Other's
Cultural/Historical Context

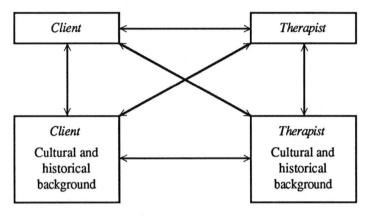

(*Autre* or "Other" in Lacanian language) rather than on the person. The client learns how he or she has been influenced unconsciously by the culture and how what seems to be individually unique behavior is actually "the discourse of the Other," in which historical factors rule behavior. Feminist therapy, in which women learn how much of their behavior is dictated by cultural expectations, follows the Lacanian Z diagram at least partially. In feminist therapy, clients learn that culture dictates

Figure 26. Lacan's "Z Diagram"

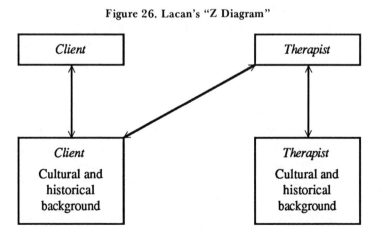

the actions of the person, and therapy is oriented toward liberating the client from the cultural discourse.

Empathy, then, from this point of view, requires a continuing development of interpersonal and intercultural awareness. Each individual is a cultural being with family, group, and cultural heritage. To conduct therapy without this awareness (which can be enhanced by reading social psychology literature) can be considered unethical and has been so labeled at the Vail Conference (Korman, 1973).

Given this frame of reference, it becomes apparent that developmental therapy always occurs within a cultural context. Issues of separation and attachment will play themselves out very differently among individuals of varying cultures. The emphasis on concrete operations as compared with formal operations undoubtedly also varies from culture to culture as it does from individual to individual and from family to family.

When we consider the world of culture and its impact on development of the individual, we become aware that patterns of our development have been determined by Others (the Lacanian *Autre* or Other) and that we have been less in control of our own development than we have believed. This exploration of the Other is a venture into the unknown. This sociocultural Other may be increased awareness of gender, sexual preference, or socioeconomic status; the impact of being mentally or physically disabled; the role of political systems; and issues of race, ethnicity, and religion.

Examination of the world of the Other implies a movement into the unknown, the exploration of what is sometimes termed the "unconscious."

The Development of the Unconscious

Is development possible beyond awareness? This section first examines the notion of the unconscious, then considers how the conscious and the unconscious are related. These two ideas are critical in an examination of how developmental therapy plays itself out at the unconscious level.

The Notion of the Unconscious. Freud used the word *das*

Unbewusste, which was translated as "the unconscious." As Bettelheim (1982) has noted, a more accurate translation would be "the unknown." Consciousness is what we know, and the unconscious is what is beyond our present awareness.

At some level, the client and the therapist remain unaware or unconscious of something beyond them. The achievement of complete consciousness is not epistemologically possible, because we are all embedded in the evolving framework of development and coevolution. As noted in Chapter Two, the outcome may be conscious, but ahead lie further indeterminant processes based on the moment, the elusive *noesis* of intelligence.

A simple definition of the unconscious that will be used in this book is "any matter of which we are currently unaware." In this sense, a client in therapy is unconscious (unaware) of a multitude of things. In the analytic sense of the term, the client is unaware of personal history that may be motivating the visit to the therapist.*

Beyond the client's awareness is how his or her current speech is influenced by what the therapist says. The client is most likely unaware that many personal constructions of the problem can be highly impacted by unique personal history. The client may also be unaware that his or her anger at the therapist may really relate to a current frustration with a superior on the job (and in turn to past frustrations with the father).

Also beyond most client awareness is the impact of cultural and social factors, such as income, past schooling, and cultural factors. White clients may be unaware that their position in the dominant culture results in certain types of unconscious sexism or racism. Conversely, female or Black clients may be at least partially conscious of these same factors of social oppression but may still be unaware of the multitude of factors that led to their present situation.

---

*The choice here is not to venture into distinctions between conscious, preconscious, and unconscious, as suggested in Freud's first topography. The preconscious elements "differ from the contents of the unconscious system in that they are still in principle accessible to consciousness (for instance, knowledge and memories that are not presently conscious)" (Laplanche and Pontalis, 1967, p. 325).

The concept of *noesis,* or intelligence, reminds us that there is always something beyond that of which we speak. The achievement of "full" consciousness may not be possible. What impels us to speak is not just what is before us, but also what is behind us and around us—that which contains the seeds of the future; these factors are all enacted in a setting of cultural and social history.

Mahoney (1980) makes the same point but uses different language: "(1) We probably learn more than we can verbalize; (2) unless we practice verbalizing them, many of our motor and cognitive skills tend to become progressively less accessible to language; and (c) stored information does not have to be communicated to exert an influence on our thoughts, feelings, and actions" (p. 163).

Perceptgenesis is an approach formulated by Kragh and Smith (1970) at the University of Lund, Sweden. Westerlundh and Smith (1983) review this work, which considers the creation of a conscious idea as a dialectic of construction between the external world and the internalized meaning system of the individual. Perceptgenesis is the perceptual process through which the senses take in (accommodate) data; the process is itself impacted and heavily overdetermined by past perceptions (assimilations) that are in the memory system—conscious, preconscious, and unconscious.

Justifying this point of view, Smith and Westerlundh cited research studies in which they and their colleagues presented stimuli to subjects using tachistoscopic techniques. In this "presentation" (Freud would use the word "verstellung"), TAT-like line drawings were presented at intervals of fifty milliseconds or less, which is below the physical perceptual threshold (see Figure 6, which shows that perception requires approximately one hundred milliseconds). The subjects do see or sense "something," and although the picture does not register on the conscious mind, the client is asked to draw a picture of what he or she thinks has been seen. In this fashion the individual must use the present new data *and* data from long-term memory (the unconscious) to construct what has been seen.

Figure 27 presents a sample stimulus that was presented briefly to subjects. Westerlundh and Smith note that the draw-

Figure 27. Instances of Defensive Transformations of a Father-Son Theme

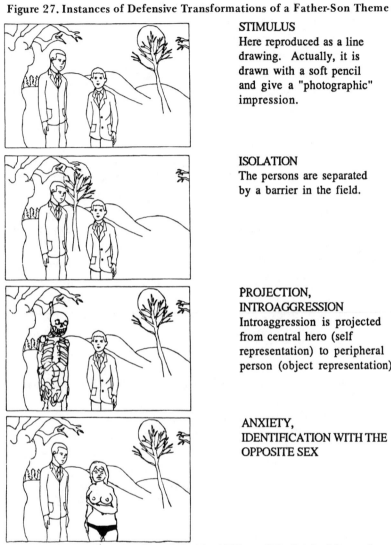

STIMULUS
Here reproduced as a line drawing. Actually, it is drawn with a soft pencil and give a "photographic" impression.

ISOLATION
The persons are separated by a barrier in the field.

PROJECTION, INTROAGGRESSION
Introaggression is projected from central hero (self representation) to peripheral person (object representation).

ANXIETY, IDENTIFICATION WITH THE OPPOSITE SEX

Source: Westerlundh and Smith, 1983, p. 613. Original figure from 1976. Reprinted by permission.

ings of the subjects represent transformational projections of these individuals. They also note that different individuals have varying patterns of perception of such ambiguous stimuli. Somewhat surprisingly, the best theoretical classification of client projections of the tachistoscopic presentations lies in

Freudian defense mechanisms. Subjects with a high level of denial, for example, tend to ignore the existence of aggression when aggression is present in the stimulus, whereas those who may use the defense mechanism of reaction formation tend to turn the aggressive action into a picture directly opposite to that presented. Such perceptual patterns tend to be automatic and repeat again and again upon stimulus presentations.

Data such as these provide strong supporting confirmation for the concept of the unconscious. Certainly, the data illustrate that "something else" in long-term memory is influencing perception. Goncalves (1985) has carefully reviewed the literature on unconscious processing and concludes that the unconscious is alive and well, perhaps more so than conscious functioning. The database elaborating the unconscious is expanding rapidly (see the work of Bowers, 1984; Shervin and Dickman, 1980; Zajonc, 1980). Cognitive behaviorists such as Bowers and Meichenbaum (1984) and Mahoney (1980, 1984) now give a prominent place to unconscious functioning in cognition.

But how does consciousness relate to the unknown beyond? Derrida's deconstruction theory provides some interesting thoughts and challenges.

The Deconstruction of the Conscious and the Unconscious

The French philosopher Jacques Derrida (1973, 1978) criticizes as metaphysical any thought system that is believed to rest on an unassailable foundation. Whether it is Piaget's strongly held beliefs about child development, Plato's conception of the nature of reality, or Freud's notion of the unconscious, Derrida suggests that all are contaminated by history. As yet, the search for first principles can only be expected to lead to failure.

Deconstruction examines the assumptions and propositions of concepts and, as such, represents the dialectic in action. Deconstruction, however, may be considered distinct from the dialectic because it includes the awareness of the futility of its own process, a concept similar to *noesis,* the elusive intelligence that is always beyond us.

If one examines first principles closely, they may be deconstructed, or as Eagleton (1983) says, "they can be shown to be products of a particular system of meaning, rather than that which props it up from outside" (p. 132). This process of deconstruction reveals internal contradictions in the structure of the idea or concept. This complex product of literary theory and philosophy very roughly parallels the situation where the therapist confronts the client by pointing out contradictions in the client's argument. In effect, the therapist helps the client deconstruct past syntheses (client's problem) through their opposition (the confrontation statement).

It can be argued that Piaget's constructivist thought, or creative transformations, as described in Chapter Five, is based on deconstruction. For the child to enter into a new thought pattern, the child must decenter (deconstruct) old ways of thinking before moving into or creating new, more complex cognitions. Derrida's deconstruction, however, is poststructuralist in nature, whereas Piaget's thought is structuralist (see Piaget, [1968] 1970). Thus, Derrida's position represents a level of analysis "above" that of Piaget's.

In the above paragraph, it may be noted that constructivism has been placed in opposition to deconstructivist theory. Placing thoughts and concepts in opposition is characteristic of deconstructive theory. Again, according to Eagleton (1983), deconstruction "is the critical operation by which such oppositions (tight constructions or ideas) can be partly undermined, or by which they can be shown partly to undermine each other in the process of textual meaning" (p. 132).

We can now turn to the deconstruction of the conscious and the unconscious. Each construct contains seeds of its own deconstruction. Just as George's thought in the interview in Chapter Six can be deconstructed (decentered) by the therapist's use of dialectical developmental therapy, so can these solid constructions be found to have internal contradictions.

Consciousness has been defined by Morris (1978) as "having an awareness of one's own existence, sensations, and thoughts, and of one's environment" (p. 283). The term derives from the Indo-European root *skei*, meaning "to cut, split, or divide"; and from the Latin *scire*, "to divide, discriminate, and hence know" (see Shipley, 1984, p. 348). Basic to the concept of consciousness is the idea that the subject is split from the object; hence the Cartesian *cogito,* "I think, therefore I am."

Basic to the idea of conscious experience (and ego psychology) is the idea that consciousness can be known. One basic assumption of developmental therapy and the underlying concept of *noesis* has been that it is impossible to separate out a knowable final truth. The client may be "conscious" of sensorimotor or concrete operational "reality," but the fact that he or she is simultaneously located in a sphere of formal operations and dialectics will be missed because these are both part of the whole.

Furthermore, driving the subject's consciousness of self and environment are impressions of that environment, which determine how the person constructs and orients self to the world. It is not a long leap to the assumption that we are but the sum total of our experiences. Thus, our consciousness is merely what is given to us from outside. As we are not aware of what comes from outside or of what comes from internal forces of biology, there is little room left for consciousness. Our awareness is not our own, but that of the Other.

Lacan ([1973] 1978) sharply criticizes the concept of consciousness and the ideas of American ego psychology. He points out that we are born into a cultural and familial script and that if there is any form of consciousness left, it is indeed very small and feeble. The concept of "I see myself seeing myself" (a variation of "I think, therefore I am") is based on the false assumption that one can see oneself in undistorted form. What one sees as good and beautiful is determined by how the family and culture describe these terms. Even the ability to recognize "face," "eyes," and "nose" requires an Other for conceptual framing. "What I look at is never what I wish to see" (p. 103).

"The unconscious is the discourse of the Other" is perhaps one of Lacan's most famous and puzzling statements, yet is also the basis of his theoretical reformulations of Freud. The Lacanian point of view takes the epistemological constructions of developmental therapy one additional step: consciousness does not exist, because when one speaks, one speaks from the position of the Other. The Other represents the sum total of the individual's social and cultural history. One does not speak; rather one is spoken. As Picasso once said, "I do not seek, I find," Lacan says, "I am not a poet, I am poem." As an author writing this text, I am not writing, I am written.

As was mentioned earlier, Lacan criticizes American ego psychology insofar as it is characterized by the revival of notions long since refuted in the field of psychoanalysis, such as the predominance of the functions of the ego" ([1973] 1978, p. 127), and for the naive Cartesian assumption that the therapist can build ego functioning and consciousness, which do not exist and are functions of the Other.

This deconstruction exercise could continue. The concept of consciousness contains too many conceptual errors and contradictions to hold together.

So, we speak from the unconscious . . . or do we? Certainly just as the idea of consciousness is helpful, so the concept of the unconscious is useful at times. Lacan is not satisfied to deconstruct consciousness; he is also intent on deconstructing the idea of unconsciousness. Lacan derives his theory of knowledge from Plotinus and appears to focus on the unity within multiplicity. In speaking of the place of the unconscious, he says: "ὄν, οὐχ ὄν, μὴὄν—(being, nonbeing, [is] not being); to use these terms is still to oversubstantify the unconscious" ([1973] 1978, p. 134).

In decoding these cryptic comments, Silhol (1985) states that the *unconscious does not exist.* The reasoning behind this surprising point is fairly simple. The unconscious vanishes the moment you "pin it down." Paradoxically, it appears in our understanding *after the fact.* In understanding the unconscious after the fact, we use conscious awareness, which itself has been deconstructed, as illustrated in the preceding paragraphs.

If neither consciousness nor unconsciousness exists, then perhaps we do not exist. *If I do not think, therefore I do not exist.* Having deconstructed existence in a possibly humorous exercise, we find ourselves in an interesting dialectic with Descartes:

$$\frac{\text{I think, therefore I am}}{\text{I do not think, therefore I am not.}}$$

The positing of one form of consciousness or unconsciousness implies the existence of another. Each proposition, one of consciousness and one of unconsciousness, contains internal contradictions. To stand, each needs the other in opposition. Just as the concept of man implies woman, good implies evil, war implies peace, and figure implies ground, so the complementary concepts conscious and unconscious form an unstable dialectical unity.

Deconstruction is a story of instability, change, and constant growth. Paradoxically, it is the examination of contradiction that, in its very action of destruction, leads to new constructions. Deconstructivist theory searches for its own beginnings, but in the act of searching, it has changed the beginning.

Let us turn now to the practical implications of these constructions in the developmental therapy model.

Developmental Therapy Beyond the Known

Mahoney (1980) has summarized the issue of gaining knowledge beyond awareness when he points out that "we probably learn more than we can verbalize" and that "stored information does not have to be communicated to exert an influence on our thoughts, feelings, and actions" (p. 163). In short, what we learn in therapy (or life) contains more than we are aware.

Thus, while working through the developmental therapy processes of concrete operations in, for example, a parent counseling session, the parent may be learning consciously the specific concrete operations of child discipline. But, the therapist's tone of voice, nonverbal state, and ultimate intent are also speaking to issues of respect for the child and the parent, the culturally appropriate behavior expected in middle-class society, and a variety of other unspoken factors. In addition, the way the therapist joins the client in empathy and terminates the interview at the end of the session are metaphors of separation and attachment. Unknown to the therapist and client is that they are enacting the cultural scripts they have been given by Others. Thus, the theoretical and observed message of therapy is only a small part of the total information transmitted in the process.

At each life developmental stage, we repeat the basic themes of separation and attachment as well as those of developmental sequences. None of these concepts exist apart from one another; together they form a whole. While we work on one of the systems, each act we take reverberates throughout the entire interpersonal system of our clients and of ourselves as well. We are, as Gilligan and Bowlby suggest, connected and attached to one another, despite our separateness. We will play the spherical game and totally separate again and again, but ultimately we are interdependent with others and our Other.

It would be possible to continue the discussion of unconscious side effects of therapy. Their existence or lack of existence is, for the most part, unknowable and indeterminate. What is unconscious can be only known after the fact, when these effects are brought out by the therapy or by self-exploration. In either case, when the unconscious is "discovered," it will be agreed that it was already there and no longer is unconscious (Picasso's "I do not seek, I find"). But something else still has been changed, for in the process of making something conscious, the underlying structure of the unconscious has already changed. Even though the unconscious does not exist, it is a fluid vessel open to expansion and contraction.

In summary, one major route toward the development of the unconscious is conscious positive development. If all goes well, the chances are that the unconscious will be positively impacted. There is a growing body of research literature on "remembering without awareness" (Jacoby and Witherspoon, 1982) in which subjects can learn or demonstrate complex skills (such as mirror writing or problem solving) and emotions (such as fear) without being consciously aware. Advertising, particularly the "sexual sell," is another obvious type of direct appeal to the unconscious. The overt conscious message may be cigarettes, but the unconscious message may be sexual attractiveness and conquest. Unconscious learning may be used for good or ill purposes.

The therapist never knows when a gesture or a word may "trigger" an unpleasant unconscious association in the client. In the early phases of Breuer's "talking cure" with the hysteric Anna O., he noted that if someone entered or left the room, she complained of gaps in her train of conscious thought and became upset. These *absences* were subsequently discovered to relate to fears surrounding her dying father (Breuer and Freud, 1893, pp. 24, 36). The metaphor of absence repeated itself in her hallucinations of black snakes. Believing that Anna O. was making satisfactory progress, Breuer absented himself and pronounced an abrupt cure. Not to be outdone, Anna O. called him urgently, saying that she was pregnant with his child. As Jones (1953) notes, Breuer hypnotized Anna O. once more and took off with his wife the next day for a second honeymoon. The side effects of unconscious development are difficult to predict.*

Anna O. and Breuer as client and therapist represent another dialectical pair. As Comfort (1984) suggests, empathy is

---

*However, Rosenbaum (1984) has carefully examined the life story of Anna O., who in real life was Bertha Pappenheim, the founder of social work in Germany. Through historical analysis of available records, it now seems possible that Jones distorted the story of Anna O.'s false pregnancy to facilitate Freud's standing in the annals of history as compared to Breuer, who many could argue is the true founder of psychoanalysis. Still others could argue it was Anna O. who founded analysis. It was she who spontaneously started free association with her able intellect and who also coined the term "chimney sweeping" as basic to the "talking cure." Nonetheless, it must be granted that Jones has a point. It does seem clear that Bertha Pappenheim did have strong transferential feelings toward Breuer, which Breuer did not recognize.

Lacan, however, perhaps has the last laugh: "Why is it we do not consider Bertha's pregnancy rather, according to my formula: *man's desire is the desire of the Other,* as the manifestation of Breuer's desire? Why do you not go so far as to think that it was Breuer who had a desire for a child?" ([1973] 1978, p. 158). Lacan considers much of transference ideas in therapy to be the desire of the analyst rather than of the patient. In effect, Bertha's false pregnancy was her fulfillment of the desire of the Other (Breuer); it was not Bertha's unconscious desire that was fulfilled, it was Breuer's.

manifested in this case in two overlapping aspects: (1) how Anna O. feels about the world is a result of incorporating particular knowledge (in this case she has incorporated absence as a basic metaphor of her existence); and (2) how she makes knowledge incorporable is determined by her past history and this, in turn, determines the nature of the content that enters in. Breuer demonstrated the first type of empathy and was able to decode Anna O.'s internal thought patterns and make them conscious. However, he was too embedded in a transferential relationship with Anna O. to note her perceptual process of making knowledge incorporable. Breuer repeated the seductive pattern of Anna O.'s father and, thus, although he cured her, he was simultaneously continuing the process of her illness. In Breuer's defense, Freud did not really outline the nature of transference in the talking cure until 1914.

Mary Bradford Ivey faces the same potential difficulties in the empathic relationship with George in Chapter Six. Clearly, she is making new data enter consciousness and is working toward an empathic understanding of the ordering patterns of the client, such as his obsessive concern for order, his desire to nurture and, most likely, to be nurtured (much of the behavior of the obsessive is a reaction formation), and so on. The second dimension of the client's perceptual patterns is less apparent, but the rapid movement of the dialectical relationship forces him to constantly accommodate to new data provided by the therapist. In this limited exchange, Ivey has not been caught in the structural repetition of behavior as was Breuer (in that he constantly used the same therapeutic method without awareness of his personal impact on the perceptual process).

Research similar to that of Westerlundh and Smith explicates the more complex definition of empathy, as outlined by Comfort, by helping demonstrate how a person's perceptions determine the structure of his or her being.

Effective empathy requires the therapist to (1) understand and uncover the structure and content of client thought and affect (these are similar to what Gregorc terms the ordering dimensions of cognitive style), and (2) understand and uncover the structure and content of client perceptual structures that lead to underlying structure and content (which Gregorc refers to as perceptual style). Without this dual dimension of empathy, therapists (and their clients) may be doomed to repeat Breuer's classic problem again and again.

Breuer worked with Anna O. at the level of the ordering of unconscious material. He kept amazing records about this client and lists, for example, 108 instances her not hearing when someone came in, 50 instances of not hearing when directly addressed, and 12 instances of deafness brought about by deep absence. "Of course all these episodes were to a great extent identical in so far as they could be traced back to states of abstraction or *absences* or to fright" (Breuer and Freud, 1893, p. 36). The instances that are not due to absences could be considered as intrusions or entry points into her experiential world. Each entry or absence upset Anna O.'s delicate equilibrium.

Breuer became quite adept at his new talking cure and was consistently able to talk away Anna O.'s symptoms as he discovered the points at which they first appeared. This uncovering of the unconscious in a relationship of love brought together the split whole. With each new gestalt or synthesis, a breakdown into splits was again inevitable, as was the constant movement of Anna O. into new symptom after new symptom.

Missing from Breuer's treatment was an examination of *how* Anna O. was taking in data perceptually beyond conscious awareness. He unfortunately failed to see that his relationship with her was repeating the cause of her problem, specifically, entry and absence, and at another level, Anna's problem with her own father. Much as in Westerlundh and Smith's work, Anna O. was transferring her past relationship with her father into her relationship with Breuer. Transference, then, is a way of transferring or utilizing one's long-term memories and consciousness in the present perceptual moment, which thus continually distorts data input. It is necessary in effective analytic treatment to not only examine the internal ordering of client data but to also evaluate the way the client takes in and assembles these data. Both processes tend to be unconscious, but the more important and more difficult issue is to clarify client perceptual input—thus, the critical importance of the transference relationship in effecting a cure.

The exceptionally difficult task, at least using the methods of Freud and the psychoanalysts, is to teach patients that they are not seeing clearly. And, until the ordering in the unconscious is made relatively conscious, it is most difficult to attack and make conscious perceptual modes of viewing the world.

However, the work of Gilligan, Lacan, and Gregorc as explored in the previous chapter points to the fact that individuals perceive the same data differently. Men have a different perceptual and ordering style from women. Those who are at the sensori-motor, concrete operations, formal operations, and dialectical levels all tend to take in and organize input differently. Thus, it theoretically should be possible to teach individuals more directly about their perceptual styles and thus make this form of unconsciousness more conscious and aware and change the nature of unconscious perception. But, as is true in therapies and educational programs that are concerned with conscious functioning, something more will exist beyond consciousness—a part that cannot be grasped.

It has been suggested that consciousness and unconsciousness do not exist, or, more accurately, that the concepts treated in isolation can be deconstructed. Perhaps a more proper formulation is that they do exist but only in relation one to another. They are bound together as tightly as the two parts of the four-legged spherical creatures of Plato. The unconscious and conscious exist in a coevolution of the dialectic, which is seldom balanced and at rest in the healthy, growing individual. However, in cases of neurosis, psychosis, and normal personal problems, the dialectic of the two has ceased to move. In a sense, the desire of the conscious and unconscious is for the unobtainable "each other."

We have seen the operation of the dialectic in George's relation to the therapist in Chapter Six. There are other dialectics occurring as well, one of the most important being the dialectic between conscious and unconscious thought within George. Much of George's conscious thought is available to us through the transcript of the interview. What is occurring in his unconscious is less apparent to us and would require another form of analysis.

One form of unconscious repetition George makes is similar to that made by Anna O., namely, absence and entry or separation and attachment. Anna O. and George are both reliving the myth of the four-legged creatures who seek to rejoin themselves. Anna O. was abused by her father and in her relationship with Breuer relived the issues of separation (Breuer's absence as he left each day and, most important, when he planned to end treatment) and attachment (the entry and re-entry of Breuer). This reliving or repeating occurred in relationship to Breuer, who came and went daily over a period of time. During this time, the attachment of the young patient for the doctor naturally increased. It seems only natural that she should hysterically become pregnant with his child when threatened by the termination of the relationship.

Many therapists repeat Breuer's error (lack of consciousness of transferential issues) when they seek to help reorder the client's world view. The client's world view must be reordered if change is to occur; so also must the perceptual system be made more flexible if repetition of the symptom in some new form is to be avoided.

Mary Bradford Ivey's transcript with George provides us with an opportunity to study dialectical shifts. The underlying issue of the unconscious is that of separation and attachment, the alternative joining and disengagement of self in relation to self and self in relation to others. A review of the transcript suggests that the unconscious movement involved separation and attachment in a constant pulsation underlying conscious thought. Consider the following analysis of Mary's and George's session:

21. *Mary:* Yeah, the same kind of thing. You know, you're doing her work for her and you're letting her get by with not doing it and then you're coming home and you know, you're taking it out on the kids . . . the same sort of thing with the kids. How does that seem to fit with you? (*Here the therapist joins with the client by using key words and constructs plus a warm, supportive vocal tone and a good deal of nonverbal mirroring as evidenced in the videotape. There is, however, simultaneously a separation in that the*

therapist is adding constructions of the situation from her frame of reference. Specifically, this is the linking of George's behavior with the secretary Georgia and the children. This separation provides the impetus for the movement of the dialectic.)

22. *George:* (*Grabs stomach*) I feel my body just sort of react to that. Yeah, I hadn't thought about that really. I do tend to be too critical of people. Ah . . . I . . . but, the thing is . . . they just aren't doing the job and . . . the thing is that it makes me feel badly again. It isn't as bad as being compulsive, but . . . on other hand . . . being critical all the time. (*The client's equilibrium has been attached and attacked. His conscious thought is challenged by new data from the therapist, which links facts that he was unconscious of to his present behavior. He has loosened tight constructs and is more ready for the movement of the dialectic. To move satisfactorily, he will need love to support this separation within himself. George's grabbing his stomach represents the moment when the unconscious physically attacks the conscious and moves to awareness.)*

23. *Mary:* Yeah, but there are some positives in that situation, George. Can you see some of the positives? I mean not only are you a critical parent, you're also a nurturing parent, you know. (*The therapist deliberately joins and attaches to the stumbling client in terms of tone of voice and paraverbals; she brings out positive dimensions of George's own attachment to the children. Paradoxically, she is simultaneously separating from George by presenting a separate view of the situation. This alternative view of the situation is a conceptual ordering process both for conscious and unconscious functioning. The perceptual issue of empathy is worked on through the movement of separation and attachment on the part of the therapist.)*

24. *George:* Positives? How's that? That doesn't make any sense. (*George is so focused on the conscious and unconscious negatives of his behavior that he has difficulty hear-*

ing the new frame of reference. His conscious behavior is in opposition to the therapist, and he seems very separate at this moment. But his need for attachment and caring is high.)

25. *Mary:*   Well, I think that you're really trying to take care of everybody when you're straightening up the house and you know people are tired.

    George: That's true. (*Note that he has incorporated the therapist's interpretation into himself at this point.*)

    Mary: You know your secretary's under a lot of pressure. You know that the kids have all kinds of work to do, and so in some ways you can almost reframe what you're doing into being a positive, ummm . . . nurturing type parent. How does that fit? (*This statement is highly oriented to attaching positive meanings [love] to client perceptions. The client has ordered the situation differently and is changing his world view. Again, the therapist is enacting loving entry into the client's world, but her enactment is beyond his [and her] awareness. It may be that the style of enactment is a better indicator of empathic understanding than the positive results that may be observed more directly.*)

26. *George:*   Yeah, nurturing comes up, it feels right because I guess I did say I like the kids . . . you know . . . they're busy and I like to help them and I know that Georgia is not really in a great spot. . . . But it sure ends up with me getting angry. . . . Ah! So, in effect, by being nurtur . . . so nurturing, I end up being [*Mary:* very critical] . . . very critical and very angry. (*The insight takes hold at a deeper level owing to the enactment of the therapist. Whereas the children or Georgia would react to George in repeating patterns, the therapist is able to stand outside the patterns and provide a new type of relationship in which George can examine his behavior and thinking more carefully.*)

Over time, George and the therapist will find that he is repeating with the therapist the behavior that is now so apparent with his children and his secretary. Just as with Anna O., this repetition will take a disguised form, but the structure of the repetition will be the same. The words may not be so nurturant and the client, caught in the discourse of the master and concrete operations, may engage in reaction formation and express a considerable amount of hostility toward the therapist. According to psychoanalytic theory, it is here in the alteration of perceptual structures that change can be truly anticipated and most likely can be best maintained over time.

The point of this particular analysis is to illustrate that the therapist's impact on processes beyond the awareness of both therapist and client is simultaneous with and perhaps stronger than her effect on the client's conscious. The enactment of the separation and attachment metaphor is basic to this process.

What the healthy personality needs is a balance or equilibration between the impossible demands of separation and attachment. This balance is often provided by the movement of the dialectic, for it is in the process of movement that we can simultaneously feel both separation and attachment as one. As has been noted earlier, if the dialectic is to be filled and ready to overturn, the therapist must fill the vessel of client need and demand. This filling or entering in represents attachment. But once the client is full, he or she will separate into a new and different human being.

But, just as in the case of Anna O., one cannot have it both ways. Anna O. was filled to overflowing with a gradually deepening understanding of her patterns of ordering her life. However, Breuer was unable to understand that her perceptual processes of separation and attachment remained the same.

The power of relational empathy, as Comfort conceptualizes the term, lies in its impossible duality, that of being within the moment but simultaneously being separate. In this way, the client can take from us and yet construct an independent being. The first dimension of Comfort's definition of empathy is "how we feel about the world, as a result of incorporating particular knowledge" (1984, p. xviii). This is the ordering process of knowledge, which is somewhat stable and the domain of much traditional therapy. It is also the basis of much successful therapy. Comfort's second dimension—"how the process of making knowledge incorporable affects the content we give to what is incorporated"—is perhaps the more complex, and it is in this place that separation and attachment are reenacted again and again in dialectical perceptual processes within the client-therapist interaction. Once again, we see Platonic knowledge (perceptual processes) and change through intelligence (awareness of internal processes constant change).

A Synthesis over the Life Span?

We exist in a coevolved, coconstructed relationship one with another and with the Other beyond our awareness. As we grow, develop, and change, we gain new knowledge and notice new things, but we shall always miss something beyond. Freud's report of the dream of the burning child summarizes this situation.

> A father had been watching beside his child's sickbed for days and nights on end. After the child had died, he went in the next room to lie down but left the door open so that he could see from the bedroom into the room in which his child's body was laid out, with tall candles standing round it. An old man had been engaged to keep watch over it, and he sat beside the body murmuring prayers. After a few hours sleep, the father had a dream that his child was standing beside his bed, caught him by the arm, and whispered to him reproachfully: "Father, don't you see I'm burning?" He woke up, noticed a bright glare of light from the next room, hurried into it, and found that the old watchman had dropped off to sleep and that the wrapping and one of the arms of his beloved child's dead body had been burned by a lighted candle that had fallen on them [Freud, (1900) 1953, p. 309].

"Father, don't you see I'm burning?" This one line summarizes the problems of personal separation one from another,
from God, and from the universe. Perhaps it is impossible to see
one another and to know God. Yet, there seem to be moments
that we can experience the attachment of creation and the
movement of the New in the dialectic that give us a sense of
being. These moments should be enjoyed to their fullest before
they deconstruct once again into the dialectics of desire and truth.

One can interpret this dream in many ways. One interpretation of the dream of the burning child is that it is about the
impossibility of gaining full knowledge or of totally understanding or noticing another human being's construction of the
world. When the child says, "Father, don't you see I'm burning?" he is noticing his father's lack of attention. But, the son
fails to notice his father's agony and sadness and that he has indeed noticed his child, more deeply than the child can imagine.
The watchman fails to notice the candle. The father fails to
notice the caring of his absent son. This dream and its images
convey more thoughts and feelings and meanings than it is possible to describe in a book. There does seem to be something
beyond our present awareness.

Theory into Practice

Development is simultaneously incredibly complex and
incredibly simple. The complexity becomes increasingly obvious as we examine the concepts of developmental therapy and
it may obscure the more basic simplicity. The simplicity may be
described as patterns that repeat themselves again and again and
to which we give a vast array of names. Development does seem,
paradoxically, to represent the One and the many.

*Construct 1: Development contains a pattern of repetition of
separation and attachment.*
1.   *Learning Objectives:* To be able to define the constructs
     of separation and attachment and to identify how they
     play themselves out repeatedly through life.

2. *Cognitive Presentation:* Pages 304–308 outline the key ideas, and Figure 20 supplements this material in important ways.

3. *Experiential Exercises or Homework:*
   a. Read again about Zeus and the four-legged spherical creatures. Imagine their joyous and somewhat bumptious behavior, which caused the gods to split them apart. Imagine also their desire to return to a union with their split selves. Do you agree that the creatures (humankind) really wish to be rejoined, or is the matter more complex than described in the story? Is separation, rather than reattachment, the basic goal?

   b. Object relations theories discussed in this chapter have been distinguished from Bowlby's attachment theory, although Bowlby is considered an object relations theorist by many. What is the connection between Bowlby's attachment theory and the theories of Gilligan? What is the relationship between Mahler and Masterson's emphasis on separation and individuation and more male-oriented constructions of the individual?

   c. Consider the twin developmental tasks of separation and individuation—what is an ideal balance of the two? Or, are they in dialectical opposition and in constant movement like the spherical creatures? Is stability in these tasks truly possible?

Construct 2: Development occurs throughout the life span.

1. *Cognitive Presentation:* Pages 308–317 summarize in brief form the ideas that developmental patterns of separation and attachment and developmental sequences repeat themselves again and again over the entire life span. Important in this presentation is the codevelopment that occurs in the family structure.

2. *Experiential Exercises or Homework:*
   a. Outline your own life-span development to this point. Think through and discuss your key develop-

mental tasks and how you worked through separation and attachment at each stage. Then describe your own movement from beginning fragments of sensori-motor experience through concrete operations and beyond.

b. Develop a chart in which your key family members are listed beside your own life-span development. Note that their developmental tasks are very different from your own. What conflicts exist between parent and child, between spouses, and what possible triangulation of two against one can you imagine within this framework? For example:

Self	*Mother*	*Father*
Age 19—task: to leave home and attach to college.	Age 38—task: to find new life goal, detach from family.	Age 45—task: cope with mid-life crisis, difficulty with job satisfaction, increased desire to attach and nurture family.

(Note that each individual has varying needs that may conflict with the needs of others. The sensori-motor, concrete operational, and formal operational issues are different in each case. Many elaborations on the family system are possible, particularly since each member is working through multiple developmental tasks.)

c. Analyze the life status of one of your clients from the above perspectives.

Construct 3: Development occurs in a cultural context, much of which is beyond our conscious awareness.

1. *Learning Objective:* To be able to describe the role of culture as part of unconscious experience that drives our thoughts and behaviors, of which we often consider ourselves "in charge."

2. *Cognitive Presentation:* Figures 22 through 26 illustrate possible relationships of culture to counseling. Full understanding of the implications of this paradigm requires thinking through and analyzing one's own experience in this framework.

3. *Experiential Exercises or Homework:*

   a. Most North American psychotherapy and counseling tends to operate in an individualistic mode and does not take adequate account of cultural dimensions. List the varying theoretical orientations with which you are familiar and note those that consider underlying cultural factors and those that do not.

   b. Provide specific examples of Figure 23, in which the therapist is talking to the client as an individual while the client is reacting to the therapist as a cultural exemplar. This could happen in counseling between people of different genders, sexual orientation, degrees of disability, race, ethnicity, and a variety of other factors. Similarly the therapist can fall into the trap of stereotyping clients.

   c. Figure 24 illustrates how client and therapist can bring culture into their interaction without conscious awareness. The two individuals may think they are talking, but the discourse is actually primarily at an unconscious level. Provide examples of this from your own experience or observations.

   d. Lacan's Z diagram (Figure 26) seeks to focus on cultural differences and the role of the Other. It has been suggested that much of feminist therapy follows this same model. Do you agree? Can you provide examples specifying these issues?

   e. Figure 25 suggests that consideration of cultural issues in conjunction with individual issues is generally the treatment of choice. List specific issues that need to be considered in each of the four points of the diagram and suggest ways in which individual or cultural (defined broadly) conflict might occur.

Construct 4: Development does not occur just at the conscious level but also at levels beyond our awareness. These levels beyond awareness are often termed the unconscious.

1. *Learning Objectives:* To be able to define how development occurs beyond our present awareness.

2. *Cognitive Presentation:* Pages 322–326 define the concept of the unconscious as the "unknown," beyond present awareness. Special attention is given to the work of Westerlundh and his colleagues on perceptgenesis.

3. *Experiential Exercises or Homework:*

    a. Compare and contrast the above definition of the unconscious with your knowledge of the concept and past experience. How might you modify the presentation here?

    b. Important to the definition of the unconscious is inclusion of cultural and social factors that impel behavior but that are often beyond awareness. Provide illustrations from your own personal experience and from observation of clients that illustrate this point.

    c. Present the first stimulus picture of Westerlundh and Smith (Figure 27) to a friend or colleague. Cover the picture with a piece of paper. Draw the paper down quickly and then put it back over the picture. Ask your friend what he or she saw. If the exercise is done smoothly, you will find that many different constructions of the picture are reported by those who view it. What has occurred is that their long-term memory (unconscious, if you will) has helped them provide gestalt closure on the picture, which they were not able to take in during the time it was presented to them.

Construct 5: The concepts of consciousness and unconsciousness can only exist in relation to one another. They exist together in opposition in an unsteady dialectic. Standing alone, they are easily deconstructed.

1. *Learning Objectives:* To be able to define and practice

deconstruction as outlined in this brief presentation, to understand the basis of Lacan's criticism of American ego psychology, and to understand the presentation of deconstruction of the unconscious and conscious.

2. *Cognitive Presentation:* Several key points are made on pages 326–330. Among them are (1) an interpretation of Derrida's deconstruction theory, (2) a Lacanian criticism of American ego psychology, and (3) the deconstruction of the concepts of the unconscious and conscious.

3. *Experiential Exercises or Homework:*

   a. Deconstruction suggests that all presentations in language are based on assumptions that can be ultimately proved to be irrational. As a first step, note Ellis-type irrational statements and how these statements can easily be deconstructed (shown to be false) due to their internal logical inconsistencies. Then evaluate more sophisticated statements of belief of individuals and the culture and note their logical fallacies in detail.

   b. Lacan is clearly not a supporter of U.S. psychological and psychiatric principles. Spend some time decoding and absorbing Lacan's statement that "the unconscious is the discourse of the Other." You will find Figures 22 through 26 useful in this process.

   c. This comparison, made in a semihumorous vein, is an attempt to point out the logical fallacy of the Cartesian dictum:

   I think, therefore I am.

   I do not think, therefore I am not.

   The deconstruction statement is, in its own way, as logical as that of Descartes. However, both statements contain logical fallacies. How does each stand stronger in relation one to another? How do the dialectics of consciousness and the unconscious play themselves out from these statements?

Construct 6: Regardless of our intent, we are impacting the unconscious of the other person. It may be helpful to attempt to plan "what happens beyond our awareness" but perhaps to do so with some humility, since there will always be a "beyond."

1. *Learning Objectives:* To be able to define examples of impact on the other person and the client without their conscious awareness; to be able to discuss how therapy operates at multiple levels beyond that on which we focus our conscious attention.

2. *Cognitive Presentation:* Pages 330-341 make the following central points: (1) we reenact themes of attachment and separation with each client (for example, in the way we meet our clients and terminate the interview, the way we join our clients in empathy, and the way we separate from them through influencing and additive empathy); (2) Breuer's case of Anna O. is a particularly rich source of how a client can be impacted negatively through transferential relationships in the separation and attachment process; (3) the case of George from Chapter Six provides us with an opportunity to study the joining and separation in the developmental therapy model.

3. *Experiential Exercises or Homework:*
   a. List the varying language frames we use in different orientations to therapy that represent forms of either separation or attachment (disengagement, enmeshment, transference, resistance). Use both individual and family therapy language systems in your descriptions. When our goal is to help the client become more separate and to individuate, our overt conscious actions are simultaneously acting also at the unconscious level. There is more happening than what we immediately observe in our conscious actions on the client.
   b. Examine the case of Anna O. for specific examples of both conscious and unconscious issues of separation and attachment. Note that Anna O. was in Haley's "leaving home" stage. What developmental

    tasks did she need to fulfill? How would you classify
her symptoms in terms of the developmental therapy model (sensori-motor, preoperational, and so
on)? How would the specific aspects of the developmental therapy model be applied to her case? What
theoretical orientations seem to be most appropriate
for work with her?

c.   Provide specific illustrations of how Mary Bradford
Ivey impacted George beyond his immediate awareness. What theoretical or practical alternatives might
you suggest for her?

d.   How would you apply each of the above exercises
to your own therapeutic practice and life experience?

e.   Apply to Freud's dream of the burning child the
central concepts from the above discussion and analyze this dream.

f.   What is your own personal reaction to Freud's presentation of the dream of the burning child? Can you
recall an early memory or a dream that it brings to
mind? How might some of the constructs and exercises presented here relate to your own personal experience of noticing and being noticed? Is it possible
that being noticed (being attached) is a necessary
precursor to being separate and individuated?

Summary

    This chapter has moved developmental therapy from an
emphasis on conscious development to a dialectic of development between the known and the unknown or the conscious and
the unconscious. Critical in this process are Bowlby's constructs
of separation and attachment and Plato's joyful spherical creatures seeking to rejoin their halves. Do we want to rejoin or do
we want to remain separate? This seems another variation of
Hamlet's "To be or not to be? That is the question."

    Basic ambivalence, our desire to be with others and to be
separate, perhaps means that we will always be engaged in the
difficult dialectics of desire. What do we want? Perhaps we want

what we do not have, and the best we can do is to follow Lacan's dictum of never giving up on our desire and the search for the impossible dream.

Life-span developmental theory was presented in this chapter in Figure 21 to suggest an overarching integration of many different developmental constructs in one chart. At the same time, this chart is not definitive; there are many other issues to explore. Perhaps the search for the meaning and place of developmental concepts in the therapeutic process is only now beginning.

Psychology, for the most part, has chosen not to deal with the concept of the unconscious. However, when retranslated as the unknown, beyond our present awareness, the unconscious can be related to solid empirical work in long-term memory studies and in learning and cognition. It may be anticipated that systematic formulations for the therapy of the unconscious will become increasingly clear to us, perhaps through the basic metaphor of Bowlby's separation and attachment, the balancing of the twin tasks of assimilation and accommodation, and our person-environment interactions, which seem the basis of the dialectics of therapy.

Culture undergirds our practice. It forms the discourse of the Other that becomes, without our conscious awareness, so much of the self. And, when the concept of culture is added to that of developmental therapy, a whole new set of enlightenments falls into place. Developmental therapy seems to be a beginning—the concepts presented here are not by any means closed.

Many like to criticize Freud as being absolutist and arbitrary. Perhaps this is an unfair characterization. Let us let Freud ([1920] 1966) have the last word, as he often does:

> Now you will no doubt conclude that a rejection such as this of all written discussion argues a high degree of inaccessibility to objections, of obstinacy, or, to use the polite colloquial scientific term, of pig-headedness [*Verrantheit*]. I should like to say in reply that when once, after such hard work, one

has arrived at a conviction, one has at the same
time acquired a certain right to retain that conviction with some tenacity. I may also urge that in the
course of my work I have modified my views on a
few important points, changed them and replaced
them by fresh ones—and in each case, of course, I
have made this publicly known. And the outcome
of this frankness? Some people have taken no notice whatever of my self-corrections and continue
to this day to criticize me for hypotheses which
have long ceased to have the same meaning for me.
Others reproach me precisely for these changes and
regard me as untrustworthy on their account. Of
course! a person who has occasionally changed his
opinion is deserving of no belief at all, since he has
made it all too likely that his latest assertions may
also be mistaken; but a person who has unflinch-
ingly maintained what he once asserted, or who
cannot be quickly enough persuaded to give it up,
must naturally be pig-headed or stubborn! What
can one do, in the face of these contradictory ob-
jections by the critics, but remain as one is and behave in accordance with one's own judgment? I am
resolved to do that, and I shall not be deterred
from modifying or withdrawing any of my theories, as my advancing experience may require. In
regard to *fundamental* discoveries I have hitherto
found nothing to alter, and I hope this will remain
true in the future [pp. 245-246].

Epilogue

Development as an Allegory

If we are indeed one in our being, then perhaps our coconstructed search for ourselves and for others and for the Other—all of our busy activity as spherical creatures of the gods or God—is really overly ambitious striving. If we will but notice, we are already there. We need look no further for the father, the mother, or ourselves.

"To move and to find we are still at the beginning"—this is perhaps the best one-line summary of developmental therapy. We are a whole, but our search for difference nonetheless helps us understand our own being and our relations with others and the Other.

Plato's four levels of consciousness and his construction of the dialectic have been critical in the formulation of developmental therapy.* At the same time, the neo-Platonic philos-

---

*The philosopher/psychoanalyst Luce Irigary (1985) has extensively criticized Plato's "Allegory of the Cave" and his conceptions of consciousness in her *Speculum of the Other Woman*. Implicitly and explicitly, she criticizes the "chain of propositions" that lead to a male-oriented search for the light of truth. In her consideration of Plato's work, she suggests that the Allegory may be considered a metaphor for the womb. Irigary points out the absence of women in the story. In this sense, the discussion in the Acknowledgments section of this book should be noted. Joyce Elbrecht of the philosophy department at Ithaca College suggested that the cave need not be considered a linear model of the "search for the highest" but rather a dialectical awareness of continually repeating tasks—to return to the beginning.

The attempt in this book has been to balance the two interpretations of Plato—the linear and the holistic, recycling into the portrayal of the developmental spheres.

351

opher Plotinus's concept of unity within the One is an important criticism and supplement.

This book began with the Greeks and perhaps it is suitable to end with them as well. Perhaps all philosophy and psychology are mere footnotes to Plato. Plato's "Allegory of the Cave" is presented here as a summary statement for developmental therapy.

"The Allegory of the Cave"
(Selections from Plato's *Republic*)

Here is a parable to illustrate the degrees in which nature may be enlightened or unenlightened. Imagine the condition of men living in a sort of cavernous chamber underground, with an entrance open to the light and a long passage all down the cave. Here they have been since childhood, chained by the leg and also by the neck, so that they cannot move and can see only what is in front of them, because the chains will not let them turn their heads. At some distance higher up is the light of a fire burning behind them; and between the prisoners and the fire is a track with a parapet built along it, like the screen at a puppet show, which hides the performers while they show their puppets over the top.

I see, said he.

Now behind this parapet imagine persons carrying along various artificial objects, including figures of men and animals in wood or stone or other materials, which project above the parapet.

Needless to say Irigary's powerful criticism of Plato is important. She suggests that Plato is too concerned with the highest good and the ordering of society. The idea of ordered, nonreciprocating hierarchies is specifically rejected. The interpretation presented here, while built from Platonic thought, ultimately criticizes and builds on Plato's point of view. Plotinus's position and his concept of multiplicity in the One seem to offer an important addition to Plato and Piaget.

Naturally, some of these persons would be talking, others silent.

It is a strange picture, he said, and a strange sort of prisoners.

Like ourselves, I replied; for in the first place prisoners so confined would have seen nothing of themselves or of one another, except the shadows thrown by the firelight on the wall of the Cave facing them, would they?

Not if all their lives they had been prevented from moving their heads.

And they would have seen as little of the objects carried past.

Of course.

Now, if they could talk to one another, would they not suppose that their words referred only to those passing shadows which they saw?

Necessarily.

And suppose their prison had an echo from the wall facing them? When one of the people crossing behind them spoke, they could only suppose that the sound came from the shadow passing before their eyes.

No doubt.

In every way, then, such prisoners would recognize as reality nothing but the shadows of those artificial objects.

Inevitably.

The preceding paragraphs represent Plato's lowest form of cognition (imagining, or *eikasia*). The prisoners chained to the walls of the cave think they have consciousness but only see confused images. In this form of consciousness, the individual is unaware of what lies behind and beyond, is unconscious of other forms. In the sense of developmental therapy, the prisoners are enmeshed in a sensori-motor consciousness. They are ruled and directed by the external environment even though they may consider themselves internally directed in their perceptions.

The treatment for this form of cognition, of course, is to provide a structured environment that may lead the prisoner or the client to the light. The therapist must act as a guide to help the client form a more comprehensive meaning of the experience he or she perceives. The therapist must join the client in his or her construction of experience and help the client separate from attachments to distorted perceptions and images.

> Now consider what would happen if their release from the chains and the healing of their unwisdom should come about in this way. Suppose one of them was set free and forced suddenly to turn up, turn his head, and walk with eyes lifted to the light; all these movements would be painful, and he would be too dazzled to make out the objects whose shadows he had been used to seeing. What do you think he would say, if someone told him that what he had formerly seen was meaningless illusion, but now, being somewhat nearer to reality and turned toward more real objects, he was getting a truer view? Suppose further that he was shown the various objects being carried by and was made to say, in reply to questions, what each of them was. Would he not be perplexed and believe the objects now shown him to be not so real as what he formerly saw?
>
> Yes, not nearly so real.
>
> And, if he was forced to look at the firelight itself, would not his eyes ache, so that he would try to escape and turn back to things which he could see distinctly, convinced that they really were clearer than these other objects now being shown to him?
>
> Yes.

In these exchanges, we have a rough analog to the problem of the preoperational child or adult, the person who insists on engaging in magical thinking. The client may see a piece of "reality" but organizes that reality and escapes from it using a basic sensori-motor frame of reference, which was internalized from old perceptions.

The following may be considered somewhat similar to the task we face as we seek to bring clients more in tune with the "reality" we see and believe will be beneficial to them. We need to identify the irrational and understand clients' constructions if they are to decenter their attachments to move to the next developmental level.

> And suppose someone were to drag him away forcibly up the steep and rugged ascent and not let him go until he had hauled him out into the sunlight, would he not suffer pain and vexation at such treatment, and, when he had come out into the light, find his eyes so full of its radiance that he could not see a single one of the things that he was now told were real?
>
> Certainly, he could not see them all at once.
>
> He would need, then, to grow accustomed before he could see things in that upper world. At first it would be easier to make out shadows, then the images of men and things reflected in water, and later on, the things themselves. After that, it would be easier to watch the heavenly bodies and the sky itself by night, looking at the light of the moon and stars rather than the Sun and the Sun's light in the daytime.
>
> Yes, surely.
>
> Last of all, he would be able to look at the Sun and contemplate its nature, not as it appears when reflected in the water or any alien medium, but as it is in itself in its own domain.
>
> No doubt.
>
> And now he would begin to draw the conclusion that it is the Sun that produces the seasons and the course of the year and controls everything

in the visible world, and moreover is in a way the cause of all that he and his companions used to see.

Clearly he would come at last to that conclusion.

The transition to the world of visible things and a more complete understanding of appearances has been achieved. Plato terms this state of mind *pistis,* or belief. It is parallel to the concrete operations stage. The child, individual, or client is able to see and experience the world of external "reality" and to contemplate linear cause and effect relationships.

The movement to this second stage has been brought about by the coaching style of teaching or therapy in which the developmental therapist works with the present cognitions of the individual and gradually helps add new ideas and concepts to past perceptions. At this point, the old consciousness may be denied and the desire for further knowledge and understanding may be initiated. In the next few paragraphs, the transition to the world of thinking and formal operations becomes apparent.

Then if he called to mind his fellow prisoners and what passed for wisdom in his former dwelling-place, he would surely think himself happy in the change and be sorry for them. They may have had a practice of honouring and commending one another, with prizes for the man who had the keenest eye for the passing shadows and the best memory for the order in which they followed or accompanied one another, so that he could make a good guess as to which was going to come next. Would our released prisoner be likely to covet these prizes or to envy the men exalted to honour and power in the Cave? Would he not feel like Homer's Achilles, that he would far sooner "be on earth as a hired servant in the house of a landless man" or endure anything rather than go back to his old beliefs and live in the old way?

Yes, he would prefer any fate to such a life.

The former prisoner has entered the world of thinking (*dianoia*) and formal operations. One may note the awareness of affect and emotion—the thinking about one's thoughts and feelings. It must be recalled that Plato notes that those in this state of awareness fail to examine their own assumptions. The danger of being unconscious of one's own assumptions is shown when the prisoner returns to the cave to share his new knowledge. There always seems something beyond our awareness.

> Now imagine what would happen if he went down again to take his former seat in the Cave. Coming suddenly out of the sunlight, his eyes would be filled with darkness, he might be required once more to deliver his opinion on those shadows, in competition with those prisoners who never had been released, while his eyesight was still dim and unsteady; and it might take some time to become used to the darkness. They would laugh at him and say that he had gone up only to come back with his sight ruined; it was worth no one's while even to attempt the ascent. If they could lay hands on the man who was trying to set them free and lead them up, they would kill him.
>   Yes, they would [quoted in Cornford, (1941) 1982, pp. 227-231].

As Cornford comments, "One moral of the allegory is drawn from the distress caused by a too sudden passage from darkness to light" ([1941] 1981, p. 227). There is need for a solid understanding of each stage of development before one is able to engage in the next level of discourse. Plato suggested the need for ten years of training in pure mathematics (at that time mathematics did not question its own assumptions) before one can bring out and examine moral questions and the dialectic.

The study of the dialectic involves the examination of the nature of the cave and the interactions therein. It requires one to examine oneself examining oneself examining oneself. It also requires the same process in the examination of others. The prisoner who returns to the cave with only "knowledge" (*dia-noia* or even the solid truth of *episteme*) is inadequately prepared for the trials of the dialectical relationship with prisoners still chained to the cave. Thus, Plato considered the study of dialectic the highest form of intelligence (*noesis*).

Plotinus has an important implied criticism of Plato at this point. Whereas Plato apparently was constantly searching for higher forms of intelligence, Plotinus focused on the concept of the One. The One may be considered a still higher principle than "highest." The concept of the One is implicit in the thoughts of Gilligan and Gregorc and is explicit in Lacan, who points out that his theory of knowledge may be found in Plotinus (1973, p. 134). The implications of Plotinus's thought for the present argument are illustrated here: "As every act of cognition, even of self-cognition, presupposes the duality of object and subject, Plotinus repeatedly and strongly states that the One is void of any cognition and is ignorant even of itself. . . . The realm of the One is 'followed' by that of Intelligence. . . . Here, for the first time, multiplicity appears" (Merlan, 1967, p. 353).

When one imposes Plotinus's concept of the One on the Platonic and Piagetian stages, another justification of the spherical codevelopment, coevolutionary concepts of developmental therapy appears. The stages of cognition do constantly enfold on themselves, resulting in a return to the beginning. The formal operational prisoner became "as a child" in his unconscious ignorance when he returned to the cave. However, when we attempt to conceptualize our being, there always seems to be a oneness and multiplicity in increasingly complicated, but unifying patterns.

The "Allegory of the Cave" is wisely incomplete and presents the need for dialectical formulations, but it is still enriched by Plotinus's concept of the One. The One reminds us that we are indeed a whole, but that, paradoxically, there is more to be found. The Allegory also can be a metaphor for the psychotherapeutic process in which the task of the therapist is to assist the client to move from darkness to light and, hopefully, to carry that light to others for whom that light is already there.

References

Altman, I., and Gauvain, M. "A Cross-Cultural and Dialectic Analysis of Homes." In L. Liben, A. Patterson, and N. Newcombe (eds.), *Spatial Representation and Behavior across the Life Span.* New York: Academic Press, 1981.

Anderson, J. *Cognitive Psychology.* New York: Freeman, 1985.

Anderson, T. *Style-Shift Counseling.* Abbotsford, B.C.: Interpersonal Effectiveness, 1982.

Appignanesi, R. *Freud for Beginners.* London: Writers and Readers Publishing Cooperative, 1979.

Atkinson, R., and Shiffrin, R. "The Control of Short-Term Memory." *Scientific American,* 1971, *225,* 82-90.

Ballou, M., and Gabalac, N. *A Feminist Position on Mental Health.* Springfield, Ill.: Thomas, 1984.

Bandler, R., and Grinder, J. *The Structure of Magic I.* Palo Alto, Calif.: Science and Behavior Books, 1975.

Bandura, A., and Walters, R. *Social Learning and Personality Development.* New York: Holt, Rinehart & Winston, 1963.

Basseches, M. "Dialectical Schemata." *Human Development,* 1980, *23,* 400-421.

Bateson, G. *Mind and Nature.* New York: Dutton, 1979.

Beck, A. *Cognitive Therapy and the Emotional Disorders.* New York: International Universities, 1976.

Beck, A., Rush, A., Shaw, B., and Emery, G. *Cognitive Therapy of Depression.* New York: Guilford, 1979.

Bekesy, G. "Bermerkungen zur Theorie der Gunstigen Nachall-
dauer von Raumen." *Annuals der Physik,* 1931, *8,* 851–873.

Bettelheim, B. *Freud and Man's Soul.* New York: Vintage,
1982.

Blumenthal, A. *The Process of Cognition.* Englewood Cliffs,
N.J.: Prentice-Hall, 1977.

Bonaparte, M. *The Life and Works of Edgar Allan Poe: A Psychoanalytic Interpretation.* New York: Humanities Press,
1971.

Bowen, M. *Family Therapy in Clinical Practice.* New York:
Aronson, 1978.

Bowers, K. "On Being Unconsciously Influenced and Informed."
In K. Bowers and D. Meichenbaum (eds.), *The Unconscious
Reconsidered.* New York: Wiley, 1984.

Bowers, K., and Meichenbaum, D. (eds.). *The Unconscious Reconsidered.* New York: Wiley, 1984.

Bowlby, J. *Attachment.* New York: Basic Books, 1969.

Bowlby, J. "Affectional Bonds: Their Nature and Origin." In R.
Weiss (ed.), *Loneliness: The Experience of Emotional and Social Isolation.* Cambridge, Mass.: MIT Press, 1973a.

Bowlby, J. *Separation.* New York: Basic Books, 1973b.

Brentano, P. *Psychologie vom Empirischen Standpunkt.* Vienna,
1874. (3rd ed., Leipzig, 1925.) (Cited in R. Chisholm, "Intentionality." In P. Edward (ed.), *The Encyclopedia of Philosophy.* New York: Macmillan, *4,* 201–204.)

Breuer, J., and Freud, S. *Studies on Hysteria.* New York: Basic
Books, 1893.

Carkhuff, R. *Helping and Human Relations.* Vols. 1 and 2. New
York: Holt, Rinehart & Winston, 1969.

Carroll, L. *Alice's Adventures in Wonderland.* Chicago: John C.
Winston, 1923.

Chesler, P. *About Men.* New York: Simon & Schuster, 1978.

Chomsky, N. *Language and Responsibility.* New York: Pantheon, 1977.

Clement, C. *The Lives and Legends of Jacques Lacan.* New
York: Columbia University Press, 1983.

Comfort, A. *Reality and Empathy: Physics, Mind, and Science in the 21st Century*. Albany, N.Y.: State University of New York Press, 1984.

Cornford, F. (trans.). *The Republic of Plato*. London: Oxford, 1982. (Originally published 1941.)

Daly, M. *Beyond God the Father: Toward a Philosophy of Women's Liberation*. Boston: Beacon, 1973.

Derrida, J. *Speech and Phenomena*. Evanston, Ill.: Northwestern University Press, 1973.

Derrida, J. "The Purveyor of Truth." In *Yale French Studies*. Vol. 52: *Graphesis: Perspectives in Literature and Philosophy*. Millwood, N.Y.: Kraus Reprint Co., 1975.

Derrida, J. *Of Grammatology*. Baltimore, Md.: Johns Hopkins University Press, 1976.

Derrida, J. *Writing and Difference*. Chicago: University of Chicago Press, 1978.

Derrida, J. *Positions*. Chicago: University of Chicago Press, 1981.

Diffily, A. "Aaron Beck's Cognitive Therapy Catches On." *Brown Alumni Monthly,* May 1984, pp. 39–46.

Eagleton, T. *Literary Theory*. Minneapolis: University of Minnesota Press, 1983.

Eliot, T. S. *Four Quartets*. New York: Harcourt Brace Jovanovich, 1943.

Ellis, A. *Reason and Emotion in Psychotherapy*. New York: Lyle Stuart, 1962.

Ellis, A. *Growth Through Reason*. Palo Alto, Calif.: Science and Behavior Books, 1971.

Erickson, M., Rossi, E., and Rossi, S. *Hypnotic Realities*. New York: Irvington, 1976.

Ericsson, K., and Simon, H. *Protocol Analysis: Verbal Reports as Data*. Cambridge, Mass.: MIT Press, 1984.

Erikson, E. *Childhood and Society*. (2nd ed.) New York: Norton, 1963. (1st ed. 1950.)

Fairbairn, W. *An Object Relations Theory of the Personality*. New York: Basic Books, 1952.

Feldenkrais, M. *Awareness Through Movement*. New York: Harper & Row, 1972.

Fleming, P. "The Family Life Cycle Model: A Paradigm for Separation and Attachment." Unpublished paper, University of Massachusetts, Amherst, October 1986.

Frankl, V. *The Doctor and the Soul.* New York: Bantam, 1952. (1st ed. 1946.)

Frankl, V. *Man's Search for Meaning.* New York: Pocket, 1959.

Freud, S. *The Interpretation of Dreams.* In J. Strachey (ed.), *The Standard Edition of the Complete Works of Sigmund Freud.* Vol. 5. London: Hogarth, 1953. (Originally published 1900.)

Freud, S. *Beyond the Pleasure Principle.* New York: Bantam, 1959. (Originally published 1928.)

Freud, S. "Negation." In J. Strachey (ed.), *The Standard Edition of the Complete Works of Sigmund Freud.* Vol. 5. London: Hogarth, 1961. (Originally published 1925.)

Freud, S. *Analysis Terminable and Interminable.* In J. Strachey (ed.), *The Standard Edition of the Complete Works of Sigmund Freud.* London: Hogarth, 1964. (Originally published 1937.)

Freud, S. *Introductory Lectures on Psychoanalysis.* New York: Norton, 1966. (Originally published 1920.)

Freud, S. "Repression." In A. Richards (ed.), *On Metapsychology: The Theory of Psychoanalysis.* London: Pelican, 1984. (Originally published 1915.)

Fry, P., Kropf, G., and Coe, K. "Effects of Counselor and Client Counselor Racial Similarity on the Counselor's Response Pattern and Skills." *Journal of Counseling Psychology,* 1980, *27,* 130-137.

Fukuhara, M. "Is Love Universal?—From the Viewpoint of Counseling Adolescents." Paper presented at the 42nd Annual Conference of the International Association of Psychologists, Mexico City, 1984.

Furth, H. *Piaget for Teachers.* Englewood Cliffs, N.J.: Prentice-Hall, 1970.

Furth, H. *Piaget and Knowledge.* (2nd ed.) Chicago: University of Chicago Press, 1981.

Gelso, C., and Carter, J. "The Relationship in Counseling and Psychotherapy: Components, Consequences, and Theoretical Antecedents." *Counseling Psychologist,* 1985, *13,* 155-243.

Gilligan, C. *In a Different Voice.* Cambridge, Mass.: Harvard, 1982.

Glass, G., and Kliegl, R. "An Apology for Research Integration in the Study of Psychotherapy." *Journal of Consulting and Clinical Psychology,* 1983, *51,* 28–41.

Glasser, W. *Reality Therapy.* New York: Harper & Row, 1965.

Goldstein, A. *Structured Learning Therapy.* New York: Academic Press, 1973.

Goncalves, O. *Intentionality in Counseling: Behavioral, Cognitive, and Unconscious Dimensions.* Unpublished doctoral comprehensive paper, Amherst, Mass., 1985.

Gray, E. D. *Patriarchy as a Conceptual Trap.* Wellesley, Mass.: Roundtable, 1982.

Gregorc, A. *An Adult's Guide to Style.* Maynard, Mass.: Gabriel Systems, 1982a.

Gregorc, A. *Gregorc Style Delineator.* Maynard, Mass.: Gabriel Systems, 1982b.

Guntrip, H. *Personality Structure and Human Interaction.* New York: International Universities Press, 1961.

Gurman, A., and Kniskern, D. (eds.). *Handbook of Family Therapy.* New York: Brunner/Mazel, 1981.

Haley, J. *Strategies of Psychotherapy.* New York: Grune & Stratton, 1963.

Haley, J. *Uncommon Therapy.* New York: Norton, 1973.

Hegel, G. *Phenomenology of Spirit.* (Also translated as *Phenomology of Mind.* (A. Miller, trans.) Oxford: Oxford, 1977. (Originally published 1807.)

Hersey, P., and Blanchard, K. *Management of Organizational Behavior.* Englewood Cliffs, N.J.: Prentice-Hall, 1982.

Ivey, A. *Microcounseling.* Springfield, Ill.: Thomas, 1971.

Irigray, L. *Speculum of the Other Woman.* Ithaca, N.Y.: Cornell, 1985.

Ivey, A. *Microcounseling.* Springfield, Ill.: Thomas, 1971.

Ivey, A. "Educational Change Planning with Psychiatric Pa- 343.

Ivey, A. *Intentional Interviewing and Counseling.* Monterey, Calif.: Brooks/Cole, 1983a.

Ivey, A. *Three Approaches to Counseling.* North Amherst, Mass.: Microtraining, 1983b.

Ivey, A., and Alschuler, A. (eds.). "Psychological Education." Special issue of *Personnel and Guidance Journal,* 1973, *51,* 581-692.

Ivey, A., and Authier, J. *Microcounseling.* (2nd ed.) Springfield, Ill.: Thomas, 1978.

Ivey, A., and Gluckstern, N. *Basic Attending Skills.* North Amherst, Mass.: Microtraining, 1974. (2nd ed. 1982.)

Ivey, A., and Gluckstern, N. *Basic Influencing Skills.* North Amherst, Mass.: Microtraining, 1976. (2nd ed. 1983.)

Ivey, A., and Goncalves, O. *The Epistemology of Intentionality: Implications for Clinical Practice and Research.* Unpublished manuscript, University of Massachusetts, Amherst, 1985.

Ivey, A., and Hurst, J. "Communication as Adaptation." *Journal of Communication,* 1971, *21,* 199-207.

Ivey, A., Ivey, M., and Simek-Downing, L. *Counseling and Psychotherapy: Integrating Skills, Theory, and Practice.* (2nd ed.) Englewood Cliffs, N.J.: Prentice-Hall, 1987.

Ivey, A., and Matthews, W. "A Meta-Model for Structuring the Clinical Interview." *Journal of Counseling and Development,* 1984, *63,* 237-243.

Ivey, A., Normington, C., Miller, D., Morrill, W., and Haase, R. "Microcounseling and Attending Behavior: An Approach to Pre-Practicum Counselor Training." *Journal of Counseling Psychology,* 1968, Part II (monograph supplement), 1-12.

Ivey, A., and Simek-Downing, L. *Counseling and Psychotherapy.* Englewood Cliffs, N.J.: Prentice-Hall, 1980.

Ivey, M. "Interpretation." Videotape selection in A. Ivey and N. Gluckstern, *Basic Influencing Skills.* North Amherst, Mass.: Microtraining, 1983.

Jacoby, L., and Witherspoon, D. "Remembering Without Awareness." *Canadian Journal of Psychology,* 1982, *32,* 300-324.

Janis, I. *Short-Term Counseling.* New Haven, Conn.: Yale, 1983.

Jaynes, J. *The Origins of Consciousness in the Breakdown of the Bicameral Mind.* Boston: Houghton Mifflin, 1976.

Jonas, H. *The Gnostic Religion.* Boston: Beacon, 1958.

Jones, E. *The Life and Work of Sigmund Freud.* Vol. 1. New York: Basic Books, 1953.

Keeney, B. *Aesthetics of Change.* New York: Guilford, 1983.

Kegan, R. *The Evolving Self.* Cambridge, Mass.: Harvard, 1982.

Kelly, G. *The Psychology of Personal Constructs.* Vols. 1 and 2. New York: Norton, 1955.

Kernberg, O. *Object Relations Theory and Clinical Psychoanalysis.* New York: Jason Aaronson, 1976.

Klein, M. *Envy and Gratitude.* London: Hogarth, 1975.

Knowles, D., and Reeves, N. *But, Won't Granny Need Her Socks?* Dubuque, Iowa: Kendall/Hunt, 1983.

Kohlberg, L. *The Philosophy of Moral Development.* San Francisco: Harper & Row, 1981.

Korman, M. *Levels and Patterns of Professional Training in Psychology.* Washington, D.C.: American Psychological Association, 1973.

Kragh, U., and Smith, G. (eds.). *Percept-Genetic Analysis.* Lund, Sweden: Gleerup, 1970.

Lacan, J. "Seminar on 'The Purloined Letter.' " In *Yale French Studies. French Freud: Structural Studies in Psychoanalysis.* Millwood, N.Y.: Kraus Reprint Co., 1975.

Lacan, J. *Ecrits: A Selection.* New York: Norton, 1977. (1st ed. 1966.)

Lacan, J. *The Four Fundamental Concepts of Psychoanalysis.* New York: Norton, 1978. (1st ed. 1973.)

Lankton, S. *Practical Magic.* Cupertino, Calif.: Meta, 1980.

Laplanche, J., and Pontalis, J.-B. *The Language of Psychoanalysis.* New York: Norton, 1973. (1st ed. 1967.)

Larson, D. *Teaching Psychological Skills: Models for Giving Psychology Away.* Monterey, Calif.: Brooks/Cole, 1984.

Lawler, J. "Dialectical Philosophy and Developmental Psychology: Hegel and Piaget on Contradiction." *Human Development,* 1975, *18,* 1-17.

Lieberson, J. "Putting Freud to the Test." *New York Review of Books,* 1985, *32,* 24-28.

Loevinger, J., Wessler, R., and Redmore, C. *Measuring Ego Development.* Vols. 1 and 2. San Francisco: Jossey-Bass, 1970.

Lorenz, K. *On Aggression.* New York: Bantam, 1966.

Løve, E. *The Self.* Oslo: Universitetsforlaget, 1982.

Lowen, A. *The Betrayal of the Body.* New York: Macmillan, 1967.

Lukas, E. *Meaningful Living.* Cambridge, Mass.: Schenkman, 1984.

Luria, A. "The Development of Constructive Activity in the Pre-school Child." (Written in 1929.) In M. Cole (ed.), *The Selected Writings of A. R. Luria.* White Plains, N.Y.: Sharpe, 1978.

McAdam, E., and Milne, G. (eds.). *Samuel Johnson's Dictionary.* New York: Pantheon, 1964. (Originally published 1755.)

McGoldrick, M., Pearce, J., and Giordano, J. (eds.). *Ethnicity and Family Therapy.* New York: Guilford, 1982.

Mahler, M. "A Study of the Separation-Individuation Process and Its Possible Application to Borderline Phenomena in the Psychoanalytic Situation." *Psychoanalytic Study of the Child,* 1971, *26,* 403–424.

Mahoney, M. *Psychotherapy Process.* New York: Plenum, 1980.

Mahoney, M. "Behaviorism, Cognitivism, and Human Change Processes." In M. Reda and M. Mahoney (eds.), *Cognitive Psychotherapies: Recent Developments in Theory, Research, and Practice.* Cambridge, Mass.: Ballinger, 1984.

Mahoney, M. "Psychotherapy and Human Change Processes." In M. Mahoney and A. Freeman (eds.), *Cognition and Psychotherapy.* New York: Plenum, 1985.

Marlatt, G. "Relapse Prevention: A Self-Control Program for the Treatment of Addictive Behaviors." Invited address presented at the International Conference on Behavior Modification, Banff, Alberta, Canada, March 1980.

Marlatt, G., and Gordon, J. *Relapse Prevention: Maintenance Strategies in the Treatment of Addictive Behaviors.* New York: Guilford, 1985.

Marshall, E., Kurtz, P., and Associates. *Interpersonal Helping Skills: A Guide to Training Methods, Programs, and Resources.* San Francisco: Jossey-Bass, 1982.

Marx, R. "Relapse Prevention for Managerial Training: A Model for Maintenance of Behavior Change." *Academy of Management Review,* 1982, *7,* 433–441.

Marx, R. "Self-Control Strategies in Management Training: Skill Maintenance Despite Organizational Realities." Symposium chaired at the American Psychological Association Annual Meeting, Toronto, Canada, August 1984.

Masterson, J. *The Narcissistic and Borderline Disorders.* New York: Brunner/Mazel, 1981.

Masterson, J. *The Real Self: A Developmental, Self, and Object Relations Approach.* New York: Brunner/Mazel, 1985.

Meara, N., Pepinsky, H., Shannon, J., and Murray, W. "Semantic Communication and Expectations for Counseling Across Three Theoretical Orientations." *Journal of Counseling Psychology,* 1981, *28,* 110-118.

Meara, N., Shannon, J., and Pepinsky, H. "Comparisons of Stylistic Complexity of the Language of Counselor and Client Across Three Theoretical Orientations." *Journal of Counseling Psychology,* 1979, *26,* 181-189.

Meichenbaum, D. *Cognitive-Behavior Modification.* New York: Plenum, 1977.

Meichenbaum, D., and Gilmore, J. "The Nature of Unconscious Processes: A Cognitive-Behavioral Perspective." In K. Bowers and D. Meichenbaum (eds.), *The Unconscious Reconsidered.* New York: Wiley, 1984.

Merlan, P. "Plotinus." In P. Edwards (ed.), *Encyclopedia of Philosophy,* Vol. 6. New York: Macmillan, 1967.

Mitchell, H., and Rose, J. (eds.). *Feminine Sexuality.* New York: Norton, 1982.

Morris, W. *The American Heritage Dictionary.* Boston: Houghton Mifflin, 1978.

Mosher, R., and Sprinthall, N. "Psychological Education." *The Counseling Psychologist,* 1971, *2,* 3-82.

Muller, J. "Hegel and Lacan." Presentation at the University of Massachusetts, Department of Comparative Literature, Amherst, Mass., Spring 1985.

Muller, J., and Richardson, W. (eds.). *The Purloined Poe: Lacan, Derrida, and Post-Structuralist Reading.* Baltimore, Md.: Johns Hopkins University Press, 1987.

Osgood, C., Suci, G., and Tannenbaum, P. *Measurement of Meaning.* Urbana: University of Illinois Press, 1957.

Ouspensky, P. *Tertium Organum.* New York: Random House, 1970. (Originally published 1920.)

Parloff, M., Waskow, I., and Wolfe, B. "Research on Client Variables in Psychotherapy." In S. Garfield and A. Bergin (eds.),

Handbook of Psychotherapy and Behavior Change. New York: Wiley, 1978.

Paul, G. "Behavior Modification Research: Design and Tactics." In C. Franks (ed.), *Behavior Therapy: Appraisal and Styles.* New York: McGraw-Hill, 1967.

Perls, F. *Gestalt Therapy Verbatim.* Lafayette, Calif.: Real People Press, 1969.

Perry, W. *Forms of Intellectual and Ethical Development in the College Years.* New York: Holt, Rinehart & Winston, 1970.

Piaget, J. *The Construction of Reality in the Child.* New York: Basic Books, 1954.

Piaget, J. *The Language and Thought of the Child.* New York: New American Library, 1955. (Original version 1923; trans. 1926; 2nd ed. 1930.)

Piaget, J. *The Origins of Intelligence in Children.* New York: Norton, 1963. (1st ed. 1952.)

Piaget, J. *The Moral Judgment of the Child.* New York: Macmillan, 1965.

Piaget, J. *Six Psychological Studies.* New York: Unilage Books, 1968.

Piaget, J. *The Principles of Genetic Epistemology.* London: Routledge & Kegan Paul, 1970a.

Piaget, J. *Structuralism.* New York: Basic Books, 1970b. (1st ed. 1968.)

Piaget, J. *The Child's Conception of Physical Causality.* Totowa, N.J.: Littlefield, Adams, 1972. (1st ed. 1960.)

Piaget, J. "Creativity." Given as a talk in the 1972 Eisenhower Symposium, "Creativity: Moving Force of Society," Johns Hopkins University, Baltimore, Maryland, 1972. Reprinted in J. Gallagher and D. Reid, *The Learning Theory of Piaget and Inhelder.* Monterey, Calif.: Brooks/Cole, 1981.

Poe, E. A. "The Purloined Letter." (Written in 1845.) In E. A. Poe, *Complete Stories and Poems.* Garden City, N.Y.: Doubleday, 1966.

Richardson, W. "Lacan's Seminar on the Ethics of Desire." Presentation at the International Lacan Conference, University of Massachusetts, Amherst, June 1985.

Ridings, D. *Neuro Linguistic Programming's Primary Represen-*

tational System: Does It Exist? Unpublished doctoral dissertation, University of Massachusetts, Amherst, 1985.

Rivera, M. *Sociological Analysis of Psychotherapy with an Application to Gestalt Therapy.* Unpublished doctoral dissertation, University of Massachusetts, Amherst, 1980.

Rodger, B. "Preoperative Preparation." In *A Syllabus on Hypnosis and a Handbook on Therapeutic Suggestions.* American Society of Clinical Hypnosis, Education and Research Foundation, 1973.

Rogers, C. "The Necessary and Sufficient Conditions of Therapeutic Personality Change." *Journal of Consulting Psychology,* 1957, *21,* 95–103.

Rogers, C. *Becoming a Person.* Boston: Houghton Mifflin, 1961.

Rosenbaum, M. "Anna O. (Bertha Pappenheim): Her History." In M. Rosenbaum and M. Muroff (eds.), *Anna O.: Fourteen Contemporary Interpretations.* New York: Free Press, 1984.

Rouse, W. (trans.). *Great Dialogues of Plato.* New York: Mentor, 1956.

Sartre, J. *Being and Nothingness.* New York: Philosophical Library, 1956.

Schneiderman, S. *Jacques Lacan: The Death of an Intellectual Hero.* Cambridge, Mass.: Harvard University Press, 1983.

Selman, R. "A Developmental Approach to Interpersonal and Moral Awareness in Young Children." In T. Hennessy (ed.), *Values and Human Development.* New York: Paulist Press, 1976.

Shervin, H., and Dickman, S. "The Psychological Unconscious: A Necessary Assumption for All Psychological Theory." *American Psychologist,* 1980, *35,* 421–434.

Shipley, J. *The Origins of English Words.* Baltimore, Md.: Johns Hopkins, 1984.

Silhol, R. "Demand and Desire in Lacan." Presentation at the University of Massachusetts, Amherst, October 1985.

Smith, G., and Westerlundh, B. "Perceptgenesis: A Process Perspective on Perception-Personality." In L. Wheeler (ed.), *Review of Personality and Social Psychology.* New York: Sage, 1980.

Spitzer, R., Skodol, A., Gibbon, M., and Williams, J. *DSM-III*

Casebook. Washington, D.C.: American Psychiatric Association, 1981.

Sullivan, J. "Franz Brentano and the Problems of Intentionality." In B. Wolman (ed.), *Historical Roots of Contemporary Psychology*. New York: Harper & Row, 1968.

Teilhard de Chardin, P. *The Phenomenon of Man*. New York: Harper & Row, 1959. (1st ed. 1955.)

Tillich, P. "The Importance of New Being for Christian Theology." In J. Campbell (ed.), *Man and Transformation*. Princeton, N.J.: Princeton University Press, 1964.

Van Den Bergh, O., and Eelen, P. "Unconscious Processing and Emotions." In M. Reda and M. Mahoney (eds.), *Cognitive Psychotherapies*. Cambridge, Mass.: Ballinger, 1984.

Ver Eecke, W. *Saying "No": Its Meaning in Child Development, Psychoanalysis, Linguistics, and Hegel*. Pittsburgh, Pa.: Duquesne University Press, 1984.

Ver Eecke, W. "Lacan, Hegel, and Dialectics." Presentation at the University of Massachusetts, Department of Comparative Literature, Amherst, Mass., Spring 1985.

Vygotsky, L. *Thought and Language*. Cambridge, Mass.: MIT Press, 1962.

Wadsworth, B. *Piaget's Theory of Cognitive and Affective Development*. (3rd ed.) New York: Longman, 1984.

Weinstein, G., and Alschuler, A. "Education and Counseling for Self-Knowledge Development." *Journal of Counseling and Development*, 1985, *64*, 19–25.

Weiskel, T. *The Romantic Sublime: Studies in the Structure and Psychology of Transcendence*. Baltimore, Md.: Johns Hopkins Press, 1976.

Westerlundh, B., and Smith, G. "Psychodynamics of Perception." *Psychoanalysis and Contemporary Thought*, 1983, *6*, 597–640.

Winnicott, D. *Through Pediatrics to Psychoanalysis*. London: Hogarth, 1958.

Woodworth, R. *Experimental Psychology*. New York: Holt, Rinehart & Winston, 1938.

Zajonc, R. "Feeling and Thinking: Preferences Need No Inferences." *American Psychologist*, 1980, *35*, 151–175.

Name Index

Subject Index

377

C

Canada, style-shift counseling in, 140

Cave, allegory of, 352-357

Centration, and creativity, 188

Change: developmentally appropriate interventions for, 209-211; and existential movement, 251; maintaining, 211-218, 223-224; process of, 205-206; structuring environment for, 206-209. *See also* Development

Client-centered therapy. *See* Person-centered therapy

Clients: assessing reactions of, to interventions, 196-201, 220-222; cognitive progression by, 201-204; developmental movement by, 179-225; and internal dialectic with therapist, 229-230

Coaching: and developmental level, 145, 146-148; in interview, 235, 237, 247

Cognition: and affect, 128-129; and assimilation and accommodation, 116-118

Cognitive balance: and person-environment interaction, 62-69; positive and negative, 64, 66-67, 74-75

Cognitive-behavioral therapy: and developmental interventions, 210; and developmental stages, 92, 102, 104, 116, 127, 145, 149-150, 171; philosophies of, 282; and reality, 21

Cognitive-developmental change, facilitating, 78-132

Communication, as adaptation, 18, 83, 227

Conceptual styles, development of, 284-290, 301-302

Concrete operations stage: and adult development, 80-81, 84, 93, 94-101, 108-109, 114; in allegory, 356; assessing level of, 163, 168; and death, 79; and development theories, 273, 274, 280, 282, 283, 287; and devel-

opmental therapy, 10-11, 23; in interview, 235, 237, 240, 245, 247, 253, 254; and life span, 310, 311, 315; and therapeutic style, 138, 141, 142, 145, 146-148

Concrete random style, 285-286

Concrete sequential style, 286-287

Confrontation: and creativity in therapy, 188-195; importance of, 250-251; and influencing skills, 194-195; in interviews, 236-248; and perturbation in dialectics, 185-187; statements for, 192-194

Conscious present, 57-58

Consciousness: concept of, 327-328; deconstruction of, 326-330, 345-346; development of, 23-26; and information processing, 54-55, 57-59; levels of, 12

Conservation, and developmental stages, 89-90, 94-95, 97-98

Construct systems: and creativity, 188; and development theories, 267, 269, 285, 290; and developmental stages, 103; and person-environment interaction, 42, 44, 70, 71

Consulting: and developmental level, 145, 148-150; in interview, 238, 239, 241, 242, 243, 244

Context, dialectic of, 159

Contradiction, confronting, 151, 172

Counseling. *See* Therapy

Creativity: and confrontation in therapy, 188-195; in dialectic with environment, 182; mechanism of, 183-185; to Piaget, 180-182. *See also* Development

Culture: as development context, 317-322, 342-344; and developmental level, 184n-185n, 204; dimensions of, 319; scripts of, 320

D

Dance therapy, and developmental stage, 146

Copyright Acknowledgments